W9-BQJ-733

Homophobia

ALSO BY BYRNE FONE

The Columbia Anthology of Gay Literature (editor)

A Road to Stonewall

Masculine Landscapes

Hidden Heritage (editor)

American Lives (novel)

Richard Edmond Flatters, The Fall of the Damned. *An all-male group of sinners, erotic even in damnation, falls into Hell. Reprinted by permission of Cliché Bibliotheque Nationale de France, Paris*

Homo
phobia

A History

BYRNE FONE

Picador USA
A Metropolitan Book
Henry Holt and Company
New York

HOMOPHOBIA. Copyright © 2000 by Byrne Fone. All rights reserved. Printed in the United States of America. No part of this book may be used or reproduced in any manner whatsoever without written permission except in the case of brief quotations embodied in critical articles or reviews. For information, address Picador USA, 175 Fifth Avenue, New York, N.Y. 10010.

www.picadorusa.com

Picador® is a U.S. registered trademark and is used by Henry Holt and Company under license from Pan Books Limited.

For information on Picador USA Reading Group Guides, as well as ordering, please contact the Trade Marketing department at St. Martin's Press.
Phone: 1-800-221-7945 extension 763
Fax: 212-677-7456
E-mail: trademarketing@stmartins.com

Library of Congress Cataloging-in-Publication Data

Fone, Byrne R. S.
    Homophobia : a history / Byrne Fone.
        p. cm.
    Includes bibliographical references and index.
    ISBN 0-312-42030-7
    1. Homophobia. 2. Homosexuality—History. I. Title.
HQ76.25 .F7 2000
306.76'6'09—dc21   99-087004

First published in the United States by Metropolitan Books, an imprint of Henry Holt and Company.

First Picador USA Edition: November 2001

10 9 8 7 6 5 4 3 2 1

For Gabriel

CONTENTS

ACKNOWLEDGMENTS

The work of those scholars whose reconstruction of lesbian and gay history has helped to transform a hidden into a visible heritage underlies this book. They are acknowledged throughout this work, but let me thank them all here.

Without the unerring eye of Sara Bershtel, my editor at Metropolitan Books, and of Riva Hocherman and David Frederickson, who also read the manuscript, and of Jolanta Benal, whose copyediting was artful, I would have fallen into traps and errors and wandered far afield.

Special thanks to Georges Borchardt, who brought us together.

Homo
phobia

"The Shepard Fence." The site of Matthew Shepard's murder, October 1999. Kevin Moloney/NYT Pictures

Introduction

The Last Acceptable Prejudice

Over time people have found sufficient cause to distrust, despise, assault, and sometimes slaughter their neighbors because of differences in religion, nationality, and color. Indeed, few social groups have been free from the effects of prejudice, but most warring factions—men and women, Jews, Muslims, and Christians, blacks and whites—have been united in one eternal hatred: detestation of a particular group whose presence is universal. Religious precepts condemn this group; the laws of most Western nations have punished them. Few people care to admit to their presence among them.

This group is, of course, those we call homosexuals. Antipathy to them—and condemnation, loathing, fear, and proscription of homosexual behavior—is what we call homophobia. Homophobia sometimes seems to be especially virulent in, and perhaps even unique to, Western culture. Studies of sexual behavior in other cultures, past and present, have rarely discovered the social, legal, moral, or religious disapproval of homosexual behavior common to so many eras of Western history.[1] Indeed, in modern Western society, where racism is disapproved, anti-Semitism is condemned, and misogyny has lost its legitimacy, homophobia remains, perhaps the last acceptable prejudice.

1 Homosexuality

"Homosexuality" describes sexual desire or relationships between people of the same sex. "Homosexuals" are individuals who engage in homosexuality or experience homosexual desire. Today, many consider both terms to imply a "sexual orientation," an unchangeable psychosexual organization that may be congenital and inherited, rather than a "sexual preference," which term suggests that homosexual behavior may be a matter of choice. Homosexuals are divided by sex and by terminology into "gay men" and "lesbians," and distinguished from "bisexual," "transgendered," and "transsexual" persons.

The word "homosexuality" was coined in 1868 by the German-Hungarian journalist Karl Maria Kertbeny in a letter written to the sexologist Karl Heinrich Ulrichs. He used it again in 1869, in an anonymous pamphlet opposing the Prussian antisodomy law. Kertbeny argued that the state had no right to penalize or even to control private consensual homosexual behavior, and that "homosexuals" ought not to be objects of derision and stigma. Kertbeny's terminology contrasted *Homosexualität*—sexual desire between persons of the same sex—with what he called *Normalsexualität*. By "normal" sexuality he meant the sexual practice of the majority of people. The term posited differing, indeed opposing, categories of sexuality but unfortunately reinforced a growing psychiatric tendency to define homosexuality as abnormal. "Homosexuality" was given medical sanction, also in 1869, in an article by the German sexual theorist Dr. Karl Westphals, in which he defined homosexual desire as "contrary sexual feeling." (This was translated into English as "inverted sexual feeling," implying that homosexuality was a reversal or the opposite of what would eventually be named "heterosexuality.")

The term "homosexual" may have been first used in English in 1883, in *A Problem in Greek Ethics,* an essay by the English critic and homosexual apologist John Addington Symonds, in which he argued that the Greeks not only tolerated "homosexual passions" but deemed them of spiritual value. The earliest known use of "homosexual" in an American text was in the May 1892 issue of the *Chicago Medical Recorder,* in an article entitled "Responsibility in Sexual Perversion" by the legal psychiatrist Dr. James Kiernan. Kiernan defined an individual whose "general mental state is that of the opposite sex" as a "pure homosexual."[2] In later medical studies, "homosexuality" came to mean, more broadly, same-sex desire, and "homosexual" was used to signify the individual. "Homosexuality" came into popular use in the 1920s; "heterosexuality" followed in the 1930s. Since then, "homosexual" and "heterosexual" have been fixed in medical terminology and public opinion as identifying two separate and definitively different kinds of sexuality, and two different and separate kinds of sexual actor.

Though the term is of relatively recent invention, the behavior it describes has always been part of human sexual activity.[3] That human beings have desired, loved, and had sex with members of their own sex over time is abundantly demonstrated in the visual art and medical, philosophical, and literary texts of all historical periods.[4]

2 Homophobia

The term "homophobia" is now popularly construed to mean fear and dislike of homosexuality and of those who practice it.[5] The word, which may have been coined in the 1960s, was used by K. T. Smith in 1971 in an article entitled "Homophobia: A Tentative Personality Profile."[6] In 1972, George Weinberg's book *Society and the Healthy Homosexual* defined it as "the dread of being in close quarters with homosexuals." Mark Freedman added to that definition a description of homophobia as an "extreme rage and fear reaction to homosexuals."[7]

One basis for this fear, many argue, is the perception that homosexuality and homosexuals disrupt the sexual and gender order supposedly established by what is often called natural law. Adverse reactions to homosexuals and to homosexuality, therefore, are founded upon fear and dislike of the sexual *difference* that homosexual individuals allegedly embody—stereotypically, effeminacy in homosexual men, mannishness in homosexual women. Another source of homophobia is the fear that the social conduct of homosexuals—rather than homosexual behavior alone—disrupts the social, legal, political, ethical, and moral order of society, a contention supposedly supported by history and affirmed by religious doctrine.

Homophobia has links with sexism as well as with anti-Semitism and with prejudice against people of color. Like sexism—denigration of women by men—homophobia employs stereotypes. If men are contemptuous of women because they accept stereotypical notions about women's alleged weakness, irrationality, sexuality, or inferiority, they are also contemptuous of homosexuals because they believe that gay men act "like" women. Skin color, race, and religion create antagonisms that are especially exacerbated when the stigmatized party is also gay or lesbian. "Faggot" and "dyke" rival "cunt," "spic," "nigger," and "kike" in offensiveness, but in a society where homophobia is not universally disapproved, it remains acceptable to utter those epithets even when the others are considered unacceptable. Indeed, "faggot" and "dyke" become the terms that unite different prejudices in familiar combinations like "Jew faggot," "fat dyke," and "nigger faggot."

Homophobia is not limited to heterosexuals, of course. It can also be found among homosexuals; indeed, it has long been a commonplace of gay lore that rabid homophobes are often repressed homosexuals. Just as homophobia exists between nonhomosexual and homosexual people, so it can exist between gay men and lesbians, both as sexism and as incomprehension or dislike of another kind of sexuality. Nor, indeed, is racism unknown among lesbians and gay men. Like other prejudices, homophobia among homosexuals may result from internalization of the lessons of a homophobic society.

Homophobia can represent multiple prejudices, and so a more accurate term might be "homophobias." In *The Anatomy of Prejudice,* Elisabeth Young-Bruehl names the primary prejudices as sexism, racism, anti-Semitism, and homophobia. She argues that they fall into one or another combination of categories: obsessional, hysterical, or narcissistic.[8]

Obsessional prejudice, by her definition, sees its objects as omnipresent conspirators, or enemies set on one's destruction, who therefore must be eliminated. Hysterical prejudice—which in Young-Bruehl's view has a strong component of sexual repression—interprets the hated individuals as "other," as inferior, and as sexually threatening. Racism is the best example of hysterical prejudice. Those who suffer from narcissistic prejudice "cannot tolerate the idea that there exist people who are not like them."[9]

She argues that homophobia, alone of all the prejudices, fits into all of these categories. Homosexuals are, Young-Bruehl notes, "all-purpose victims": clannish and dangerous "like" Jews; sexually obsessed and predatory "like" people of color. They are "like" women and therefore not like real men, or they are women who "do what men do—they compete for women."[10]

This book will demonstrate that homophobia has taken various forms and arisen from many sources. Invented, fostered, and supported over time by different agencies of society—religion, government, law, and science—it tends to break out with special venom when people imagine a threat to the security of gender roles, of religious doctrine, or of the state and society, or to the sexual safety and health of the individual.

3 History

The history of homosexuality has been much chronicled by devoted laborers in the field of lesbian and gay studies, but the history of homophobia has had less comprehensive attention.[11] I will survey the social and religious, legal and political, moral and philosophical dimensions of homophobia over time. I will examine judgments made about those who engage in same-sex sexual practice, and consider the consequences those judgments have had for those who were judged. The scenes of this exploration will be historical events and literary, religious, philosophical, and scientific texts. My assumption is that even if homophobia is imagined by most homophobes to be an intellectualized name for an innate antipathy to homosexuals, it nevertheless represents a product of nurture and socialization.

A historical survey of homophobia will necessarily be primarily a story of prejudice against male homosexuality. Abhorrence and persecution of same-sex practice, and their documentation, have traditionally been the domain of male privilege; likewise, male homosexuality has been the primary target of homophobia. Indeed, until recent times, lesbians were nearly invisible in history. Where I find historical prejudice against lesbians, I will examine it. But just as sexism aimed at men is different from sexism aimed at women, so prejudice against lesbians is a very different subject from prejudice against male homosexuals, and manifests itself in different ways. Because this is so, the larger story of homophobia against lesbians demands a book of its own.[12]

Our history begins in antiquity. Part One, "Before Homophobia?," considers the Greco-Roman period, when there is ample evidence to show that homosexual behavior between men as well as between women was common and—within clear conventional limits—approved.[13] Homosexual behavior became a subject of concern only when its practitioners were seen to have broken certain sexual and social rules, and to have threatened conventional ideas about gender.

Part Two, "Inventing Sodom," looks at the sacred books, laws, and customs of Judaism and early Christianity. Though contemporaneous with Greek and Latin writings, these texts reflect a more general aversion to homosexual behavior, which is seen as an emblem of decadent paganism—godless, debauched, and heretical. For both Jews and early Christians, the Old Testament story of the destruction of Sodom became the foundation text of homophobia, even though neither Jews nor early Christians, including Christ himself, unanimously interpreted it as a text condemning homosexual behavior.

In the early days of Christianity, the writings of St. Paul consolidated the rejection of homosexual behavior; his definition of such conduct owed much to the Jewish Scriptures, but was also indebted to the ascetic and antisexual moral teachings of some Jewish and Christian philosophers, especially Neoplatonists, who tried to retune ancient philosophy to play in harmony with the music of the new faith.

Part Three, "A Thousand Years of Sodomy," surveys the period between the fall of Rome and the beginning of the Renaissance. During this period, "sodomy" was defined in the canon law of the Roman Catholic Church as any nonprocreative act between persons of either sex, though it came to be understood primarily as a forbidden sexual act between males. In the thirteenth century, Pope Gregory IX called sodomites "abominable persons—despised by the world [and] dreaded by the council of heaven." It remained only for the avenging flames of Sodom actually to be kindled beneath a sodomite, which was done in 1292 when the first recorded victim of state-sponsored homophobia was burned at the stake.

By the Renaissance, the definition of sodomy had expanded. Once only sexual, the sin had now become conflated with all kinds of social deviance. Sodomites were accused of being heretics, traitors, sorcerers, or witches, the cause of plagues and civic disaster. But during the Renaissance—the subject of Part Four, "Lighting Bonfires"—the rebirth of classical studies brought about a reconsideration of the morality of intimate social, and sexual, relations between males. Consequently, some Renaissance literature celebrates eroticized friendship between males, often described as "masculine love." But other texts reveal a powerful antisodomy discourse, derived from religion and law and manifest in popular satire and philosophy.[14] Though erotic same-sex friendship was celebrated, the period also saw a sharp rise in the persecution and execution of suspected sodomites.

The seventeenth and eighteenth centuries, discussed in Part Five, "Sodomy and the Enlightenment," produced much literature deriding homosexual behavior and little literature approving it. Protestantism was as rigorous in its prohibitions as Rome was. While the churches condemned sodomy as a sin, the state passed even harsher statutes punishing sodomy as a crime. Convictions of sodomites increased yet again; between 1750 and 1830, homophobia turned into hysteria, as sodomites were arrested, tried, and, more often than ever before, executed.

Social discrimination and harsh legal repression paradoxically gave rise to a distinct identity based on sexual desire, and a way of publicly expressing that identity began to develop. Sodomites were defined as social outcasts, monsters and effeminates, and ostracised. Some men who engaged in homosexual behavior also behaved effeminately and cross-dressed. Called "mollies," these men made their manner of dress and style of expressing their sexuality a style of life. The mollies questioned male social and sexual roles, as sodomites never had before.

Others also questioned the ethics and morality of the regulation of private sexual conduct by the state. One man, apprehended for attempting sex with another man, asked by what right the police interfered with the use of his "own body." The philosopher Jeremy Bentham (1748–1832) argued that consensual sodomy ought not to be a crime. In the 1830s, an anonymous poem that claimed to detail the homosexual life of Lord Byron asserted that of many sexual crimes daily committed in England, the least was sodomy.

Part Six, "Victorian Secrets," concerns the period from 1850 to 1910. It was then that England, America, and Europe witnessed the most remarkable period of homoerotic self-expression since the Renaissance. Writers advocated equality for homosexuals: in France—where after the Revolution all sexual acts had been decriminalized—Rimbaud and Verlaine scandalized the nation by advocating sex between men. Even earlier in Germany, Heinrich Zschokke and Heinrich Hössli wrote essays (in 1821 and 1836–38, respectively) on homosexual eros and the manly love of the Greeks, arguing that such love was no crime. In Austria, the term *homosexualität* was invented, to describe sexual difference.

In England, homoeroticism became a subject for all manner of texts, most famously Lord Alfred Douglas' "Two Loves." It was Douglas who, in this poem, coined the phrase "the love that dare not speak its name." Whitman's American songs of the love of comrades were heard by sympathetic listeners in England and echoed by John Addington Symonds and Edward Carpenter, who asserted the need for social and sexual equality for homosexuals and demanded that homosexual acts be decriminalized. In the 1890s, however, this ferment was extinguished by the trial and conviction of Oscar Wilde. For the Victorians,

Wilde stood as proof that homosexuality was pernicious and even infectious, dangerous to the nation, its youth, its families, and its image of manhood.

Part Seven, "New World Homophobia," shifts the focus to the history of American attitudes toward homosexuality. Homophobia can be discovered as far back as the original conquest of the Americas by a variety of European adventurers in the sixteenth and seventeenth centuries. Protestant moral opinion led to the institution of laws condemning homosexual behavior, laws that became ever more draconian during the nineteenth century. During this time, some homosexual writers, such as Walt Whitman, Bayard Taylor, and Xavier Mayne, created fictions in which manly men unashamedly loved equally manly men.

Part Eight, "Normal Homosexuals," turns to the beginning of the twentieth century, when some writers invented outrageous parodies of the male in female clothes, as in the pseudonymous novel *The Scarlet Pansy* and the lurid sexual autobiography *The Female Impersonator*. Whichever paradigm they chose—homosexuals as real men, or homosexuals as imitation women—all resisted the increasingly vocal American homophobia. By the beginning of the century, homosexuality had come to be understood as a "perversion" rather than as "inversion"; thinking had departed from the idea that homosexuality was simply a reversal of sexual attraction to the notion that it was pathological and that homosexuals might be insane. To "cure" them, homosexuals were subjected to "treatment" that included involuntary incarceration and drug and shock therapies, an approach that lasted well into the 1950s.

By the mid-twentieth century homosexual behavior was also seen as subversion. Senator Joseph McCarthy and his homosexual assistant, Roy Cohn, searched out and exposed "known homosexuals" in government service, some of whom lost their jobs while others took their own lives. In an America in which homosexuals had become the target of state-sponsored persecution, homophobia was an absolutely acceptable prejudice. By the 1960s, 82 percent of American men and 58 percent of American women surveyed believed that only Communists and atheists were more dangerous than homosexuals. Contemporary writers characterized homosexuals as perverts, girlish, sinister, decadent, unmanly, insane, degenerate, criminal, and un-American. From the 1940s to the 1960s, a startling number of novels and plays dealt with homosexuality and homosexuals. A few were positive, but most offered a troubling vision of sensitive, vaguely effeminate young men or wicked, mannish, and scheming lesbians. Literature usually saw to it that these characters met some ignominious end, often involving murder or suicide. Life echoed art, as violence against homosexuals, who were just beginning to call themselves gay, escalated.

Perhaps in resistance, gay liberation movements began to appear. Both in literature and in social activism, homosexuals began to revolt, first in the 1950s and then definitively in 1969 with the rebellion at New York City's Stonewall Inn. Liberation produced a new gay culture, which took root in manifold areas of American life. In the 1970s, gay culture often took the form of social protest and political activism, but it also potently influenced education, religion, entertainment, the media, and material culture in what was called the homosexualization of America.[15]

So successful was this culture in establishing itself that it encountered a conservative backlash, which continues to this day. The most recent expressions of homophobia draw upon age-old fears about the dangers that homosexuality and homosexuals pose to the stability, the morality, and the health of society. Those who fear and despise homosexuals—homophobes—believe that homosexuals are predators who molest children, seduce young people, flaunt their sexuality, and proselytize for their sexual practice and "lifestyle." Homosexuals, they assert, encourage promiscuity, spread disease, and advocate the destruction of the family. Many homophobes allege the truth of fundamentalist biblical arguments that are said to prove and condemn homosexuality's sinfulness and substantiate its status as a perversion. Some Christian fundamentalists even insist that homosexuals afflicted with AIDS are sinners appropriately punished by divine retribution.

Many homophobes, whose political views are colored by their religious convictions, crusade to deprive gay people of certain civil rights that at present are guaranteed to all, gay and straight. Though private, consensual sodomy—often characterized as "homosexual sodomy"—remains criminal in most U.S. states, some extreme homophobes advocate even harsher legal sanctions against gay people, sanctions that would be based simply on their known sexual orientation; some seek the death penalty for those who commit any homosexual act.

For homophobes, the terms "homosexual" and "heterosexual" register absolute concepts of sexual difference, and pit "abnormality" against "normality." To such people, "homophobia" is not an abstract belief, a religious doctrine, or a political argument (though homophobes employ it in all those ways); it is a fear and distaste so deeply felt as to seem ordained by natural law, even inscribed in the genes. For them, homosexuality subverts the lifestyle of decent Americans. These homophobes argue that homophobia should not be considered bigotry or intolerance, but an aspect of their version of the values of society. They can, indeed, proudly embrace homophobia.

Yet homosexuality has gained some measure of acceptance. Gay people, as gay activists proclaim, are everywhere. In public life, gay people make their presence known not only through public protest but daily on the job, in the army and in the police, in church, in politics. So urgent has the need to come out seemed, that many well-known people have risked—and sometimes enhanced—their celebrity by publicly proclaiming their real convictions about gay rights along with their identity. So too, countless less well known gay people—risking, perhaps, even more—have chosen no longer to hide their sexual orientation from their families, friends, and employers.

Images of marching gay activists clearly offend and enrage homophobes and may disquiet even more-tolerant Americans. But the media present a more generous picture of gay people and of homosexuality. Influential newspapers, such as the *New York Times,* and mass circulation newsmagazines, such as *Time* and *Newsweek,* no longer routinely denigrate homosexuals. Even more remarkable is the positive portrayal of lesbians and gay men in movies and on television. Films have realistically and sympathetically portrayed the tragedy of AIDS and dealt with the problems of being gay in a straight environment; occasionally, positive comedies about gay life have appeared. Television offers a variety of programming, including situation comedies that feature amusing (and usually rather loopy), nice gay boys and sharp, witty lesbians. Far from being monsters or perverts, these characters are, such programs tell us, just folks, nothing if not lovable. Their sexual lives, if alluded to at all, are presented as "different strokes" and never pictured on-screen. Perhaps in part because of these images, it sometimes seems that straight Americans have come to accept the homosexuals in their midst.

However, in 1999, forty states still allowed known homosexuals to be summarily fired from their jobs, without cause.[16] In 1998, 54 percent of Americans still believed homosexuality to be a sin, and even more—59 percent—believed it to be morally wrong; 44 percent believed that homosexual relations between consenting adults should be illegal.[17] Though a trial like that of Oscar Wilde may be inconceivable, gay people are still metaphorically on trial in Congress and in state legislatures, where civil rights are denied, and in the streets, where the verdict is often death. The 1999 murder of Matthew Shepard, a gay

twenty-one-year-old college student, by two self-proclaimed homophobes stands as gruesome testimony to the viciousness of homophobia
in America. The killing shocked most Americans. Across the nation
vigils and rallies were held to protest violence against gay people. Bills
penalizing hate crimes were introduced in a number of state legislatures. When they came to a vote, however, all of the bills were
defeated.[18]

To any observer of sexual history and social attitudes, homophobia
must seem a constant and even ineradicable presence. The history of
homosexuality seems to confirm that same-sex behavior has long been
the object of legal, social, and religious persecution; just as homosexuality seems to be a ubiquitous aspect of human behavior, it may
sometimes seem that homophobia is as well. Yet, like "sexuality" and
"homosexuality"—concepts and terms only recently invented, and
both of which have undergone reevaluation—homophobia may prove
to be a construction responsive to historical and social forces. Like so
many of the seemingly immutable forces of history, it may be open
to change, even to eradication. This book is intended as a contribution
to that enterprise.

(Top) A bearded man wearing women's clothing dances, as does a
second bearded man wearing male attire, a cloak, and a garland.
(Bottom) Two bearded men wearing women's clothing and carry-
ing parasols dance to music provided by a woman.

PART ONE

Before Homophobia?

*"Homosexuality" and "Homophobia"
in Antiquity*

Chapter One

Inventing Eros

Nearly every age reinvents Greece in its own image. Rome appropriated Grecian glory to ornament Roman grandeur. The rediscovery of Greek literature and art gave the Renaissance a new aesthetic and propelled Europe from the medieval into the modern age. In the eighteenth and nineteenth centuries, Greece was the ideal upon which many modern nations modeled their systems of education, ethics, and government, and even their architecture. Now, at the turn of the century, ancient Greece is still popularly lauded as the ideal democracy, and the ancient Greeks as the best examples of physical and moral achievement, to which all men and nations ought to aspire.

Figuring in the imaginative re-creation of Greek antiquity has been the perception of those centuries as a golden age in which homosexual behavior was not just condoned but associated with the highest social, spiritual, and moral values. The idea of Greece as a utopia in which homosexual love flourished without blame or censure has been central to the defense of same-sex love from the Renaissance to the present day. And that view contains much that is true. The reality, however, is more complex.

Classical Greek had no word for "homosexuality" nor any word equivalent to our "homosexual," though a number of terms described those who engaged, frequently or exclusively, in homosexual behavior.[1] Nor was there a Greek word to express the special concept of homophobia, at least not as we understand it today. But even without a word for it, antiquity may have known something very much like homophobia; men who engaged in certain homosexual acts sometimes became the objects of general derision and abhorrence. Indeed, as we will see, many believed that the sexual activities and the demeanor of such people were indubitable signs of a different—and contemptible—sexual nature.

Locating Greek homophobia in antiquity means locating it in Greek writing. It is best to note, however, that the Greek texts available to us are only a small part of a literature now mostly lost. And as the classicist John J. Winkler cautions, the surviving Greek texts do not represent ancient society as a whole.[2] Rather, they reflect the conventions of a small coterie of educated upper-class adult male citizens and the theories of a few philosophers whose ideas and writings may have been ignored or even ridiculed by most Greeks. When we say that we know what the Greeks believed about homosexual behavior, we are saying that we know what Plato and Xenophon, Aristophanes and Aristotle wrote about the matter. For the sake of brevity, I will refer to "the Greeks" when in fact I am usually concerned with those few writers whose texts have been taken over time to speak with that people's collective voice.

The Greek voice is far from uniform. Much of the extant Greek literature—epics and dramatic tragedy, for example—retells ancient myths and legends. Some reflects the contemporary concerns of philosophers, scientists, or politicians. The poetry, lyric, erotic, and romantic, embodies—or perhaps invents—the social conventions that governed both affectional and sexual attitudes. Attic comedy, on the other hand, often satirizes those same attitudes. To better understand what kinds of homosexual behavior generated anxiety among the Greeks, we must first begin with an overview of what some ancient writers said about love and sexual relations between men.

1 Imagining Eros

In ancient Greece the *ideal* of same-sex desire was encompassed within the philosophical concept of *paiderastia,* a term derived from the combination of *pais* (boy or child) and the verb *eran* (to love), the source of *eros* (desire). This ideal imagined a relationship between an older and a younger male, the former an adult citizen, experienced in life, conversant with proper conduct and civic duty, wise in the ways of warfare, exemplary in his management of his household and of his wealth, dutiful to his parents, virtuous, brave, honorable, and devoted to truth. The younger male, commonly described as a youth whose beard had not yet begun to grow, was expected to be modest in demeanor, athletic and brave, eager to improve himself, and willing to learn what his mentor and lover could teach about the general conduct of life and love. *Paiderastia* implied a relationship that combined the roles of teacher and student with those of lover and beloved, and it carried the expectation of sex between the two.

The Greek language provided specific terms for each role. The beloved or desired boy is sometimes called *pais* or the related *paidika*. Often he is *eromenos,* "one who is loved or desired"; *aitas,* "the listener, receiver"; or *kleinos,* "the famous" or "the admired." The mentor is called *erastes,* "the lover"; or *eispnelos,* "the inspirer"; or *philetor,* "the befriender" of the *kleinos.* The *erastes* was presumed not only to woo and seduce the *eromenos* but also to instruct him in the arts of the hunt and of war, in the right conduct of life, and in proper behavior as a citizen. It was assumed that the *erastes* would also eventually take a wife—which did not necessarily mean that he would abandon homosexual practice—and that the *eromenos* in his turn would become an *erastes* to other youths. According to Greek legend, this pederastic or transgenerational homosexual relationship was invented either by Zeus, when he kidnapped the young Ganymede, or by Laius, father of Oedipus, when he kidnapped the youth Chrysippus.[3]

Paiderastia, which should not be confused with pedophilia, did not involve the sexual use of children, a practice that antiquity viewed with as much horror as we do today. When men pursued younger males, those they pursued were theoretically ready for the chase—that is, they had reached puberty. Such relationships were governed by centuries of tradition handed down from father to son, ratified in an extensive philosophical, heroic, and erotic literature, and, it is claimed, ordained in law by Solon the lawgiver himself, who decreed that before marrying, a citizen had the obligation to take as a lover and pupil a younger male and train him in the arts of war and citizenship.[4] Many ancient sources suggest that the erotic relationship between a man and a boy was both a social ideal and a common practice; this judgment, confirmed by modern classical historians, is based on a substantial body of visual evidence (Greek vase paintings, of older and younger males in

various relationships, including sexual intimacy), and on ancient literature (the poems of Book Twelve of the Greek *Anthology*, for example,
are almost exclusively dedicated to the love of boys).[5] Of course, our
knowledge of *paiderastia* comes primarily from the literature and visual
art produced by the literate, the aristocratic, and the wealthy. Because
what we know about many Greek homosexual customs comes from
such sources, it can be argued that *paiderastia* was an idealized convention, even a toy, of a handful of Greek upper-class males.[6] What men
who were not literate or who were not aristocrats, who could not write
about their desire or did not have the means to picture it, may have
done is a matter for speculation. This having been said, however, in
recent years classical historians have produced extensive evidence to
show that the homosexual behavior that the Greeks called *paiderastia*
was a common and even conspicuous feature of Greek daily life among
all classes by the sixth century B.C.E.[7] Speaking about classical Athens,
David Halperin observes that no one who studies classical antiquity
will doubt that "paederasty was a social institution in classical
Athens—an institution often thought, moreover, to serve a variety of
beneficial purposes." Nor, he continues, should anyone doubt that it
was also "an expression of a deeply felt sexual desire."[8]

But *paiderastia* was not the only kind of homosexual relationship in
the ancient world.[9] Love and sex between adult males are evident in literature and visual art, and there is ample evidence that intimate and
permanent relationships existed between men of relatively close ages.[10]
Age may have mattered to some Greeks; to others it apparently did not,
for Socrates loved the adult Alcibiades. Some men remained lovers into
mutual adulthood: Pausanias and Agathon, speakers in Plato's *Symposium,* appear to have been lovers of long duration. In the second century C.E. the poet Strato confessed that though he liked boys at any age
from twelve to seventeen, he knew very well that when they were older
the relationship became more serious, for "if anyone likes older boys,
he is not playing any more, but desires someone to respond."[11] Obviously, youth enhanced male beauty and spurred desire, but—perhaps
summarizing a general opinion of his time about the age at which men
could be desirable—Xenophon observes, "Beauty is not to be condemned . . . that it soon passes its prime, for just as we recognize beauty
in a boy, so we do in a youth, a full-grown man, or an old man."[12]

Greek visual art also shows scenes of sex between men of near equal
ages and, presumably, status. The historian K. J. Dover discovered sev-

eral vase paintings that show such couples: in one, two youths are wrapped in a cloak—that is, they are about to have sex; in another, two youths lie together, one caressing the other as he swings his leg over him in preparation for sex.[13]

Whether literary and pictorial evidence reveals, in Dover's words, "what actually happened" or instead reflects "an ideal pattern of sentiment and practice that dominated public utterance and convention," there can be no doubt that homosexual activity was an accepted part of the lives of Greek males at an early age and that it could continue without qualm in adulthood.[14] If an adult male introduced a handsome boy to sex—and if, in doing so, he introduced his young lover to a world of responsible citizenship—then the ideal was served and desire satisfied. Since much Greek literature, such as the poems in the *Anthology*, suggests that sex and not altruism was the more driving motive, it may be naive to imagine that a handsome face provoked only the contemplation of philosophy. Nevertheless, lust was not all that motivated Greek men. If that were the case, then Achilles would not have lamented Patroclus with so much anguish nor would ancient literature detail valor, love, and fidelity between male couples like Harmodius and Aristogiton, Orestes and Pylades, or Damon and Pythias, who live—and die—for each other. Nowhere in Greek thought can we find condemnation of homosexual activity between two males of any age, as long as it conformed to fairly simple guidelines of sexual propriety, which prohibited prostitution, sex with underage boys or slaves, and certain forms of lovemaking.

2 Legitimating Eros

The Greek preoccupation with appropriate forms of homosexual activity is reflected in discussions that attempt to define "legitimate" *eros*, the proper sexual and social conduct between lovers. The most comprehensive and detailed theory of the origins, nature, social value, and metaphysical meaning of homosexual love appears in Plato's dialogue the *Symposium*.

The *Symposium*, written sometime around 385 B.C.E., concerns the nature and the right conduct of an erotic relationship between the lover and the beloved. The piece is cast as a conversation at a drinking party given by the tragic poet Agathon about 416 B.C.E. The topic of love is addressed in turn by Phaedrus, a writer; by Pausanias, the lover of

Agathon; by the comic poet Aristophanes; by the doctor Eryximachus; and by Socrates himself. In the *Symposium,* love is always construed to be homosexual love, and it is the unquestioned presumption that love between males is the highest form of love. While it can be—and, according to Socrates, even *should* be—expressed spiritually rather than physically, none of the speakers are troubled that such love can be accompanied by sex.

Phaedrus proposes a parallel between healthy love-relationships and the healthy life of the state. He argues that Love is the oldest of the gods and "the most powerful to assist men in the acquisition of merit and happiness." Love between a youth and his lover promotes virtue in the youth, he argues, inspires ambition in the lover, and leads to happiness for both, as each sets an example of merit and worthiness for the other to follow. Phaedrus declares that "there can be no greater benefit for a boy than to have a worthy lover . . . nor for a lover than to have a worthy object for his affection." In such a relationship, both lovers will acquire not only virtue but also the "ambition for what is noble," without which "[neither] a state nor an individual can accomplish anything great or fine." Phaedrus expresses his high opinion of the value of intimate relationships between male lovers when he asserts that a state made up only of lovers and their beloveds "could defeat the whole world" (178b–180e).[15]

Pausanias adds to Phaedrus' praise of male love by explaining the circumstances under which it is permissible for a beloved to gratify— that is, to have sex with—his lover. He claims, first, that love between males is not only different from love between men and women but superior to it, because it is discriminating, faithful, and permanent and because men are superior to women in both intelligence and strength.[16] Pausanias makes a distinction between men attracted by both women *and* young men and those only "attracted by the male sex"; this distinction suggests the existence in ancient Greece of men who engaged exclusively in homosexual acts. These men, indeed, "do not fall in love with mere boys" (that is, certainly not with underage boys, nor even with youths who had reached the accepted sexually available age of fourteen), but wait until "they reach the age"—about seventeen or eighteen—"at which they begin to show some intelligence, that is to say, until they are near to growing a beard." For these men's "intention is to form a lasting attachment and a partnership for life" (180e– 182a).[17] Pausanias considers love between males that has as its object both intellectual satisfaction and the creation of a lasting partnership to be nobler than the indiscriminate search for temporary and merely sexual satisfaction with women or boys.[18]

Like Phaedrus, Pausanias links love between men to the presence of democracy in the state. He asserts that "in parts of Ionia . . . and elsewhere under Persian rule," such love is condemned because of "the absolute nature of their empire; it does not suit the interest of their government that a generous spirit and strong friendships and attachments should spring up among their subjects, and these are the effects which love has an especial tendency to produce" (182a). But in Athens, "the universal encouragement which a lover receives is evidence that no stigma attaches to him; success in a love-affair is glorious, and it is only failure that is disgraceful" (183b–183c).

Pausanias observes that "the truth about every activity is that in itself it is neither good nor bad." This theme of circumstantial morality is central to his view that the beloved can without dishonor grant favors—that is, sex—to the good man, the "man of noble nature."

> There is, as I stated at first, no absolute right and wrong in love, but everything depends upon the circumstances; to yield to a bad man in a bad way is wrong, but to yield to a worthy man in a right way is right. . . . According to our principles there is only one way in which a lover can honorably enjoy the possession of his beloved. . . . If a person likes to place himself at the disposal of another because he believes that in this way he can improve himself in some department of knowledge, or in some other excellent quality, such a voluntary submission involves by our standards no taint of disgrace or servility. . . . This is the Heavenly Love which is associated with the Heavenly Goddess, and which is valuable both to states and to individuals because it entails upon both lover and beloved self-discipline for the attainment of excellence (184d–186a).

Athenian intellectuals devised various theories to explain same-sex desire; in the *Symposium,* the comic poet Aristophanes recounts (or invents) a legend to explain sexual difference. When the human race was created, he says, there were three sexes—the androgynous, the female, and the male—and each sex had four hands, four feet, one head with two faces, and two sets of genitals. The gods, angered by these formidable and proud creatures who dared to attack them, split them in two, thus creating new beings. Those who were the male half of the original androgyne became lovers of women, the female half lovers of men. Women who were halves of the female "direct their attention towards women and pay little attention to men," and "those [men] who were halves of a male whole pursue males." Aristophanes' explanation of the existence and the nature of men who love men, like Pausanias' remarks, suggests that exclusive homosexuality was a category of desire recognizable to the Greeks. Because such men are exclusively devoted to the male sex, Aristophanes continues, "when they grow to be men, they become lovers of boys, and it requires the compulsion of convention to overcome their natural disinclination to marriage and procreation; they are quite content to live with one another unwed." Aristophanes argues that it is physiology and nature that prompts their exclusivity: "Such persons are devoted to lovers in boyhood and themselves lovers of boys in manhood, because they always cleave to what is akin to themselves. . . . The reason is that this was our primitive condition when we were wholes, and love is simply the name for the desire and pursuit of the whole" (191c–192e).

When it is Socrates' turn to speak, he proposes a theory of love from which sex seems to be absent, although, like the other speakers in the *Symposium,* he assumes that significant love relationships are those between men. Socrates reports a dialogue with the wise woman Diotima, in which she leads him to agree to two essential points: first, that love is the desire for the perpetual possession of the good and the true; second, that the highest wisdom lies in the attainment of the knowledge of absolute beauty.[19] Diotima also argues that all men desire immortality. For most men, immortality is achievable only through procreation. But since procreation perpetuates only the flesh, it has no part in the ideal world of truth and beauty. However, there are those who seek to engage in a nobler kind of procreation, men "whose creative desire is of the soul, and who long to beget spiritually, not physically, the progeny which it is the nature of the soul to create and bring to birth. And if you ask what that progeny is, it is wisdom and virtue in general." Those who beget such progeny include "all poets and such craftsmen as have found out some new thing" as well as those who seek the "greatest and fairest branch of wisdom," which is concerned with the "due ordering of states and families" and with "moderation and justice." Diotima makes it clear who such men are:

> When by divine inspiration a man finds himself from his youth up
> spiritually fraught with these qualities, as soon as he comes of due

age he desires to procreate and to have children and goes in search of a beautiful object in which to satisfy his desire. . . . If in a beautiful body he finds also a beautiful and noble and gracious soul, he welcomes the combination warmly, and . . . takes his education in hand. By intimate association with beauty embodied in his friend, and by keeping him always before his mind, he succeeds in bringing to birth the children he has long desired to have, and once they are born he shares their upbringing with his friend; the partnership between them will be far closer and the bond of affection far stronger than between ordinary parents, because the children that they share surpass human children by being immortal as well as more beautiful (205e; 208c–209e).

However, Diotima continues, even such noble procreation is only a prelude to setting forth on the road to enlightenment that leads from the love of individual beauty to the comprehension of moral or absolute beauty. The lover who attains the enlightened state will understand that true love is not the possession of a beautiful person but the "desire for perpetual possession of the good," and that the highest form of wisdom is the contemplation of "absolute beauty." In Socrates' speech, then, Plato legitimates homosexual *eros* by making it the source of aesthetic inspiration and right conduct. But there should be no doubt that, even for Plato, what ends in chaste meditation has had its origin in the consummation of desire.

3 Greek Homosexuality and Homophobia

Greek custom did not condemn nonprocreative sex, nor did Greek law comment on same-sex relationships, except for specific prohibitions such as rape and congress between slaves and freeborn boys or between adults and underage boys. Nor did the Greeks find homosexual desire or practice to be a matter for religious regulation. However, they did pass judgment on homosexual acts and relationships in terms of their effect on social convention, and on the status of Greek society's most important individual, the adult male citizen.

For the Greeks, warrior, citizen, husband, and lover of boys were all facets of masculine identity. The ideal male who appears in heroic, romantic, popular, and philosophical literature is warlike and brave, scrupulous in his duty to his wife, family, and parents. He is pious and eager to serve the city and participate in civic life, through political activity and through marriage by which he perpetuates his own line and creates new members of the body politic. He practices self-control and moderation in all that he does, conserves and increases his inheritance, and avoids extreme behavior in public and personal life. He does not demean his manhood by selling his body for sex. He does not allow himself to be implicated in any sexual act other than as the dominant partner, nor does he exhibit any mannerisms, adopt any costume, or engage in any activities that might suggest effeminacy by imitating the activities, the mannerisms, or the appearance of women. He enjoys sexual relations with his male lover only under the "right" circumstances, at the right time, in the right situation, and in the right way.

We now generally tend to think of homosexuality as irreducibly opposed to heterosexuality, as a preoccupation with same-sex desire and dedication to same-sex practice. The Greeks, however, would have been perplexed by the idea that one could judge a person by *exclusive* reference to the object of sexual desire, without reference to a particular sex act, or that one could be "a homosexual" or "a heterosexual."

The Greeks attached more importance to the sexual instinct than to the sex object.[20] What most concerned the Greek male was not whether the object of desire was male or female, but what place that object occupied in the social and sexual hierarchy. Boys and women, so some modern commentators assert, taking their cue from Michel Foucault's argument in *The Uses of Pleasure,* were socially defined as passive and were thus legitimately desirable. As Foucault explains, "For the Greeks, it was the opposition between activity and passivity that was essential, pervading the domain of sexual behaviors and that of moral attitudes as well."[21] Some evidence suggests that the Greeks believed that it was the duty of passive males—that is, boys and sexually available younger men—to accept penetration, but not their obligation to enjoy it. Only women were imagined to naturally receive pleasure from being penetrated. For younger men it was a necessary indignity, associated with their inferior sexual status.[22]

Adult males were expected to take the active—that is, penetrative—role in sex, because as adult males they had superior status in society. As David Halperin points out, sex in classical Athens was not "knit up in a web of mutuality." Instead it was "a deeply polarizing experience," which divided, classified, and distributed its participants into "distinct and radically opposed categories." It was "a manifestation of personal status, a declaration of social identity," not a sign of some presumed sexual identity or even of an inclination.[23] Within those boundaries, the propriety of active homosexual activity was seldom questioned. In any sexual encounter, whether between males or between male and female, the adult male had the unquestioned right to penetrate and dominate his presumably weaker, usually younger, and socially inferior partner. Indeed, most Greeks would probably have described such a right as derived from the observable fact that adult males were physically stronger than women and young men; they were temperamentally more aggressive and warlike than either, and as citizens enjoyed many rights denied to them.

Some recent commentators, however, have argued that the active-passive theory misreads Greek practice and reflects instead a "modern way of looking at sex" as an act of "domination, aggression, and subjugation." In *Courtesans and Fishcakes: The Consuming Passions of Classical Athens*, James Davidson insists that the Greeks did not "see a gulf between a desire to penetrate and a desire to be penetrated" and considered both pleasurable sex acts.[24] Henderson's assertion is intriguing. Nevertheless, Greek literature and art overwhelmingly suggest that the relationships between men and women or youths, while possibly a source of pleasure to each, were neither socially nor sexually equal.

Few Greeks would have considered "proper" homosexual activity to be in any sense unnatural. More likely, they would have believed male superiority and male prerogative in these areas to be appropriate to the "nature" of the male. It may be that not all Greek males engaged in homosexual relationships, but nothing in Greek society, religion, or law would have condemned the desire to consummate those relationships. Homosexuality was not problematic as long as it was manly, active, and controlled. Some men's exclusive devotion to homosexual liaisons, however, even as active participants, could make them vulnerable to condemnation, because it might lead them into resisting the conventions of proper conduct. On the question of exclusivity and convention, Aristophanes comments in the *Symposium,* as we have seen, that for some men "it requires the compulsion of convention to overcome their natural disinclination to marriage and procreation; they are quite content to live with one another unwed."

Not only the *Symposium* but much other Greek literature praised long-term and faithful relationships between men. It was not exclusivity, as we shall see, but sexual passivity, insatiability, and effeminacy that were not considered natural or acceptable. Though it was presumed that most men could not, and probably should not, enjoy being penetrated, the Greeks also believed that some men did enjoy it. It is upon this question of what was pleasurable to whom—what was the nature of that pleasure and the nature of that individual—that much of the structure of Greek homophobia rests.

Chapter Two

Against Nature

Greek opinion did not associate *approved* homosexual acts with unmanliness or "effeminacy." In fact, classical Greek lacks a precise equivalent for our own concept of effeminacy. A man deemed unmanly was described as *malakos* ("soft") or as *androgynos* ("manly-womanly"), but *malakos* does not mean "homosexual," and it most often denotes some type of moral weakness.[1] What the Greeks thought of as unmanliness could include a variety of flaws, including physical or moral weakness and cowardliness as well as sexual promiscuity, and these flaws did not necessarily imply devotion to passive homosexuality or to women's dress or mannerisms.[2] But men who were exclusively devoted to passive homosexual acts and who adopted the mannerisms or the dress of women were especially open to imputations of lewdness, weakness, or unmanliness. Since it was presumed that women and boys were naturally and socially subordinate to men and sexually passive, any male adult who accepted or sought the passive role was unnaturally subordinating himself to other men. And if no "real" man could enjoy such subordination, then one who did must be constituted differently from other males. Aristotle, in the *Nichomachean Ethics,* implied that some men were *by nature* more inclined to passive homosexuality than others.[3]

Furthermore, the man who sought submissive homosexual sex had surely, in the Greek view, been overpowered by his urges and lost his self-control and sense of moderation, if he was willing to suffer social condemnation and neglect his duty as soldier, citizen, and husband. If he also behaved or dressed like a woman, his shame would be complete, for he had abdicated his natural role as a male and betrayed the sexual and social expectations accompanying that status.[4]

1 Imagining Effeminacy

In a surviving fragment of Euripides' play *Antiope*, written about 410 B.C.E., Zethos, warrior and farmer, confronts his brother, the poet Amphion, and accuses him of effeminacy and cowardice: "You flaunt an outward appearance that mimics a woman. Give you a shield, and you would not know what to do with it, nor could you defend others by bold and manly counsel." In Zethos' eyes, Amphion's unmanly appearance necessarily implies cowardice and ineptitude. Zethos broadens his attack to include Amphion's muse, whom he calls "disturbing, useless, drunken, idle, and spendthrift"; by extension, Amphion—and poets like him—are responsible for the worst ills of social disorder.

Zethos charges that a man who "delights in music and pursues that always . . . will achieve nothing for his family and city and will be no good to his friends," since "inborn qualities are lost when a man is worsted by the delights of pleasure."[5] Those inborn qualities are exactly those that define the ideal citizen and the real man—that is, bravery, industry, usefulness, sobriety, financial moderation, loyalty to family and friends, and fulfillment of civic duty. When Zethos equates the specific delights of music with more general "delights of pleasure," he does not explain how such pleasure might wreak social havoc, but he does not have to. Even though music and poetry were acceptable pursuits for a man, Amphion's devotion to them suggests his deliberate eschewal of other manly activities. This is all the evidence Zethos needs to condemn Amphion and, because he is effeminate, to accuse him of being dangerous to social stability. Zethos' accusations will become increasingly familiar in the language of homophobia.

By a generation or so after Euripides, the effeminate man and the transvestite had become stock characters, as had the adult male who enjoyed passive homosexual sex. Such characters often appear in the satires of Aristophanes, who between about 425 and 388 B.C.E. wrote over forty plays, eleven of which survive. Aristophanes aimed his broad satire at many Greek social conventions and at politicians, the rich, and the upper classes. But one of his chief targets was sex and its conventions. In his play *Plutus,* for example, he even satirized the rituals of homosexual *eros,* suggesting that idealized eroticism is often a mask for common lust. In a dialogue between Carion and Chremylus, the latter differentiates between youths who have sex for money and youths who have sex with their lovers in return for gifts, such as horses or dogs. The erotic theory of *paiderastia* asserted that such gifts from the *erastes* could be accepted without shame by the *eromenos.* Carion will have none of that; he dismisses the argument by saying that boys who accept gifts are no better than those who have sex for money.

However, Aristophanes does not censure other men's admiration of male beauty or condemn their desire for sex with youthful males. Indeed, as Dover points out, there is no passage that "demonstrably ridicules or criticizes any man or any category of men for aiming at homosexual copulation with beautiful young males."[6]

But if Aristophanes is largely silent about one of the central erotic preoccupations of Greek life, he is extremely vocal about one of its chief anxieties. He capitalizes on the comic value of effeminate or transvestite male characters and on the imputation of passive homosexual sex. The objects of his satire are often men like Amphion, artists, intellectuals, and philosophers, or politicians, like the tyrant Cleon in *Knights,* who is accused of being a passive homosexual. Aristophanes wrote for a class that was neither rich nor aristocratic, nor perhaps even literate, and when he satirizes the social or sexual snobbery of the aristocrat, the pretensions of the plutocrat, the hypocrisy of the politician, or the effeminacy or sexual preferences of any of these, he echoes the opinion of his audience. This audience particularly appreciated the implication that politicians, aristocrats, and philosophers were not "real men" at all, but effeminate monsters who would take any man who wanted them, as Aristophanes would surely have put it, up the ass.[7]

The openly effeminate male provoked even more anxiety than the tyrannical, corrupt politician and the lustful aristocrat. In *Thesmophoriazusae,* Aristophanes offers a devastating satirical portrayal of Agathon, a contemporary poet and the host of Plato's *Symposium.* The play opens shortly before the Thesmophoria, a festival devoted to the goddesses Demeter and Persephone in which only women may participate. The celebrants intend to try the playwright Euripides for insults to their sex. Euripides begs Agathon to go to the festival disguised as a woman and speak for him at the trial. Agathon refuses, but eventually Mnesilochus, Euripides' kinsman, volunteers to go. Euripides and Agathon dress him as a woman, using clothes and makeup from Agathon's apparently large supply.

Though Agathon is reluctant to attend the festival, he is less hesitant to don women's garments: he is wearing them when he first appears onstage, though he also carries such manly accoutrements as a sword and oil for use after exercise at the gymnasium.

Mnesilochus, confused, addresses him:

Young man, whoever you are, permit me to address you in the style of Aischylos:

"What woman, or what man, or both combined, with cosmetic art betrays the stigma of his youth in the costume of a virile tart?" I understand the lyre, of course; but what are you doing with a hair-net? A bottle of gymnasium oil, yes; but why the girdle? Why a hand-mirror and a sword at the same time? What are you, you recumbent paradox? A man? Show me; or, if that makes you blush, where are your Spartan boots, your cavalry cloak? Or are you a woman? If so, where are your breasts? No answer. Bashful. If I want to find out, I suppose I'll have to read your *Collected Poems*.

Agathon: Greybeard, greybeard, your malicious envy bombards my ears, but I heed it not at all. However, if you must know, I wear this particular costume by design. A dramatist embarked upon his art should prepare for the voyage; and since my best characters are female, my manner suggests the Heroine. Do you follow me?

Mnesilochus: More or less. I take it you're bare-ass when you go to work on a *Phaedra*.

Agathon: Again, a male role calls for male properties. Thus art makes up for natural defect.

Mnesilochus: Remember me when you write a satyr play: I've a fundamental art that will enchant you.

Agathon: Furthermore, who wants a hairy poet? Bah, these rugged artists! No, let me have Ibykos—there's a writer for you!—or Anakreon or Alkaios, all of them simply a-swim with music. Those boys liked pretty hats and pretty manners, and that's the reason their songs are pretty, too. Or take Phrynichos—you've heard of him, surely: He was a fancy poet with a fancy taste, and his fancy poems go fancying down the ages. It's a law of nature: Art is the perfect mirror of character.[8]

Agathon insists that he wears women's clothes in order to better realize the female characters about whom he writes. As for male roles, Agathon announces that art makes up for nature's defects; this unblushing admission of female tendencies reveals Agathon's rejection of Greek conventions of masculinity. Finally, Agathon places himself in a homoerotic tradition by rejecting "rugged artists" and "hairy poets" and instead invoking Anacreon, Ibycus, and Alcaeus, all known for their love poems to boys.

Agathon is proud of his status as a poet, and is even imperious in his persona as an effeminate male; he seems to consider himself superior to the less imaginative, the "rugged," and the "hairy." He proclaims that as a poet he is a member of an elite, but he also hints that he is special because he can inhabit two genders rather than one, and he suggests that such duality enhances rather than weakens his art. Aristophanes' satire is founded upon the presumption that everything that Agathon *appears* to be also implies what he *is* and what he *does*. Behind the veils, behind the pose of the poet, but reflected in the mirror, appears a man who, sexually submitting for the sake of pleasure, is willing to violate the rules governing the social and sexual behavior of an adult male citizen. As Zethos said of Amphion, Agathon has lost his maleness because "inborn qualities are lost when a man is worsted by the delights of pleasure." And these delights are read as sexual.

Agathon was no doubt known personally to many in Aristophanes' audience, who could appreciate the point of the satire. But Agathon also stood for a *class* of people with whom the audience was familiar as well. Aristophanes' point is that men like Agathon—neither male nor female—disrupt the order of society; the corrupted male body introduces chaos and corruption into the body politic. Of course, Aristophanes wrote comedy, not philosophy. But the Greeks who watched these plays might well have read his satire of effeminacy not only as uproarious comedy but as a more sober warning about the consequences that such betrayal of the self—a form of loss of control—could have for both the individual and the state.

Plato, though, *did* write philosophy. Only a few years separate *Thesmophoriazusae* (411 B.C.E.) from his declaration, in the *Symposium*, that those who "long to beget spiritually" the progeny "which it is the nature of the soul to create," as Diotima says, should search for a youth with a "beautiful and gracious soul," and educate him, since this "partnership" will be "far closer and the bond of affection far stronger than those between ordinary parents."[9] Euripides' Amphion and Aristophanes' Agathon are the comic reverse of Plato's noble man, who inhabits a realm wherein neither women nor effeminacy have any place. Plato's lovers are real men, while Agathon, his gender blurred and dubious, is no man at all.

2 Unnatural Crimes

In the last years of his life, around 350 B.C.E., Plato wrote his final major work, the *Laws,* in which he seems to contradict the opinions about love between men expressed in the *Symposium.* Indeed, in the *Laws* Plato appears to renounce that ideal homoerotic spirituality in favor of the argument that homosexual behavior is unnatural.

The speakers are Megillus of Sparta, Cleinias the Cretan, and an unnamed Athenian stranger, probably intended to be Plato himself. In outlining a plan to establish Magnesia, a utopian state, on Crete, this stranger expounds on civil and legal administration, marriage, education, the arts, sports, agriculture, punishment, religion, and sexual conduct. Magnesia is to be governed upon the principle that there are unchanging and absolute moral standards that can be discovered and translated into a code of law. Correct moral conduct is to be further enforced by religion. Magnesian religion will allow no moral relativism; it is to be founded upon three absolute articles of faith: the gods exist; they are concerned for the welfare of mankind; and they will not forgive human sin and wrongdoing, even if implored to do so by prayer, supplication, or sacrifice. A strict regime of education will teach the precepts of the law, and obedience will be imposed from the earliest years. The foreigner, slave, or citizen who disobeys the law will be subject to the loss of rights and a variety of punishments, including death.

In the course of imagining this state, the question of sexual conduct arises. The Spartan observes that in Sparta the sexes are segregated in order to promote virtue among young men, who eat together and engage in rigorous gymnastic exercises. The Athenian objects that groups of young men might foment revolution. But his real objection is based on the possibility of improper homosexual activity among them. Such segregation, he argues, seems to have "corrupted the natural pleasures of sex" because of the homosexual activity it fosters.[10] The Athenian insists that when man and woman come together to have a child "the pleasure seems to arise entirely naturally." But homosexual intercourse and lesbianism are "unnatural crimes of the first rank," the result of men's and women's inability "to control their desire" (636a–c).

Why is same-sex intercourse "unnatural"?[11] First, argues the Athenian, because the only legitimate purpose of sex is to produce children. Second, homosexual sex is the result of overpowering urges, which are the enemy of individual right conduct and of civic and social order; therefore, the thirst for pleasure must be disciplined. And whereas procreative sexual intercourse produces natural gratification, sex between men or between women is unnatural because it entails gratification for its own sake and does not lead to procreation. Those who seek sexual satisfaction as an end in itself are seeking pleasure without responsibility, that is, without self-control. Thus sex between men or between women is not condemned because it is homosexual per se, but because it does not contribute to the propagation of the race, and can lead to irresponsibility in the citizenry.

The Athenian includes people who engage in homosexual acts among the "inferiors," people who have fallen victim to their own appetites and have lost control of themselves. Just as it is the duty of each individual to control his urges, so a state must control such chaos within itself, for "sometimes evil citizens will come together in large numbers and forcibly try to enslave the virtuous minority" (I, 627). Indeed, a state has not only the right but the duty to stamp out homosexual activity, since such lack of discipline is dangerous to the state.

The Athenian adduces justifications that will echo in all future homophobic discourse: Homosexual behavior is unnatural; in the animal world "males do not have sexual relations with each other, because such a thing is unnatural." It is incompatible with social virtue: if a man is seduced by another male, the Athenian asks, will "the spirit of courage spring to life in the seduced person? Will the soul of the seducer learn habits of self-control?" The seducer who has gratified himself by taking pleasure with another man instead of with a woman has abdicated his role as procreator, and, as the Athenian says, "everyone will censure the weakling who gives in to temptation, and condemn his all too effeminate partner who plays the role of a woman" (836). Euripides and Aristophanes implicitly objected to some types of homosexual activity; Plato is explicit in his objection to *uncontrolled* homosexual activity.

Since the dangers of unbridled homosexual conduct are so great, Magnesia's law guardians, whose role has been simply to administer existing laws, must take the drastic step of becoming legislators. They must enact a law "which permits the sexual act only for its natural purpose, procreation," and forbids homosexual sex and masturbation on the grounds that in them "the human race is deliberately murdered" (838). To ensure compliance, people must be persuaded that, like incest, homosexual acts are "absolutely unholy, an abomination in the sight of the gods, and that nothing is more revolting" (838). If the law is given "sufficient religious backing," claims the Athenian, "it will get a grip on every soul and intimidate it into obeying" (839).

Greek religion, however, did not condemn any form of sexual behavior but incest. The Athenian proposes to associate shame with sex. "If we were incapable of having sexual intercourse without feeling ashamed, our shame would lead to infrequent indulgence, and infrequent indulgence would make the desire less compulsive" (841).

Finally he suggests linking sexual morality to personal ambition. The chief object of Greek athletics, he points out, is victory in the Olympic contests, a victory achieved through iron discipline and self-control. The Athenian reminds his listeners of the commonplace that the great athletes "never had a woman or even a boy" while in training, and then goes on to propose an even greater achievement: "the conquest of pleasure" (840). Just as physical athletes are spurred by ambition for fame, so spiritual athletes, through determination and ambition to succeed in the conquest of pleasure, will forgo all sex and embrace chastity until the time comes for them to have sexual intercourse for the purpose of procreation. The reward: "They will have a happy life."

If the Athenian speaks with the voice of Plato—and most argue that he does—how can we explain the seeming contradiction between the *Symposium*'s apparent approval of homosexual relations and the declaration in the *Laws* that they are an "unnatural crime"? Has Plato changed his opinion?

One answer is that he has. As Trevor Saunders observes, "as Plato grew older and wiser his optimism turned to pessimism, and his idealism into realism."[12] According to this argument, in the *Symposium* Plato offered an ideal pattern for human conduct, in which men would relinquish desire and carnality voluntarily so as to achieve a higher good. In the *Laws*, Plato recognizes that this ideal is unrealizable. Irrationality, loss of self-control, continued desire for sexual indulgence, and the irresponsible search for self-gratification "affect society and the character of the individual" (636). The ideals of the *Symposium*, Plato came to feel, are contradicted by the reality of human desires and appetites.

Realistically, Plato argues in the *Laws,* society must be protected from anything that might endanger it. Realistically, procreation is necessary for the maintenance of the race; homosexual relations do not produce children. Sex is the most irrational and potentially uncontrollable of all appetites. It must be strictly controlled, and Plato therefore proposes realistic laws to control it. As Dover notes, Plato's main concern is to reduce to a minimum "all activity of which the end is physical enjoyment in order that the irrational and appetitive element of the soul may not be encouraged and strengthened by indulgence."[13] However, this proscription is not aimed only at homosexual sex; it applies as much to heterosexual relations. If uncontrolled, both can lead to social disorder.

It can, however, be argued that Plato has not changed his view of love between men. Some of the speeches in the *Symposium*—notably those of Phaedrus, Pausanias, and Aristophanes—obviously approve homosexual sex. Nor does Socrates seem to condemn it. But he values chastity more, and he urges, with Diotima, that physical love is only a step, and one soon necessarily abandoned, on the ladder to self-mastery, wisdom, and the contemplation of the good and beautiful. In the ideal world of the *Symposium,* men who seek the higher good can achieve it in company with a male lover, but only if their love is chaste.

In the *Laws,* in fact, Plato also approves and advocates chaste love between men. In the discussion of friendship that begins his discussion of sexual conduct, he describes the kind of friendship that "is particularly ardent," so much so that "we call it love" (837). There are, he says, three kinds of friendship between men: The first, between men who are "widely different," is often "violent and stormy"—that is, sexual; the second, between men who are alike, produces "a calm and mutual affection that lasts a lifetime" and is chaste. The third category is compounded of the first two. The problem is to discover "what the lover is really after." He is "torn between two opposing instincts: one tells him to enjoy his beloved, the other forbids him. The lover of the body, hungry for his partner who is ripe to be enjoyed, like a luscious fruit, tells himself to have his fill, without showing any consideration for his beloved's character and disposition." But for the lover of virtue, "physical desire will count for very little and the lover will be content to gaze upon his beloved without lusting for him." He "will want a life of purity, chaste lover with chaste beloved." Isn't it obvious, he continues, "that in our state we'd want to see the virtuous kind spring up—the love that aims to make a young man perfect?" (837).

Therefore, though homosexual behavior is to be forbidden and homosexual desire suppressed because they can lead to loss of self-control, not forbidden is the ideal form of love that Greek tradition had always approved, the form that Diotima advocates in Plato's *Symposium:* a calm, lifelong "mutual affection" between two men, predicated on spiritual rather than sexual attraction.

Just how important Plato's ideas were for those Greeks who knew of them is difficult to assess. Philosophers and their speculations were often satirized in Greek literature, so it will not do to presume that the Greeks accepted what Plato proposed. The Athenian, Plato's spokesman, suggests the limits of Plato's influence when he expresses doubt that his project would be put into practice. Even if "sufficient religious backing" were available and the laws strongly enforced, he fears that the citizens of his utopia, "corrupted by seeing and hearing how most other Greeks and non-Greeks go in for 'free' love on a grand scale . . . may prove unable to keep themselves in check." As the Athenian says, "we've reached a point where people still think we'd fail"; there is little hope of "a whole state" endorsing a law forbidding "unnatural" sexual relations (839). The Athenian is well aware that what he proposes is impossible precisely because homosexuality is ubiquitous in his culture. John Winkler observes that this passage "was clearly a thought-experiment on the same order as censoring traditional poetry in *The Republic,* one that went against the grain of the values, practices and debates of Plato's society."[14] Plato did not convince his contemporaries to abandon what they considered harmless pleasures sanctioned by the gods, but he influenced later writers to scrutinize homosexual relationships through the disapproving optic many believed he had provided.

3 Indicting Effeminacy

In 346 B.C.E., just a few years after Plato wrote the *Laws,* the city of Athens concluded a peace treaty with Philip of Macedon. Among the envoys charged with delivering the treaty to Philip and accepting his assent were the orator Demosthenes and the politician Aeschines. Lauded for his bravery in battle in his earlier years, and later distinguished as a tragic actor, Aeschines had entered politics and had made enough of a mark to be chosen for the sensitive mission. However, Philip's machinations brought Aeschines' conduct as envoy under suspicion and led Demosthenes to disassociate himself from the peace process. When Aeschines returned to Athens, Demosthenes denounced him and formally charged him with treason, enlisting the support of Timarchus, a man of considerable wealth who, by virtue of his distinguished political activity, was one of a small number of citizens who had spoken often before the Athenian assembly. He had written many laws and was, as Aeschines observes, noted for his beauty.[15]

In order to delay the treason proceedings against him, Aeschines brought a countersuit against Timarchus, who had achieved notoriety in his early years as a spendthrift and was generally believed to have prostituted himself. Prostitution was not illegal, but any Athenian citizen who had mistreated his parents, avoided military service, shown cowardice in battle, squandered his inheritance, or prostituted himself to another male was forbidden to speak in the assembly and denied the rights of a citizen. If Aeschines could prove that Timarchus, having prostituted himself, had nevertheless spoken in the assembly, then Timarchus would be disenfranchised.

Aeschines won his suit, Timarchus was disenfranchised, and Demosthenes was discredited by association. (Three years later, when Aeschines himself finally came to trial on the treason charge, he was acquitted.) *Against Timarchus* is a written version of the speech given by Aeschines at the first trial. It is also one of the few surviving works of Greek literature entirely concerned with homosexual relationships.[16]

Aeschines proposes to inquire into the character of Timarchus by detailing his past history. He warns the jury that Timarchus' life "has been so shameful that a man who is describing his behavior is unable to say what he wishes without sometimes using expressions that are likewise shameful. But I will try my best to avoid doing this."[17] Aeschines is not simply reluctant to utter offensive or obscene language. No Greek familiar with the comedies of Aristophanes would have been shocked by what we would call obscenity, nor was spoken obscenity considered offensive. As Jeffrey Henderson points out in *The Maculate Muse: Obscene Language in Attic Comedy,* "it was the shame of exposure that made obscenity obscene for the Greeks."[18] Aeschines warns the jurors that they will witness just such an exposure and will hear of actions that are shameful and "unclean by nature" when committed by a male like Timarchus who "had reached the years of discretion" and "knew the laws of the state" (37–39).

Aeschines reports that as soon as Timarchus was past boyhood he went to live in the house of the physician Euthydicus. There, pretending

to be a medical student, he offered himself for sale to merchants, foreigners, and even to "our own citizens" (40). Aeschines names some of
the men who kept Timarchus. First among these is Misgolas, who, finding Timarchus too expensive, dismissed him. Then followed Anticles,
and when Anticles could no longer afford to keep him, Timarchus
found Pittalacus, who had more than adequate resources. Finally, leaving Pittalacus, Timarchus took up with Hegesandrus. All of these men
are characterized as profligate and some as exclusively interested in
homosexual behavior.

Misgolas, for example, though "otherwise honorable and beyond
reproach," has "an extraordinary enthusiasm for homosexual relationships."[19] The point of this observation is not to discredit homosexual
acts, but rather to present Misgolas as a man unable to control his
desire. Aeschines also reports that Misgolas "surrounded himself with
singers and cithera players" (41)—a sure indication of "what sort of
man" Misgolas is (Euripides' Amphion also played the cithera). To further discredit Misgolas, Aeschines points to his youthful appearance:
"Some men, old by count of years, seem mere youths. Misgolas is such
a man. He happens, indeed, to be of my own age. . . . I am quite gray,
as you see, but not he. Why do I speak of this? Because I fear that seeing him for the first time, you may be surprised" and think he "is not
much older than Timarchus" (49). Misgolas has counterfeited youth,
undoubtedly through artificial means. Finally Aeschines notes that
Timarchus "was already past boyhood" when he lived with Misgolas,
so the relationship was one of two adult males, in which sex, however,
might well have played a central role.

Though Aeschines attacks Timarchus' homosexual activities, he
does not dispute the propriety or morality of homosexual acts themselves, nor ever imply that they are any less natural than heterosexual
acts. Indeed, Aeschines notes that he himself has loved handsome boys
and written erotic poems to them; he says he is a devotee of such desire,
describing it in himself as a "habit"—possibly to draw a distinction
between what is merely habitual for him but natural for Timarchus. He
stresses, however, that his desire is governed by self-control, directed
toward proper objects, and ruled by a code of sexual conduct that
rejects both unmanly submission and the acceptance of money for sex.

Timarchus, on the other hand, has violated the code: what Misgolas
wanted to do, Timarchus wanted to have done. That he wanted to submit to anal penetration, rather than merely accepting it, makes the alle-

gation even more serious. No real man could enjoy penetration, but it was not impossible to imagine what kind of man might.

If honor and manhood are outraged by Timarchus' acts, the outrage is exacerbated when Aeschines notes that Timarchus did not sell himself because he needed the money; indeed he "had income enough to satisfy all reasonable desires." Instead, Timarchus behaved as he did "because he was a slave to the most shameful lusts," which ought not "to have mastery over a man who is well born and free" (42).

Deliberately embracing excess, rejecting self-control, willingly accepting an unspeakable sexual role, Timarchus must, Aeschines implies, be a sexual reprobate, a promiscuous *kinaidos*. This "etymologically mysterious" word has the sense of "lewd weakling."[20] Aeschines at one point accuses Demosthenes of *anandrias kai kinaidias,* "unmanliness and lewdness," and describes him as wearing soft, pretty garments about which people would be at a loss to say "whether they had in their hands the clothing of a man or of a woman."[21] In Plato's *Gorgias,* Socrates discusses the evils of a life devoted to excess. As an example, he names *kinaidoi,* who are defined by their insatiable sexual desires, and who embody the evils of a life devoted to the excessive pursuit of pleasure.[22] A man could be, as one Greek observer said, "*kinaidos* in front or behind."[23] However, the term was primarily used to refer to those who engaged in homosexual acts. Thus *kinaidoi*—imagined to be deviant by nature, lewd, weak, sexually insatiable, and of doubtful gender, men who also sometimes adopted the costumes and the submissive sexual role of women—became the opposite of citizen-soldiers, of real men. *Kinaidoi* gave effeminacy a name.[24]

The fact that Timarchus sold himself to several men, Aeschines argues, proves that he has not "merely been a kept man, but . . . a common prostitute" (52). And to make matters worse, one of his clients, Pittalakos, though apparently a man of means, was not a citizen but a slave, the property of the city. He encountered Timarchus at a gambling house and took him home. As Aeschines indignantly says, Timarchus was "not disturbed by the fact that he was going to defile himself with a public slave, but thought only of getting him to be paymaster for his disgusting lusts, to the question of virtue or of shame he never gave a thought" (54). Another potential lover, Hegesandros, catching sight of Timarchus at the house of Pittalakos, also "lusted after" the youth; when Pittalakos refused to give Timarchus up, Hegesandros asked Timarchus directly. Timarchus accepted and became Hegesandros' kept

lover. This, of course, led to violence between Hegesandros and Pittalakos, and to a complex lawsuit. Aeschines' point is not only that
Timarchus associates with disreputable men, gamblers and slaves, but
also that his very presence in the body politic disrupts the civil and public order.

As if all that were not enough—Aeschines continues—once Timarchus "lost his youthful charm" and could no longer attract men to pay
for the demands of his "lewd and depraved nature," which "still craved
the same indulgence," he resorted to "devouring his patrimony, selling
his lands, and even depriving his mother of the burial plot she desired
on the family farm, so eager was he to secure funds for his depravity"
(79). Next to honor and civic responsibility, the wise conservation of an
inheritance and filial care of his parents were a man's primary duties.
Aeschines knew that little elaboration was needed to horrify the jury.

In his concluding remarks, Aeschines voices what he has up till now
only implied: not only is Timarchus an irresponsible citizen, he is that
monstrous thing, "a creature with the body of a man defiled with the
sins of a woman" (185). Aeschines asks the all-male jury, "Who of you
will punish a woman if he finds her in wrongdoing? Or what man will
not be regarded as lacking intelligence who is angry with her who errs
by impulse of nature." It is woman's nature to sin by being sexually
promiscuous or adulterous, but it is not, Aeschines implies, man's
nature. A promiscuous man, such as Timarchus has been, is acting
against his male nature. He is a "man who in despite of nature has
sinned against his own body," and in allowing himself to be used as the
passive object of male desire, he has become a *kinaidos*, virtually a
woman.

Earlier in his oration, Aeschines had contrasted men who "have had
many lovers" and "who have lived the life of free and honorable men"
with men who "have prostituted themselves shamefully and notoriously" (155). Timarchus' particular transgressions now become the
basis for a much broader accusation: "We recognize the prostitute even
without being present at his act, by his shamelessness, his effrontery,
and his habits. For he who despises the laws and morality in matters of
supreme importance comes to a state of soul which is plainly revealed
by his disorderly life. Very many men of this sort have overthrown cities
and fallen into the greatest misfortune themselves" (189). As a class,
Aeschines says, men like Timarchus threaten the youth of Athens, the
hope of the future. Aeschines insists that it is the duty of the law and of
those who administer it to protect youth from these predators. The

most effective means is "to remove from among us such natures," for by doing so Athens' leaders "will turn the aspirations of the young towards virtue" (190–192). Translating Timarchus from individual to type, Aeschines has now moved far beyond his original accusation that Timarchus' sexual transgressions ought to cost him his rights of citizenship.

The motive behind Aeschines' prosecution of Timarchus is, of course, the pursuit of a political enemy more than that of a sexual outlaw. However, Aeschines' choice to destroy his enemy with allegations of sexual deviancy is a technique that has become sadly familiar in the history of homophobia.

Aeschines' condemnation of effeminacy in males, and his contempt for certain kinds of same-sex practices, marks, along with the works of Euripides, Aristophanes, and Plato, an important development in the historical construction of homophobia. Though sex between men under the right conditions was accepted, the abdication of manhood that effeminacy and passivity marked, though also free of legal penalty, carried with it profound social opprobrium. The opinions expressed in these works foreshadow the institution of legal penalties against homosexual behavior, and assert the special responsibility of homosexually active persons for civil and social disorder. They offer an early stereotype of the promiscuous, sexually passive, sexually obsessed, effeminate molester of the young. That special monster, created by homophobia, has long haunted the dreams of those whose chosen mission it is to defend youth, the sanctities of the family, public virtue and order, and, most of all, masculinity.

Chapter Three

Making Monsters

Homosexual Behavior in Roman Society

In his *Satire II,* written about 85 C.E., the Roman poet Juvenal portrays a Roman citizen, once a priest of Mars, who now "decks himself out in a bridal veil" in order to marry another man. Juvenal comments, *"horreres maioraque monstra putares"*: "you may shudder and consider such men even greater freaks"—greater, that is, even than such evil omens as women giving birth to calves, or cows to lambs. Invoking the shades of Roman ancestors, Juvenal argues that the presence in society of such men bodes no good for the Roman people; indeed, it has brought them to a "pitch of blasphemous perversion."[1]

Juvenal's horror is directed at effeminacy and at the sexual passivity he believes it implies. Like Greek literature, the literature of the Roman republic and empire generally celebrated love and sex between men, and in Rome as in Athens, homosexuality was widely practiced and, within certain parameters, generally accepted by both the exalted and the humble. Latin poets presumed that all men at one time or another felt homosexual desire, and Roman art, as the historian John Clarke has documented in *Looking at Lovemaking: Constructions of Sexuality in Roman Art 100 B.C.–A.D. 250,* pictured that desire openly, showing sex between men and boys and between adult males on wall paintings in Roman houses, on coins, and on artifacts—jewelry, terra-cotta lamps, flasks—made for the elite as well as for the masses.[2] Indeed, visual depictions of homosexual acts between men and boys and occasionally between age mates (for example, on the Warren Cup, where the two male partners seem to be of the same age) clearly suggest, as Clarke affirms, that the Romans liked looking at scenes of sex between males just as they liked looking at scenes of sex between men and women. As in Greece, the propriety of sexual acts had more to do with power and the status of penetrator and penetrated than with the latter's sex.[3] So we might heed Clarke's warnings—applicable to sexual practice throughout pre-Christian antiquity—that we should not imagine that because what we see in Roman art is familiar that it necessarily meant to them what it means to us.[4] After all, as Clarke notes, this was a world "before Christianity, before the Puritan ethic, before the association of shame and guilt with sexual acts."[5] However, shame could still attend on men who conducted their homosexual activities in ways outside of what was accepted and approved. That shame left enough room for the satiric creation of a male sexual monster, promiscuous, passive, and effeminate. Even more than their Greek counterparts, Roman writers targeted effeminate men as visible examples of a special tribe.

1 Imperial Desire

No Roman law has been discovered that categorically prohibited homosexual acts, nor have historians found any indication that such a prohibition ever existed. What did regulate homosexual activity, and indeed all sexual activity, was the distinction made in custom and in law between sexual relations with slaves, and sexual relations with citizens or freeborn Romans. Sex with slaves was considered simply the acceptable use of property. As Craig Williams explains in *Roman Homosexuality*, violation of the "sexual integrity of freeborn Romans of either sex" was a heinous offense, often designated by the term *stuprum*.[6] In early Roman texts, *stuprum* can refer to a wide variety of sexual activities from general fornication to debauchery in brothels; it eventually came to signify what Romans deemed most shameful: violation, in some sense, of the freeborn. *Stuprum* condemns not homosexual or heterosexual relationships, but the sexual violation of status.

Stuprum could imply anything from sex with a freeborn youth (even if by mutual consent), to rape, to anal penetration of one freeborn man by another. In the latter case, both the shame visited upon the man penetrated, and the penetrator's sexual use of a freeborn male could be called *stuprum*.[7] Again, at the heart of *stuprum* was violation of the status of a freeborn Roman, or violation of the sexual status of a male—what the Romans called a *vir,* a real man who penetrates but is not penetrated.

Punishment of *stuprum,* whether homosexual or heterosexual, may have been mandated by the Lex Scantinia. This law may have been enacted around 226 B.C.E. and has been thought by some to have punished homosexual activity. However, no copy survives, and no prosecution under it has been satisfactorily documented. Since no Roman law of the republic or early empire is known to have punished homosexual activity, it is more likely that the Scantinian Law was generally directed at a broader variety of sexual misconduct, but with specific reference to misconduct with protected minors of either sex.[8]

That Roman law did not punish homosexual behavior is attested to by Clement of Alexandria, a Greek Christian writer of the second century C.E., who notes that in his lifetime homosexual acts were legal in Rome.[9] Little specific regulation of homosexual behavior can be discovered in Roman law until the third century C.E., when the emperor Philip attempted to outlaw homosexual prostitution.

Nor did custom condemn romantic love between men. It was a common subject in literature—admittedly, a literature written by an elite class. Most of the major Roman poets—Catullus, Virgil, Horace, Tibullus, Ovid, Martial, Juvenal—wrote of homoerotic sentiments, and although homosexuality, like most other human appetites, was often satirized, love between men was a central and sometimes idealized subject. In the first century before the Common Era, Catullus, Horace, and Tibullus celebrated and lamented their love for handsome boys, as did Martial a century later. Virgil's *Aeneid,* the foundation epic of Rome, includes the episode of Nisus and Euryalus, which celebrates the fidelity and loyalty of two Greek lovers who died for each other on the plains of Troy. Perhaps the greatest and most influential homoerotic poem of the ancient world, Virgil's *Second Eclogue,* tells the story of Corydon's unrequited love for Alexis. In his *Metamorphoses,* Ovid transforms the homoerotic Greek legends of Ganymede, Narcissus, Apollo and Cyparissus, and Apollo and Hyacinthus into Latin homoerotic romances. Catullus' love for Juventius—however cruel the response from that thoughtless, seductive youth—provides, if not the pleasure of viewing love triumphant, at least the pleasure of hearing it described in the best Latin verse. In popular prose romances of the time, some written in Greek during the early years of the empire, same-sex couples lead lives of such exemplary devotion that they could well be considered bound by formal ties. Charicles and Klinias in Achilles Tatius' romance *Clitophon and Leucippe* are lovers, and Hippothoos and Cleisthenes in Xenophon of Ephesus' novel *Ephesiaca* apparently intend a relationship of mutual and lifelong fidelity.

One of most popular and most homoerotic of these romances is the *Satyricon* of Gaius Petronius (d. 66 C.E.), the elegant "arbiter of taste" at the court of Nero, who calmly took his own life upon being falsely accused of plotting against the emperor. The *Satyricon* is devoted to the exploits of Giton, a handsome youth who is constantly unfaithful to his devoted lover, Encolpius, the book's narrator. Though everything is seen through the eyes of Encolpius, who is madly in love with Giton, Petronius no more judges that madness than he judges Giton's promiscuity. Their story is about sex and the variations of desire, but it is also about love: no matter how often Encolpius vows to free himself from Giton, he always goes back to him; no matter how often Giton strays, he always returns. Far from an ideal couple, they are a couple nevertheless, whose devotion is in its way exemplary.

But even though Greek models influenced Latin literature, and some Romans admired and imitated Greek ways, Greek and Roman attitudes toward homosexual love differed significantly: the Greeks idealized same-sex relationships between men and freeborn youths and gave them an important place in the political life of the nation and the spiritual and ethical life of the individual; the Romans held no such exalted view and, at least in theory, discouraged men from having sex with freeborn youths. They did not, however, condemn or discourage pederasty, or even imagine it to be especially "Greek"; as their literature shows, they practiced it and sought it out. But few Roman writers, unless modeling their work on Greek texts, would have maintained that sexual relations between men or between men and boys would benefit the state or improve the mind and the conduct of the boy.[10] For the Romans, sex began with desire and ended with gratification.

The object of gratification was of less moment than the experience itself. Sex with slaves was a prominent feature of Roman life. Roman men of rank or wealth often had a male slave called a *concubinus*, whose function was to provide sexual satisfaction before marriage and who often continued to do so thereafter. A common satiric jibe had it that a man found more pleasure with his slave than with his wife. No law prohibited relations with male slaves or with prostitutes; indeed, in Augustan Rome (27 B.C.E.–14 C.E.), homosexual prostitution was taxed and prostitutes were granted their own holiday, on April 25. Male prostitutes were often employed to perform multiple services; Juvenal's *Satire IX* portrays Naevolus, a male prostitute who attends to both his client Virro and Virro's wife. Male prostitutes sometimes became the object of romantic attachments; Tibullus and Catullus both loved male prostitutes and wrote about their loves. Some writers asserted that boys were better love objects than women; others, Martial, for example, argued that using both sexes provided far more pleasure than restriction to one.[11] Martial (11.29) sums up Roman attitudes toward homosexuality: "Nasica raped the doctor's pretty lad; / But then, they say, the fellow's raving mad. / Mad? I maintain / He's very sane."[12]

There is evidence that some lasting relationships between men were accorded more formal status. Occasionally, such relationships were construed as similar to heterosexual marriages, though often this opinion was sarcastic or satiric. Cicero, who approved of little, alleged that Curio the Younger was united to his friend Antonius "just as if he had given him the matron's stola," the garment worn by married Roman women.[13] Both Martial and Juvenal mention public marriages between men. Martial reports that "the bearded Callistratus married the rugged Afer / Under the same law by which a woman takes a husband"—though he wonders if this is not too much even for Roman morality: "Does this not, Rome, seem enough? Do you expect him to bear a child?"[14] Juvenal, in *Satire II,* considers another example of Roman decadence: noting that one man has "got his boyfriend to the altar at last," he charges that "soon such things will be done in public."[15] Indeed, two emperors, Nero and Elagabalus, publicly married men.[16]

For a real man, it was deemed appropriate to penetrate another anally or to receive oral sex. Martial often contrasts the *viro* with the weak and womanly *cinaedus* (the Greek *kinaidos,* Latinized), the effeminate male who engages in passive homosexual behavior.[17] It was considered disgraceful for a citizen to engage in prostitution, to submit to anal penetration, or to perform fellatio. To submit to anal penetration was tantamount to relinquishing not only manhood but also the moral (if not the legal) right to be a citizen of the Roman state. For an adult male to perform oral sex was thought both reprehensible and impure, reprehensible because, like passive anal intercourse, it indicated a willingness to submit to sexual mastery; impure because making the mouth a receptacle like the anus or vagina defiled both mouth and man. A body of satire derided some men because they deviated from the sexual habits of the majority, eagerly engaged in passive homosexual activities, provided oral sex, and seemed effeminate in their mannerisms or physical appearance. Derisory language directed at the specific homosexual activities of *certain* men in some Latin satire would subsequently be generally used to condemn *all* same-sex activities, and the men who engaged in them.

2 Naming Perverts

When a beautiful boy was the subject of admiring poetry, he might be charmingly called the *puer* (youth), *puer delicatus,* or *ephebus* (from the Greek *ephebe,* "youth"). In a relationship with another youth (as between Giton and Encolpius) he might be a *frater*—a word that meant but implied more than "brother." However, when sex instead of love was the subject, the language was far less elevated.

Prostitution flourished in Rome and was legal, and homosexual prostitutes were often identified according to their sexual specialty. A boy or a youthful male prostitute, sexually passive and available to older lovers, was called a *catamitus* (a Latin corruption of the Greek name Ganymede, the youthful companion of Zeus), and sometimes, if he was the constant companion of an older man, a *concubinus.* The *exoleti,* usually slaves and adults rather than boys, covered all bases— they serviced both women and men actively or passively. A *spintria,* or male prostitute (the term was derived from the word for the sphincter muscle), might perform any action his client desired, from passive receptivity to active anal penetration. Male prostitutes with especially large genitals were called *drauci* and were sought out by both men and women. Martial (3.73) describes some youths as "well-hung boys," and others (11.63) as "heavy-hung smooth-cheeked young men," the equipment suggesting that they are *drauci,* the smooth cheeks that they are homosexual.[18] The active *drauci* were imagined to be more reprehensible than men who enjoyed *pedicare* with boys, because *drauci* were often employed by adult male *pathici* (men who preferred passive anal sex) or by adult males who enjoyed performing fellatio.[19] *Cinaedus* is the term in Latin that most closely approximates "effeminate adult male homosexual," "queen," or "fag." Effeminate *cinaedi* and *pathici* were often homosexual male prostitutes, as were *fellatores* (men who provided oral sex to other men).

Latin satire often associated sexual activity with notions of foulness, dirtiness, and obscenity. The genitalia are frequently described as obscene (*obscenus*). Any form of sexual activity is likely to be described as *spurcus* (foul), *turpis* (shameful, dirty, lewd, foul, disgusting), or *improbus* (indecent), and homosexual acts almost always are. Passive homosexual acts are often called *infamis* (notorious); Juvenal depicts passive homosexuality as *turpis* and men who engage in it as *monstra* (freaks).[20] *Obscenus* especially is applied to *pathici* or *fellatores*. *Pathici*, especially if adult, were condemned because what they allowed obscenely violated their manhood. The mouth of a *fellator* was an *os impurum,* literally a "dirty mouth." Catullus observes in Epigrams 97 and 98 that Aemilius is such a notorious *fellator* that there is (literally) no difference between kissing his mouth and kissing his ass, and because he is also a well-known *pathicus,* his mouth and ass perform the same job.[21]

Martial (2.28), wondering about the sexual interests of one Sextillus, decides to accept the rumor that Sextillus is a *fellator.* But rumor is quite specific: Sextillus is a *fellator* but not an *irrumator. Irrumo,* "to offer the penis for sucking," implies forcible oral intercourse.[22] It is often used as a sexual threat. Catullus begins one poem, *"Pedicabo ego vos et irrumabo, / Aureli patheci et cinaedi Furi"*—translated loosely as "I'll bugger you and fuck you in the mouth, / Aurelius you sodomite, Furius you faggot." Martial (3.82) notes that he cannot take revenge against one Zoilus by irrumation because Zoilus is a *fellator*—that is, since he *enjoys* oral sex, irrumation would be no punishment. Irrumation, the active version of fellatio, is understood as a violent act, oral rape performed for pleasure or as punishment against a passive male. Therefore condemnation is rarely directed against the *irrumator.*

As in Greece, it was the *cinaedus,* effeminate and sexually promiscuous as *fellator* and *pathicus,* who provoked the most derision and the most anxiety. Among the graffiti of Pompeii one individual is memorialized as *magnus cinaedus et fellator*—though "a big fag and a cocksucker" does not precisely provide an equivalent. As in Greek, Latin words used to indicate effeminacy implied unmanliness, weakness, self-indulgence, and vanity. So large was the lexicon of effeminacy that any number of unpopular or deviant acts could be so labeled, including the adoption of women's clothing, exclusive preference for one or another form of sexual activity, or even allowing oneself to be too much dominated by women. Some asserted that it was effeminate to shave the face or remove hair from the body. Seneca condemns both men who dress like women, and men who try to make themselves look younger by depilation, asserting that such habits imply the desire to be sexually used by other men.[23] The belief that effeminacy was a characteristic of men who preferred passive sex made it a frequent charge and the common coin of satire. By the time of Juvenal—the end of the first century C.E. and the beginning of the second—passive homosexuality and effeminate appearance or mannerisms were often linked.[24] But it would be inaccurate to presume that the *cinaedus* was the Roman equivalent of a modern effeminate "homosexual," or that the modern "fag" renders the term. Whether he preferred passive sex, or prostituted himself, or simply affected effeminate garb, the *cinaedus* was first of all a gender deviant. It was his abdication of the role of *vir* and the sexual rituals of masculinity, or his mockery of the appearances of manhood, or his sexual promiscuity, that caused him to be derided and portrayed as a dangerous, socially unacceptable monster.

When Catullus attacks Aurelius and Furius by calling them *patheci et cinaedi,* he employs the two most common and most pejorative terms for men who had sex exclusively with males. The *cinaedus* advertised his sexual availability by effeminate mannerisms—certain gestures, lisping speech, and a rolling or seductive walk. To describe this walk, Roman writers sometimes used the verb *ceveo,* "to move the haunches as if in sexual intercourse."[25] In *Satire II,* Juvenal objects to men who hide their homosexual preferences under a veneer of ultra-masculinity; he prefers those effeminate men whose walk reveals their inclinations as at least more honest. In *Satire VI,* he distinguishes between "proper-sounding men" and "lispers," and Martial describes the Greek Charmenion as having a lisping mouth and a weak tongue (*"os blaesum tibi debilisque lingua est"*).[26] The effeminate gestures of *cinaedi* included holding their hands in front of their hips, or scratching their heads or buttocks with one finger. In Juvenal's *Satire VI* the effeminate stereotype is embodied in a male prostitute who masquerades as a *cinaedus* so as to lure married men, who like effeminate males, away from their wives: "He may line his eyes with kohl, / And wear a yellow robe and a hairnet—but adultery / Is the end in view. That affected voice, the way / He poses, one arm akimbo, and scratches his bottom, shouldn't / Lull your suspicions."[27]

Pathici and *cinaedi,* it was asserted, favored green, yellow, saffron, and purple clothing.[28] *Cinaedi* enhanced their effeminate appearance by plucking their eyebrows, beards, hands, and buttocks, or their entire bodies, employing makeup for skin and eyes, and smoothing and softening their skin with pumice stones; in this, they reflected the Roman judgment that effeminate men were *mollis* and *tener,* soft and delicate or dainty.[29] In *Satire II* Juvenal uses *molles* to distinguish a class of homosexually inclined men when he asserts *magna inter molles concordia*, "among the soft ones the harmony is great"—that is, "all queers stick together." A few lines later Juvenal attacks them and their effeminate mannerisms:

> After a while you will find yourself taken up
> By a very queer fraternity. In the secrecy of their homes
> They put on ribboned miters and three or four necklaces,
> . . . . . .
> You'll see one initiate busy with eyebrow-pencil, kohl
> And mascara, eyelids aflutter; a second sips wine
> From a big glass phallus, his long luxuriant curls
> Caught up in a golden hairnet. He'll be wearing fancy checks
> With a sky-blue motif, or smooth green gabardine.

Along with *effeminatus, mollis* and *tener* are the adjectives most commonly used to describe sexually deviant men. But others occasionally appear—words that express weakness or suggest that homosexual acts are connected with disease: *debilis* and *debilitas* (weak; weakness); *tremulus* (quivering, limp); *inbellis* (unwarlike, hence passive). *Morbosus* (sick, perverted) and *morbus* (vice or perversion) are applied to *pathici* and *cinaedi*, though rarely if ever to active homosexuality.[30]

Martial, who in other poems celebrates his own enjoyment of homosexual sex, has little patience with effeminate men. The manner and appearance of one Charmenion disgust him:

> Since you're always bragging that you're a citizen
> Of Corinth, Charmenion—and no one denies it—
> Why are you always calling me "brother"? I hail from
> The land of Iberians and Celts and the River Tagus.
> Do you think that we even look alike?
> You wander around looking sleek with your curly hair,
> While mine is wildly unruly in the Spanish style.
> Every day a depilator makes your body smooth,
> While I sport hair on my thighs and cheeks.
> Your mouth is lisping and your tongue is faltering,
> But I speak deeply from my guts;
> We're more different than a dove from an eagle

Or a timid doe from a raging lion.
And so, Charmenion, stop calling me "brother"
Or else I'll start calling you "sister."[31]*

Both Juvenal and Martial also satirize men who try to disguise their desires by wearing beards, cutting their hair short, and assuming a false aspect of virility. Martial skewers them in a number of epigrams, especially attacking Stoic philosophers with shaggy beards and uncombed hair as *pathici* or *cinaedi* in disguise (even though, in the poem just quoted, he describes himself as bearded and wild-haired). Martial derides one Maternus, who "thinks that anyone who wears pink is not a man, / And believes that violet-colored clothes are for queens." But Maternus protests too much. Though he wears conservative clothes, Martial charges, Maternus is devoted to *drauci* and "is always devouring the private parts of butch fags."[32] Juvenal notes in *Satire II* that though "shaggy limbs and bristling hair" may "suggest a fierce male virtue" and though some men "talk in clipped laconic style, and crop their hair crew-cut fashion," yet it is clear from their activities that they prefer men to women.[33]

Of all the satirists, Juvenal is the most indignant concerning the general decay of ancient Roman virtue; he focuses on effeminate men and rampant homosexual sex as special signs of that decay. *Satire II* shows little of the tolerance accorded to homosexual acts and desire by other Roman writers. Juvenal professes to detest the hypocrisy of men who pretend to virtue while embracing vice, who profess philosophy without exercising its rigor, and who act one part while living another. Like Martial, he castigates the august Stoic philosophers who conceal pederastic lust beneath their dignified demeanor. With horror Juvenal sees one well-born man marry another: male brides will soon want to have their wedding notices published in the paper, he predicts. At a gathering, men put on makeup and hair nets and women's clothes: Juvenal asks what has brought Rome to such a pass.[34] So often does Juvenal attack effeminate *cinaedi* as a class that he appears to think of them as a separate sexual species, whose effeminate mannerisms are the outward

---

*Juvenal and Martial mock masculine women, too, accusing them of being lesbians, whose promiscuity and vulgarity make them repellent. Of Philaenis, Martial (7.67) says that she "hurls the heavy ball with ease," drinks excessively, and devours women while being disgusted with men. Juvenal (6.313) is also appalled by lesbians, whom he describes as drunken voluptuaries who engage in orgies of feasting and "take turns riding each other."

mark of their homosexual desire. Juvenal, like many in late antiquity, thinks in terms of two distinct types of sexual preference and two distinct types of men. Real men have sex with women and, actively, with boys, but the *cinaedi* are not real men. Lisping, perfumed, and made-up, smooth and hairless, seductively walking the streets of Rome and promiscuously importuning men for a moment of sex, they draw from Juvenal indignation and condemnation. Indeed Latin satire generally treats them with disdain, so much so that it sometimes seems single-mindedly devoted to constructing them as the *monstra* that Juvenal despised. All this derision of *pathici* and *cinaedi* foreshadows some darker chapters in human history, in which the caricatures of Latin satire come to be taken as universal truths about the "nature" of homosexual desire.

3 Diagnosing Deviance

The effeminate and passive male also drew medical and scientific attention. His ways were chronicled, his mannerisms classified, his physical characteristics enumerated, for better recognition. Once classified and investigated, he also became the object of speculation concerning the physiological, emotional, or spiritual cause of his desire.

A number of explanations were advanced in ancient texts as to why some men preferred to engage in passive homosexual relations with other men or even preferred sex with men exclusively. In Plato's *Symposium,* as we have seen, Aristophanes claims that homosexual desire is part of the natural order of creation—as we would say, the cause is biological. In the *Nicomachean Ethics,* Aristotle considers homosexual desire to be what he calls a disposition; the "disposition of sexual intercourse for males" is subsumed under that disposition which is "disease-like or as a result of habituation."[35] That is, Aristotle speculates, some men take pleasure in intercourse with males because they first engaged in it when they were boys and grew to prefer it. However, Aristotle also suggests that some men desire homosexual sex because it is in their nature to do so; it is natural for them.

Aristotle's comment is in the context of his discussion in the *Ethics* of those who cannot refrain from doing what they believe to be wrong. If someone believes that having intercourse with males is wrong, but it is in his nature to do so, he cannot be accused of lacking self-control. Aristotle compares such men with women, who cannot be described as lacking in self-control because "they do not mount sexually but are mounted."[36] He seems to believe that those who are inclined by nature to intercourse with males are those who are sexually passive. When Aristotle links exclusive and passive homosexual behavior, he appears to be concerned to investigate the suspect and disturbing *kinaidos*.

In the *Problemata,* a work sometimes mistakenly attributed to Aristotle, the focus is exclusively on that troublesome figure; a scientific attempt is made to explain why some men enjoy being "subjected to sexual intercourse."[37] Some men, the *Problemata* speculates, are physiologically so constituted that the conduits for sperm lead through the rectum rather than the genital organs, and rectal ejaculation follows rectal stimulation. Recollecting the pleasure this afforded when they were young—that is, when it was acceptable for them to be penetrated by an adult male—these men continue to seek it as adults. They are "naturally" disposed to such desires. The writer of the *Problemata* describes such men as "effeminate by nature," because like women's sexual pleasure, theirs involves the desire for penetration. They are also physically defective, for they have a larger portion of female characteristics than most "normal" males.

Neither Aristotle—whose evaluation of the morality of homosexual acts tends to be more cautious and less judgmental than that of his teacher Plato in the *Laws*—nor the author of the *Problemata* condemns desire for a handsome youth or the consummation of that desire by an adult male exercising an active role. Nor does either writer consider this a defect of masculine nature.[38] Both texts focus on passivity, but the *Problemata* also emphasizes what might be called the physiological effeminacy of such men. Aristotle explains passive homosexuality as a consequence of nurture and nature, physiology and habituation. The *Problemata* also offers a physiological explanation. But whether the desire for passive sex with men is construed as a diseaselike disposition, or the irresistible result of irreversible habit, or the natural activity of a defective or impaired male nature, it leads in every case to the construction of a separate sexual species, neither women nor real men.

The ancient theory of physiognomy, which held that character is written on the body, offers perhaps the most detailed description of this new species. For physiognomists, the *kinaidos* is an object not only of curiosity but of loathing; it is the intention of their treatises to explain just how to recognize and protect against these creatures.

The earliest text in which the *kinaidos* is subjected to detailed classification is the fourth century B.C.E. *Physiognomonics,* collected in the works of Aristotle though not written by him.[39] The presumption of the

Physiognomonics is that people *are* what they look like; thus the coward, hero, or wise man can be identified by certain physical signs: gestures, facial characteristics, bodily anomalies; his manner of walking, speaking, or looking. The *kinaidos,* too, reveals himself not only by what he does but by how he looks, and the decent citizen can, with the help of this manual, know one when he sees one. The *kinaidos* has an "unsteady eye, and knock knees; he inclines his head to the right; he gestures with his palms up and his wrists loose; and he has two styles of walking—either waggling his hips or keeping them under control. He tends to look around in all directions."[40] Hands aflutter, this limp-wristed, mincing creature from the fourth century B.C.E. will reappear again and again in everything from the satires of Juvenal to twentieth-century films.

The *kinaidos* turns up in the writings of the Greek physiognomists Loxos and Polemo. No original text of Loxos, a physician who wrote during the Hellenistic period (c. 350–325 B.C.E.) has survived. However, his work was apparently used by Polemo, a rhetorician of the second century of the Common Era, in his *Physiognomy.*[41] Polemo opens his discussion by identifying masculine and feminine characteristics in human beings: "The male is physically stronger and braver, less prone to defects and more likely to be sincere and loyal. He is more keen to win honor and he is worthier of respect. The female has the contrary properties: she has but little courage and abounds in deceptions. Her behavior is exceptionally bitter and she tends to hide what is on her mind. She is a rebellious oppressor with a tremendous fondness for quarreling." When it comes to physical characteristics, Polemo polarizes even more:

> Now I will relate the signs of male and female physique and their physiognomical significance. You will note which prevails over the other [in any individual] and use this to guide your judgment. The female has, compared to the male, a small head and a small mouth, softer hair that is dark in color, a narrower face, bright glittering eyes, a narrow neck, a weakly sloping chest, feeble ribs, knock-knees, dainty finger tips and toes, the rest of the body moist and flabby, with soft limbs and slackened joints, thin sinews, weak voice, a hesitant gait with frequent short steps, and limp limbs that glide slowly along. The male is in every way opposite to this description, and it is possible to find masculine qualities also in women.[42]

Ancient medical commentators often maintained that an anatomical male or female need not necessarily display masculine or feminine characteristics. Polemo agrees that in the masculine there is something of the feminine to be found, and in the feminine something of the masculine: "The name 'masculine' or 'feminine' is assigned according to which of the two prevails."[43] The job of the physiognomist was to discover which characteristics prevailed in a given individual.

Why did anatomical sex not determine masculine or feminine gender traits? Some ancient medical writers suggested that the proportions of male and female sperm present at conception would determine where on the spectrum of gender, from the ideal male to the ideal female, an individual would fall. Polemo explains that "you may obtain physiognomic indications of masculinity and femininity from your subject's glance, movement, and voice, and then, from among these signs, compare one with another until you determine to your satisfaction which of the two sexes prevails."[44] The "glance, movement, and voice" of the *kinaidos* are especially revealing: "You may recognize him by his provocatively melting glance and by the rapid movement of his intensely staring eyes. His brow is furrowed, while his eyebrows and cheeks are in constant motion. His head is tilted to the side, his loins do not hold still, and his slack limbs never stay in one position. He minces along with little jumping steps; his knees knock together. He carries his hands with palms turned upward, he has a shifting gaze, and his voice is thin, weepy, shrill, and drawling."[45] Armed with this description and Polemo's picture of the dangerous female, an amateur physiognomist would have had no trouble in recognizing a *kinaidos,* nor in knowing that within that suspect male body the cowardly, quarrelsome, and bitter female, against whom he has also been warned, awaits to practice her deceptions on innocent males. As the fourth century C.E. Latin version of Polemo additionally warns, effeminates "set themselves up in a woman's role and an elaborate and effected style of deportment in order to attract other men."[46]

Though some *kinaidoi* are obvious, others attempt to hide their effeminacy from censorious eyes: "They actually try to remove suspicion from themselves by straining to assume a more virile appearance. They imitate a youthful stride, hold themselves with a peculiar firmness, intensify their gaze and voice, and with their whole body adopt a rigid bearing." But these impostors can be detected by the accomplished practitioner of the physiognomist's art: "They generally slacken both voice and neck, relaxing their hands and feet, and are easily betrayed by other transient signs. It is by the twitching of their lips and the rotation of their eyes, by the haphazard and inconsistent shifting of their feet, by the movement of their hips and the fickle motion of their hands, and by the tremor of their voice as it begins with difficulty to speak, that effeminates are most easily revealed."[47] Indeed, few *kinaidoi* can long hide their "true nature" from the practiced physiognomist, for even the smallest sign—an unguarded glance, a too-curious stare, a slight loosening of the wrist—can expose them.

In the second century C.E., the Greek physician Soranos added to the store of characteristics that define *kinaidoi* and offered a new diagnosis of what caused their special form of desire.

> People find it hard to believe that effeminate men, or pathics, really exist. The fact is that though the practices of such persons are unnatural to human beings, lust overcomes modesty and puts to shameful use parts intended for other functions. That is, in the case of certain individuals, there is no limit to their desire and no hope of satisfying it; and they cannot be content with their own lot, the lot which divine providence had marked out for them in assigning definite functions to the parts of the body. They even adopt the dress, walk, and other characteristics of women. Now this condition is different from a bodily disease; it is rather an affliction of a diseased mind. Indeed, often out of passion and in rare cases out of respect for certain persons to whom they are beholden, these pathics suddenly change their character and for a while try to give proof of their virility. But since they are not aware of their limitations, they are again the victims of excesses, subjecting their virility to too great a strain and consequently involving themselves in worse vices. And it is our opinion that these persons suffer no impairment of sensation. For this affliction comes from a corrupt and debased mind. Indeed, the victims of this malady may be compared to the women who are called *tribades* because they pursue both kinds of love. These women are more eager to lie with women than with men; in fact they pursue women with almost masculine jealousy.[48]

Soranos' commentary preserves the now-familiar description of homosexual men as effeminate and of lesbians as masculine but, unlike earlier medical texts, which were more tentative about the question, categorically asserts that the desires and practices of such men and women are unnatural. His argument that "pathics" are ruled by uncontrollable lust is equally familiar in the catalogue of charges against effeminate men and mannish women. But his assertion that such loss of control signifies not a physiological defect but a diseased mind is a new proposition, an early and confident harbinger of later medical explanations for homosexuality: homosexual desire is a species of insanity.

The writings of the physiognomists contributed to the classification of *kinaidoi* as a separate sexual species. *Kinaidoi*, it was claimed, promiscuously preyed upon innocent youth and endangered the family and the state. But fortunately for society, *kinaidoi* were identifiable by certain ineradicable signs: their inner sexual desire was marked outwardly, by contempt for masculinity and by wanton effeminacy. The stereotype of the effeminate but dangerous homosexual predator, ever on the hunt for *viri*, would, in years to come, justify the search for ways to segregate them, to control them, and even to eradicate them.

Since neither Greeks nor Romans condemned homosexual behavior of the approved kinds described above, we cannot strictly claim to find homophobia as we know it in Athens or in Rome. What the Greeks and Romans feared was what some kinds of homosexual behavior, and some kinds of sexualized role-playing, might do to corrupt ideal masculinity and to compromise the active sexual dominance of "real men," whether over women or over other males. Indeed, it was the fear that homosexual desire *itself* might be demasculinized and effeminized that provoked sexual anxiety in the ancient world.

Chapter Four

The End of Antiquity

*Changing Attitudes About Homosexuality,
100 B.C.E. to 400 C.E.*

From Homer to Martial the literature of antiquity celebrated love between men. The notion that this was the highest form of love, and that sex between men under the right circumstances was honorable, was a staple theme in ancient texts and would shape all subsequent homoerotic mythology. Sex between males was suspect only when one partner manifested an exclusive preference for passive homosexuality, or behaved effeminately. Indeed, most discussion of appropriate sexual conduct in ancient texts had as its subtext the seemingly unbridgeable distance between masculinity and effeminacy, between being sexually active and sexually passive, not the difference between homosexuality and heterosexuality.

In later antiquity, though, prompted perhaps by a narrow reading of Plato's *Laws,* some began to argue that *any* sexual relationship between men was unnatural and a menace to social stability; these writers denied that love between men could be anything but base desire, and insisted that only love and sex between men and women were natural and socially acceptable. Those eager to defame all forms of love between men—as even Plato in the *Laws* had not done—inflexibly debated those who continued to defend what once had seemed unexceptionable; the very existence of the debate testifies to a change in

common opinion concerning sexual practice. Homosexual sex and heterosexual sex were increasingly construed as opposing, rival, and even
mutually exclusive.

During the first century of the Common Era, Plutarch in the
Erotikos opines that "the union of male with male . . . is rather not a
union, but a lascivious assault" and that therefore "one would be right
to say: 'This is the work of Hubris [pride], not of Cypris [love].' That is
why we class those who enjoy the passive part as belonging to the lowest depth of vice and allow them not the least degree of confidence or
respect or friendship."[1] Daphnaeus, a character in the *Erotikos,* is willing to outlaw homosexual behavior entirely as he outlines both new
and old terms in the general debate. He contrasts "union contrary to
nature with males" with "love between men and women," describing
the latter as "normal and natural" and arguing that among those who
"consort with males" there is "weakness and effeminacy." He identifies
all homosexual behavior with effeminate homosexual profligacy. The
distinction he makes between the sexual "union" of men and the nobility of the "love" that exists only between men and women establishes
an even more exclusionary category: any man who sexually consorts
with other males is excluded not only from friendship, confidence, and
respect but also from the very emotion of love. In the centuries since
Phaedrus urged that "there can be no greater benefit for a boy than to
have a worthy lover . . . nor [than] for a lover to have a worthy object
for his affection," the ancient world had gradually but radically
changed its opinion of the value and the virtue of homosexual desire.

1 Affairs of the Heart

By the beginning of the Common Era, the debate about the merits of
homosexual behavior—begun in texts like Plato's *Laws* and supported
by scientific and moral categorization of homosexual types—had also
become a fashionable literary genre in writings like Plutarch's *Erotikos.*
But the very fact that the subject was debated suggests the existence of
anxiety about the question. Formal dialogues argued the relative
virtues of sex with boys and sex with women. In some debates, like the
Erotikos, despite powerful arguments for homosexual relations of the
approved Greek kind, the debate was decided in favor of conjugal ties.

Among Greek prose literature of the late Roman Empire, the
Erotes—attributed to Lucian of Samosata (died c. 180 C.E.) but probably written as much as a century after his death—offers an especially

complex and suggestive instance of the debate. In it each of two men, exclusively devoted to their respective sexual passions, argues that his own practice is superior, not only in terms of physical and emotional pleasure but in terms of moral worth.[2] The *Erotes* proposes that sexual desire is not a preference guided by occasion, undifferentiated lust, or availability, but instead is governed by the promptings of something very much like sexual orientation; in effect, the *Erotes* declares that men who love women, and men who love men, are separate, almost irreconcilable species.

The *Erotes* was written in a time when tolerance for homosexuality was decreasing. What was once deemed to be the highest form of love had come under attack by the growing asceticism of a crumbling and increasingly unstable empire. This asceticism derived partly from the antisexual arguments of Neoplatonist and Jewish philosophers, partly from the doctrine of the new Christian sect, which clamored against the worship of the ancient gods. Though the old gods still held sway when *Erotes* was written, the next century saw more fundamental changes. In 313 C.E. the emperor Constantine declared the empire Christian. In 342 C.E. an edict was promulgated by the emperors Constantius II and Constans I that mandated "exquisite punishment" for men who offered themselves "in a womanly fashion" to other men.[3] The scope of the edict is unclear. It may have been intended to outlaw the kind of legal union between same-sex couples that Juvenal had satirized, or it may have been directed at prostitute *cinaedi*.[4] By this time, both Roman jurists and Christian theologians had begun earnest speculations about the legality and the place of homosexual sex in daily and spiritual life— speculations that would eventually culminate in the legal prohibition of homosexual acts in an edict of 390 C.E. and the subsequent declaration by the Church that such acts were sinful because they were unnatural. Against this background, the author of *Erotes* wrote his urbane and sophisticated book. Despite its place in a genre usually read as light entertainment, the author seems to intend a more serious message concerning the rival claims of ancient and modern conceptions about the nature of love.

The characters of the *Erotes* are the narrator, Lycinus, apparently chaste and asexual; Theomnestus, an old-style pagan hedonist who declares his equal passion for males and females; Charicles, a single-minded champion of love between men and women; and Callicratidas, an enthusiastic devotee of Greek-style pederasty. Theomnestus has been entertaining Lycinus with some rather lewd reminiscences of his love affairs with "women at their fairest and boys at the flower of their beauty."[5] Now he asks Lycinus to pass judgment on which kind of lover is superior to the other, "those who love boys or those who delight in womankind" (4). Theomnestus is confident that Lycinus can be an impartial judge, "since you incline to neither type of passion." Notably, Theomnestus does not ask Lycinus which form of love but which type of *lover* he believes to be superior. Earlier debates offered homosexual and heterosexual *behavior* as largely unjudged sexual alternatives. But Theomnestus' query is framed in terms of superiority and implies the existence of different and opposed sexual types, even though he himself is happily made up of both.

Lycinus recognizes the tension inherent in Theomnestus' question: he observes that the debate may have been introduced "as a matter of sport and laughter" but the subject is "far from a laughing matter," and he recounts a conversation between his friends Charicles, a Corinthian, and Callicratidas, an Athenian, on the same subject.

> I heard two men arguing heatedly with each other about these two types of love, and I still have the memory of it ringing in my ears. They were opposites, not only in their arguments but in their passions, unlike you who, thanks to your easy-going spirit, go sleepless and earn double wages, "one as a herdsman of cattle, another as tender of white flocks." On the contrary, one took excessive delight in boys and thought love of women a pit of doom, while the other, virgin of all love of males, was highly susceptible to women. So I presided over a contest between these two warring passions and found the occasion quite indescribably delightful. . . . I shall retail to you exactly what I heard the two of them say (5).

Charicles brings a dark and negative tone to the discussion, for he not only claims superiority for heterosexual sex, but in rabid and almost hysterical terms condemns homosexual behavior as immoral, contrary to nature, and dangerous to the state and the individual. Indeed, Charicles may well be the first full-scale fictional portrayal of a homophobe. Callicratidas is an almost equally enthusiastic defender of love between men. Rarely in the literature of antiquity have the two positions been so definitively argued; the two men are virtual archetypes of opposed sexual desire, each single-mindedly and obstinately arguing for his own sexual position. In the end, the *Erotes* guardedly finds homosexual behavior superior to heterosexual, but it seems almost to be intended as a defensive action in favor of homosexual desire at a time when a general reevaluation of all sexual conduct was taking place.

That Charicles comes from Corinth—a city especially noted in antiquity as a center for prostitution of all types, but especially heterosexual—reinforces the picture of his sexual appetites. Lycinus describes him as one who is "not only handsome but [who] shows some evidence of the skillful use of cosmetics because, I imagine, he wishes to attract women" (9). The use of cosmetics by men had long been a subject of derision, as in Juvenal's *Satire II,* where it is a sign of the effeminate *cinaedus,* and in Aristophanes' portrait of Agathon. That cosmetics here are associated with a womanizer may reflect real practice, but more likely it suggests the author's less than total admiration for Charicles as well as being an ironic notation of the ambiguity attached to the male use of cosmetics. In contrast to the made-up, dandified Corinthian, Callicratidas the Athenian is presented as a real man "of straightforward ways." Plato's Athenian would surely have approved of his social demeanor: "pre-eminent among the leading figures in public speaking and in this forensic oratory of ours. He was also a devotee of physical training." But he would probably have agreed with Lycinus that Callicratidas "was only fond of the wrestling schools because of his love of boys. For he was enthusiastic only for that, while his hatred for women made him often curse Prometheus" (in classical mythology credited with inventing woman). Lycinus portrays Charicles and Callicratidas as bitter rivals in their contest for sexual superiority; indeed so completely does this topic rule their lives that, as Lycinus says, often "short skirmishes broke out between them without the point at issue being settled" (10).

Their style of life mirrors their inclinations. Callicratidas surrounds himself with handsome beardless slave boys whom he properly sends away, in accordance with ideal Greek pederastic practice, when their beards begin to grow. The description of Callicratidas—an exemplary citizen, a practitioner of *paederastia*—exaggerates his masculinity and shows him to be the physical and moral opposite of the effeminate homosexual *kinaidos.* In contrast to Callicratidas, Charicles surrounds himself with dancing and singing girls. However, his houseful of women is no guarantee of masculine virtue. Rather, it suggests something of the indolence and excessive devotion to pleasure that brought the wrath of Aeschines down upon Timarchus and provoked Zethos' contempt for Amphion. Charicles' sexual excess, the ambiguous detail concerning his use of cosmetics, his perhaps too pleasing demeanor, all tend to unfavorably contrast him with the straightforward Callicratidas, the rough and simple idealized "real man" who avoids excess of any kind.

Lycinus' patience is sorely tried by the constant "skirmishes," which break out again when the friends contemplate a visit to the city of Cnidus and the temple that holds Praxiteles' nude statue of the Cnidian Aphrodite. Though both Lycinus and Charicles are enthusiastic, Callicratidas is reluctant to go to a place where he will "see something female"; he would rather go to the temple of Eros at Thespiae, which contains Praxiteles' equally famous statue of Eros, and where the god who presides over love between males is venerated. He does, however, finally agree to go to Cnidus.

Upon seeing the statue of Aphrodite, Charicles runs to it and kisses it feverishly. When Callicratidas circles the statue and views it from the rear, he too claims to be overcome by the fine detail of the buttocks and back, which, he says, suggest to him how Ganymede must have looked to Zeus. This amusing enunciation of opposite desires embodied in one statue naturally provokes an argument between the two men on their favorite topic. Lycinus declares himself weary of their "snarling argument" and proposes to end the "disorderly, inconclusive contentiousness" with a debate "to defend your own opinion," after which the loser will "never again vex our ears on similar topics" (17).

Charicles begins, advancing the argument that males have innate masculine qualities and sexual desires and that to deviate from these is contrary to nature. He prays to Aphrodite to "allow men to remain male, as they were born to be." He insists that "it is a sacred law of necessity" that each sex should not transgress "against their inborn nature": "neither should the female grow unnaturally masculine nor the male unbecomingly soft."[6]

Charicles maintains that in the beginning of time men linked themselves to women, obeying "the laws made by nature." However, "luxury . . . transgressed the laws of nature." Some nameless transgressor was "the first to look at the male as though at a female, after using violence like a tyrant or else shameless persuasion," and "the same sex entered the same bed. Though they saw themselves embracing each other, they were ashamed neither at what they did nor at what they had done to them, and, sowing their seed, to quote the proverb, on barren

rocks, they bought a little pleasure at the cost of great disgrace (20)."
To bolster his case, Charicles repeats the common (and false) argument
used in many ancient debates, that there is no homosexuality among
animals; this, he insists, proves that homosexual behavior is contrary to
nature. Indeed, it is a human invention, a consequence of social decadence and "self-indulgence" that has brought men to that "infection"
that "cannot even be mentioned with decency" (21).* Charicles' reluctance to mention the details of homosexual practice is not simply a matter of modesty or linguistic delicacy; it forecasts the language of
antihomosexual legal proscription, which will designate homosexuality
the sin that cannot be named. His allegation that homosexual practice
is an "infection" derives from the speculation, familiar from Aristotle,
that homosexuality might be a sickness that could be caught through
habitual exposure.

Employing a familiar argument against *paiderastia,* Charicles maintains that many who profess the ideals of Plato's *Symposium* in reality
lust for the bodies of beautiful boys and have no desire to attain beauty,
wisdom or truth, for "lovers of youth rather than of wisdom . . . give
honorable names to dishonorable passions and call physical beauty
virtue of the soul" (24). So besotted by male beauty do such men
become, Charicles insists, that they are willing to forgive even the most
heinous crimes committed by those they adore; they would forgive an
Alcibiades for blasphemy against the gods and treason against Athens.[7]
Thus Charicles sides with Aeschines and the Plato of the *Laws,* calling
homosexual behavior a danger to the state and to civil peace.[8] But
while the earlier writers proscribed only effeminacy and passive homosexuality, Charicles' condemnation includes all homosexual acts, especially the idealized homoerotic relationships that both Aeschines and
Plato (even in the *Laws*) celebrated as exemplary.

Charicles' tone becomes increasingly shrill. He now attacks Callicratidas himself, in order, he says "to vent his hatred" (24), and
announces that he will now "descend somewhat to your level of pleasure, Callicratidas," in order to demonstrate that the "services rendered
by a woman are far superior to those rendered by a boy." Thus he
implies that where pleasure is concerned Callicratidas is no idealistic

---

*The English text I use here is less precise than the Greek concerning "luxury," "self-
indulgence," and "infection." The Greek words are somewhat more pointed and can be
translated as, respectively, "wantonness," "softness or effeminacy," and "disease."

and philosophical boy-lover, but simply a lecherous pederast. Pleasure with women, Charicles argues, is long-lasting, for "from maidenhood to middle age . . . a woman is a pleasant armful for a man to embrace" (25). But "the very man who should make attempts on a boy of twenty seems to me to be unnaturally lustful and pursuing an equivocal love" (26). "Boys" of twenty, of course, have become men; their limbs, Charicles notes, are "large and manly" and their "well-developed thighs are sullied with hairs . . . as for the parts less visible than these, I leave knowledge of them to you who have tried them" (26). The last sally clearly conveys Charicles' contempt and, perhaps, his eagerness to disassociate himself from Callicratidas' pleasures.

Charicles concludes with the sarcastic demand that if "male intercourse with males" is acceptable then "henceforth let women too love each other" and let "wanton lesbianism—a word seldom heard, which I feel ashamed even to utter—freely parade itself." And although he detests lesbians, he even asserts that it is better for them to practice sexual wantonness than for "the male sex . . . [to] become effeminate and play the part of a woman" (28).

Lycinus reports that "in the midst of this intense and impassioned speech Charicles stopped with a wild fierce glint in his eyes"—he has almost lost control of himself. The urbane Lycinus adds that "it seemed to me that he was also regarding his speech as [a] ceremony of purification against the love of boys" (29). Lycinus may mean to suggest that Charicles views homosexual behavior as a spiritual evil against which ritual purification is called for. Such a belief could make Charicles a fanatic adherent of any of a number of ascetic cults of the time, including Christianity. However, given what we know about Charicles' character, Lycinus may mean that Charicles' love of women dominates him as irrationally as religion dominates others. Alternatively, he may be making an astute psychological point: that Charicles' anger betrays fear about his own sexual interest.

In his answer to Charicles, Callicratidas employs the familiar apologia for homosexual love: it is "a noble duty enjoined by a philosophic spirit," the product of "divine philosophy" (33–35). Animals do not engage in homosexual acts, because "they have been condemned by nature not to receive . . . the gift of intellect" afforded to males, and so they have also been "deprived of the desire for males." Love does not "walk in a single track" but is "a twofold god." Love of women alone is "completely childish"; reason does not guide it and it is "the companion of violence," leading men to seek "unreasoning" gratification of their desires. But love of men is "hedged around with sanctity, and is a dispenser of temperate passions" (37).

Callicratidas compares women unfavorably to boys. Women are vain and self-centered. They employ cosmetics to hide their age or ugliness. They bedeck themselves with jewels and expensive clothes, demand rich foods and luxuries, and engage in secret and sexually orgiastic religious ceremonies open only to women, the intent of which is only to bring disaster down upon their husbands and other men. They are not capable of loyalty or honor or friendship. In contrast to women, boys have simple needs; they are innocent, honest, modest, loyal, and true, concerned with developing their bodies, their martial skills, and their minds. Who, he asks rhetorically, "would not fall in love with such a youth" rather than with the designing women he has described (46)?

Callicratidas' diatribe against women is no more temperate than Charicles' against homosexual lovers. However, in saying that love is a "two-fold god," Callicratidas assumes a more measured tone. He answers Charicles' charge that homosexual love is prompted only by lust by invoking all the familiar praises of love between men, asserting its honor, value, and utility both for the individual and for society.

Charicles' and Callicratidas' speeches have one thing in common: both offer definitions of homosexual practice and those who engage in it. When Callicratidas describes his own behavior, we are meant to believe that he is testifying to what he *is,* and the moderate Lycinus confirms this. Charicles, however, inaccurately describes Callicratidas as what he is not: he ignores Lycinus' testimony on behalf of Callicratidas and asserts that the latter is promiscuous, plays the woman sexually, and engages in unnatural acts. In effect Charicles describes Callicratidas as a *kinaidos,* the sexual monster Charicles most despises. Charicles is Callicratidas' avowed enemy, surely capable of calumny and distortion. His efforts to discredit Callicratidas make him as much a monster as the creatures he imagines.

Though Lycinus purports to be impartial, his report clearly reveals his antipathy to Charicles. The suggestion of derangement—the detail about the "wild fierce glint" in Charicles' eyes, his anger and intolerance, his refusal to countenance dissent, and his black-and-white view of the nature of love—all mark Callicratidas' opponent as a fanatic, not an example of the rational and balanced ideal. Charicles' self-confessed hatred of love between men reflects obsession with it and fear of it, pos sibly in himself. Charicles is the real target of the author's satire, and he is also a precise emblem and living embodiment of homophobia before it had a name.

2 The Triumph of Charicles

At the end of the debate, Lycinus delivers his carefully worded judgment: "Marriage is a boon and a blessing to men when it meets with good fortune, while love of boys [which affirms the hallowed duties] of friendship, I consider to be the privilege only of philosophy. Therefore all men should marry, but let only the wise be permitted to love boys, for perfect virtue grows least of all among women" (51). Lycinus' decision must reflect the opinion of the unknown author of the *Erotes,* but it was a position under threat, in a world of waning tolerance, where Pan was dying if not dead and where love between men would soon encounter rigorous official and ecclesiastical prohibitions. Near the end of the debate, Callicratidas eloquently recalls a better world:

> I thought that our merry contest had gone as far as jest allowed, but since Charicles in his discourse has been minded also to wax philosophical on behalf of women, I have gladly seized my opportunity; for love of males, I say, is the only activity combining both pleasure and virtue. For I would pray that near us, if it were possible, [were growing] that plane-tree which once heard the words of Socrates, a tree more fortunate than the Academy and the Lyceum, the tree against which Phaedrus leaned, as we are told by that holy man, endowed with more graces than any other. Perhaps like the oak at Dodona, which sent its sacred voice bursting forth from its branches, that tree itself, still remembering the beauty of Phaedrus, would have spoken in praise of love of boys. But that is impossible,
>
> > *"For in between there lies*
> > *Many a shady mountain and the roaring sea,"*
>
> and we are strangers cut off in a foreign land, and Cnidus gives Charicles the advantage. Nevertheless we shall not be overcome by fear and betray the truth (31).[9]

Callicratidas movingly characterizes himself as a stranger in a foreign land—the land of the Cnidian Aphrodite, the land of the enemies of love between men. He vows not to betray the truth. But what is this truth? Is it his belief in the virtue of his desire? Or a subtler assertion about the truth of what he *is*? It is probably anachronistic to speculate that the author of the *Erotes* intended to depict a man who sees desire as identity. It is possible to speculate, however, that in Charicles' diatribe the author outlined a future he feared, when men such as Callicratidas would become strangers "in a foreign land" ruled by the goddess of exclusive heterosexual love. The "truth" that Callicratidas vows to defend is the principle he himself enunciated: love does not walk "in a single track." This opinion would soon be challenged by the spiritual, intellectual, and social changes that were already reshaping sexual attitudes in late antiquity.

The natural disasters and political upheaval of the first centuries of the Common Era were serious enough to drastically unsettle the daily life of the empire. So too, disturbances in intellectual and spiritual life—of little interest to the majority but involving bitter dispute and pitched battles among a minority—precipitated tumultuous changes in philosophical and religious belief in general, and in opinions about sexual practice in particular. Asceticism was growing more prominent, influencing philosophy, religion, and sexual conduct. The ancient world was the domain of many gods whose example—polymorphous, indiscriminately erotic, and tolerant of any form of desire—justified the actions of men. Newer religions, among them Christianity, saw the world as a battlefield between good and evil. In such a world, sex itself became dichotomized and battle was joined between opposing notions of proper sexual practice.

So while much ancient opinion urged that no pleasures, taken in moderation, could be deemed culpable, the management of those pleasures—and their appropriateness—became an ever more involving preoccupation in late antiquity. Plato's recommendations in the *Laws* may not have represented or influenced many of his Greek contemporaries, but they accurately predicted the varieties of antisexual asceticism that appeared in the Hellenized Roman Empire. Neoplatonists, Stoics, and Cynics all warned about the consequences of excessive sexual pleasure, though no ascetic philosophical school urged the suppression of homosexual desire—only, as for all pleasure, its control. Austere religious cults like Christianity argued for a more strict interpretation of the uses of pleasure, and increasingly focused on sexual pleasure as suspect, possibly even harmful. Assenting to the dualistic vision of a moral universe governed by unalterable natural laws—a view subscribed to by a number of religions—Christianity insisted that asceticism and celibacy, not pleasure and sex, marked the earthly conduct most likely to be rewarded with a place in the life to come. Nowhere in such a scheme was there room for any kind of homosexual behavior: neither for the promiscuous vice enjoyed by "passive" males, nor for the approved practices of "real men" who found both virtue and pleasure in the arms of boys, nor even for those who enjoyed sex with male partners with whom they had lived lovingly, faithfully, and long.

The new asceticism preached a dichotomy of flesh and spirit, denigrating the flesh and its uses, and glorifying the spirit; advocating abstinence and celibacy, and asserting that procreation was the only justification for sexual desire. Adultery, pederasty, and all varieties of prostitution—by women, by passive or active homosexuals, by heterosexual males—threatened the conceptual primacy of procreative sex. If this attitude was generally antisexual, it was also specifically homophobic. The *Erotes* is one of the last pagan apologias for same-sex love, and the author may have felt he was fighting a rear-guard action. Despite the urbane assurance of his argument for love between men, the *Erotes* offers a glimpse of the world to come, in which Charicles, not Callicratidas, would triumph.

The Destruction of Sodom. *Twelfth-century mosaic. Duomo, Monreale, Italy. Alinari/Art Resource, NY*

PART TWO

Inventing Sodom

*Sodom and Homosexual Behavior in the
Old and New Testaments*

Chapter Five

The Sodom Story

T hose who live in turbulent days—raging with moral, religious, and philosophical battles and disrupted by wars, plagues, persecutions, and portents of a crumbling empire or even the end of time—often claim that such events must reflect divine displeasure with human conduct. Jewish and Christian theorists writing in the early years of the Common Era blamed social chaos on immoral sexual conduct, especially the homosexual behavior of the pagans who surrounded them. As proof that such behavior was an abomination, Jewish and Christian theologians cited ancient Hebrew scriptures and the opinions of the scholars who interpreted them, finding support there for their own abhorrence.

1 Fire from Heaven

The story of Sodom in Genesis 18 and 19 is generally accepted as the biblical source for prohibitions against homosexual behavior; its practitioners came to be called sodomites, after the city. Though many who read the biblical account believe they know precisely what sin caused Sodom's destruction, in the text God is less explicit. Determined to discover whether the scandalous reputation of Sodom and Gomorrah is accurate—"the cry of Sodom and Gomorrah is great, and . . . their sin is very grievous"—God decides to "go down now, and see whether they have done altogether according to the cry of it, which is come unto me; and if not, I will know."[1] God sends two angels disguised as travelers to Sodom; there they encounter Lot, who, though not a native, lives in Sodom with his wife and two daughters. The author of Genesis 19 (King James Version) then swiftly recounts the events that earn the most famous punishment in Western moral history.

1   And there came two angels to Sodom at even: and Lot sat in the gate of Sodom: and Lot seeing them rose up to meet them; and he bowed himself with his face toward the ground;

2   And he said, Behold now, my lords, turn in, I pray you, into your servant's house, and tarry all night, and wash your feet, and ye shall rise up early, and go on your ways. And they said, Nay; but we will abide in the street all night.

3   And he pressed upon them greatly; and they turned in unto him, and entered into his house; and he made them a feast, and did bake unleavened bread, and they did eat.

4   But before they lay down, the men of the city, even the men of Sodom, compassed the house round, both old and young, all the people from every quarter:

5   And they called unto Lot, and said unto him, Where are the men which came in to thee this night? bring them out unto us, that we may know them.

6   And Lot went out at the door unto them, and shut the door after him,

7   And said, I pray you, brethren, do not do so wickedly.

8   Behold now, I have two daughters which have not known man; let me, I pray you, bring them out unto you, and do ye to them as is good in your eyes; only unto these men do nothing; for therefore came they under the shadow of my roof.

9   And they said, Stand back. And they said again, This one fellow came in to sojourn, and he will needs be a judge: now will we deal worse with thee, than with them. And they pressed sore upon the man, even Lot, and came near to break the door.

10   But the men put forth their hand, and pulled Lot into the house to them, and shut to the door.

11   And they smote the men that were at the door of the house with blindness, both small and great: so that they wearied themselves to find the door.

12 And the men said unto Lot, Hast thou any here besides? Take thy sons-in-law, and thy sons, and thy daughters, and whatsoever thou hast in the city, bring them out of this place:

13 For we will destroy this place, because the cry of them is waxen great before the face of the Lord; and the Lord hath sent us to destroy it.

God apparently finds adequate reason in the conduct of the Sodomites to take vengeance. As the angels have promised, there "rained upon Sodom and upon Gomorrah brimstone and fire from the Lord out of heaven; And he overthrew those cities, and all the plain, and all the inhabitants of the cities, and that which grew upon the ground."

For nearly two millennia it has been accepted that the Sodomites intended some sexual encounter with the angels, that this intent defined the general wickedness of the Sodomites, and that they were destroyed solely for this wickedness. The Sodom story is popularly believed to demonstrate God's abhorrence of homosexual acts and to embody his most profound prohibition against them. It is also generally accepted as a dire warning to mankind, detailing what calamities will befall a society that allows homosexual behavior to flourish, and as scriptural justification for the belief that the extreme punishment is just recompense for the sin. The authority of the Church has supported this reading and has considered it sufficient justification for condemning those whose sin is believed to be like that of the men of Sodom.

The traditional reading of Genesis 19 hinges on the crucial verb "to know"; the Sodomites' demand to "know" the angels is interpreted as the cause of their devastating punishment. In the Hebrew text the verb is *yadha*. *Yadha* appears some nine hundred times in the Old Testament, and almost always it means "to become acquainted with." In a handful of cases, however, *yadha* can also be understood, perhaps euphemistically, to imply sexual activity with someone.[2] Traditional translations from Hebrew to Greek or Latin or English render *yadha* as "to know" with the implication of carnal knowledge, or in later translations, more directly as "to have intercourse with" or "to abuse." Thus the King James Version (KJV) of the Sodom story reads "to know," the Jerusalem Bible (JB) "have intercourse with," the New English Bible (NEB) "abuse."[3] It is argued that this translation of the verb is supported by Lot's description of his two daughters as having "not known [*yadha*] man." The use of the same verb in an indubitably sexual context seems to confirm the sexual translation of *yadha* in its first appearance and to demonstrate that the story is concerned primarily with the consequences of sexual activity.

But although *yadha* does, on a handful of occasions, imply sexual knowledge, on every one of these occasions it refers to heterosexual sex. Only in the Sodom passage—and in one other curiously parallel story in the Book of Judges—has it been construed to refer to a homosexual act.[4] The question then arises, Why has *yadha* been assumed to imply a homosexual act only in this instance? And is there any other evidence to support the contention? Skeptics argue that since the translation of *yadha* is the only basis for the conclusion that homosexual behavior is the root of Sodom's evil, then doubt about its meaning must also cast doubt on the traditional interpretation. Indeed, some commentators point out that no text in Genesis 19 unequivocally supports an interpretation of the Sodom story as a prohibition of homosexual behavior, a testimony to its just punishment, or a declaration that the actions of the Sodomites were unnatural.[5] And nowhere in Genesis 19 does any homosexual act actually take place. In fact, these commentators urge, the text clearly suggests another sin as the wickedness for which Sodom was destroyed.[6]

Let us look briefly at Lot's conduct. It is generally assumed that Lot believes the Sodomites desire homosexual intercourse with the angels and will use violence to get it. Lot's startling response is to offer instead his two daughters, who "have not known man." This offer has several possible explanations. Lot may simply be trying to save his own skin. One commentator suggests that "the surrender of his daughters was simply the most tempting bribe Lot could offer on the spur of the moment to appease a hostile crowd."[7] However, if he knows that the visitors are divine emissaries, he may believe that his duty to God overrides his duty to his kin, and that it is better to surrender his daughters than to allow the Sodomites to harm the visitors to whom he has offered hospitality. In surrendering the visitors he would incur God's wrath. Lot's position would be justified in Genesis 22 by Abraham's willingness to sacrifice Isaac, for which obedience God blesses Abraham. Whereas Isaac is Abraham's heir, Lot's daughters occupy a rather different and lesser position in terms of their relative value to Lot. Though they may be sexually desirable because of their virginity, and therefore useful for trade, barter, or bribe, or as bearers of children, they are not Lot's heirs. Their inferior status as women might make his offer of them as sexual commodities—or possibly as slaves or servants—acceptable in the eyes of contemporary readers of Genesis.[8] But the notion that Lot is sacrificing his children in the service of the Lord hinges on his recognition that his visitors are angels, and the only indication of this is that when he first encounters them, he "bow[s] himself with his face to the ground" in deference. So, unfortunately, the text offers little basis for any interpretation.

But if Lot's motives in offering his daughters remain obscure, his response to the Sodomites' demand that he bring out the visitors so "that we may know them" seems quite clear. To that Lot replies, "Do not do so wickedly." He virtually commands the Sodomites, "Unto these men do nothing; for therefore came they under the shadow ["shelter"—NEB] of my roof." Lot protects the angels from violence because he has given them hospitality and shelter. In reaction, the Sodomites try to do violence to Lot, who is in turn saved by the angels. After the brief appearance of the dubious *yadha,* there is nothing in the story to support any further "homosexual" interpretation. If Lot's offer of his daughters is intended as a sexual bribe, then this is the only element suggesting *any* sexual desire on the part of the Sodomites, and that desire is not homosexual.

The men of Sodom do not accept Lot's offer, nor do they show any further interest in the angels. Rather, they threaten Lot with violence. The Sodomites warn Lot that they will "deal worse with thee" than with the angels; they attack him, and "pressed sore upon the man, even Lot, and came near to break the door." But they are deterred when the angels blind them. A traditional view is that the Sodomites intend to rape Lot.[9] But they do not attempt rape; they try to break down Lot's door. The Sodomites' threat may allude not to rape, but to more murderous violence. In fact, there is no sexual conduct at all on the part of the Sodomites. Though the language of Genesis makes it difficult to assess their motives, it is clear about what they do. If the Sodom story advocates the punishment of homosexual acts, it does so even though no such acts are committed.

Another biblical text points to an alternative reading: the story of the outrage at Gibeah in Judges 19–20. Probably written later than the Sodom text, and perhaps derived from it, this text uses the verb *yadha* in a strikingly similar context.[10] In this story a Levite, a resident of the highlands of Ephraim, has taken as a concubine a woman of Bethlehem. After an argument with the Levite she returns to her father's house, staying there four months, until the Levite comes to bring her back. On their return journey they come to the Israelite town of Gibeah, home of the tribe of Benjamin, where they seek lodging for the night. However, no one in Gibeah welcomes them or offers them lodging, and they are left sitting in the public square. An old man—who, like the Levite, is from the highlands of Ephraim—takes pity and welcomes them into his house, saying that he cannot allow them to spend the night in the streets. (The fact that both Lot and the old man are "sojourners" may indicate their essential difference from the native townspeople.) During the evening meal, the men of Gibeah—described in various translations as sons of Belial (KJV) and more simply as "scoundrels" (JB, NEB)—attempt to batter down the door, demanding that the old man "bring forth the man [the Levite] that came into thine house, that we may know him" (Judges 19:22, KJV; "abuse him," JB; "have intercourse with him," NEB).

Like Lot, the old man resists the request, and for the same reasons: "Do not commit this crime. This man is my guest" (19:23, JB). Then the old man offers his daughter, saying, "Here is my daughter, she is a virgin. . . . Rape her and do to her what you please, but you shall not commit such an outrage against this man" (Judges 19:24, NEB; in the Hebrew text the old man offers both daughter and concubine). The men of Gibeah will not listen. Rather than sacrificing his host's daughter, the Levite thrusts his own concubine out the door and the men rape and kill her.

When he is asked how the crime came to occur, the Levite replies: "I had come with my concubine to Gibeah in Benjamin to spend the night there. The men of Gibeah rose against me that night, surrounded the house where I was, intending to kill me, and they raped my concubine and she died" (Judges 20:4–5, NEB). Though the men of Gibeah demanded to "know" him, the Levite clearly understands that their intention was to kill him, not to carnally abuse him. The story does not target their homosexuality but their inhospitality and murderous brutality to strangers.

As Mark D. Jordan affirms in *The Invention of Sodomy in Christian Theology*, both tales "narrate a terrible violation of the obligations of host to traveler."[11] Violence against strangers, breach of the rules of hospitality—these violations are at the heart of both texts.

Lot is a "sojourner" in Sodom—in Hebrew, a *ger,* or, as it were, a resident alien.[12] What his obligations might be to his Sodomite hosts is not clear from the text; nor is what restrictions might be placed upon him as a sojourner. But the Sodomites' anger, evidenced by their pointed comment that Lot's alien status does not give him the right to judge them, suggests that he has violated some obligation that relates to his status in Sodom. Is it that Lot the visitor has taken it upon himself to admit strangers illegally to the city? And once having done that, has he been arrogant enough to refuse the legitimate request of the permanent residents to identify the unknown foreigners? When Lot lectures the Sodomites on their obligation to be hospitable to the strangers—judging them, as they say—has he, in their eyes, far overstepped his bounds? For the men of Sodom to inquire about unknown visitors arriving late at the house of a foreign resident—making *yadha* pertain to a query about identity rather than to a sexual threat—may not be so unusual.

The Sodom story is probably the Western text most often cited to justify homophobia, and yet this interpretation depends upon the disputed translation of a single verb.[13] But the obligation to give shelter to travelers was a common, powerful, and respected convention in the ancient world. That an individual, a household, or a city must offer hospitality to a stranger is one of the primary tenets of nearly all ancient moral and ethical systems—an imperative reflected in ancient texts besides the Bible. The Sodomites' wickedness—like that of the men of Gibeah—lies in their disregard for the ancient laws of hospitality, wickedness proven when they reject God's command as it is spoken by Lot: "Unto these men do nothing; for therefore came they under the shadow of my roof."

2 Sodom and Homosexuality in Other Old Testament Texts

The destruction of Sodom was clearly a monumental disaster, which much impressed the writer or writers of Genesis. That the story is more than myth has been confirmed by modern archeology: a disaster did occur, and the Cities of the Plain, near the Dead Sea, were destroyed—probably by a powerful earthquake that may also have ignited subterranean gases seeping from the asphalt deposits common in the region, so that fire burned what the earthquake did not destroy. Though Genesis 19 attributes this catastrophic destruction to the wickedness of the Sodomites, the text does not describe the precise nature of that wickedness.

For the history of homophobia, what the Sodom story was meant to convey is less important than how it has been read, and with what consequences. As John McNeill eloquently argues, "In the Christian West, the homosexual has been the victim of inhospitable treatment. . . . In the name of a mistaken understanding of the crime of Sodom and

82 *Inventing Sodom*

Gomorrah, the true crime of Sodom and Gomorrah has been and continues to be repeated every day."[14] Certainly, as John Boswell points out, it is anachronistic to imagine that "the sexual preoccupations of modern or even early Christian ages were of interest to the writers of the Old Testament."[15]

If Genesis 19 is not about homosexuality, then Judeo-Christian disapproval of homosexual acts is based possibly upon a mistranslation and certainly on a tragic misunderstanding. But the overwhelming majority of Christians believe that the story of Sodom condemns homosexual behavior. What is the source of this judgment? Has the story always been interpreted thus? An answer may be discovered by locating Sodom in other Old Testament texts.

Given the usual interpretation of the story, one might expect later Old Testament books to use Sodom and the Sodomites as synonyms of or metaphors for homosexual behavior. Especially, one might expect that Sodom would be employed as a cautionary image in contexts where homosexual acts are specifically prohibited or condemned.

Only two texts in the Old Testament by common assent clearly refer to homosexual conduct; one explicitly prohibits it, and the other decrees its punishment. Leviticus 18:22 (NEB) says, "You shall not lie with a man as with a woman: that is an abomination." Leviticus 20:13 (NEB) reads, "If a man has intercourse with a man, as with a woman, they both commit an abomination: they shall be put to death; their blood shall be on their own heads."[16]

Leviticus is the collection of laws governing the conduct of the Jewish people, probably compiled sometime between the seventh and fifth centuries B.C.E.—that is, several hundred years later than the presumed composition of Genesis 19, which describes events of roughly 1850 B.C.E.[17] It is not known whether the passages in question are contemporary with the rest of Leviticus, older than the general body of Leviticus, or interpolated at a later date.[18] The prohibitions against homosexuality occur in the portion of Leviticus known as the Holiness Code. Chapter 18 has to do specifically with offenses against conjugal relations and with sexual offenses. Chapter 20 enumerates the penalties for those offenses. But even though the text of Leviticus contains the most explicit expression of Old Testament repugnance to homosexual behavior, and demands extreme punishment for it, it does not appeal to the Sodom story.

The Holiness Code decrees that what the heathen Egyptians and Canaanites do, the Jews cannot: "You shall not do as they do in Egypt where you once dwelt, nor shall you do as they do in the land of Canaan to which I am bringing you; you shall not conform to their institutions. You must keep my laws and conform to my institutions without fail. I am the Lord thy God."[19] A large number of sexual practices are listed among the customs common in heathen nations but prohibited to the Jews—sexual intercourse with a variety of blood relatives, sexual relations with animals, and sexual relations "with a man as with a woman." That is, God prohibits penetration of one man by another. God warns the Jews that "the heathen whom I am driving out before you, made themselves unclean" through illicit sexual behavior, and "that is how the land became unclean, and I punished it for its iniquity so that it spewed out its inhabitants. . . . Observe my charge, therefore, and follow none of these abominable institutions customary before your time; do not make yourselves unclean with them." The Jews are therefore commanded not to be corrupted by heathen examples. It is clear, though, that rather than being a uniquely horrendous crime uniquely punishable by death, homosexual intercourse of a specific kind is included among a large number of prohibited sexual offenses, *all of which* are punishable by death, and the performance of *any of which* is an abomination that will make the Jews unclean, like the Canaanites and Egyptians. As for failure to mention Sodom, either the compilers of Leviticus presumed that the story was so well known that it was unnecessary to refer to it explicitly (perhaps Sodom is the land that "spewed out its inhabitants") or they did not believe that Sodom had been punished for sexual iniquities and so found it irrelevant.

In Leviticus 18:22, the prohibition against homosexuality immediately follows a prohibition (18:21) against "let[ting] any of thy seed pass through the fire to Molech"—that is, surrendering children for use (possibly sexual) or sacrifice in rituals devoted to Canaanite gods. Though textual proximity is not a definitive argument, some modern commentators have suggested that since verse 21 prohibits participation in heathen rituals, verse 22 does not prohibit homosexuality generally but ritual homosexual prostitution in particular.[20] There is evidence of such prostitution in the religious practices of various peoples of the ancient Near East, and a number of Old Testament texts describe attempts by various Judaean and Israelite kings to evict homosexual male prostitutes from the temple in Jerusalem.[21] The proscription in Leviticus, then, may be aimed at the particular rituals of a heathen religion.[22] Significantly, the word used to describe the forbidden act in Leviticus—*toevah*, "abomination"—is used throughout the Old Testament to describe idolatrous practices. Like the Sodom story, the Leviticus text may well condemn something other than what later readers have imagined.

Nowhere in the Old Testament is Sodom clearly associated with homosexual behavior. However, the city is mentioned many times as a general symbol of evil and as an example of sudden and massive divine retribution. Genesis 13:13 and 18:20 (KJV) both speak about the sin of Sodom, though only to say that the men of the city were "wicked" and that their sin is "very grievous."[23] Deuteronomy, probably written in the fifth or fourth century B.C.E., twice refers to Sodom, but only to warn that, if the Israelites do not adhere to the covenant God proposes, their lands will become "as desolate as Sodom and Gomorrah." The book of Jeremiah, written between 608 and 587 B.C.E., accuses the "prophets of Jerusalem" of being "adulterers and hypocrites" and claims that in Jerusalem "no man turns back from his sin": "To me all her inhabitants are like Sodom and Gomorrah" (23:14, NEB). Jeremiah also fulminates against the towns of Edom, which, he prophesies, will become objects of horror and be "overthrown like Sodom and Gomorrah" (49:18, JB). In the oracle against Babylon, Jeremiah prophesies that as God overthrew Sodom so Babylon will be destroyed—"to repay her arrogance against Yahweh," and also because it is a country of sages, diviners, and idols (50:29, 35–38, JB). The poet of Lamentations (4:6, JB) protests that the "crimes of the daughter of my people have outdone the sins of Sodom." Lamentations suggests that Jerusalem's sin is even greater than Sodom's, though it nowhere says that the holy city was ridden with homosexual vice. All of these texts cite Sodom as an example of extreme wickedness and warn that Israel or Jerusalem or Edom or Babylon will suffer a similar fate because of their own iniquity, but the iniquity is always described as pride, arrogance, and idolatry, never as homosexuality.

The prophet Ezekiel, in a passage that can be dated near 593 B.C.E., is quite specific about the sins of Jerusalem and Sodom:

> Dealers in proverbs will say of you, "Like mother, like daughters."
> You are a true daughter of a mother who loathed her husband and
> her children. You are a true sister of your sisters who loathed their
> husbands and their children. You are all daughters of a Hittite
> mother and an Amorite father. Your elder sister was Samaria, who

lived with her daughters to the north of you. Your younger sister, who lived with her daughters to the south of you, was Sodom. Did you not behave the way they did and commit the same abominations? You came very near to doing even worse than they. As I live, says the Lord God, your sister Sodom and her daughters never behaved as you and your daughters have done. This was the iniquity of your sister Sodom: she and her daughters had pride of wealth and food in plenty, comfort and ease, and yet she never helped the poor and wretched. They grew haughty and did deeds abominable in my sight, and I made away with them, as you have seen. . . . Your sins are so much more abominable than theirs that they appear innocent in comparison with you (16:44–52, NEB).

Even if the prophet believes that homosexuality was the principal sin of Sodom, he asserts that the sins of Jerusalem are greater; the implication is that homosexuality is not the most serious of all sins against God. In any case, however, Ezekiel says nothing about homosexuality. Rather, Sodom's sins were pride, haughtiness, and unwillingness to share her luxury and wealth with the poor and wretched. This list clearly suggests that Ezekiel believed that Sodom was destroyed because of its inhospitality to strangers.

Other prophets use the fate of Sodom to caution Israel about the consequences of apostasy and pagan worship. Amos warns the Israelites that God will destroy them just as he overthrew Sodom and Gomorrah if they persist in idolatry (4:11). Reminding Israel about the retribution due to pagans, the prophet Zephaniah points out that Moab—a pagan city—will become like Sodom because it has insulted God; it will be "a waste land for evermore" as a "retribution for their pride" (2:9, 10, NEB). Here arrogance and idolatry are the sins that will bring down destruction like that of Sodom.[24]

Two other books of Scripture, both rejected as apocryphal by Jewish and Protestant traditions but accepted as canonical by the Greek Orthodox and Roman Catholic churches, also mention Sodom. These are the Book of Ecclesiasticus, written in Hebrew about 190–180 B.C.E., and the Book of Wisdom, written in Greek in the late first century B.C.E. In a passage describing the punishment that will befall wicked people, Ecclesiasticus notes that fire will be kindled against a disobedient nation and remarks that "God did not pardon the giants of old who in their confident strength rebelled. He did not spare the people with whom Lot lived, whom he abhorred for their pride"

(Ecclesiasticus 16:8, JB). The Book of Wisdom—the most explicit, extensive, and possibly latest pre-Christian scriptural explanation of the story of Sodom—describes the Egyptians as even more culpable than the Sodomites. The Israelites have fled from the Egyptians—the sinners—across the Red Sea, protected by the Lord:

> *On the sinners, however, punishments rained down*
> *not without violent thunder as early warning;*
> *and deservedly they suffered for their crimes,*
> *since they evinced such bitter hatred towards strangers.*
> *Others had refused to welcome unknown men on their arrival,*
> *but these had made slaves of guests and benefactors.*
> *The former moreover . . .*
> *had shown the foreigners hostility from the start;*
> *not so the latter: these welcomed your people with feasting*
> *and after granting them equal rights with themselves*
> *then afflicted them with forced labor.*
> *Thus they were struck with blindness like the former at the door of the*
>   *virtuous man . . . [Wisdom 19:13–18, JB]*

Written more than a thousand years after Genesis 19, the Book of Wisdom is notable for making no reference to homosexuality in Sodom and for repeating the usual Old Testament accusation of inhospitality.

Leviticus, the only biblical text to directly prohibit homosexual intercourse, is presumed to have been compiled sometime after the Babylonian captivity began in 586 B.C.E. As Sodom seems to have no homosexual resonance in Old Testament texts written before Leviticus, it is therefore possible to presume that the Jews had no prohibition against homosexuality until after the exile.[25] In addition, if the Sodom story is never cited in connection with homosexual practice in any Old Testament text, its interpretation as a warning against the evils of homosexuality may be a comparatively late reading—even a misreading—of an ancient text.[26]

3 Interpreting Sodom

What, then, is the source of the almost universal antihomosexual interpretation of the Sodom story? During the centuries after the return from the Babylonian captivity, a number of historical currents influenced Jewish thought—in particular, the Hellenization of the Mediterranean world and the incursion of Hellenistic influence into the heretofore closed world of the Jewish people. Suspicious of Hellenistic culture, intent on protecting the traditions and purity of Judaism, Jewish commentators were especially scandalized by what they saw as pagan sexual licentiousness.

Jewish texts from the Hellenistic period concur on the imperiled state of Judaism. Lustfully following the examples of pagans, Jewish men were said to be devoted to fornication, their daughters and wives to licentious conduct. The inordinate luxury of the wealthy, it was said, contributed to this sexual chaos and resulted in the abandonment of traditional religion and the precepts of the Law. Elaborating upon the Levitical prohibitions of all kinds of sexual irregularities, Jewish writers increasingly advocated celibacy, asceticism, and sexual abstinence, even going so far as to rewrite the Ten Commandments to prohibit both nonprocreative sex with one's wife and homosexual behavior.[27] As the ills of both Jewish and pagan societies were especially attributed to sexual license, writers began to invoke the Sodom story less as an example of inhospitality and more as an example of the consequences of general sexual misconduct. During this period a number of Jewish texts also begin to specifically attack homosexual behavior, particularly among Gentiles, who are seen as especially prone to homosexual behavior, commonly manifested in pederastic practice. The Sybilline Oracles, a book of prophecies from the second century B.C.E. predicting the dire consequences of Roman oppression, compares Jews with Gentiles. Jews are "mindful of holy wedlock, and they do not engage in impious intercourse with male children, as do Phoenicians, Egyptians, Romans, specious Greece, and many nations . . . Persians, Galatians, and all Asia."[28]

In the first century B.C.E.—about the time that Ecclesiasticus and Wisdom were written—another set of noncanonical writings began to reinterpret the story of Sodom as a specific warning about sexual transgression. These writings, known as the Pseudepigrapha, comprise several Jewish texts, of which one, the Book of Jubilees, mentions Sodom repeatedly. In 13:17 "the men of Sodom were sinners exceedingly," and in 16:5–6 "the Lord executed his judgments on Sodom . . . and he burned them with fire and brimstone [because] they defile themselves and commit fornication in their flesh, and work uncleanness on the earth." In 20:5–6 Abraham warns his sons "of the judgment of the giants and the judgement of the Sodomites," both of whom had died because of their "fornication, uncleanness, and mutual corruption through fornication." (Sodom's men in their wickedness are compared to the "giants" or the immortal "sons of God," as they are called in Genesis 6:2 and 4, or the Watchers, as they are sometimes called in Jewish legend, who unlawfully engaged in sexual acts with mortal women and whom God consequently destroyed.)[29] While nowhere mentioning homosexuality, the Book of Jubilees does explicitly identify the sin of Sodom as sexual. And though the text refers to the heterosexual sin of the Watchers, the "mutual corruption through fornication" attributed to the Sodomites in the third passage hints that the sins may have been homosexual, mutually engaged in by men alone.

The Testaments of the Twelve Patriarchs, a group of texts that purport to be prophecies and admonitions of the Jewish patriarchs but, with interpolations over time, were probably written sometime during the first century B.C.E., also contain several references to Sodom. In the Testament of Benjamin, God warns the Israelites to beware that they do not "commit the fornication of Sodom" for fear that they will perpetrate "wanton deeds with women" (9:1). In another, the Testament of Levi (written around 50 B.C.E.), God prophesies that "wedded women ye shall pollute, and the virgin of Jerusalem shall ye defile, and with harlots and adulteresses shall ye be joined, and the daughters of Gentiles shall ye take to wife, purifying them with unlawful purification, and your union shall be like unto Sodom and Gomorrah" (14:6). In both these texts, the sins of Sodom are obviously heterosexual. In the Testament of Naphtali, written close to the time of Christ, the analogy of the Watchers and Sodomites reappears. God enjoins that "ye become not as Sodom, which changed the order of nature. In like manner the Watchers also changed the order of their nature, whom the Lord cursed at the flood" (3:4–5). One interpretation of this is that just as the Watchers changed the order of their nature by having sexual relations with mortal women, so too did the Sodomites by engaging in homosexual acts, but nowhere does the text specifically say so. More persuasive is Naphtali 4:1, which warns "ye yourselves shall also depart from the Lord, walking according to the lawlessness of the Gentiles, and ye shall do according to all the wickedness of Sodom." As mentioned, many Jewish writers of this period associated sexual licentiousness, especially pederasty, with Gentile sinfulness.

Another Jewish text, the Secrets of Enoch, usually called the Second Book of Enoch, probably written in Egypt before 70 C.E., claims to be the writings of the prophet Enoch, who inveighs against idolatry and sexual profligacy and prophesies punishment for the wicked and reward for the righteous. Idolators, the text says, have "laden the whole earth with untruths, abominable lecheries, namely one with the other, and all manner of unclean wickednesses" (34:2), a passage more accurately translated as "they engage in abominable intercourse," that is, "friend with friend in the anus, and every other kind of wicked uncleanness which it is disgusting to report."[30] And 2 Enoch 10:4 describes the several levels of the afterlife, where a region is made ready for those "who dishonor God, who on earth practice sin against nature, which is child corruption after the Sodomitic fashion." The two texts from Enoch may be the earliest in the Jewish scriptural tradition to identify Sodom with homosexual behavior, which is explicitly named a "sin against nature" and clearly defined—"child corruption"—as pederasty.

4 Sodom and Sexual Deviance

The antihomosexual vision of Sodom that would become so familiar to later ages finally emerges in the writing of Philo Judaeus. A Hellenized Jewish scholar who lived in Alexandria and died about 45 C.E., Philo was as familiar with the Greek classics as he was with the scriptures and scholarship of Judaism, and he was clearly influenced by the anti-sexual ascetics of both traditions. Hellenistic Neoplatonism, a synthesis of the thought of Plato, Aristotle, and Pythagoras, leavened with a large portion of mysticism, arose near the end of the last century B.C.E. and had, by the third century C.E., become the most influential philosophy of the ancient world. Neoplatonism shared with other ascetic philosophies a general suspicion of sex and a particular distaste for homosexuality. In a number of treatises, among them *On Abraham, The Special Laws,* and *The Contemplative Life,* Philo, echoing Plato's *Laws,* asserts that homosexual acts are contrary to nature.[31] In *The Special Laws,* for example, Philo associates effeminacy with pederastic homosexual desire, finding it everywhere in the streets of Alexandria. But his pederasty is not the idealized Attic *paederastia.* Its object is not the youthful and appropriately boyish *eromenos* but something much more like the always questionable *kinaidos.* He condemns both effeminate, passive homosexuals ("those who transform the male nature to the female") and those who engage in active homosexual behavior—"the lover[s] of such."

In former days the very mention of [pederasty] was a great disgrace, but now it is a matter of boasting not only to the active but
to the passive partners, who habituate themselves to endure the
disease of effeminization, let both body and soul run to waste, and
leave no ember of their male sex-nature to smolder. Mark how
conspicuously they braid and adorn the hair of their heads, and
how they scrub and paint their faces with cosmetics and pigments
and the like, and smother themselves with fragrant unguents. . . .
In fact the transformation of the male nature to the female is practiced by them as an art and does not raise a blush. These persons
are rightly judged worthy of death by those who obey the law,
which ordains that the man-woman who debases the sterling coin
of nature should perish unavenged, suffered not to live for a day or
even an hour, as a disgrace to himself, his house, his native land
and the whole human race. And the lover of such may be assured
that he is subject to the same penalty. He pursues an unnatural
pleasure and does his best to render cities desolate and uninhab-
ited by destroying the means of procreation.[32]

Applying his extensive knowledge of classical texts to an interpretation of Mosaic law, Philo argued that the law of Moses and the law of
nature were the same and that both concurred in condemning homosexual acts of all kinds. In a curious synthesis, Philo argues that since
homosexuality was contrary to nature (as he believed Plato insisted),
and since biblical prohibitions—derived from the story of Sodom and
expressed in other Old Testament texts—decreed death for homosexual
acts, then the law of nature itself must impose the same decree.

Philo's *On Abraham* offers a particularly lurid account of the "land
of the Sodomites,"

brimful of innumerable iniquities, particularly such as arise from
gluttony and lewdness. . . . The inhabitants owed their extreme
license to the never-failing lavishness of their sources of wealth. . . .
[I]ncapable of bearing such satiety, . . . they threw off from their
necks the law of nature, and applied themselves to deep drinking
of strong liquor and dainty feeding and forbidden forms of intercourse. Not only in their mad lust for women did they violate the
marriages of their neighbors, but also men mounted males without
respect for the sex nature which the active partner shares with the

passive; and so when they tried to beget children they were discovered to be incapable of any but a sterile seed. Yet the discovery
availed them not, so much stronger was the force of their lust
which mastered them. Then, as little by little they accustomed
those who were by nature men to submit to play the part of
women, they saddled them with the formidable curse of a female
disease. For not only did they emasculate their bodies by luxury
and voluptuousness, but they worked a further degeneration in
their souls and, so far as in them lay, were corrupting the whole of
mankind.[33]

Philo's elaborate fantasy of daily life among the Sodomites bears little
relation to the description found in the book of Genesis, but this passage and others like it would come to be taken as accurate.

In a discussion of Genesis, Philo may have been the first to give the
Hebrew *yadha* a specifically homosexual connotation, translating it to
mean "servile lawlessness and unseemly pederasty."[34] Philo's description of the sin of Sodom—far more detailed than any biblical passage—
draws not only upon accreted tradition but also upon his own fertile
invention and possibly upon the sexual life he saw around him in Hellenistic Alexandria. But since Philo must derive his condemnation of
homosexual acts from its Old Testament source, his account gives the
chief sin of Sodom as excess of all kinds, including gluttony and lewdness, consequences of the Sodomites' vast wealth. Though consonant
with Old Testament depictions of Sodom as prideful and inhospitable,
Philo's ascetic presumption is that material excess leads to the general
degeneration of the moral nature and thus to the perversion of nature
itself. Emasculated by luxury, Philo's Sodomites indulged in indiscriminate sexual debauchery. Not only did these fatally emasculated men
pursue homosexual acts, being incapable of rejecting that debauchery
once they had experienced it, but worst of all, they seduced or forced
those "who were by nature men" to "play the part of women." Such
corruption of real men is like a disease—Philo calls it the "female disease"—and can soon spread to the whole of mankind.

Philo invented Sodom as we now know it; his retelling of the Sodom
story forecasts all later interpretations of both the sin and its punishment. His condemnation of homosexual acts stands as the most elaborate expression of homophobic sentiment at the dawn of the Common
Era. Derived from Old Testament prohibitions, themselves based on a

misreading of the Sodom story old even in Philo's time, supported by the ancient condemnation of effeminacy in men and by Jewish convictions that same-sex behavior was in itself emblematic of paganism, Philo's treatises first array the charges that would be levied against homosexual acts in the writings of the early church. His belief that the monsters he invents ought to be put to death would eventually be ratified by the law of the newly Christian Roman Empire.[35]

Chapter Six

Gospel Sodomy

Sodom in the New Testament

T he New Testament is as imprecise as the Old about the significance
of Sodom. Were the Sodomites homosexual sinners or inhospitable
and violent neighbors? Jesus of Nazareth mentioned the wicked city
only once, and he seems not to have construed its sin as homosexual.
As reported in the Gospels of Matthew and Luke, Jesus warned the seventy people he appointed to go out before him and deliver his message
that "whosoever shall not receive you, nor hear your words, when you
depart out of that house or city, shake the dust off your feet. Verily I say
unto you, it shall be more tolerable for the land of Sodom and Gomorrah in the day of judgment, than for that city" (Matt. 10:1). Indeed, for
the writers of the New Testament, as for those of the Old, Sodom is not,
as Mark Jordan argues in *The Invention of Sodomy in Christian Theology*, a story about same-sex copulation but rather about "some combination of arrogance and ingratitude."[1]

1 The Unnameable Sin

In the New Testament writings that claim to report Jesus' words, most
scholars find no hint of what he believed about the morality of homosexual acts. Some scholars' readings of the passages in the Gospels of

Matthew and John concerning the "beloved disciple" have led them to
speculate that Jesus was sympathetic to love between men, but those
texts in fact offer little to suggest that Jesus' affection for John extended
to encompass what modern homophile writers hoped that it did.[2] The
latter have argued that the absence of positive evidence does not prove
the negative; some have even asserted that Jesus' opinions about homosexuality have suffered textual corruption or censorship.[3]

However, there is a New Testament passage that may indeed throw
light on Jesus' view of same-sex behavior. In Matthew 5, during the Sermon on the Mount, Jesus says that he has not come to abolish the
ancient commandments but to fulfill and complete them. To support his
assertion, he addresses a number of Mosaic and Levitical laws concerning murder, adultery, divorce, and oath-breaking, as well as the ancient
maxim that demands an eye for an eye and the popular admonition that
a man should love his neighbor but hate his enemy. In his gloss on the
commandment against murder, he says:

> Ye have heard that it was said by them of old time, Thou shalt
> not kill; and whosoever shall kill shall be in danger of the
> judgment.
> But I say unto you, That whosoever is angry with his brother
> without a cause shall be in danger of the judgment: and whosoever
> shall say to his brother, Raca, shall be in danger of the council: but
> whosoever shall say, Thou fool, shall be in danger of hell fire.
> [Matthew 5:21–22, KJV]

Just as the old Law declares that murder will be punished by "the judgment" of God, so in the new dispensation that Jesus preaches, certain
other sins will be considered equally serious—on a par, in fact, with
murder. These are unjustified anger, saying "Raca" to one's brother,
and (even worse) saying "Thou fool," also presumably to a brother,
that is, a friend. But what does this mean?

Jesus seems to be saying that just as murder, a violent sin against the
body, deserves the extreme punishment, so unjustified anger will be
punished as a kind of murder of the spirit. The curious word *raca*, however, and the odd warning that one who calls his brother "fool" shall be
in danger of hellfire are more problematical. The Gospel of Matthew
was written in Aramaic and then translated into Greek.[4] *Raca*—sometimes *racha*—appears in both versions. In more recent translations of
the verses, *raca* continues to appear untranslated; it is glossed in foot-

notes as derived from Aramaic *raqa,* translated as "empty-headed, brainless."[5] Textual scholarship has suggested that *raca* comes from a Semitic root word implying something "fit to be spat upon," that is, something despicable, and that it is also related to the Hebrew *rakh,* meaning "soft" (used in modern Hebrew to mean "gay").[6] In addition, *raca* may have been translated into Greek as *racha,* meaning "a worthless or wicked man." In support of this thesis, Warren Johannson quotes a Greek source from the second century B.C.E. that mentions "those" about "Antiochus the *rachas,*" some of whom are described as *kinaidoi.* Johannson speculates that *rachas* may also have been synonymous with Greek *malakos,* "soft" or "effeminate."[7] Whatever its precise sense, *raca* is clearly a contemptuous epithet. And to use it against a literal or figurative brother merits severe punishment. This crime is so serious that he who commits it will be judged by the supreme council, the Sanhedrin.

Jesus next warns that the man who calls his brother "fool" will be in danger of hellfire. "Fool" translates the Greek *moros*—"foolish" or "absurd"—and seems intended as a parallel to *raca.* Johannson suggests that *moros* renders the Aramaic text's *nabhal,* "a sexual wrongdoer and aggressor."[8] Other translations use "renegade," one who is, in Jewish usage, "impious."[9] Impiety is an accusation made against those who engage in homosexual behavior. If Jesus intends a parallel construction pairing *moros*—impious and aggressive—and *raca*—despicable, soft, and even effeminate—he may be alluding to active and passive homosexuality. If this is so, then the hellfire that Jesus threatens against the man who accuses another of being an active sexual aggressor may be the same fire that destroyed the presumed homosexual aggressors of Sodom. In other words, the accuser deserves the punishment given to the accused.

These speculations may not hold up under closer scrutiny.[10] Nevertheless, if Jesus' comments in Matthew 5 are intended as a gloss upon the Law, it is at least possible that he was prohibiting his followers from making the worst possible false accusation—that is, that a man engages in homosexual behavior. He seems to forbid even the use of the contemptuous word. Heeding Jesus, later versions of the Gospels persistently leave *raca* untranslated, suggesting the horror with which they viewed, or believed Jesus viewed, the activity that *raca* appears to describe. Here is an illustration of the homophobic dictum—which has been a formula in both ecclesiastical and civil law—that homosexuality is the sin not to be named among Christians.

2 Testifying to Perversion

Even though Christ did not accuse Sodom of the sin we now call
sodomy, the Gospel of Matthew suggests that it is unlikely Jesus would
have condoned what Jewish tradition since Leviticus seemed universally to condemn. Three passages in the New Testament refer more
directly to homosexual behavior; all of them appear in the letters of the
Apostle Paul. (In none of the letters, incidentally, does Paul mention
Sodom.) The three passages occur in the Epistles to the Corinthians
(c. 52 C.E.), to the Romans (c. 57 C.E.), and to Timothy (c. 65 C.E.).
These texts, the only clear condemnation of homosexual acts to be
found in the New Testament, have come to be cited as the definitive
Christian scriptural justification for abhorrence toward homosexual
acts and homosexuals, and have been taken by some as a license for
persecution.

In the King James Version, I Corinthians 6:9–10 reads: "Be not
deceived: neither fornicators, nor idolaters, nor adulterers, nor effeminate[s], nor abusers of themselves with mankind, / Nor thieves, nor
covetous, nor drunkards, nor revilers, nor extortioners, shall inherit the
kingdom of God." A similar warning is delivered in I Timothy 1:9–10,
where Paul declares that "the law is not made for a righteous man" but
for all manner of sinners, including "them that defile themselves with
mankind."

In Greek Paul uses *malakoi,* rendered in the King James translation
of Corinthians as "effeminate[s]." In both Corinthians and Timothy he
uses *arsenokoitai,* translated in the King James Version as "abusers
[or "defilers"] of themselves with mankind." *Malakoi*—from the verb
meaning "to make soft" or "to enervate," with a secondary meaning of
"to be weak or effeminate"—can take various forms, including
"*malakos, malakon:* soft, in a bad sense soft, effeminate; *malakia:* softness or tenderness, of men effeminacy or weakness."[11] The word
appears in Attic Greek as well as in biblical and patristic Greek. In the
play *Oi Malathakoi* by Cratinus, an early contemporary of Aristophanes, it seems to have referred to effeminate men.[12] Plato employs
it in the *Phaedrus* when he comments that an older, stronger lover will
look for and pursue weaker or effeminate boys.[13] The word usually
suggests weakness and often has a sexual overtone; it can be used in
relation to both homosexual and heterosexual desire.[14] However, Paul's
use of the word in Corinthians, where he enumerates the kinds of sin-

ners who will not enter heaven, has consistently been interpreted by translators to mean effeminate homosexual males.

Paul's use of *malakoi* seems to condemn passive homosexual activity. It is not improbable, therefore, that *arsenokoitai* is used in parallel, to refer to men who engage in active sex with other men. The word does not occur in Attic Greek, and since there is no word in Greek for homosexuality, it may have been a coinage of Paul's own time; perhaps Paul himself coined it, to make clear to Greek Christians the antihomosexual prohibitions of Leviticus. It is presumably derived from *arsen*—"male"—and *koit*—"a place to lie down" or "the marriage bed." *Arsenokoitai* can also signify unspecified lewdness or sexual activity; it is defined in Liddell and Scott's *Greek-English Lexicon*—perhaps reflecting Pauline usage—as indicating those "guilty of unnatural offenses."[15] Most commentators attribute a sexual, and specifically homosexual, sense to *arsenokoitai*. Some suggest that it refers exclusively to those who engage in active homosexuality, while others think it means only men who patronize those deemed to be *malakoi*—that is, *arsenokoitai* were lovers of boys, or the clients of boy prostitutes, or the clients of the adult passive male prostitutes sometimes called *kinaidoi*.[16] Paul's list of those who will not enter heaven includes several groups engaged in irregular sex; given Paul's emphasis on sexual sin elsewhere and the Corinthians' ancient reputation for sexual license, it is not surprising that he would include an objection to homosexual acts, which he considered emblematic of paganism. He fears that pagan sins will corrupt the purity of the newly converted Christians, just as the compiler of Leviticus feared that they would corrupt the purity of the Jewish people. As a Hellenized Jew, Paul could hardly have been ignorant of pagan views on the proper sexual role for a male, and his use of *arsenokoitai* and *malakoi* reflects this. Paul makes it clear that these individuals represent both exclusive passive and active homosexual behavior, a distinction with which his age was long familiar, and neither will inherit the kingdom of God.[17]

3 Paul on Punishment

In I Corinthians Paul lists ten sins that would keep a person out of heaven; of those, three—idolatry, passive homosexual acts, and active homosexual acts—might be considered specifically pagan, since in pagan eyes they were not sins. In his later epistle to the Christians in Rome, Paul continues his attack on paganism, citing sexual excesses

similar to those described by Philo and specifying the punishment that
will befall participants:

> For we see divine retribution revealed from heaven and falling
> upon all the godless wickedness of men. In their wickedness they
> are stifling the truth. . . . There is therefore no possible defense for
> their conduct; knowing God, they have refused to honor him as
> God, or to render him thanks.
>
> For this reason God has given them up to the vileness of their
> own desires, and the consequent degradation of their bodies,
> because they have bartered away the true God for a false one.
>
> Their women have exchanged natural intercourse for unnat-
> ural, and their men in turn, giving up natural relations with
> women, burn with lust for one another; males behave indecently
> with males, and are paid in their own persons the fitting wage of
> such perversion.
>
> Thus, because they have not seen fit to acknowledge God, he
> has given them up to their own depraved reason. This leads them
> to break all rules of conduct. They are filled with every kind of
> injustice, mischief, rapacity, and malice; they are one mass of envy,
> murder, rivalry, treachery, and malevolence; whisperers and
> scandal-mongers, hateful to God, insolent, arrogant, and boastful;
> they invent new kinds of mischief, they show no loyalty to parents,
> no conscience, no fidelity to their plighted word; they are without
> natural affection and without pity. They know well enough the
> just decree of God, that those who behave like this deserve to die,
> and yet they do it; not only so, they actually applaud such prac-
> tices. [Romans 1:18–32, NEB]

Paul contends that the pagans have persisted in idolatry despite
God's manifest revelation; in response, God "has given them up to the
vileness of their own desires," so that women and men turn aside from
sexual relations with each other to engage in homosexual acts. It is only
after God abandons the pagans that they become enslaved to the most
degraded elements of their nature. Homosexual desire, then, can be
present only in God's absence. And so the sin becomes the punishment.

Once sins against God, including homosexual acts, are committed
they become so attractive, even addictive, that though the sinners
"know well enough the just decree of God, that those who behave like
this deserve to die . . . yet they do it; not only so, they actually applaud

such practices." Philo, we recall, similarly observes that "in former days the very mention of [pederasty] was a great disgrace, but now it is a matter of boasting not only to the active but to the passive partners." Paul takes this one step further: homosexual desire seems to be not only a sin but also a disease. The pursuit of "vileness" brings about the "degradation" of the body, almost as if the infection of homosexuality were already present deep in the blood. Plato, Aristotle, and other scientific commentators had speculated that the desire for passive homosexual sex could be explained by a congenital defect or a physiological predisposition to such desire. For Paul, *all* homosexual desire is such a defect, located within the darkest recesses of man's vile nature.

And homosexual behavior is intimately tied to all the other sins of which men are capable, and which follow in short order: their reason becomes depraved; they become guilty of "envy, murder, rivalry, treachery, and malevolence"; they become "whisperers and scandal-mongers, hateful to God, insolent, arrogant, and boastful; they invent new kinds of mischief, they show no loyalty to parents, no conscience, no fidelity to their plighted word; they are without natural affection and without pity." In short, every decent and moral human impulse falls before the onslaught of homosexual passion, and homosexual sin leads inexorably to all sin. These terrible effects are the "divine retribution revealed from heaven," perhaps Paul's metaphoric reference to Sodom and its punishment.

It is in Romans that Paul first mentions women as abandoning the natural for the unnatural. He could mean either that women abandoned the sexual passivity traditionally expected of them and adopted active sexual roles with men, or that they engaged in lesbian sex. He is not explicit, but St. Ambrose, writing in the fourth century, had no doubt of his meaning: that "a woman would desire a woman for the use of foul lust."[18] As for men, however, Paul certainly means that they abandoned women and engaged in sex with other men. Paul's Greek phrase for "unnatural" is the familiar "contrary to nature," the phrase Plato used to condemn homosexual relations between men. Plato meant that since homosexual acts are unprocreative, they are contrary to nature; Paul may have been echoing that tradition.[19] Neither Paul nor his contemporaries had a fully formed concept of a cosmic "natural law" like that of later Christian theologians; he probably employed the term "natural" as many Greek philosophers used it, to refer to "the nature *of* something."[20] Thus, these sinners have abandoned the sexual roles that are "in the nature of" the male and female to perform. But

Paul was also certainly influenced by the Jewish tradition that God irrevocably established the order of the universe at the creation; consequently, he began to argue that the order of God's universe is offended by this wholesale abandonment of the natural for the unnatural.[21]

Like contemporary Christian writers, schools of pagan asceticism, and Jewish scriptural interpreters, Paul condemned sexual pleasure and argued that sex ought to be engaged in solely for procreation. To define the sexually orthodox meant defining the sexually unorthodox as well. As we have seen, antiquity did so. Though Paul's tradition did not require that he imagine innately homosexual people in order to abhor homosexual acts, there is no reason to think he would have had any difficulty in imagining such a class; Philo and many of his contemporaries saw them everywhere. If the Corinthians knew the *kinaidoi* in their streets and the Romans ridiculed the *cinaedi* who haunted the temple precincts, Paul must have noticed them too. Adhering to the letter of Leviticus, influenced by the world he saw around him and the varieties of sexual practice that antiquity afforded, Paul chose to condemn them all, save for the relationship between man and wife.[22]

Whatever the nuances of Paul's intentions, his later translators have had little doubt about the meaning of *malakoi* and *arsenokoitai*. The King James translation, as we have seen, translates the terms in I Corinthians 6: 9–10 as "effeminate" and "abusers of themselves with men." The Revised Standard Version, of 1946, reads more simply: "Neither the immoral, nor idolaters, nor adulterers, nor homosexuals" will inherit the kingdom of heaven. A footnote adds that "two Greek words are rendered" by "homosexuals." The translation of Corinthians in the New English Bible (1971) warns: "Make no mistake: no fornicator or idolater, none who are guilty either of adultery or of homosexual perversion, nor thieves or grabbers or drunkards or slanderers or swindlers, will possess the kingdom of God." As to Roman Catholic versions of the Bible: the Rheims-Douai of 1609–10 offers "the effeminate, liars [*sic*] with mankind," while the Confraternity edition of the New Testament (1941) employs "effeminates and sodomites," and the Jerusalem Bible of 1966 translates the two Greek words simply as "catamites and sodomites."*

---

*The KJV names the sinners of Timothy as those who "defile themselves with mankind." The Revised Standard Version translates the phrase in Timothy as "sodomites." In Roman Catholic versions, the Rheims-Douai translates Timothy as those "who defile themselves with men." The Confraternity edition: "sodomites." The Jerusalem Bible: "those who are immoral with boys or with men."

. . .

Just as conclusions concerning Old Testament opinion about homosexuality have been based upon the interpretation of the single word *yadha,* and attempts to fathom Jesus' view of homosexual activities have focused on his unusual utterance of *raca,* so the reasons for Paul's choice of *malakoi* and *arsenokoitai,* their precise meaning, and the accuracy of their translation have occasioned considerable commentary by biblical scholars and great and painful consequences for people who engage in same-sex sexual behavior. Paul's *malakoi* and *arsenokoitai* are not what we "mean" by homosexual. But his comments have been taken to identify certain of those against whom the gates of heaven are closed.

4 Reinventing Sodom

Early Christianity was torn by conflicting beliefs and doctrines; factions within the Church were variously influenced by Judaism, Neoplatonism, Stoicism, Gnosticism, and Manichaeanism. Their attempts to put Christ's simple precepts into practice produced bitter controversies, accusations of heresy, and violent confrontations. The doctrine of the early Church was located in the Gospels, in the Epistles of Paul and other Apostles, and in a text describing the history of the Church that would come to be called the Acts of the Apostles. In the first century, of course, none of these texts had been collected into what we now call the New Testament. Despite its doctrinal disunity and incessant arguments over major and minor points of doctrine, early Christianity was nevertheless largely of one mind concerning homosexual acts, rejecting them as unnatural and as inimical to marriage and to the only appropriate end of marriage, procreation.

Early Christians knew of the pederastic attachments common in Hellenistic communities; one of the earliest Christian texts explicitly prohibited this kind of homosexual act. The Epistle of Barnabas (c. 130 C.E.), accepted as canonical by many early Christians, commands that "thou shalt not become a corrupter of boys." The *Didache,* a second-century manual of Christian conduct sometimes called *The Teachings of the Twelve Apostles,* includes a similar prohibition.[23] In *Paidagogos,* a handbook of advice written for Alexandrian Christians in the second century, Clement of Alexandria echoes Barnabas, Philo, and Paul. A convert to Christianity who is now numbered among the Greek fathers

of the Church, Clement used his extensive knowledge of classical literature and his zeal as a convert to argue that classical Greek culture and
philosophy were inferior to Christianity. Following the Neoplatonists,
he proclaimed the unnaturalness of homosexual behavior, and
explained the congruence between Plato's teaching and his own Christian beliefs by the revelation that Plato was in some way instructed by
Moses. Referring to Barnabas, Clement insists that "physical relations
between males, fruitless sowings, coitus from the rear, and incomplete
androgynous unions all ought to be avoided; and nature herself should
rather be obeyed who discourages [such things] through an arrangement of the parts which makes the male not for receiving the seed but
for sowing it."[24] Those who act otherwise disobey not only the law of
the Bible but the law of nature as well. Yet in a commentary on the
Gospel of Matthew 19:12—where Christ notes that some eunuchs are
born, others made, and still others self-made—Clement seems to think
that Jesus means homosexual males; he observes that "some men, from
birth, have a natural aversion to women, and those who are naturally
so constituted do well not to marry."[25]

In *Paidagogos*, Clement sets out to apply the teachings of Christ to
the conduct of daily sexual life, lessons he apparently feels that the dissolute Alexandrians need. He reminds them that the Sodomites "had
through much luxury fallen into uncleanness, practicing adultery
shamelessly and burning with the insane love of boys."[26] They were
punished for this by "the angels who came to Sodom" and "burned
those who were trying to dishonor them . . . demonstrating with a clear
sign that this—the fire—is the fruit of lust."[27] He explained to the
Alexandrians how to recognize the sodomites in their midst. Employing
the theories of the physiognomists, Clement preached that hidden sin
can be detected in outward appearance. A suspicious lack of facial hair
or an effeminate manner, for example, will allow the watchful Christian
to identify a doubtful passerby as an *androgynous*—a man-woman.
Clement warns: "He who disowns his manhood by day will surely be
shown to play the woman at night."[28] By linking the biblical story with
second-century androgynes, Clement transforms the familiar *kinaidos*
into a Hellenistic sodomite. For him the androgynes of Alexandria are
the same as the inhabitants of Sodom—a monstrous and unnatural
species, possibly deranged, surely effeminate and promiscuous, who go
so far as to deny their masculine nature by playing the woman at night.

A century after Clement two Church councils took up the subject.
The doctrinal views of the Eastern and Western churches were rarely

unified, but their similar beliefs about homosexual acts were expressed in the enactments of two Church councils, one held in Elvira (now Granada) in Spain, the other in Ancyra (now Ankara, Turkey). The Council of Elvira (305–306) may be the earliest such assembly to attempt to regulate Christian sexual practice. Among the many regulations adopted, nearly half dealt with sexual conduct, and one specifically barred those who continually and unrepentantly had sex with boys or youths from being admitted to the solace of Communion, even on the verge of death. Equally harsh penalties were directed at women who were apprehended in adultery or who engaged in prostitution; this association suggests that the council assumed that homosexual behavior was prompted only by lust or cash, and that the heroic or tender feelings that pagan tradition attributed to it were inadmissible.[29] The deliberations of the eastern Council of Ancyra (c. 314) vaguely proscribe "shameful and offensive" conduct. But later, Latin interpretations of the Council's Greek canons render this as "defilement . . . with males" and ratify the punishment of homosexual acts earlier specified: exclusion from the Sacraments for fifteen years for unmarried men under twenty, for life for those married and over fifty.[30]

These punishments echo Paul's admonition in Corinthians and Timothy that homosexual sinners cannot inherit the kingdom of heaven. The Church fathers took up this theme. Tertullian, a Roman writing in the second or early third century, castigates those who practice "all frenzies of lust which exceed the laws of nature" and urges that they "be banished from the church," for their sex acts are "not sins so much as monstrosities."[31] The fourth-century pronouncements of the Greek Church father John Chrysostom are a landmark in the development of homophobia. Like Tertullian, he accuses those who engage in homosexual acts of monstrosity and insanity, but he goes further, recommending that they be "driven out and stoned." In his commentary on Paul's Epistle to the Romans, Chrysostom presents a full-scale list of objections to homosexual behavior. Observing that "the soul is more damaged by sin than the body is by illness," he insists that the most heinous sins are those Paul describes as "vile affections," typified by women who "did change the natural use into that which is against nature" and by men who, "leaving the natural use of the woman, burned in their lust one toward another" (Romans 1:26–27, KJV). Of these vile affections, the worse is the "mania for males." "There is absolutely nothing more demented or noxious than this wickedness," Chrysostom holds. "What shall we say of this insanity?"[32]

Since homosexual affections are sins against nature, there can be no
pleasure in them, insists Chrysostom: "Real pleasure is only in accordance with nature." Therefore, those who engage in homosexual acts
do so not for pleasure but because they are in the grip of insane lust, a
sure sign that God has abandoned them: "When God has abandoned
someone, everything is inverted." Such a reversal of the natural order
of God's sexual creation becomes the very opposite of the divine: the
sinners' "beliefs are satanic" and "their lives . . . diabolical." So attractive is their sin, so powerful its obsessive temptation, that even though
God offered them the chance to reject their passion, "they refused and
they were unpardonable." Christ extends his mercy to sinners who
truly repent, but those who are seized by the mania for men do not
repent; they are insane, and in their refusal to give up their inverted
desires "they have outraged nature herself."

After Paul, Chrysostom insists that those seized by this mania are
dead to the legitimate affections; their desire, merely lustful, knows
nothing of love. Though he admits that pagan literature documents an
honorable history of homosexual love, Chrysostom argues that this history must be rejected because the pagans did not know God or his law.
Being ignorant of God's law, the pagans may be worthy of compassion,
but not so those who have rejected God's dispensation and continue
their homosexual practice: "They are even worse than murderers, and
it would be better to die than to live dishonored in this way. The murderer only separates soul from body, but these people destroy the soul
within the body. Whatever sin you mention you will not name one
which is the equal of this."

Males who practice homosexual acts suffer, in Chrysostom's view,
the most horrible of all consequences: "I maintain that not only are you
made [by it] into a woman, but you cease to be a man: yet neither are
you changed into that nature, nor do you retain the one you had. You
become a betrayer of both, and are worthy of being driven out and
stoned by both men and women, since you have brought injury upon
both sexes." So commission of a homosexual act physically transforms
a man into an especially ambiguous creature—more woman than man,
but neither male nor female. While not ceasing to be male, he ceases
to be a "man." He becomes an androgynous monster whose sexual
nature, gender, and even biological sex are somehow altered and who
inhabits a separate and unnatural sexual realm.

In the treatise *Against the Opponents of the Monastic Life*, Chrysostom adds to the catalogue of horrors connected with homosexual acts:

A certain new and illicit love has entered our lives, an ugly and incurable disease has appeared, the most severe of all plagues has been hurled down, a new and insufferable crime has been devised. Not only are the laws established [by man] overthrown but even those of nature herself. Fornication will seem a small matter in the reckoning of sexual sins and just as the arrival of a more burdensome pain eclipses the discomfort of an earlier one, so the extremity of this outrage causes lewdness with women, which had been intolerable, to seem so no longer. Indeed to be able to escape these snares seems desirable, and there is some danger that womankind will become in the future unnecessary, with young men instead fulfilling all the needs that women used to.

Writing about the Christian community in Antioch, Chrysostom charges that so prevalent is homosexual promiscuity that "this outrage is perpetrated with the utmost openness." Far from being ashamed, "they take pride" in their activities, and indeed "in the middle of cities men do these unseemly things to each other, just as if they were in a vast desert." Evidently homosexual desire is rampant even among Christians, those "seemingly rational creatures, the beneficiaries of godly learning" who instruct others in God's word. Brazen in the extreme, they "do not consort with prostitutes as fearlessly as with young men. . . . [A]s if there were no final judgment, as if darkness covered all and no one could hear such things, they dare all this with absolute frenzy."

Chrysostom's remarkable tirades, like those of Philo and Clement, are of course the opinions of an individual rather than the official pronouncements of the Church or the opinions of a still largely pagan populace. But they concentrate the hostility of the millennium in a full-scale portrait of the homosexual monster.

Though less willing to impose the death penalty than Chrysostom was, Basil (c. 329–379), whose rule still governs Eastern Orthodox monastic life and whose liturgy is still sung in its rites, also comments harshly on the temptations of homosexual desire. For Basil, such desire is a trap set by Satan himself, and the sexual attraction of young men, rather than being something the devout Christian can easily resist, is powerful enough to shake the faith of even the most avowed ascetic. In *On the Renunciation of the World,* he urges young monks to "fly from intimate association with comrades of your own age and run away from them as from fire. The enemy has indeed set many aflame through such means and consigned them down into that loathsome pit . . . on the pretext of spiritual love."[33] Basil warns young monks to have no close physical contact with their brothers. And "when a young man converses with you . . . make your response with your head bowed lest perchance by gazing fixedly into his face, the seed of desire be implanted in you by the wicked sower and you reap the sheaves of corruption and ruin."[34] Basil seems to know just how attractive a boy can be.

For those who actually engage in what he calls unseemliness with males, he prescribes the same discipline as for adulterers: they are to be excluded from receiving the Sacrament for fifteen years, and are to perform an elaborate series of penances.[35] Significantly, this penalty was less severe than that imposed for incest, murder, and apostasy, sins that excluded the sinner from the company of the faithful until the very hour of death.

The era's antihomosexual literature is augmented by an influential contribution from Augustine (354–430), the bishop of Hippo in Roman North Africa, who voiced in his *Confessions* a special detestation of homosexual acts. Augustine's early affection for a young man whom he "passionately loved," and his later revulsion against all sexual desire and practice, are the elements of an oft-told story.[36] He shared the general Christian belief that sexual intercourse was lawful only within marriage, though he insisted more sternly than most that even marital sexual pleasure ought not to be countenanced. Sharing also the general misogyny of both pagan antiquity and the Judeo-Christian tradition, Augustine maintained that since "the body of man is as superior to that of a woman as the soul is to the body," for a man to "use his body like a woman" was to undermine masculine superiority as well as to commit the sin punished in Sodom's flames.[37] "These foul offenses," he insisted, "which be against nature," ought to be "everywhere and at all times detested and punished, just as were those of Sodom." All nations that permit such acts "stand guilty of the same crime, by the law of God, which has not so made men that they should so abuse one another."[38] Augustine's pronouncements on homosexuality in particular, and his rigorous interpretation of Christian sexual morality in general, powerfully influenced the sexual attitudes of the Christian Church in the West.[39]

Despite the antihomosexual utterances of canonical and apocryphal scriptures and Church fathers, and the antisexual ascetic traditions of

Hellenistic philosophy, homosexual practice flourished. Many people openly engaged in homosexual relationships, and in literature those relationships were both satirized and celebrated, as they always had been. Homosexual prostitution was licensed by the state. No pagan law or spiritual guide was as hostile to homosexuality as were Jewish Scripture and the new Christian Gospels, nor did any pagan state issue harsh decrees against homosexual acts. The speculations of ascetic philosophy and the admonitions of minor religious sects in the first three centuries of the Common Era probably had little impact on the sexual conduct of the vast, largely pagan majority of the empire's citizens. Certainly for those who were not Christians—and perhaps even among those who were—the fulminations issued by philosopher-ascetics in faraway cities, disseminated among a few of the faithful, may have had less weight than the custom of centuries that rarely frowned upon dalliance with a handsome youth.

However, by the fourth and fifth centuries of the Common Era, attitudes toward homosexual acts had shifted from broad tolerance to widespread suspicion. Once, imaginative literature had treated homosexual relations often and approvingly; now homosexuality began to vanish from literary texts, instead appearing as the object of furious detestation in religious and moral polemic. The end of classical toleration for homosexual love can be symbolically marked by the appearance of a final nostalgic and valedictory epic, probably written between 390 and 405, the *Dionysiaca* by Nonnus of Panopolis, who may have been a Christian. Dionysus loves the handsome Ampelos, woos him, makes love to him, loses him, and mourns him. Almost a thousand years were to pass before literature again celebrated such passion in such an uninhibited way.

Taddeo di Bartolo (1363–1422), The Last Judgment; *detail,* "Sodomite and Adulterer." *Collegiata, San Gimignano, Italy. Alinari/Art Resource, NY*

PART THREE

A Thousand Years of Sodomy

Defining Sodomy, 500–1400

Chapter Seven

Avenging Flames

At the beginning of the Common Era, Rome triumphantly governed the ancient world; relative stability allowed for toleration of diverse religious and sexual practices. But that stability was soon shaken by political and natural events. In the Hellenistic cities and provinces of the eastern portion of the empire—in Greece, in Alexandria, in Antioch—numerous ascetic philosophies, pagan mystery religions, and other cults challenged the ancient gods. Though it was the religion of a tiny minority in a vast pagan empire, Christianity increasingly attracted the hostile attention of Roman authority. In 64 C.E., the persecutions of Christians began.

For those who believed that new religions and new philosophies were endangering age-old verities, there was much to be made of such dire portents as the destruction of Pompeii in the year 79 C.E. by the eruption of Mount Vesuvius, and the plague that swept the empire in 80. Plague struck again in 125, in 165, in 189, and in 255. Christians were sometimes scapegoated as the cause of such disasters. Because Christians refused to participate in the state religion of emperor worship, they were believed to be disloyal to Rome and dangerous to the stability of the state. In 177 the emperor Marcus Aurelius instituted a persecution that forced Christians to practice their rites secretly, in the relative safety of the catacombs. In 250 the emperor Decius, in an attempt to restore the religion of ancient Rome, launched an even larger attempt to exterminate them, and in 303 Diocletian, also eager to revive the old religion, decreed a wholesale persecution of Christians throughout the empire. The persecutions ended when the emperor Constantine converted to Christianity in 312 and decreed toleration for all religions, including Christianity, throughout the empire.

Though Christianity had achieved a political triumph, Rome had been under siege for some time. Throughout the second century, revolts by subject peoples and barbarian incursions against the city marked the decay of Roman power. The increasing instability of the throne was dramatically demonstrated in 193, when the army auctioned the empire to a merchant senator, who reigned for three months before he was murdered. In the next century a succession of emperors, often ruling jointly with political rivals, was elevated and deposed with equally murderous rapidity.

Constantine's accession in 312 gained Rome only a brief respite from approaching chaos. The empire was further weakened when he left Rome and established Byzantium, renamed Constantinople, as the capital of the empire, in 330. Constantine died in 337 and was succeeded by three sons, who ruled as co-emperors in east and west. Constantine II was murdered in 340. Constans was murdered in an army rebellion in 350; after defeating the rebels in 351, Constantius was left sitting alone on the throne of the Caesars. Perhaps to celebrate or to secure this triumph, in 356 Constantius decreed the closing of pagan temples and banned the celebration of pagan rites, but he enjoyed the demise of paganism for just five more years; he died in 361.

Successive emperors resisted ever more determined barbarian invaders, among them the Huns, who first raided the empire in the year 360. Co-emperors continued to rule, one in the east from Constantinople, and one and sometimes more—so quickly were emperors chosen and deposed—in the west. In Rome Gratian assumed power in 375, but he moved his capital to Milan; his co-emperor, Valens, governed the eastern provinces. At Adrianople on August 9, 378, in what is still deemed one of the most decisive military encounters in history, the Visigoths disastrously defeated the hitherto invincible Roman legions and killed Valens.

Gratian was assassinated in 383 and succeeded by the co-emperors Valentinian II and Theodosius. By this time Christianity had become the dominant religion of the empire; pagans became the object of official persecution. Theodosius, especially suspicious of non-Christians, was always ready to find reasons to persecute pagans and in doing so brought further disruption to the empire. In 390 the Roman military commander in Thessalonica imprisoned a popular charioteer who had raped or attempted to seduce a male servant of the commander or the commander himself.[1] The largely pagan populace rose in revolt. Whether they were outraged that their Christian governors should punish their popular hero for what (if mere seduction) would have seemed a minor infraction or whether they simply took the imprisonment as an occasion for political insurrection is not clear. The commander was murdered in the uprising, which Theodosius saw as an attack against his throne. He ordered a massacre; seven thousand people were killed, by some accounts.[2]

Theodosius continued his campaign against pagan culture. After a fire completely destroyed the great Alexandrian library in 391, taking with it vast numbers of pagan texts, he ordered the destruction of those that remained. In 393 he also ordered the cessation of the Olympic games, which had been celebrated for a thousand years. This marks the triumph of ascetic Christianity over the pagan glorification of the body.

At the death of Theodosius in 395, for ease of governing, the Roman Empire was officially and irrevocably split. In the east, Theodosius' son Arcadius ruled in Constantinople as a *basileus*—in Greek, "a king"— while in the west, his other son, the ten-year-old Honorius, assumed the purple of the Caesars, ruling now from Milan. The city of the Caesars, Rome itself, abandoned by its emperors, continued to decay.

The divided empire would never be reunified, though the fiction of unity would long be maintained. The Western Empire sank into chaos, its provinces captured by barbarians. In 401 Italy itself was invaded by the Visigoths. In 410 the Huns invaded the empire; Rome was attacked by Alaric, by Attila the Hun, and then by the Vandals, who sacked the city in 455 with such ferocity that their name became synonymous with wanton destruction. The last of the Caesars, the emperor Romulus Augustulus—ironically if diminutively named after the empire's legendary and actual founders—was briefly elevated to the purple in 475, and deposed a year later by the Saxon prince Odoacer. The empire established by Augustus in 27 B.C. fell on August 28, 476 C.E. Roman Italy was now ruled from Ravenna by Saxon conquerors, who still styled themselves Roman emperors. By the beginning of the sixth century, the city that had given the empire its name was in ruins, its treasures looted, its palaces and temples destroyed, its population shrunk.

The "Roman" Empire was henceforth centered in Constantinople. As the Western Empire declined, the Eastern grew strong. Governed from behind the city's impregnable walls, the Eastern Empire was oriental, Greek, and Christian; from the ancient name of its capital, it was called Byzantium. For another thousand years its rulers attempted to recapture what had been lost in the west; they imposed Roman law wherever they could, maintained the fiction that they ruled the world, and continued to call themselves Roman emperors.

1 Avenging Flames

Though the fathers of the Church could not agree upon the nature of Christ or the wording of a creed, they were united in their detestation of homosexual acts. Initially, only the most devout of the laity and the strictest of the clergy subscribed to these views and those expressed by the councils of the Church, but the weight of their opinion began to be felt in civil laws that increasingly reflected Christian doctrine. No pre-Christian Roman law had forbidden homosexual acts; some Roman legal opinion had been suspicious of them, but only when they infringed on the rights of freeborn minors.[3] But by the fourth century the empire had become officially Christian, and legal condemnation based on religious precept became possible. In 342 the co-emperors Constans and Constantius II promulgated an edict that read: "When a man submits to men, the way a woman does, what can he be seeking? . . . We order the statutes to arise, and the laws to be armed with an avenging sword, that those guilty of such infamous crimes, either now or in the future, may be subjected to exquisite penalties."[4]

Whether this statute refers exclusively to homosexual marriages, as has been urged, or to homosexual acts generally, it is clearly a *legal* prohibition; what the Church fathers insisted was a sin had now become a crime.[5] And in 390 the Theodosian Code, promulgated by the co-emperors Theodosius and Valentinian II, specified that the crime deserved the punishment of Sodom. Directing their edict to Orientius, the vicar of the city of Rome, the emperors commanded:

> We shall not suffer the City of Rome . . . any longer to be defiled
> by the pollution of effeminacy in males. . . . Praiseworthy is your
> practice of seizing all who have committed the crime of treating
> their male bodies as though they were female, submitting them to
> the use becoming the opposite sex, and being in no wise distin-

guishable from women, and, as the monstrosity of the crime demands, dragging them out of the brothels (it is shameful to say) for males. . . . In the sight of the people shall the offender expiate his crime in the avenging flames, that each and every one may understand that the dwelling place of the male soul should be sacrosanct to all and that no one may without incurring the ultimate penalty aspire to play the part of the other sex by shamefully renouncing his own.[6]

In 527 the emperor Justinian began his long reign at Constantinople. Continuing the policy of his predecessors, he set out to eradicate the last vestige of pagan intellectual freedom. In 529 he ordered the closing of the Athenian academy, founded by Plato in 347 B.C.E., and began the work of codifying—and revising—Roman law. One of the laws he revised was the ancient Lex Julia, which punished adulterers with death; in 533 Justinian decreed that the death penalty be extended to homosexual acts. The prohibition against homosexual behavior is spelled out in the Institutes, the part of Justinian's code that summarizes the essential provisions of the law: "The *Lex Julia* . . . punishes with death not only those who violate the marriages of others, but those who dare to commit acts of vile lust with [other] men."[7] In 538 and 544 two additional *novellae,* or new laws, elaborated on this decree.

The first, Novella 77, was directed against both blasphemy and homosexual acts, which Justinian blamed for natural disasters:

Since certain men, seized by diabolical incitement, practice among themselves the most disgraceful lusts, and act contrary to nature: we enjoin them to take to heart the fear of God and the judgment to come, and to abstain from suchlike diabolical and unlawful lusts, so that they may not be visited by the just wrath of God on account of these impious acts, with the result that cities perish with all their inhabitants. For we are taught by the Holy Scriptures that because of like impious conduct cities have indeed perished, together with the men in them. For because of such crimes there are famines, earthquakes, and pestilences; wherefore we admonish men to abstain from said unlawful acts, that they may not lose their souls. But if, after this our admonition, any are found persisting in such offenses, first, they render themselves unworthy of the mercy of God, and then they are subjected to the punishment enjoined by the law. For we order the most illustrious prefect of the Capital to arrest those who persist in the aforesaid lawless and impious acts after they have been warned by us, and to inflict on them the extreme punishments, so that the city and the state may not come to harm by reason of such wicked deeds.

Nevertheless other catastrophes, natural and military, followed: in 540 the Eastern Empire was invaded by the Persians; for nearly a decade, starting in 541, bubonic plague spread across the empire; and in 543 terrible earthquakes destroyed major cities. In 544, either to strengthen with even sterner warnings the existing proscription of homosexual acts, or to allay the fears of subjects panicked by catastrophe, Justinian issued Novella 141. This new law did not mention blasphemy but decreed that commission of homosexual acts alone was sufficient for extreme punishment:

Instructed by the Holy Scriptures, we know that God brought a just judgment upon those who lived in Sodom, on account of this very madness of intercourse, so that to this very day that land burns with inextinguishable fire. By this God teaches us, in order that by means of legislation we may avert such an untoward fate. Again, we know what the blessed Apostle [Paul] says about such things, and what laws our state enacts. Wherefore it behooves all who desire to fear God to abstain from conduct so base and criminal that we do not find it committed even by brute beasts. Let those who have not taken part in such doings continue to refrain in the future. But as for those who have been consumed by this kind of disease let them not only cease to sin in the future, but let them also do penance, and fall down before God and renounce their plague. . . . Next, we proclaim to all who are conscious that they have committed any such sin, that unless they desist . . . they will bring upon themselves severer penalties, even though on other counts they are held guilty of no fault. For there will be no relaxation of enquiry and correction so far as this matter is concerned, nor will they be dealt with carelessly who do not submit themselves during the time of the holy season, or who persist in such impious conduct, lest if we are negligent we arouse God's anger against us. If, with eyes as it were blinded, we overlook such impious and forbidden conduct, we may provoke the good God to anger and bring ruin upon all—a fate which would be but deserved.

Justinian's edicts were the first laws to declare *all* homosexual acts illegal and to punish them by death. Civil authority had only rarely focused attention upon homosexual acts in the centuries between the Church councils of Elvira and Ancyra in 305 and 314 and Justinian's time, but the *novella* of 544 introduced into civil law both the story of Sodom and Paul's abhorrence, thus translating Judeo-Christian condemnation of same-sex practice into Roman law. Homosexual practice was now defined in law as a threat to the common good, to the state as well as the soul, and those who engaged in it were the cause of social, civil, and natural disorder. That the state, prompted by the word of God and supported by legal precedent, was obliged to identify, punish, and even destroy such creatures for the good of the majority, was the harsh and unarguable basis of the law.

It has been argued that the laws promulgated in the fourth and fifth centuries constituted a "veritable crusade" against homosexuality. But this notion is as overstated as the opposite assertion, that Christianity played but a minor role in the foundation of homophobic attitudes.[8] It is true that what we would call homophobic sentiment can be discovered in antiquity. Still, it is also true that neither pagan nor ascetic philosophers would have found homosexual practices sinful, nor did any pagan state declare them criminal, nor did any pagan rite name damnation as their eternal punishment.[9]

In the antihomosexual pronouncements of the early Christian era, altar and throne always agree. The *novellae* echo the antihomosexual Christian ascetics, especially Chrysostom, Basil, and Gregory. Although Christian emperors rarely enacted antihomosexual laws, the laws they did enact were harsh. Apparently the emperors did not believe moral suasion sufficient to enforce the laws of God and the teachings of the Church; seizing upon the language of Christian condemnation, they translated their hostility into law.

Whether most Christians shared the laws' abhorrence, whether those laws reflected an ancient hostility to homosexual acts, is less important than that the hostility *did* become law. And the law proscribed for everyone what only a few may have heretofore detested. In a world shaped by the triumphant doctrine of the Christian Church and the equally triumphant emergence of the Christian empire, homophobia of an intensity never before seen in Western culture was for the first time institutionalized as the law of the land.

2 Rooting Out Depravity in the West

With the formal dissolution of the Roman Empire in 476, no central authority remained in the west. During the fifth and sixth centuries, Europe was an almost constant battleground. Tribes gained ascendancy over tribes, only to be defeated by revolt or by still stronger enemies; rudimentary nations appeared and disappeared; large territories held together by allegiance to a charismatic ruler were divided among weaker sons; kings were crowned only to be murdered by more ruthless rivals, sons, or brothers. Germanic invasions divided the former empire into territories governed by Lombards, Saxons, Goths, Visigoths, Alemanni, Bavarians, and Franks. By 480, the Visigoths had conquered lands extending from the Loire to the Mediterranean and established their capital at Toulouse. In Italy Odoacer, heir to Rome, in his turn was besieged by Ostrogoths and in 493 murdered by the victorious Ostrogothic leader Theodoric. In the Frankish kingdoms—part of modern France—Clovis I succeeded to the throne and founded the Merovingian dynasty. Converted to Christianity in 496, Clovis established his capital at Lutetia (Paris) in 508.

Clashes among these tribes and between them and the forces of the Byzantine Empire made peace rare and security dear. Justinian dreamed of restoring Italy to Byzantine rule and sent his general Belisarius to retake Rome, which Belisarius did in 536, taking Ravenna in 539. The resurgence of Roman rule was brief; Belisarius, defeated by the Ostrogoths in 540, abandoned Rome. When the conquerors reentered the city they found it nearly abandoned, its population reduced to a few hundred, its grandeur destroyed, only its legend remaining.

The Germanic tribes that succeeded Rome brought with them definite views about homosexuality. The Roman historian Tacitus (c. 50 C.E.), whose *De origine et situ Germanorum* offers a comprehensive picture of their customs, reported that those accused of bodily infamy (*corpore infames*) were buried alive in swamps with wicker baskets placed over their heads.[10] This "infamy" is a translation of a term—variously *argr* or *ragr* or *ergi*—that could easily refer to cowardliness in battle, but some have believed it meant effeminacy or even passive homosexual behavior. If it does reflect anxiety about effeminacy and possibly transvestitism, that may be because both were often associated with magical powers, sorcery, and shamanistic practices in some Norse and Germanic customs and legends.[11] Though little is known about Germanic attitudes toward active homosexuality, a number of ancient commentators, such as Procopius, in the *History of the Wars of Justinian,* have claimed that some tribes celebrated masculine comradeship and may have, like the Greeks, encouraged pederastic relations between adults and youths as part of the latter's preparation for adult and warrior status.[12]

Throughout the fifth century, Christianity advanced into the Germanic states, and many tribal leaders were, even if only nominally, converted to the new faith. The leaders of the Germanic states could not officially approve what the Church condemned. Nevertheless, it is noteworthy that in the territorial laws passed by a number of Germanic tribes in the years after 476—the so-called *leges barbarorum*—there is a general absence of comment about homosexuality. Only in Visigothic Spain was homosexual behavior strictly prohibited and severely punished. After being defeated by Clovis in 507 and losing their territory in southwestern France, the Visigoths retreated to what remained of their kingdom in the Iberian peninsula. There they ruled, harshly, over a population of Spanish Romans, Celts, and other natives of the peninsula, who vastly outnumbered their masters and considered the Visigothic brand of Arian Christianity heretical.[13] Whether because of a sudden conviction about the inadequacy of their own Christian beliefs, or thanks to a revelation concerning the higher truth of the Roman faith, or because the majority of their subjects were Roman Christians, the Visigothic kings converted to Roman Christianity in 587—thus, they may have hoped, enlisting the growing power of the majority church in support of their precarious rule.

Even before their humiliating retreat to Spain, the Visigothic kings had proscribed all homosexual behavior. The law, as revised in 650, makes no appeal to Scripture or to Sodom, nor does it refer to sin; rather, it defines homosexual behavior as a civil crime and draws upon a familiar antihomosexual vocabulary, describing it as "that crime that ought always to be detested," forever beyond exculpation. Homosexual acts are decried as "an execrable moral depravity"; those who engage in them are totally corrupt, lost to human decency, and blind to moral distinction. For both active and passive homosexuals—"those who lie with males and those who participate passively in such acts"— the law stipulates castration and adds the ancient penalty suggested by Plato and by Jewish and Christian antihomosexual writings: "Those who are known to have perpetrated such unlawful acts voluntarily may be subjected to forcible expulsion" by excommunication, banishment, or both. By severely penalizing "those who lie with males," the law transfers the burden of punishment from the act that anyone might perform to the deviant actor. That is, in its emphasis on "those who perpetrate such acts voluntarily," on "the man who is known to have sunk to this madness of his own free will," the law invents an individual who chooses to embrace sexual crime, and defines homosexual behavior as a deliberately perverse choice. That this creature is "well-known" to embrace "madness" makes him more monstrous still. The Visigothic edict targets those who break the law even once, but it is especially bent on identifying those who do so continually and exclusively; their repeated depravity is the mark of a separate race that must be banished from the unstained human family.

Forty years later, another Visigothic ruler, King Egica (687–701), found it necessary to reiterate and strengthen these pronouncements, perhaps because he saw homosexual practice increasing in his kingdom and feared God's wrath. In 693 Egica demanded that a Church council in Toledo confront the problem of homosexuality in his kingdom: "Among other matters see that you determine to extirpate that obscene crime committed by those who lie with males, whose fearful conduct defiles the charm of honest living and provokes from heaven the wrath of the supreme Judge." Egica's almost quaint observation that "fearful" homosexual acts defile the "charm of honest living" suggests their imagined monstrosity; they become not simply individual acts that violate the specific prohibition of Scripture but dangerous disruptions of the social fabric. This is a distant forecast of the contemporary accusation that homosexuality destroys heterosexual family values. To prevent such defilement, extirpation of the crime—and, as will be seen, of the criminal—was, in Egica's opinion, ideal.

The Toledan council agreed to punish harshly all clerics who "had committed this vile practice against nature" and warned that offenders would surely be "struck down by damnation." Those "implicated in the evils of another's filthy doing, let them be punished none the less without respect of order, rank, or person" by castration; they must be "excluded from all communion with Christians, and in addition have their hair shorn, receive one hundred stripes of the lash, and be banished in perpetual exile."[14] To ensure that God would be placated and to conform to "the teaching of the orthodox faith," Egica issued a civil edict that elaborated the ecclesiastical decree. In order to "serve the interest of our people and country," he stated his determination to "root out crimes of depravity" and end "evil acts of vice," especially the "detestable outrage of that lust by the filthy uncleanness of which men do not fear to defile other men." Of those who "pollute themselves by the mutual defilement of this crime," he decreed that if "any man, be he cleric or layman, whatever his state or birth, is clearly detected (by whatever evidence) in the crime aforesaid, let him endure castration" and "undergo the extreme penalty for these offenses." No defense remained to a homosexual offender in Visigothic law, for any defense was obviated by the provision that allowed guilt to be proven "by whatever evidence." And Egica's insistence that homosexual behavior be "extirpated" and "rooted out" advocates not simply the punishment of individual criminals, but the persecution of an entire sexual population for the good of "our people and country." Whether "the extreme penalty" was death, as has been surmised, or excommunication and damnation—to the faithful, an even more dreadful punishment— Egica's law was the most severe antihomosexual statute enacted in the West up to that time.[15]

Egica's efforts to protect his kingdom from God's wrath were apparently unavailing, for Visigothic rule lasted only another twenty years. God's wrath, he may have thought, was embodied in the huge armies of Muslims gathering on the southern shores of the Mediterranean. In 610 in Mecca, Mohammed had begun to preach; at his death in 632 his followers began their conquest of the Near East and North Africa. In 682 they occupied Tripoli, Carthage, and Tangier, and their leaders now patiently waited across the Straits of Gibraltar to unleash their armies—military representatives of a culture never hostile to homosexuality, as Egica must have known—upon Christian Spain. The invasion came in 711; the Muslims defeated Roderick, the last Visigothic king, and the conquest effectively canceled the repressive Visigothic laws. Muslim rule lasted for nearly seven hundred years throughout southern Spain, longer in Granada and Valencia—a brilliant era of intellectual, religious, and sexual tolerance during which homoerotic literature flowered and homosexuality was generally accepted, a culture unmatched by any in Christian Europe before the Renaissance.

But although the triumphant Moorish armies had conquered southern Spain, their incursions into northern Spain and then into the Frankish territories were not so successful. In 732, at the battle of Tours, the Moors were defeated by Charles Martel and retreated beyond the Pyrenees. This victory allowed the Frankish state to consolidate itself and by 800 Charlemagne, now emperor of the Franks and the Romans, undertook various reforms in law. Homosexual acts once again came under the scrutiny of secular authority, but Frankish lawmakers were content to issue warnings against sexual unorthodoxy, without going so far as to punish it. Most Carolingian legislation is addressed to the clergy, not the laity; in one capitulary, or ordinance, Charlemagne reminded the monastic orders that he "dared not permit any such ills [homosexual behavior] any longer in any part of his kingdom."[16]

This relative inattention to the sin of Sodom must have seemed unforgivable to those who sought a scapegoat for the calamities descending upon Christendom. To remedy lapses in the law, fraudulent "laws" against homosexual acts were created. Such forgeries—documents intended to enhance political power or to substantiate a claim for land or influence on behalf of a person, state, or church—had a long history and were often accepted at the time as genuine. The spurious Donation of Constantine, for example, written in the eighth century but purporting to date from the fourth, allegedly guaranteed to the Church land and power and absolute authority over the rulers of Christendom. Another forgery, written around 850 by one Benedict Levita, purported to be a collection of edicts issued by Charlemagne himself in 779. These, later revealed to be fabrications and called the False Capitularies, asserted the temporal and spiritual power of the Christian Church over the Frankish kingdom and its rulers; among the edicts were three that addressed homosexual acts. Levita's edicts theorized that men who engaged in homosexual acts endangered both kingdom and Church and repeated Justinian's warning that cities had been destroyed for tolerating such behavior. They cited the invasion and conquest of Spain by Muslims as clear evidence of what awaited a Christian nation that did not adequately punish homosexual acts. Levita advocated the definitive solution first proposed in the fourth century: burning at the stake.[17]

During the five centuries between the publication of Justinian's edict in 544 and the advent of the second Christian millennium in 1000, both civil and ecclesiastical authority, both east and west, took greater notice of homosexual acts and those who engaged in them. Some of their pronouncements appeared as civil laws, others as enactments of Church councils; still others dealt with the kind of penance that ought to be assigned for a homosexual offense. Nearly all assertions about the culpability of homosexual acts, whether instituted as civil or canon law, appealed to the authority of Scripture, referring variously to the judgment of Sodom, the opinion of Leviticus concerning the punishment of such sinners, or the warnings of Paul about who might be shut out of heaven's gates.

3 Repenting for Pleasure

In the Western Church during the sixth century and after, two developments had a significant impact upon codes governing sexual morality: the appearance of strict Eastern-style monastic communities and the increasing centralization of papal power. Even as, in 519, the schism between the Eastern Church and the Western was briefly mended, the administration of the Western Christian Church was beginning to be centralized in Rome. In 590 Pope Gregory set about to establish the papacy as both spiritually and temporally supreme over all of Christendom. With the emperor supreme in Constantinople, the pope claiming rival and equal supremacy in Rome, and the great European monarchies ruling in various parts of Europe—Lombards in Italy, Merovingians and Carolingians in France, Visigoths in Spain, Franks in Austria and Burgundy—the lineaments of modern Europe began dimly to appear.

The Christian Church became more influential in the new states in the sixth through the ninth centuries. One locale for this influence was in the monastic communities that had begun to appear during this period, among the first of which was the Benedictine monastery at Monte Cassino in Italy founded by Benedict of Nursia in 529. Christian asceticism was institutionally supported by Christian monasticism. Both men and women entered a life of segregated and cloistered religious duty, prayer, and meditation. The rules of monastic life recognized the possibilities of sexual temptation among groups of men or women who lived closely together, and prescribed means to curb it. These rules were reflected in the penitentials—lists of sins and their corresponding penances—that local branches of the Church began to compile. Primarily intended to regulate the conduct of individual monastic establishments, penitentials, not surprisingly, concerned themselves more with homosexual than heterosexual offenses. But they were, in time, applied to the laity as well.

The penitentials are lists of sins that *might* be committed, so they cannot be used to document actual practice. But their writers no doubt learned what could happen by observing what did happen. They discovered evidence of ancient sexual tendencies, much at variance with Church teachings about the exalted state of virginity and celibacy, and the sinfulness of all sex that did not result in procreation.

The antihomosexual laws of the Christian Roman Empire were promulgated from the distant eminence of the emperor's throne; the condemnations of the Church were delivered in the writings of patriarchs and saints. The penitentials, on the other hand, were the product of local bishops or monasteries, and their provisions were delivered directly to both clergy and laity by their confessor priests. The presumed utility of the penitentials—or perhaps the ubiquity of sin—is suggested by the fact that Charlemagne himself insisted that every priest have a copy of a penitential and that sinners be forced to perform the penances they contained.[18]

Various penitentials—such as the Canons of the Synod of Llanddewi-Brefi, the Penitential of Columban, Ecgbert's Penitential, and the Penitential of Thorlac Thorhallson, to name four ranging in date from the sixth to the eleventh century—list a large variety of sinful deeds and thoughts, often describing them in considerable detail upon the principle that to know a sin is to conquer it. As Haltigar, bishop of Cambria, observes in his preface to the Pseudo-Roman Penitential (c. 830), just as "no physician can treat the wounds of the sick unless he comes in contact with their foulness, so also no priest or pontiff can treat the wounds of sinners" without knowing and describing them.[19] The sins catalogued range from minor to major transgressions, from the neglect of minor religious observances to the commission of forbidden sexual acts. The penitentials that deal with homosexual behavior are fairly detailed. While they disagree on the precise severity of the appropriate penance, all treat homosexual acts as grave offenses and declare them unnatural and abominable.

Some writers distinguish between active and passive homosexuality in assigning penance. Others concern themselves with lesbian activity, a penance for which first appears in the penitential of Theodore, Archbishop of Canterbury at the end of the seventh century. Augustine had warned against lesbian activities in a famous letter cautioning nuns that "the things that shameless women do to other women . . . are to be avoided."[20] Hincmar of Reims, that city's ninth-century archbishop, confides that women who engaged in lesbian sex often used "certain instruments of diabolical function to incite desire." Theodore prescribed three years' penance for a woman who "practices vice with a woman," unless artificial instruments were employed, for which doubly unnatural practice the penance was presumably more severe. However, the penances assigned to lesbian sex (even when it involved mechanical aids) were generally less harsh than those assigned to males.[21]

Almost all the writers ranked homosexual sins. Kissing was less sinful than kissing with seminal emission, and the latter was worse if the
sinners were over twenty years of age. Mutual masturbation was less
culpable than fellatio or anal penetration; a single offense was more
leniently regarded than habitual practice; and passive homosexual acts
were less offensive than active, especially if the passive offender was a
boy under ten or a youth under eighteen or twenty. Theodore of Tarsus
fitted the punishment to the crime, he apparently felt, when he decreed
that effeminate passive homosexuals ought to be punished as adulteresses.[22] Theodore also relished describing fellatio; he observed that
swallowing semen was the "worst of evils," though he did not penalize
it as severely as anal penetration. We have seen that the Romans were
apparently horrified by fellatio; Theodore felt it his duty to warn
monastics about the too enthusiastic enjoyment of an oral practice
abhorred even by godless pagans.

A penance might consist of bodily mortification, of fasting or abstinence or prayer, or of exclusion from the rites of the Church; all varied
according to the type of sexual experience involved, and the age, rank,
and degree of culpability of the individual offender. Penances assigned
to laypersons tended to be more lenient than those given to clergy for
the same act. Thus for habitual homosexual behavior one penitential
demanded five years' penance for a layman, ten for a priest, and twelve
for a bishop. Penitentials also varied in their assessment of the sinfulness of homosexual acts; some required ten years' penance, others
twenty, still others life. It is likely that imaginative or sympathetic confessors exercised some freedom in imposing penance. Indeed, Peter
Damian, writing in the eleventh century, complained that sodomite
confessors imposed lenient penances on similarly inclined fellow monks
and, worse still, on those monks with whom they themselves had
sinned.[23]

St. Basil ruled that profligate monks accused of molesting boys
should be flogged, shaved, chained in prison for six months and given
only bread and water, and spat upon by all who encountered them.[24]
His penance for "sodomy"—a term that could refer to any number of
sexual acts, including bestiality and "unnatural" sex with a woman,
but which increasingly came to imply anal intercourse between men—is
the same as that for adulterers: exclusion from the Sacrament for fifteen
years, during which time the penitent was obliged to wear special garments marking him as a sexual sinner. During the first five years he was
to be denied admission to the church building itself; after five years he

could enter the church porch and listen, from a distance, to the comforting words of Scripture; he had to spend the next four years in fasting and occasional acts of physical mortification; finally, in the last year he might enter the church but had to sit apart from other, less sinful believers. A priest who had committed "natural fornication or sodomy," according to the Welsh penitential of St. Gildas, "shall do penance for three years. He shall seek pardon every hour and keep a special fast every week, except during the fifty days following the Passion. He shall have bread and water without limitation and a refection with some butter spread over it on Sunday."[25]

The penitentials recommend penances but do not record what confessors actually imposed. There is evidence that an easier punishment could substitute for the more severe. Thorlac Thorhalsson's penitential allowed a lengthy fast to be commuted if the penitent genuflected a hundred times a day; others allowed him to substitute the frequent repetition of psalms for a fast. Still others permitted the penitent blessed with worldly goods to donate alms so as to be relieved of fasting. Indeed, a rich man might share his penance with others, so that, for example, he might quickly accomplish a three-year fast by paying 365 men to fast with him for three days.[26]

Significantly, homosexual acts were judged in early penitentials to be no more or less heinous than other kinds of nonprocreative sexual activity. Nevertheless, that homosexual acts were regulated in such detail suggests that this sexual practice was of increasingly urgent and anxious concern to the early medieval Church. Homosexual acts are regularly described as "detestable," as "abominable," as "sins against nature." Pope Gregory III, commenting in the early eighth century on the variety of penances assigned to "the crime of sodomy," calls it a "vice so abominable in the sight of God that cities in which its practitioners dwelt were appointed for destruction by fire and brimstone."[27]

As an eighth-century Irish penitential chillingly asserted, sodomy is the sin "not forgiven either in the present world or that which is to come."[28] The penitentials essentially sought to provide a cure for sinners, among them those who allowed homosexual desire to triumph over the stern warnings of doctrine and discipline. While the penitentials did not amount to persecution, they did contribute to the invention, marginalization, and eventual criminalization not only of sodomy but of the "sodomite." Moreover, by assigning specific penances for many sexual acts deemed to be homosexual, the penitentials enlarged the range of sin associated with homosexuality so that *any* tender contact between people of the same sex—a glance, a simple kiss, a fond embrace—could be considered a grave and detestable sin.

4 Something Shameful

Civil and ecclesiastical laws tell us what people should do. For a hint concerning what they may have done, we can look at literature. While the Church and the law were beginning to stigmatize sodomy and invent the sodomite, literary texts showed far less unanimity of opinion. Though there is no body of medieval European homoerotic literature to compare with that of classical Greece and Rome, in the early Middle Ages a few texts—almost all written by clerics—speak of friendship between men and hint at intense and even physical affection. These writings are often couched in terms reminiscent of classical homoerotic poetry, even as they employ language drawn from the humane and loving precepts advocated by Christ.[29] There is also a body of writing, modeled upon Latin antihomosexual satire, that reflects the Christian horror of homosexual desire, condemning sodomy as sin and conflating homosexual conduct with effeminacy.

Because some medieval writers commanded Greek as well as Latin, they were able to consult the remnants of ancient literature that had found their way into monastic libraries all over Europe. There they found pagan celebrations of homosexual love as well as pagan satire against it. Translating them, or employing them as models, they produced homoerotic declarations of affection, addressed to fellow clerics or sometimes to handsome youths. Sometimes a writer who had produced poems declaring homoerotic desire for a friend next translated doctrine into verse condemning the hated sodomite.

The fourth-century poet and scholar Ausonius (c. 310–395 C.E.), born in Bordeaux, was a civil servant and eventually the tutor to the emperor's son; he wrote in the classical tradition, of which he may be the last and best exemplar. Ausonius professed Christianity, but his style and subject looked back to pagan authors with both fascination and doubt. His imitation of the Greek poet Meleager (who wrote circa 95 B.C.E.) shows the moral distance between the two ages. Speculating on the mechanics of a homosexual ménage à trois, Meleager describes the scene without judgment: "In one bed two submissive and two in action. Four in all you think. No, there are three. The man in the middle swings back and forth and provides sport in either port."[30] The tone of Ausonius' imitation is different:

> *"There are three men in one bed.*
> *Two are taking something shameful,*
> *And two are giving it."*
> *"Well, that should make four."*
> *"No, you're wrong.*
> *The two on the ends are guilty of just one crime,*
> *While the one in the middle is having it two ways."*[31]

In another poem he describes one Marcus as a pedophilic seducer of males and compares him to a dung beetle. Some of his works, though, hint that Ausonius may have been captivated by beautiful boys. In a memorial epigram dedicated to a sixteen-year-old youth, Ausonius laments his death and compares the "mingled beauties of thy face" to Ganymede's.[32] In another poem he notes: "While nature was wondering whether to make you male or female, / You were made half-girl, my beautiful boy." Here, even as he admires, Ausonius employs the common association of homosexuality with effeminacy and androgyny.

Some of Ausonius' poems appear to distinguish between love and friendship on the one hand and sexual promiscuity on the other, categories drawn from pagan asceticism. A similar distinction is made by Ausonius' contemporary St. Augustine. In the *Confessions* Augustine recalls his intimacy with a friend and the intense grief that followed the friend's death. He accuses himself of having tainted the friendship with sensuality and desire—a recollection that may have contributed to his obdurate detestation of homosexuality. Indeed, Augustine's doctrinal definition of homosexual activity as *the* sin against nature was central in shaping the antihomosexual attitudes of the Western Church. Ausonius, humane student of the classics, although beset by Christian doubt about the sexuality he observed in the ancient writers, exemplified the order that was passing. Augustine, strict theorist of Christian asceticism, proclaimed the world to come.

While some early medieval writers doubted or denied the morality of homosexual desire, a few others seemed to hope that friendship, love, and even sex between persons of the same sex might be touched by the message of Christ's love. A hint of homoeroticsm can be detected in the popular medieval genre of saints' lives, intended to support the faith and educate and edify the faithful. Some possibly dating from as early as the fourth century, these stories celebrated the exemplary lives and exploits of pairs of saints such as Perpetua and Felicity, who were martyred in Carthage by the Romans; Sergius and Bacchus; Polyeuct and Nearchos, the latter described as "brothers not by birth but by affection."[33] These tales describe the piety, bravery, and inevitable martyrdom of the saints and often include fervid descriptions of intimate friendship and love between men and between women. Not unlike the stories of male lovers found in Hellenistic prose romances like *Clitophon and Leucippe,* or earlier Greek legends of heroic male lovers like Aristogeiton and Harmodios or Orestes and Pylades, saints' lives place their protagonists in mortal danger, confront them with implacable enemies, and separate them, often by martyrdom. These privations are endured and made more bearable by the love between the protagonists and by the prospect of joyous reunion in heaven. Like the pagan prose romances, saints' lives demonstrate that love conquers all. And saints' lives show that the love of brave men for each other can not only lead to triumph over adversity but to attaining the kingdom of heaven.

The legend of Saints Sergius and Bacchus, for example, details their holy life and triumphant martyrdom at the hands of the emperor Maximian. Described as "being at one in their love for Christ," they are also portrayed as a devoted couple; when Bacchus is martyred first, he returns to Sergius in a dream to remind him that although "I have been taken from you in body, I am still with you in bond." Bacchus encourages Sergius to quickly effect his own martyrdom so that, once dead, he can "pursue and obtain me . . . for the crown of justice for me is to be with you."[34] This legend and others like it, including the story of the exemplary devotion of Felicity for her companion in sanctity, Perpetua, suggest intimate and even eroticized relations between same-sex couples in the service of Christian doctrine. Not only are they reminiscent of tales of pagan relationships but they also recall the biblical stories of David and Jonathan and Christ and John, the Beloved Disciple, tales that by the late Middle Ages were being read as homoerotic.[35]

However, images and allegations of monstrosity, androgyny, effeminacy, and promiscuity began to predominate in fifth- and sixth-century poems about same-sex desire. Stylistically indebted to the epigrams of Martial, these poems are notable for their contemptuous detestation of the monsters they invent. The French writer Ennodius of Arles (c. 473–521), bishop of Ticinum (Pavia), wrote of one man, "There is a constant deception at play in his double sex"—"[he's a] woman when passive, when active in lust he's a man." Another example of sexual deception: "Your face is masculine, your gestures feminine, but your thighs are both: / You resolve an opposition in nature by negating the difference." With such creatures abroad, no sexual or gender distinction is safe. In another poem Ennodius urges, "Look at this monster, created by promiscuous rule"—a man who is "of common gender, rather of all genders." Ennodius' horror may well be founded in personal dislike of effeminacy or in ascetic disapproval of sex, but his vehemence derives from the conviction that confusion of gender represents a clear danger to the natural order. The objects of his detestation are not simply fallen men whose transgression might be washed away through penance, but rather creatures neither male nor female. That sodomites are characterized by deceit and that they choose deviance are central to his image of them: one is "created" by promiscuity; another seems to have chosen to resolve the opposition of nature by deliberate negation of the difference between male and female; yet another plays out an equally deliberate deception as he is first passive and then active with different partners.

Luxorius, a Christian of the early sixth century who may have lived in Carthage, found homosexuality and effeminacy, if not too horrible to contemplate, then certainly worthy of vitriol. In one of his poems he invents an effeminate lawyer more interested in sex than the law. Calling him a "model of castrated men," an "utter disgrace of nature," "an object of filthy lust," and a "Paris to be used as a woman," he charges that the lawyer chooses to handle useless causes and impossible-to-argue cases because "you want good stuff entrusted not to your mouth, I think, but to your asshole." The lawyer's homosexual obsession and promiscuous sexual passivity have corrupted his commitment to the practice of law. Of a woman who may have been a lesbian—Luxorius describes her as a hermaphrodite—he says she is a "double-membered monster of the female sex / Whom unnatural desire makes a man." A young man named Becca is castigated for squandering his inheritance on a series of "husbands" to whom he passively submits; Luxorius cannot help wondering "what wretched thing you're hiding" and speculates that "if you were offering good pieces of meat, you should have sold them for a goodly return." A charioteer named Vico, who, like a modern sports hero ought to be an exemplar of masculinity, is warned that he will never win a race unless he gives up his apparent addiction to sexual submission: he will always be "unmanned by this wretched practice."

Another sixth-century poet, this one anonymous, addresses one Martius, similar to the passive youths of Ennodius and Luxorius. The poet charges that "Venus itches in your notorious ass" and calls Martius a "tale of unknown sex: / Though you're not a woman, you still cannot be a man."[36]

Products of the last days of the declining Roman Empire, these texts reveal a classical culture almost wholly overwhelmed by the Christian presence. Echoing the distaste of Martial and other Latin poets for effeminacy and passivity in males, animated by antihomosexual Christian doctrine, they urge that men who engage in homosexuality be viewed as neither male nor female. If they are not quite sure whether homosexual activity is a choice or a compulsion they generally agree that it is despicable and unnatural, and that the alarming mannerisms and sexual desires of certain males mark them as definitively a race apart.

In secular and ecclesiastical law, in the admonishments of local penitentials, in the declarations of Church councils, and in literature, homosexual acts were generally considered heinous and occasionally described as the worst of all sins. Punishment ranged from a few years of penance to excommunication for life. Though Christendom enacted only a handful of antihomosexual statutes in the five centuries after Christ announced his gospel of tolerant love, the following five centuries, between Justinian's edict and the millennium, saw more than a hundred antihomosexual civil and ecclesiastical pronouncements emanate from a dozen nation-states and numerous local churches. Some have argued that this represents a relatively small amount of regulation of sexual behavior by a negligent and uninterested Church and an even less interested state, but in comparison with the Church fathers and the Apostles, it is a significant attempt at control. What official attention to the morality and social implications of homosexual acts shows is that they had begun to generate increasingly intense and negative concern.[37] As the millennium approached and Christendom fearfully awaited the Second Coming and the Last Judgment, some also eagerly awaited the moment when sodomites, the worst of sinners, would receive exquisite and appropriate punishment.

Chapter Eight

The Plague of Sodomy

The Eastern Empire, as we have seen, had thoroughly demonized and criminalized homosexual acts, but in the West the homosexual sinner was just beginning to be invented by the Church, the homosexual criminal to be imagined by the state. The deviant creature—sometimes taken from life, sometimes borrowed from Latin satire—was also entering literature. By the millennium, medieval Christianity, building upon pagan and Judeo-Christian asceticism, had been reasonably successful in transforming natural sexual desire, homosexual or heterosexual, into sin.

As the millennium passed without Christ's returning to save the righteous and punish sinners, the great states of Europe—France, the Holy Roman Empire, Spain, Portugal, and Norman England—continued battling to acquire new territory or protect old, or to settle the claims of rival monarchs to disputed thrones. Kings began to centralize their realms by wresting power from both minor lords and regional princes, claiming the absolute authority once possessed only by the Caesars.

The Church, too, began to centralize its power, in the person of the pope, and as part of this process it codified the haphazardly accreted doctrines and laws of the past thousand years. The codification allowed the church to designate more clearly who was an enemy of the faith. In the two centuries after the millennium, both heretics and those whose sexual practices were deemed contrary to the dictates of natural law began to be classified, prosecuted, and persecuted.

Christian sources preached a consistent lesson: effeminacy was a sign of deviance; homosexual pleasures were snares to trap the unwary and destroy the soul. No jurist, king, or pope would have disagreed with the now-universal interpretation of the story of Sodom or questioned the need to punish sodomitical sinners. But what the majority of early medieval people thought or felt about homosexual activity we can only guess. Those who were neither clergy nor gentry knew no Latin and could not read; they may have known nothing of scriptural condemnations, and they surely understood none of the intricacies of current law, much less the laws of vanished Rome or distant Byzantium. In the early Middle Ages, their lives were often threatened by barbarians, hunger, and natural calamity, and if they thought about sex at all, they probably felt that theorizing about sodomy was best left to monks and magistrates. The lure of an occasional moment's pleasure with a friend, a servant boy, a male prostitute, or a passing stranger may well have been more compelling than solemn priestly warnings against the evils of *sodomitica luxuria* or vice *contra naturam*—and certainly more comforting.

1 Theorizing Sin

After the millennium, battle was joined in Christian Europe between the claims of temporal and spiritual power. Temporal rulers felt that as heirs to the Roman Empire or to ancient tribal jurisdictions they ought to take precedence over a church that had no warriors and little power, and they claimed the right in their own domains to appoint clergy and appoint and depose bishops. By the end of the eleventh century it was common practice for local nobles to sell Church livings in their possession to the highest bidder. A baron might have among his holdings a dozen churches, or a monastery, or even a bishopric, each intended to minister to local inhabitants and supported by a few tenant properties. The man granted such a church—perhaps a man with no priestly vocation, and likely with a wife and even children—gathered the income from the land and from the faithful, and thus enjoyed a decent living. Such a priest, abbot, or bishop would naturally offer greater allegiance to the secular lord who had appointed him than to the Church superior who claimed spiritual authority over him, but who had little practical power to discipline and none to depose.

The papacy sought to extend its religious authority into dominion over nations, kings, and princes as well as over the spiritual lives of their subjects. But for the Church to exercise such power legitimately, it had to be morally and spiritually unassailable. It would have to discipline strictly the morals of its own clergy, abolish simony—the sale of clerical offices—and, enforcing the fifth-century papal edicts on the subject, end the marriage of priests.

At the beginning of the new millennium, many priests were married and some kept concubines, even boys. This seriously weakened the moral authority of the Church. Anticlerical sentiment was strong; disgusted by a profligate priesthood and a hierarchy that seemed more concerned with worldly wealth than spiritual perfection, many believers gravitated to new if unorthodox expressions of Christianity—the Church called them heresies—that preached simplicity and purity.

Determined to cure the ills of the priesthood, a number of clerics pressed for reform. While offering general denunciations of clerical sexual misconduct, the reformers focused on sodomy as an emblem of the sickness afflicting the Church. Sodomy was not a new outrage, nor was suppressing it a new cause. But the premillennial Church had considered it a sin that could be addressed by penance; the sodomitical sinner was a man who had fallen and who, once repentant, would no longer be sinner or sodomite.

Now, however, the Church set out to strengthen its doctrine. The various premillennial laws and edicts, penitentials, and literary texts became the foundation for more stringent ecclesiastical and civil laws. To these must be added one of the earliest collections of canon law, one in fact made before the beginning of the reform movement, by Regino of Prum in 906. His *De ecclesiasticis disciplinis libri duo* ("Two Books on Ecclesiastical Discipline"), of which the first volume addresses the clergy and the second laymen, was a most valuable source for later reformers. Regino, for example, quotes the admonitions of the Council of Ancyra against shameless sexual conduct, but unquestioningly presumed that those vague prohibitions are aimed at homosexual acts. Those "who pollute others with the leprosy of this branded crime," he writes, ought to be considered unclean in body and spirit. Refusing to mention even here the name of the unspeakable crime, Regino perpetuated the characterization of homosexual acts as a disease of both body and spirit.[1]

The *Decretum* of Burchard of Worms (c. 1007) continued the work of codification and listed penances for all manner of transgressions, including homosexual acts. Burchard, it seems, did not consider homosexual behavior more serious than other sexual transgressions; his penances for heterosexual and homosexual offenses were comparable. Heterosexual adultery, for example, was punishable by a strict fast of eighty days on bread and water, followed by fourteen years of lighter fasting; for sodomy engaged in by a married man, forty days of bread and water and twelve years of fasting would expunge the sin.[2] As a penitential, the *Decretum* is not markedly different from earlier texts. However, Burchard, like Regino, offered an unusually detailed discussion of homosexual activity. He proposed a series of questions concerning sexual conduct to be used by confessors: "Did you," for example, "commit fornication as the Sodomites did, so that you put your penis in the back of a man?"[3] Solitary and mutual masturbation as well as "fornication with a man between the hips" are assigned penances, whose severity depends on whether the act is a single instance or habitual, and on the age and rank of the offender: masturbating boys suffer only ten days' penance, while men over fifty who persist in performing anal intercourse are condemned to do penance for life.

Perhaps the most zealous advocate of Church reform was the cleric Peter Damian (1007–1072) of Ravenna. Damian had allied himself with an especially vehement group of reformers, among them Hildebrand, who as Pope Gregory VII fought to establish the supremacy of the Church over all civil authority. Damian denounced clerical marriage, asserted that all clergy ought to be celibate, and demanded that married priests divorce their wives and reject their families. He was a ferocious theorizer on the nature of sodomitical sin, as well. Everywhere around him Damian saw convincing evidence that sodomy was the most ubiquitous of sexual sins, its abominable signature writ large upon the body of the Church. About 1050, he wrote the *Liber gomorrhianus,* a furious condemnation of clerical sodomy, defined specifically as homosexual behavior. It is in this book that Damian used *sodomia* to describe what he so detested: "If blasphemy is the worst sin, I do not know in what way Sodomy is better." As Mark Jordan has observed, "*Sodomia* does not make its appearance [in Damien] as a neutral description of acts." Rather, the word itself condemns the acts; it links those who performed them in Damian's time with the ancient Sodomites, "who suffered the most severe divine punishment."[4]

The clergy both secular and monastic licentiously engaged in all kinds of homosexual acts, Damian thundered. He cited solitary and mutual masturbation, interfemoral sex, and sodomy; he defined the last as anal intercourse, calling it the sin that "surpasses all others in uncleanness."[5]

> This vice is in fact the death of the body, the destruction of the soul; it pollutes the flesh, extinguishes the light of the mind, casts out the Holy Spirit from the temple of the human breast, and replaces it with the devil, the rouser of lust; it removes the truth utterly from the mind; it deceives and directs it toward falsehood; it sets snares in a man's path and, when he falls into the pit, blocks it up so there is no escape; it opens the doors of hell and closes the gates of heaven.[6]

Damian demanded that Pope Leo IX, to whom he dedicated the book, bring the power of the Apostolic See and the full weight of canon law to bear on such sinners. He also argued that canon law is not rigorous enough; he cites the death penalty exacted by Leviticus, urging that clerical sodomites ought to do penance for fifteen years if not for life, and ought to be beaten, spat upon, bound in chains, imprisoned, and starved.[7] The pope did not accede to Damian's harsh demands. Indeed, many clerics, the pope probably among them, seemed to feel that Damian's blanket characterization of the whole Church as a body infected with sodomitical vice was more harmful than healing.[8]

In time, however, Damien's assertion that sodomy is worse than all other sexual sins became a commonplace of canon law. When Ivo of Chartres (1040–1116) assembled his collection of canon law, he echoed Augustine's concept of unnatural intercourse, asserting that "to act against nature is always unlawful, and beyond doubt more flagrant and shameful than to sin by a natural use in fornication or adultery."[9] A similar judgment was made by an Italian monk named Gratian who, in 1140, compiled the *Concordia discordantium canonum* and thus earned the sobriquet "Father of Canon Law." Deriving his text from Augustine, early councils, Scripture, and Roman law, Gratian ranked sins against nature in order of their seriousness. Though he found fornication, adultery, and incest serious, he saw them as lesser evils since they used the sexual member in a "natural" way. Homosexual acts, however, were patently unnatural in the Augustinian sense and irredeemably sinful. Not only did they not result in procreation, but fellatio and anal intercourse were contrary to the penis's "natural use" which, according to Gratian, was taught by the Scriptures and the Prophets, upheld in canon law and in the deliberations of the Church, justified by the example of nature, and commanded by God.

Alain of Lille (ca. 1128–1202) linked sodomy and homicide as the two most serious of all crimes in his *Sermones de peccatis capitalibus.* Albert of Cologne, called Albertus Magnus ("the Great") (1206–1280), wrote a *Summa theologiae* in which he labeled *sodomia* a sin against nature with peculiarly unwholesome effects.[10] Sodomy is more detestable than any other sin, Albert argues, because it is characterized by uncontrollable frenzy (an emotion that does not reflect the rational order of nature), a condition so powerful and so alluring that it can neither be rejected nor cured. Sodomy is also marked by a special foulness—Albert calls it a "stink"—that rises to heaven. Finally, it is contagious, spreading from one man to another until the whole world is in danger of infection.[11] Albert introduces—more accurately, he reintroduces—the language of medicine, to create a physiology of sodomy and of sodomites.

The definitive canonical statement on sodomy was made by Thomas Aquinas (1225–1274), a pupil of Albert. In his own *Summa theologiae,* begun about 1265, Thomas establishes nature as the touchstone of Roman Catholic sexual ethics.[12] Thomas classifies sins against nature as a species of *luxuria,* that is, excessive and uncontrolled desire for carnal pleasure. *Luxuria*—let us call it lust—subverts both natural order and reason, which dictate that procreation is the only proper end of sex. So any sexual act in which lust is dominant subverts order and is irrational; therefore it is unnatural. Even adultery, fornication, seduction, rape, and incest do not fall into the category of unnatural acts, because although they may cause harm, they can nonetheless result in procreation, the ultimate purpose intended by God.

Thomas lists four kinds of sinful and unnatural sexual acts: those engaged in with the wrong species (animals), with the wrong gender (homosexuality), in the wrong position and with the wrong organ (oral and anal intercourse), and masturbation. Sex with the wrong gender, the "vice of sodomy," is second only to murder in its seriousness. Thomas, like Damian, understands sodomy as exclusively homosexual and seems to imagine the sodomite as a special kind of sexual offender. At one point, he suggests that men who prefer sex with men are a unique species: "Something which is against human nature, in regard to either reason or to the preservation of the body, may become natural to a particular man, owing to some defect of nature in him."[13] From

Thomas and Damian, Alain and Albert, the sodomite emerges as an infected and innately sinful creature, for whom there would be no salvation.

It has been argued that in medieval eyes sodomy and homosexuality were not necessarily the same, and that the suppression of sodomy was not necessarily the suppression of homosexuality.[14] Yes and no. In its earliest and broadest definition, sodomy included any nonprocreative sexual act and could therefore be committed by either sex with either sex or by a person with an animal; it was also defined more narrowly as anal intercourse by a man with either a man or a woman. In any case, homosexual sex was always sodomy, and (most narrowly) some commentators saw sodomy only as homosexual, whether engaged in between women or between men. The most common meaning, "the anal penetration of one male by another," was the one that would come to preoccupy moralists. For though the broadest meaning always obtained, it was the narrower association of sodomy with homosexual acts that carried the most powerful opprobrium.

Such an association is made in a scientific definition of same-sex sexual behavior written around 1310 by Peter of Abano, a teacher of natural philosophy and medicine. He summarized what may have been widespread scientific and medical, as opposed to moral and theological, opinion about sodomitical behavior. Peter addressed the subject in his commentary on the *Problemata,* the work attributed to Aristotle that proposed a range of questions concerning problems in natural science and medicine. As we have seen, the *Problemata* made a distinction between men who engaged in homosexual behavior because they had learned to do so in their youth and therefore continued to do so from habit, and those for whom such behavior might be in some way "natural." Peter's discussion divides men, as did the *Problemata,* into those who enjoy both "acting" and "being acted upon," and those who enjoy only being acted upon. Why they enjoy it is the question he tries to answer.

The *Problemata* had explained that some men desire sex with men because they experienced the pleasure it afforded when they were young, continued to seek this sensation as adults, and have become habituated to it. Others are so constituted that sperm is secreted by the anus rather than by the genital organs, so that anal ejaculation follows anal stimulation. These men are thus "naturally" disposed to such desires. The writer of the *Problemata* believed such men to be physically defective, for they have a larger portion of female characteristics than most "normal" males. He therefore described such men as "effeminate by nature" because, like women's sexual pleasure, theirs involves the desire for penetration.

Peter differs only slightly. Like the Aristotelian text, Peter suggests that anal stimulation is what "such men"—he categorizes them by that phrase—enjoy. In men who prefer to be "acted upon," the pores and passages that convey the sperm to the penis are blocked, and sperm accumulates around the anus; men who both act upon other men and are acted upon have only a partial blockage, so that sperm accumulates in both penis and anus. Thus, in an individual anatomical sense, the desire for anal intercourse is natural to both sets of men. However, since the pores are blocked, or deformed, though the desire is natural to the individual, it is caused by an irregularity, what he describes as "a disorder and monstrosity happening by birth." As Joan Cadden summarizes his position: "It is possible for men to be born this way, for them to be this way by nature and in nature."[15]

Though strict logic might suggest that such men could neither be judged nor condemned for the irregular structure of their anatomy, others, who engaged in homosexual behavior through habit and by choice, could be. Peter uses traditional moralizing rather than scientific language to describe them: such men are "sodomites"; their habits are "perverse" and "filthy," and their desires "abominable." He describes their behavior clearly: "Some exercise the wicked act of sodomy by rubbing the penis with the hand; others by rubbing between the thighs of boys, which is what most do these days; and others by making friction around the anus and putting the penis into it in the same way as it is placed in a woman's sexual part."[16] As Cadden says, Peter is not discussing "'homosexuality'—an abstract construct to describe a state of being or identity that transcends particular acts and desires."[17] But he supports, with scientific inquiry and with some of the ferocious disgust of religious discourse, the idea that "such men" were sexually different and that they possessed, as he says, "a monstrous nature."[18]

Pope Gregory IX, writing around 1230, summarized the position of the medieval Church concerning the nature of sodomy. His definition, which justified extreme punishment, clearly addressed not only sin but a race of sinners: "They are abominable persons—despised by the world, dreaded by the council of heaven, who have become more unclean than animals, more vicious than almost anything alive, who have lost their reason and destroyed the kindness of nature, who are deprived of interior light and do not discriminate one sex from the other." Sodomy, once a sin any man could commit, became in Pope

Gregory's formulation the specific and ineradicable vice of men called sodomites. Penance might once have wiped away its stain and ushered the sinner back into the arms of the Church, but now sodomites were outcasts, despised both on earth and in heaven, their sin the one for which there was no forgiveness. A terrible punishment awaited sodomites after death: "What will the arbiter of eternal salvation and damnation provide for the enemies of nature who falsify its custom. . . . When they come to that terrible judgment, will He not command that they be tortured in hell with some unimaginable type of pain worse than that given to other damned souls?"[19]

2 Criminalizing Sodomy

As part of the general attempt to reform the clergy during the twelfth and thirteenth centuries, various Church councils addressed the question of sodomy and proposed punishments of increasing severity. Though primarily concerned with the clergy, some councils also ruled on such conduct among laypeople as well. One of the earliest edicts against the "shameful sin of sodomy" was promulgated in England in 1102 by the ecclesiastical Council of London. Though it is not clear whether by "sodomy" the council meant a specifically homosexual act or any nonprocreative sex, the timing of the edict, coming shortly after the death of King William Rufus, suggests that homosexual behavior may have been intended.

Henry I had ascended to the throne in 1100, succeeding William Rufus, son of William the Conqueror. One chronicler of his reign, Ordericus Vitalis, asserts that during Rufus' reign "the effeminate predominated everywhere . . . and filthy catamites, fit only to perish in the flames, abandoned themselves shamefully to the foulest practices of Sodom."[20] No other chronicler mentions such homosexual excess, though several claim that William Rufus was "given insatiably to obscene fornication and frequent adultery."[21] Whatever his sin, the council of 1102 may well have been convened in response to the behavior of Rufus' court.

The law of 1102 called for "weighty anathema" against those convicted of committing the "shameful sin": clerics were to be deposed, while laypersons were to be "deprived of [their] legal status and dignity in the whole realm of England." Singled out were "those who of their own free will take pleasure" in sodomy. That sin was so serious that only a bishop could absolve it.

Anselm, Archbishop of Canterbury, in a commentary on the edict addressed to his archdeacon, described the prohibited sin specifically as the sin of Sodom and noted—perhaps with Rufus in mind—that "this sin has been hitherto so public that hardly anyone is embarrassed by it, and many have fallen into it because they were unaware of its seriousness."[22] It is unlikely that the far more common sins of heterosexual adultery and fornication would have elicited this comment, which recalls Peter Damian's charge that sodomy was everywhere—a common complaint of moral reformers. There is some doubt that the edict was ever enacted, but it marks an early attempt by the English Church and state to translate sin into crime. And, significantly, it is among the earliest attempts in the medieval West to deprive a layperson of his legal status for acts of sodomy.

Perhaps the most ferocious laws against homosexual activity actually enforced in medieval times were those promulgated by a council of lords and bishops in the Kingdom of Jerusalem. The First Crusade had captured the city in 1099. The crusaders slaughtered most of the city's inhabitants, burned its mosques and synagogues, and founded upon the carnage a Christian kingdom under the rule of Godfrey of Bouillon. In 1120 Baldwin II, the Norman king of Jerusalem, along with his patriarch and his bishops, convened the Council of Nablus. The sermon that opened the proceedings attributed recent local calamities, including earthquakes and continued attacks by the Saracens, to the sexual promiscuity of Baldwin's subjects. In response the council passed twenty-five canons, condemning all manner of carnality. Four addressed sodomy. The first read: "If any adult shall be proved to have defiled himself voluntarily by sodomitical vice, whether actively or passively, let him be burnt."[23] Meanwhile, the enemy Saracens, whose Islamic religion was popularly believed to encourage and reward the commission of sodomy, patiently waited outside the walls.

The Council of Nablus also classified varieties of sodomites. The adult who "defiled himself voluntarily . . . whether actively or passively" was one kind. Another was he who seduced or forcibly violated a minor or "anyone else." In a third category was anyone who, after having been "forcibly compelled to submit to the crime of sodomy," nevertheless concealed his shame and allowed himself "to be polluted again." Earlier opinions about sodomy implied that men who engaged in sodomitical acts could rejoin the faithful if they repented, but according to the canons of Nablus, once tainted, never changed. The law does offer mercy to "any sodomite" who "comes to his senses" and "renounces the abominable vice"; he can at least be received into the Church. But "if he fall a second time," even though he again repents, such is the nature of his pollution that he must be "expelled from the Kingdom of Jerusalem" so as not to contaminate its holiness or call down upon it the divine wrath that had punished Sodom.[24] For the Council of Nablus, sodomites are hardened sexual sinners, devoted to illicit pleasures and acting upon the sinful promptings of their own free will.

The enactments of Nablus, jointly passed by representatives of both Church and state, declared that the state ought to enforce Church prohibitions against homosexual acts. These canons would not, however, have much effect on the larger Church, because the council that passed them was local. The Third Lateran Council, on the other hand, represented the entire Church. Held at Rome in 1179, it was the first ecumenical council to enact canons against homosexual acts.[25] Somewhat more temperate than the council of the other Holy City, Lateran III merely ruled that any cleric found guilty of the "incontinence which is against nature"—defined as the sin that brought down the wrath of God on Sodom—ought to be deposed from office, while laymen ought to be excommunicated and "completely isolated from contact with believers."[26] Though the vague language could suggest that homosexuality was not the only nonprocreative sexual act being condemned, the antisodomitical fulminations of reforming clerics must have been fresh in the memory of those deliberating. Writing at about the same time, Peter Cantor, in *De vitio sodomitico*, had equated sodomy and murder, asserting that the biblical Sodomites were "spastic and feeble" men who "change[d] themselves from males to females" and engaged in acts clearly contrary to nature. Peter angrily asked why it was that "the church leaves untouched" sins so spectacularly punished by God and proscribed by both Scripture and Roman law; he quoted the Theodosian edict of 342 that demanded "when a man marries as a woman, let the laws be armed, let justice come forth."[27]

The Fourth Lateran Council (1215) decreed both ecclesiastical and civil penalties against those who engaged in homosexual acts. Noting that the clergy must avoid the "sin of lust—particularly that on account of which the anger of God comes from heaven upon the sons of disobedience"—the council demanded that any "caught giving way to the sin of incontinence" shall be punished "according to the rules of canon law." But those "whom the fear of God does not hold back from evil" have an added inducement: "Temporal punishment at least may restrain [them] from sin." Lateran IV engaged the entire Church against sodomites and invited all the states of Christendom to join the battle.

Civil punishment of sodomy allowed temporal rulers to use accusation and punishment as weapons to control political enemies, dissidents, and troublesome populations—including but not limited to sodomites. Various Italian city-states, influenced both by Lateran IV in 1215 and by the Inquisition—established in 1232 by Pope Gregory IX to search out and punish heretics—introduced stringent and often capital measures against the "plague of sodomy." In some cities, where the newly created Dominican and Franciscan orders were especially energetic in pursuing heretics, prosecutions for sodomy were also frequent.

The complex political and religious wars that bloodied Italy during the thirteenth century lie beyond the scope of this book, but the contest between the somewhat liberal and the more conservative factions—the former the aristocratic Ghibellines; the latter the more middle-class Guelphs, allied with friars and pope—provide the background for the harsh antisodomy legislation of the time.[28] In some Italian cities, such laws—often enacted at the behest of orders of friars who had achieved political influence and power—called for banishment or the amputation of limbs for first or second offenses, and burning for third offenses, or for habitual offenders. Between 1245 and 1267 statutes in Bologna created governmental (rather than ecclesiastical) forces to cooperate with the local Inquisition in searching out heretics and sodomites, often taken to be one and the same. One Italian town offered a reward to anyone who denounced sodomites or heretics. In Bologna in 1250— where university scholars specialized in the interpretation of the newly rediscovered corpus of ancient law, which had prescribed death for homosexual acts—convicted offenders were exiled from the city, but in 1259, under pressure from the Dominicans, they were condemned to be burned.[29]

France, Spain, and England also acted against sodomites in the thirteenth century. In France, alleged outbreaks of sodomy occasioned the introduction of a law in Orléans about 1260. *Li Livres de Jostice et de Plet* applied to both males and females, demanding that a man "who has been proved to be a sodomite must lose his testicles, and if he does it a second time, he must lose his member, and if he does it a third time, he must be burnt." Women too, were to be mutilated and executed.

In 1261 the Bishop of Amiens asserted that he, not the city's burghers, had the sole right to judge cases of sodomy. A royal decree settled the matter in favor of the civil authorities: "A better case has been made for the town . . . than for the bishop"—an indication that judgment of sodomites was in fact passing from ecclesiastical to civil courts.[30] In 1283 a French civil law code, *Coutumes de beauvaisis,* declared that those convicted of "sodomiterie" were to forfeit their property and die by burning.[31]

In Spanish Castile, a law code of 1265, *Las Siete partidas,* decreed that "when one man desires to sin against nature with another . . . both [were to] be castrated before the whole populace and on the third day after be hung by the legs until dead, and that their bodies never be taken down."[32] *Las Siete partidas* took care to define the sin it criminalized: "Sodomy is the sin which men commit by having intercourse with each other, against nature and natural custom." Like Justinian's sixth-century *novellae,* the Castilian law notes that "for such crimes our Lord sent upon the land guilty of them famine, plague, catastrophe, and countless other calamities." The antisodomy law meant to prevent the "many evils" that arise "in the land where it [sodomy] is perpetrated."[33]

The English Church had proposed depriving sodomitic laypeople of their legal status in 1102; by the end of the thirteenth century and at the beginning of the fourteenth, some legal treatises instead recommended death. One of them, *Britton,* specifies burning for "sorcerers, sorceresses, renegades, sodomists, and heretics." Another, the *Fleta,* dealt with social and sexual deviations: "Apostate Christians, sorcerers, and the like should be drawn and burnt. Those who have connection with Jews or Jewesses, or those who are guilty of bestiality or sodomy, are to be buried alive."[34] The association of sodomy with heresy was by this time firmly established in both law and the popular mind. Again, we do not know whether these legal opinions ever became civil law, but their mere existence suggests that many in England thought the prescribed punishment was appropriate.[35]

In many parts of Europe at the end of the thirteenth century, then, sodomites, heretics, and other social and sexual deviants were demarcated from the rest of the population. Those who once were only sinners now were criminal; their behavior was not only sinful but antisocial, and thus appropriately punished by loss of rights, property, and life. In 1292 John de Wettre, a knifemaker, was executed for sodomy in Ghent, burned alive for engaging with another man in an act "detested by God."[36] This is the earliest known execution for that act. We don't know whether the other man was a lover or a passing stranger, whether the act was habitual or unique. All that we can know about John de Wettre is how his age defined him as it burned him—in Pope Gregory's words, an "abominable" person whom "the world despises." John's execution, if it was the first, would not be the last.

3 Identifying Sodomites

Who were sodomites? As the Church began to conflate sexual with doctrinal deviance, sodomy with heresy, all manner of the religiously unorthodox, the politically suspect, and the simply foreign—Muslims, Jews, heretics—were routinely accused of sexual crimes, among them sodomy. Sodomy was already construed as the worst of all sins save murder, perhaps amenable to penance but certainly deserving severe punishment. The suspicion had also arisen that some men were inveterate, perhaps incorrigible sodomites. If heretics and non-Christians were sodomites, and if, as some theorized, sodomy was a sin that, like disease, was contagious, then it followed that any group of people could be sodomites. At various times in the Middle Ages, any number of Christian groups (the nobility, the clergy, the educated, the wealthy) as well as some Christian peoples (the Lombards, the French, the English) were accused of sodomy and said to have special sodomitical tendencies. The citizens of certain large cities, for instance Orléans, Paris, Chartres, and Venice, were accused of sodomy. Even such a hamlet as Montaillou in southern France had its entire population accused, apparently with some reason, of engaging in a variety of sexual sins, not least among them sodomy. According to Hildebert of Lavardin (1055–1133), "more common than any other lewdness is the plague of sodomy. / Men pay what they owe their spouses to other men. / Countless Ganymedes tend countless hearths."[37] Hildebert's early-twelfth-century picture of a world overrun by "Ganymedes" may be discounted as the wild overstatement of a zealot, but many other texts of the period also insisted that sodomites were everywhere. It became even more essential to identify and categorize these people, so that the world would be aware of who they were, what they did, and where they were to be found.

In some graffiti added to a ninth-century German manuscript of poems, whole cities—usually French—were said to be inhabited solely by sodomites. One anonymous poet urges that "Chartres and Sens should be destroyed, where Adonis prostitutes himself / According to the laws of the whorehouse. The foul acts of sodomy are there." And "the noble city of Paris" is "infected with the same evil." Another poem charges that "the men of Orléans are the best—if you happen to follow / The customs of men who go to bed with boys." Chartres was again accused in a poem of the thirteenth or fourteenth century, which warns "if anyone in this life chooses not to live as a sodomite, / Then he'd better get out of Chartres—unless he wants to become a woman."[38] While French cities were said to be prone to sodomy, the charge could be made against any city. Florence and Venice were reputed to be especially rife with it. An English document from around 1192 paints a picture of the London underworld in which ganymedes— and their protectors—flourish. In his *Chronicle of the Times of King Richard the First,* Richard of Devizes lists some of the inhabitants of the London underworld. He mentions mimes, beggars, magicians, and *noctivagae*—night walkers, or prostitutes—as well as *glabriones, pusiones, molles,* and *mascularii.* Each of these terms has a homosexual connotation. The first may mean a smooth-cheeked effeminate boy or catamite, the second a young hustler (Latin: *pusio,* "catamite"). The third, *molles,* is a version of a familiar Latin term usually translated as "soft," and implying effeminacy. The last, *mascularii,* seems to mean "man-lovers." That such specific erotic types could be identified may suggest the existence of a homosexual subculture.[39]

Sodomy might be imputed to almost anyone. Walter of Chatillon, a student in Paris and later a teacher in Chatillon, found sodomites among all classes of men: "The sons of the nobility / Are sent away to France to learn scholarship; / Corrupters of youth recruit them with coaxes and cash / and so they bring their obscene habits" home with them when they return. Sodomy is the practice of "barbarians, Romans or Greeks," and "the priesthood is just like the laity"; "men make women of themselves, and stallions turn into mares" while "rulers turn this crime into common practice."[40]

Sodomy was imagined to be especially widespread among the clergy, who ought most vehemently to have condemned it. This was a particular cause for alarm among moralists and the faithful, as well as a fertile subject for the satirist. "You will find," one poem says, "many who say that wickedness with boys / Should be cursed, but they do not shrink from the deeds."[41] An eleventh-century German poem insists, in Latin, that the local bishop is more Ganymede than Ganymede himself; it goes on to assert that a sodomite is more vile than a prostitute and that "when a sodomite copulates, he leaves behind only pollution."[42] Another poem—apparently rebellious parishioners' complaint to a bishop about sodomitic clergy—insists: "Either remove this smelly flock or be informed that we're going to leave, dear Bishop." This small manifestation of social unrest, dated sometime in the eleventh or twelfth century, hints at how antisodomitical sentiments could be mobilized against authority.

Ambitious clergy may have been quite as willing as the laity to use the charge of sodomy to their own advantage. Ivo of Chartres, a cleric determined to eradicate sodomy, reported in his correspondence that Ralph, Archbishop of Tours, had schemed with King Philip of France to elevate Ralph's friend John to the bishopric of Orléans, a city that also had a sodomitical reputation. John, who was apparently known to many as Flora, a name sometimes given to homosexual prostitutes— was not only Ralph's lover but had also allegedly been the lover of the previous archbishop of Orléans. Horrified at this connivance, Ivo appealed to Pope Urban II, noted for his reforming zeal, to prevent this iniquity. The pope, however did nothing, and John was consecrated in 1098.[43]

Reformers saw sodomy among the aristocracy. The rapidly expand- ing middle class found it both comforting and politically useful to believe in the sexual decadence of the nobility. We might say that John of Salisbury (1120?–1180) was engaging in both sexual and class war- fare when he contemptuously described what he saw as the effeminacy of life at the Norman court:

> When the rich wanton is preparing to satisfy his passion, he has
> his hair elaborately frizzled and curled; he puts to shame a courte-
> san's make-up, an actor's costume. Thus arrayed he takes the feet
> of the figure reclining by him in his hands, and in plain view of
> others caresses them, and not to be too explicit, the legs as well.
> The hand that had been encased in a glove to protect it from the
> sun and keep it soft for the voluptuous purpose extends its explo-
> ration. Growing bolder, he allows his hand to pass over the entire
> body with lecherous caress, incites the lascivious thrill he has
> aroused, and fans the flame of languishing desire. Such abomina-
> tions should be spat upon rather than held up to view.[44]

Though John does not reveal the gender of the person being so eroti- cally caressed, the obvious effeminacy of the subject and the shame- lessness of the caress strongly suggest that the object is male. The punishment John imposes—that the two be spat upon—echoes the

familiar monastic punishment of sodomites. The phrase "abomination" leaves little doubt as to which horrors John wants to describe.

Kings were accused of sodomy. Philip II of France was said to have
sodomitical leanings, and contemporary chroniclers insisted that he
and Richard I (the Lion-Hearted) of England shared what one called
"passionate love." We have seen that William Rufus, an earlier occu-
pant of the English throne, was accused by contemporaries of effeminacy and shameful behavior. Though the nature of Rufus' shame is
alluded to in only one account, most contemporary observers treat his
behavior with general if euphemistic condemnation, sometimes a hint
that the sin not to be named among Christians is nevertheless the one
meant to recognized.[45]

The case of Edward II of England—who reigned from 1307 to 1327,
and whose story would later be so famously portrayed in Christopher
Marlowe's *Edward II* (1594)—is familiar enough to need only a brief
reminder that his thirteen-year association with Piers Gaveston led to
the latter's murder by Edward's resentful barons and to the king's own
assassination, approved by Isabella, his slighted and vengeful queen.
Sodomy was the charge leveled against Henri III of France (r. 1574–
1589), whose inordinate attachment to a group of effeminate young
men he called his *mignons* created scandal and provoked disgust. Even
popes fell in the face of such allegations. The antipope John XXIII,
elected by schismatic cardinals in 1410, resigned his throne in 1415,
destroyed by accusations that included incest and sodomy.[46]

4 Sodomite and Heretic

A weapon effective against political enemies, the charge of sodomy
could also be employed against entire peoples and systems of belief.
The identification of spiritual enemies had long been a preoccupation
of the Church, and the theater in which such enemies might act was
effectively enlarged in 1095 when the attention of all Europe was
focused upon the Holy Land, now in the hands of Muslims. Pope
Urban II proclaimed a crusade to recapture Jerusalem, heralding it as
the ultimate battle between good and evil, fidelity and heresy. During
the next two centuries, Christian armies warred over the barren lands
and holy places—sometimes capturing them from, but more often losing them to, the Muslim forces. Though the First Crusade had established a Christian kingdom in Jerusalem, where the most severe laws

against homosexual acts would be promulgated, the seven more Crusades—the last came in 1270—finally failed to retain the city.

Muslims had, of course, been demonized by Christian Europe long before the Crusades. Their conquest of Spain and southern France had introduced into Europe Muslim concepts about same-sex love, in part through an extensive body of Hispano-Muslim texts that celebrated love between men and boys. Perhaps because of their unusual tolerance for religious and sexual diversity, Muslims were often accused of sodomy, portrayed as inveterate sodomites whose sole desire is to pervert and ravish innocent Christians. Arabs appear so in the tenth-century *Passion of St. Pelagius,* by Hrosvitha of Gandersheim, a German nun whose poetry is perhaps the earliest written by a woman in the Middle Ages. The *Passion* tells the story of St. Pelagius, who chooses to die rather than submit to the repeated sodomitical demands of the Caliph of Cordoba. The saint even strikes the irritated Caliph in defense of his virtue, though his horror seems to be directed more at the possibility of a union between Christian and Muslim, between heretic and true believer, than at one between males. The frustrated Caliph, blind to such nice distinctions, murders Pelagius.[47]

Once Arab armies captured Jerusalem, it was not hard for Christian Europe to fasten the label of "sodomite" upon the monsters who had ravaged the most sacred sites in Christendom—in the process, it was alleged, desecrating churches, raping and murdering holy virgins, and sodomizing priests of God. The literature that helped to rouse the crusading zeal of Europe depicted Muslims not only as a threat to Christianity and to the safety of European nations but as profligate sodomites. The Dominican friar William of Adam, upon his return from infidel Egypt, reported that Muslims, "forgetting human dignity, go so far that men live with each other in the same way that men and women live together in our own land."[48] A twelfth-century letter— almost certainly a forgery, purporting to have been written by the Byzantine emperor Alexius I Comnenus to Robert, Count of Flanders, begging for his help against the incursions of Turks—alleges that the Muslim Turks have "degraded by sodomizing them men of every age and rank—boys, adolescents, young men, old men, nobles, servants, and, what is worse and more wicked, clerics and monks, and even— alas and for shame—even bishops."[49] Muslims, it was asserted, with the encouragement and approval of their faith, engaged in "any sexual act whatever" and were reputed to have "effeminate men in great number who shave their beards, paint their faces, and put on women's clothing." Muslim men "freely resort to these effeminates or live with them as among us men and women live together openly." The devious infidel—taught by Mohammed himself, who was claimed to have "popularized the vice of sodomy among his people"—was thus seen as the embodiment of both heresy and sexual deviance, combining in one monster two horrendous sins and indelibly linking them.[50] The anti-Muslim propaganda of the age turned an entire people already damned as heretics into sodomites as well.

European xenophobia was also directed at other national minorities, at non-Roman Christians, and especially at Jews. In 1204, for example, the Fourth Crusade found it better to capture Constantinople and slaughter its Greek Christians than to keep course for Jerusalem and save its Christian populace. Other crusading armies on their way to liberate the holy places in the name of Christian charity detoured to slaughter Jews in Germany. Accused of being usurers, Jews were also said to murder Christian children in their mysterious rituals. The Third Lateran Council enacted measures against the economic interests of European Jews, and the Fourth Lateran barred them from public office and demanded that they wear special clothing to distinguish them from faithful Christians. In 1182 Jews were banished from France, in 1290 from England, and later from Germany and Spain.[51] Christians who had sexual relations with Jews in England suffered the penalty attached to sodomy: burial alive.[52] Indeed, it was alleged that Jews living in Muslim nations engaged in sodomy, as their Muslim rulers did.[53]

The suppression of heresy, justified as a struggle to purify the Church and protect its faithful from doctrinal corruption, in fact provided one group the opportunity to extirpate another for political and economic reasons. The same heretics who resisted the discipline of orthodox belief were often also seen as troublesome by secular authority. By the simple expedient of calling rebels heretics and slaughtering them in the name of doctrinal purity, Church leaders and nobles could enrich themselves with confiscated lands and wealth.

At the beginning of the thirteenth century, Pope Innocent III—who had insisted that popes ought to have supremacy over kings—decreed that convicted heretics should forfeit their property and be put to death. This edict justified a bloody campaign, begun in 1208, to extirpate the Albigensian heresy. The Albigensians, or Cathars, flourished in southern France and Provence; adherents included peasants and the middle class as well as the aristocracy. The great cities of Albi, with its monumental fortified cathedral, and Carcassonne, ringed by nearly impregnable walls, were among their chief strongholds. In the eyes of Rome, Albigensian doctrine was undeniably heretical: it was a version of Manichaeanism, the ancient doctrine that preached the equal duality and power of good and evil and the endless battle between them. Since matter, in the Albigensians' theory, was evil, man could not hope to participate in the eventual triumph of good. Thus they rejected the Christian Eucharist and the power of infant baptism, and instituted instead a single sacrament, the Consolamentum, which offered forgiveness for all the sins of one's life and which was generally received shortly before death. Also, since the body was physical and therefore evil, the Cathars could neither accept the doctrine of its resurrection nor approve the act of reproducing it. They taught that procreation only continued material pollution, and thus that those who engaged in sex ought to avoid procreation. Though the elevated ranks of the Cathars were celibate—these *perfecti* having received the Consolamentum and therefore having also vowed physical purity until death—most Cathars, knowing that the sacrament would eventually expunge their sin, were content to occasionally commit it. Their orthodox enemies claimed they engaged in orgiastic sexual rites, not the least of which involved sodomy. As Guibert of Nogent breathlessly reported, "They condemn marriage and the begetting of offspring through intercourse. And surely, wherever they are scattered throughout the Latin world, you may see men living with women but not under the name of husband and wife, and in such fashion that man does not dwell with woman, male with female, but men are known to lie with men, women with women."[54] Since Christian Rome had elevated procreation as the greatest—the only—good to be derived from sex, it was consistent in imagining that a religion that declared procreation sinful and the pleasures of sex at least provisionally acceptable could spawn that erotic monster, the sodomite.

The Cathars also possessed some of the richest land in southeastern France. That as much as their heresy made them an obvious target for the pious wrath of the Italian Church and the greed of the northern French nobility. The Crusade against them, preached by Pope Innocent in 1208 and led by the Norman Simon de Montfort—whose reputation for bloody viciousness and love of indiscriminate slaughter remains intact in southern France—captured Carcassonne in 1209, as well as the cathedral at Albi, on whose walls horrific murals show the Cathar heretics writhing in retributive flame. It would take another decade for the Albigensians finally to be defeated. The last brave remnants died by their own hand in their remaining mountain stronghold, Montségur. Their enemies searched in vain for the fabulous Albigensian treasure, which would have forever enriched the Church and eased the consciences of those who had shed so much innocent blood.

The Albigensians probably derived the core of their belief from what was called the Bulgarian heresy, for its origins in Slavic Bulgaria. In numerous decrees and edicts, the Albigensians and other heretics are referred to as Bulgars, Bulgari, Boulgres, or Bougres. Thus the various forms of "Bulgar" became synonymous with the idea of heresy, and indeed the word itself came to mean heretic. A French legal document from the period rules that "if anyone is suspected of *bougrerie* the magistrate must seize him and send him to the Bishop, and if he is convicted he must be burnt and all his goods confiscated to the Baron. And the heretic ought to be dealt with in the same way."[55] This document intends to distinguish between Albigensian *bougres* and other kinds of heretics. Whether the Albigensians engaged in sodomy cannot be definitively known. But they were accused of doing so as a product of their heresy, and the accusation inflamed popular hysteria against them and conflated the sexual with the doctrinal sin. Thus, over time, *bougrerie* gradually became synonymous with sodomy. Sodomy is first described as "buggery," an anglicized form of the French word, in an English law of 1533. The term originally applied in Europe to doctrinal dissent was now used in England to indicate a sexual sin.

Once the Cathars were suppressed, the Church determined to put down all heresy, for which purpose Gregory IX created the Inquisition in 1233. In its campaign the Church employed its new orders of Dominican and Franciscan friars as spiritual avengers; their actions against heresy were often as ferocious as those of the civil armies that also served the Church. The Dominicans, charged with overseeing the Inquisition, were especially determined to stamp out doctrinal impurity.

Though the Inquisition was primarily concerned with heresy, sodomy increasingly came into the question. Not all heretics were found to be sodomites, but each charge became useful to exacerbate or prove the other. Indeed, since proper sex and correct doctrine were marks of both faithful layman and model cleric, it is hardly surprising that imputations of sexual immorality and doctrinal infidelity came to be linked, and that sodomite and heretic could turn out to be the same.

Perhaps the most infamous and effective use of heresy and sodomy charges to destroy a group occurred under King Philip IV of France, who arrested all the Knights Templars in France. The Poor Knights of Christ of the Temple of Solomon, founded in Jerusalem in about 1120, was one of the three great military orders of the Middle Ages—the others were the Knights of the Hospital of St. John of Jerusalem and the Teutonic Knights—and for the next two centuries remained perhaps the most powerful independent military, financial, and political force in Europe. The Templars admitted to their order only men of noble birth, preferably unmarried, though married men could be initiated with the donation of half their property. Their avowed purpose was to protect the hordes of pilgrims who came to visit the holy sites in Jerusalem, when that city was in Norman hands. The Templars vowed service and obedience to Christ and to the Benedictine Rule, every knight swearing to lead a life of poverty, chastity, and unquestioning obedience to those the order served and to the grand master of the order, who ruled it with absolute authority. So impressive was their presence, so deep their secrecy, and so powerful those who supported them, including the fanatical Bernard of Clairvaux and a succession of popes, that the Knights were soon recognized to be independent of any king and were granted immunity from excommunication by mere priests or even bishops. They received donations, bequests, and subsidies from both the poorest and the wealthy, so that in a few years they were the richest of the military orders. They were also trusted, and because of their vast wealth—rumor had it they were richer than all the empires of Europe—and their international reach, they became in effect the continent's bankers. In small towns and great cities, Templar Houses came to be where people left their money and possessions for safekeeping. Furthermore, the Templars were wealthy enough to lend money to those who needed it—including, it was believed, King Philip IV.

Understandably, the Templars were also envied and feared. Better organized than most monarchies, the four thousand Templars throughout Europe must have seemed to some harried kings, especially those who owed them favors or money, to be a nation above nations, answerable only to God. And indeed the Knights Templars comported themselves with a hauteur befitting their exalted station, demanding—and usually receiving—the right to advise kings and counsel popes. Any group so powerful and secretive necessarily inspired curious speculations; it was inevitable that rumor would invent what curiosity could not discover, and that fear and envy would color the invention. Rumor said that the Templars worshiped a disembodied head called Baphomet, that initiates were required to renounce Christ, spit upon the cross, and kiss the buttocks of the master who received them into the order. Rumor whispered that in the secret depths of their fortresses and in the sacred precincts of their chapels, these noble and celibate knights engaged in sodomy among themselves and allied themselves with all kinds of devils, both heretical and sodomitical.

It did not help their cause that the Templars—always thirsty for glory and eager to engage in military exploits, no matter how hopeless and foolhardy—were in part responsible for the loss of Jerusalem in 1187 to Saladin, the Muslim prince whose descendants were to rule the Holy City for another nine hundred years. Though the Templars fought with spectacular bravery during the Crusades, they were outnumbered; in 1291 the last Christian fortress, at Acre, fell to the Mameluke Egyptians. The few Templars left in Palestine scattered to the order's houses across Europe. With no Christian presence in the Holy Land, the Templars now had no mission and no country. They were a powerful and potentially dangerous group of haughty, aristocratic knights occupying splendid palaces in all the great capitals of Europe, filled, everyone agreed, with unimaginable treasure. There, it was said, when they were not professing heretical beliefs and engaging in unspeakable acts of forbidden sex, they were plotting to influence popes and kings to further their own mysterious ends.

No wonder, then, that Philip IV—having robbed, murdered, and exiled the Jews, having banished the Lombards as usurers, and being in financially perilous waters as well as indebted to the Templars—determined that ridding himself of the troublesome Knights would with one stroke eradicate a rival power in his very capital, enrich his treasury with Templar gold, and bring to him their vast lands. Acting swiftly and brutally, Philip arrested the Templars all over France on a single night, October 13, 1307.

The Templars and their grand master, Jacques de Molay, were charged with blasphemy, heresy, and sodomy—charges endorsed by popular rumor, though deemed false by many contemporaries and by most modern historians.[56] Over the next five years, Philip's campaign against the Templars progressed efficiently and effectively; he engineered the election of his puppet Pope Clement V and suborned witnesses against the Templars. Tortured beyond bearing by the king's officials and by the Inquisition, many Templars confessed to whatever was demanded of them; the grand master, after having the skin stripped from his body and his bones broken, confessed that he had indeed spat upon the cross. Despite the torture, de Molay never confessed to sodomy; throughout the persecution, only three Templars did.[57]

The order of the Knights Templar was finally abolished in 1312, destroyed by the unanswerable, largely unproved, but fatally potent charges of heresy and sodomy—leveled not in the interest of purified doctrine or elevated morality but in order to neutralize a rival power and satisfy greed. When de Molay and many of his Templar brothers faced death by burning in March 1314, they recanted their confessions. Tradition says that as the flames engulfed him, de Molay called out that within the year King Philip would be called to account by God. Philip died on November 29, 1314.

5 The Trial of Arnald of Verniolle

About 1317 a revival of the Albigensian heresy prompted the Bishop of Pamiers (later Pope Benedict XII) to undertake a new investigation and to build a special prison, Allemans, to house heretics and other felons.

One of those arrested was Arnald of Verniolle, of the parish of Mercadel in Pamiers, accused of heresy and sodomy. Arnald was a Franciscan and a subdeacon, a rank that permitted him to assist a priest at mass but not to officiate. Nor could he hear confessions or give absolution. Arnald was accused of telling certain young men that he was authorized to hear their confession, and of committing sodomy with several of them. The young men described in detail their sexual encounters with Arnald and the circumstances under which he claimed the authority to hear their confessions and even, on one occasion, to say mass. The witnesses also testified that Arnald had denied the gravity of sodomy, attempting to convince them that it was no more serious than simple fornication and less serious than incest and rape, and that he knew of a friar who would absolve them. By this time, though, it was generally accepted that sodomy was, after murder, the most heinous of *all* sins. The crime of sodomy had long been defined in canon law as anal intercourse with emission of semen, but the acts that Arnald enjoyed with his young partners seem to have been interfemoral intercourse—that is, insertion of the penis between the legs—and perhaps mutual masturbation. The depositions nowhere state that they engaged in anal intercourse, which Arnald himself at one point calls a mortal sin. But it may have been out of fear of confessing to the serious crime of true sodomy that both Arnald and his partners admitted the lesser offenses.

At Arnald's trial in June 1323, the court heard the testimony of Guillaume Roux, Guillaume Bernard, Guillaume Boyer, and Guillaume Pech, all of whom testified to having engaged in sodomy with Arnald on several occasions. Each claimed that Arnald lured him into a sexual encounter by promising some favor. To Roux, Arnald promised to arrange a position with a canon of the church of St. Saturnin in Toulouse; only later did Roux learn that he would probably have to commit sodomy with the lascivious canon. Roux claimed that Arnald then suggested that Roux accompany him to his rooms, where he would show him a book wherein it was written that "if a man plays with another, and because of the warmth of their bodies semen flows, . . . it is not as grave a sin as if a man carnally knows a woman. Because, so he said, nature demands this and a man is made healthier as a result."[58] Roux then claimed that Arnald threw him down on the ground and placed his penis between Roux's buttocks—not, note, into the anus—and that the semen flowed "between his legs." When he had finished, Arnald made Roux swear to tell no one and assured him that he could bring him to a Franciscan who would absolve him. A week later, Roux encountered Arnald again, and following him to a field was raped once more, this time at knifepoint. A week after that Roux again accompanied Arnald to his rooms and was raped a third time. He confessed to the lord bishop that he had engaged in sodomy with Arnald on several other occasions. Similar confessions were elicited from the other Guillaumes, some asserting that Arnald offered them gifts or a position with the canon of Toulouse, others that he offered to hear confession, but all agreeing that Arnald denied the gravity of the act.

The court also heard the testimony of a soon-to-be-defrocked friar, Pierre Recort, with whom Arnald was imprisoned in Allemans. To the friar Arnald had confessed—or boasted—that he had been in the habit of having sex with three of the boys at once, two engaging in sodomy while Arnald and the third watched. Arnald explained to Recort that these experiences marked only his most recent sodomitical adventures. He had actually begun practicing sodomy before he became a cleric. After a disastrous experience with a female prostitute, he developed a loathsome skin disease; believing women to be the source of his malady, and fearing to be thought a leper, Arnald determined to have sex only with boys. He regaled the friar with a number of homosexual exploits, telling him how he met and had sex with a boy from Toulouse, and how when he himself was a student at Toulouse he had several sexual encounters with a boy who had come to him for religious instruction. Arnald also told the friar that he kept company with a young man named Raymund, with whom he traveled to Tarascon, where he convinced two church attendants to allow him to celebrate mass secretly in the church.

Arnald's confession also provides his own, sometimes quite different version of the events described by the other witnesses, as well as a detailed account of his own sexual history. Rather than pointing to women and disease as the reason for his activities, Arnald declared that "he believed that his nature inclined him to commit sodomy." Seduced as a youth of ten by a schoolmate, one Arnald Auriol, and then by his schoolmaster, one Master Poncius, Arnald amassed extensive homosexual experience. In addition to the encounters with the Guillaumes, he disclosed adventures with myriad youths whom he apparently met in the streets of Toulouse and Pamiers. On one occasion he was followed into a garden by an eighteen-year-old who volunteered to tell him "how he satisfied his lust when he had no woman." The two embraced but nothing happened, so the youth told Arnald that he would "teach him another method, that is, . . . he would place his penis between Arnald's legs in order to commit sodomy. . . . The youth told him that many good men did this, and Arnald replied that it was so, as he heard said, even the religious"—that is, priests and monks—did it.[59] Arnald's complicated sexual life suggests the truth of what he had observed to Recort: "The bishop would have enough on his hands if he were to apprehend everyone in Pamiers who had been infected with that crime [of sodomy] because there were more than three thousand persons."[60]

A year after his confession, Arnald was again brought before the court. As the trial record reports:

> On 1 August 1324, Arnald of Verniolle, taken from the prison in the tower of Les Allemans, and brought before the lord bishop . . . swore again to tell the whole truth and nothing but the truth concerning heresy and sodomy, about himself and all persons living and dead; when this oath was completed, he was asked if what he had confessed to the bishop on 23 June 1323 was full and complete and true. Arnald replied that everything in his confession was true and complete. . . . Asked if he wanted to add or subtract anything in his confession, concerning himself or others living or dead, he replied in the negative.

Asked if he told anyone or believed that because his nature required him to satisfy his lust either with a man or a woman it was not "sinful to have relations with men or women, or that these may be minor or venial sins, he replied that he believed that his nature inclined him to commit sodomy, though he always believed that sodomy is a mortal sin."

Fatally, he continued by saying that he believed sodomy was "as sinful as simple fornication and that illicit deflowering of a virgin and incest may be graver sins, and is, in any case the same as men carnally knowing other men." Unfortunately for Arnald, the Church did not concur.

Arnald was then questioned again about celebrating the mass and hearing confessions and admitted to doing so.

> Asked if he were penitent for having believed and uttered the above errors and for the fact that he taught them, initiating others into error, and if he wanted to turn back from those errors, he replied in the affirmative and he said that he was prepared to undergo that penance which the lord bishop would impose on him for the aforesaid.

Arnald was then informed that if he "made full confession and was penitent," the bishop would "absolve him in accordance with the rules of the church from the sentences which he had incurred for the crimes of heresy and sodomy." But apparently his confession was not deemed full enough or his penitence sincere: for heresy he was deposed from the diaconate, and for sodomy the bishop promised a more rigorous sentence.

> You, Arnald of Verniolle, have fallen into the horrible and damnable crime of sodomy, as is noted above in your full confession, and because of which you are to be gravely and harshly punished. . . . You should therefore be degraded and placed in iron chains in the strictest prison, to be fed a diet of bread and water for life . . . so that no one may grant you grace in future, neither the bishops nor inquisitors who succeed us.[61]

The sodomites who appear in the satires, legal decrees, and penitential recommendations of the period are mythical monsters, creations meant to frighten and to warn. But Arnald was a real sodomite, who found his desire for sex with young men more compelling than the sanctity of his vows and his fear of sin. That sex was the primary subject of this heresy trial may suggest how intense was the medieval fascination with the subject. Arnald seems to have been as profligate in speaking about sex as he was in the commission of it, and the extent of his testimony suggests that the subject was of considerable interest to the bishop as well. Arnald's insistence that his sodomy was prompted by nature, not by choice, may not mean that he was in some sense resisting his accusers, and it would be wrong to imagine him as a medieval activist. But he surely was a medieval sodomite, and not simply a man guilty of sodomy.

The record of this trial illustrates the intimate connection that the Church was busy weaving between sodomy and heresy. According to witnesses, Arnald insisted that "sodomy and fornication were equal sins." The crux of the trial can be located in a question that, though unrecorded in the text, the bishop nevertheless must have asked, for Arnald answered it: "Did either Guillaume Roux or Guillaume Bernard ask you if the sin of sodomy was a sin of heresy?" Arnald said he told them that "said sin was not a sin of heresy but rather equal to carnal knowledge of women or prostitutes." Unfortunately for Arnald, this opinion *was* heresy. It established what the lord bishop intended to prove: that Arnald was both sodomite and heretic, and that sodomy and heresy were the same.

6 Is It a Sin to Love?

The eleventh and twelfth centuries were perhaps the most brilliant period of the Middle Ages.[62] As nation-states established themselves, urban culture began to revive throughout Europe; in the cities, great universities, like that at Paris, were revivified or established. In both the churches and the universities, rediscovered classical texts were often at the center of discourse. Many of these addressed the subject of love. The proper conduct of romantic love between men and women, between husband and wife, and between lovers became a central theme of theory and debate, of art, music, and poetry. This theorization of what has come to be called courtly love has led some to suggest that "love" itself was in the process of being reinvented. It can also be argued that homoerotic love was reevaluated as well.[63]

A body of writing from the eleventh and twelfth centuries does suggest that homosexual relations were approved and actively advocated by some, though it is not so clear that these writings can substantiate the presence of an organized "homosexual" subculture that existed to support its own members and to resist the antihomosexual position of state and Church.[64] What is evident is that the visibility of homosexual acts and those who engaged in them seems to have dramatically increased. Side by side with the body of homoerotic literature is a large body of antihomosexual satire, which suggests that because homosexuality was more visible it was also more despised.

Language that approved love between males and between women can be found in poems, letters, and even doctrinal treatises. Some writers openly defended homosexual desire, producing texts such as the late-twelfth-century "Ganymede and Hebe," which asked whether the love of boys or of women was more pleasurable; similar debates, like "Ganymede and Helen," condemned homosexual desire.

Writing about love between men was, of course, privileged by the male-dominated culture, and so there is only a small literature reflecting love between women. If male writers considered lesbian sex at all, they usually dealt with it by recourse to the misogynistic cliché that women were sexually rapacious, more lustful and even more debauched than men.[65] One crude poem, certainly written by a man, attacks a woman who is "a strange mixture of the female gender / Whom driving lust makes male." The author argues that when she submits as women ought—"when you have given that part by which you are judged a woman"—then "you will be a girl."[66] Two anonymous letters from a German manuscript of the twelfth or thirteenth century, however, were apparently written by a woman. One, written to the mysterious C——, who is "sweeter than honey and the honeycomb," describes C—— as a "unique and special one." The author "sighs for you at every hour" and does not want "to hear or see anyone else but you." I look around, she says, "and do not find my lover." Another, to G——, wonders how the writer can "endure your absence" when she remembers "the kisses you gave me" and the way "you refreshed my little breasts with sweet words."[67]

Poems of obvious male homoerotic content are typified by one anonymous work, perhaps from the thirteenth century, which describes a complicated triangle that ended happily:

A maiden loved Graecinus and Graecinus loved a boy,
But the boy was taken only with the maiden.
Graecinus handed her over to the boy, and the boy gave himself to
   Graecinus,
So both man and boy enjoyed the fruits of their prayers.[68]

Godfrey of Winchester, who was prior of St. Swithin's around 1082, seemed certain about his opinion concerning sex between males:

Whoever looks at you, Grosphus, sees two men in one:
*   From behind, he sees a boy; from the front, a man.*
If you play, you're a boy; give your rear, and it's all right,
*   But you're holding up the game, turn around and you'll be free.*

Some writers were clerics of tremendous influence, like Anselm (1033 or 1034–1109), Archbishop of Canterbury, whose letters to friends and students glorified friendship between men as one of the pillars of monastic life. To Gondulph, another monk, Anselm wrote: "Thy spirit and mine can never bear to be absent from each other, but unceasingly are intertwined. . . . What is thy love for me but the image of mine for thee?" In another he laments that because his friend Gilbert has apparently found another friend, there is "nothing left to me but heartbreak."

Aeldred of Rievaulx's discussions of Christianity and friendship posited "a concept of Christian friendship which, in its emphasis on human affection, surpassed any earlier theological statements and explicitly expressed in prose" the "implicit correlation" between human and spiritual love.[69] Aeldred gave love and friendship between persons of the same sex an essential and indeed central role in a Christian life. In *On Spiritual Friendship,* he argued that "God is friendship"; to justify his idealization of love between men, he invoked the example of Jesus with John, the Beloved Disciple. It may have been that Aeldred knew homosexual desire and the physical expression of it: he reports that as a youth he had experienced "a cloud of desire . . . from the lower drives of the flesh and gushing spring of adolescence," and "the sweetness of love and the impurity of lust combined to take advantage of the inexperience of my youth." In later years Aeldred apparently loved at least two monks; one of them, Simon, is described in *The Mirror of Charity:* "The rules of our order forbade us to speak, but his face spoke to me, his bearing spoke to me, his silence spoke to me." When Simon died, Aeldred rebuked those who felt that his grief was too carnal: "Let them think what they wish . . . others see what is done outwardly; they cannot perceive what I suffer inwardly." After Simon's death, Aeldred became attached to another young man, of whom he said: "We had but one mind and one soul. . . . I deemed my heart in a fashion his, and his mine, and he felt in a like manner toward me."[70]

Two other clerics, Marbod (c. 1035–1123), later Bishop of Rennes, and his pupil Baudri of Bourgueil (1046–1130), who would become Archbishop of Dol in Brittany, in unmistakably passionate terms praise friendship between men and describe ideal masculine beauty. Both seem to have thought that the love of women and the love of boys were equally interesting, or frustrating. Marbod, for example, complains that "those dearer to me than my eye, either he or she, / Scarcely want to talk as long as they are loved." He sadly concludes that the "embraces of both sexes displease me now."[71] Marbod wrote poetry to both women and men. He praises the beauty of girls and boys equally, but in one poem lets the reader know that it is the girl's suitor he loves—"that spectacular youth whose beauty is my fire"—not the girl herself.[72] In another poem he confesses his debt to classical texts: "Horace wrote an ode about a certain boy / Who could easily have been a pretty girl. . . . His brow was white as snow . . . his eyes black as pitch . . . his lips blazing. . . . Anyone wondering about the body which lay hidden under his clothes / Would be gratified, for the boy's body matched his face."

Baudri wrote over two hundred poems, most addressed to men, fifteen addressed to women. In one poem he describes the beauty of one who took his eye and recalls or imagines how "your bright clear eyes touch my breast and heart . . . the touch of hands plays over your snowy body."[73] His poetry is sometimes more erotic than Marbod's, and often very personal. A young man named John, the subject of a number of his poems, arouses Baudri's anxiety: "I wonder and cannot stop wondering / Why my friend, that John, has not returned quickly / Since he pledged me over and over that he would return. / Either the boy is sick or, out of his mind, has been stolen, / He is really out of his mind if he has forgotten me."[74] Elsewhere he confesses that "I wrote of certain things which treat of love / And both sexes are pleased with my songs."

All that is known about an Englishman named Hilary is that he studied for a time with Abelard at an abbey near Paris, and that he wrote a number of poems passionately praising handsome young men. His images are conventional—the white brow, the golden hair—and he makes the stock complaints that had been familiar in classical poetry and were again becoming so: a boy is cruel, indifferent, not chaste enough, too chaste. Hilary's love poems to an English boy bring to medieval poetry a new kind of direct homoeroticism: his love is a sickness that only the boy can cure, no other mortal is as beautiful, the boy's power over him is like that of the hunter over the hunted, the whims of the boy hold him in thrall.

In medieval homoerotic poetry, the commonest image of youthful beauty was Ganymede. In the early Christian period some writers had allegorized Greek myths to conform them to Christian doctrine; in both the visual arts and literature, Ganymede became a symbol for the soul's ascent into heaven. But Ganymede as the ideal of a beautiful youth beloved by an older man was ultimately a more powerful reading. By the later Middle Ages his name was invoked not only in texts sympathetic to male-male love but in those that attacked it: an eleventh-century bishop, for instance, was excoriated as *"ganimedior est Ganimede"*—"ganymedier than Ganymede." A poem attributed to Hildebert of Lavardin describes Jove's passion: "Eyes, neck, cheeks, waves of blond hair— / These were the features of Ganymede that lit a blazing fire in Jove. / Wanting to allow himself a few liberties with this lad, / The god decreed all things shall be permitted with boys."[75] Ganymede is the subject of or appears as an allusion in a remarkably large number of poems written to boys by men in praise of homosexual desire: "Believe me, if the golden age should come again / Jove's cupbearer would thou be: / Not Ganymede but thee / Caught up by Heaven: / By day to give sweet drink, / by night sweet kisses and delight."[76] By the beginning of the thirteenth century, Ganymede—the androgynous and somewhat wanton boy—had become the symbol of homosexual love and "a ganymede" had come to mean a male used by other males for sex.

Though boys are the subject of many homoerotic poems of the twelfth century, adult same-sex love often appeared in epics and heroic romances, just as it had in the subtexts of saints' lives. Tales such as the *Song of Roland,* the medieval Latin *Lantfrid and Cobbo,* the Old French *Amis and Amile*—one of the most famous and constantly rewritten legends of the period—and the Old French *Lancelot Grail,* in which Lancelot and his friend Galehut share knightly quests and manly devotion, and reveal the world of men at war to be one also of passion and desire. Amis and Amile, eternally devoted, live together and even reject wives and sacrifice children for each other. They die together and are interred together. Lancelot and Galehut, from the moment of their meeting in battle, are bound together not only by loyalty but by an outspoken and specifically described passion, that of Galehut for Lancelot. The tale describes their adventures together and the gradual growth of a reciprocal passion for Galehut in Lancelot's heart. Lancelot is the center of Galehut's life, and although Lancelot loves Guinivere, as the legend binds him to do, there can be no doubt that even she and King Arthur must recognize and honor the knights' intimacy.

The conventions of literary expression in the High Middle Ages were well suited to an exaggerated profession of feeling between friends as well as between lovers. The poetic conventions evident in courtly love poetry demanded such eroticized address, and in poetry and letters, in the language of hymns and in devotional literature, such highly charged language often blurs the division between friends and lovers. Many writers believed that love, whether for a man or a woman, was the greatest of all the gospels. And it is hard to believe that Baudri, writing to a man, did not have some sense of the difference of his desire when he said, "God made our natures full of love. . . . What we are is a crime, if it is a crime to love, / For the God who made me live made me love."[77]

7 The Plague of Sodomy

The homoerotic literature that had flowered in the eleventh and twelfth centuries virtually disappeared after the middle of the thirteenth. Intolerance of sexual deviation was mirrored in literary texts as writers limned new and horrific pictures of the sodomite. Some writers exhibited confusion and ambivalence, praising male love in one poem, damning sodomy in another. Marbod notes in one poem that nothing is "as valuable as a boy who plays fairly with his lover," while in another he mounts a vehement attack on homosexual acts, arguing, orthodoxly, that sodomy is more serious than any other sin and detailing the punishment that awaits it.[78] Though there are "a hundred thousand sins invented by the Devil," for which the sinner will be "roasted by a perennial flame," he writes, those whose sin involves "guilty hips and an accomplice cock never grow cool."

> And although the vengeance of Hell is hard on everyone,
> There are, nonetheless, degrees of punishment.
> As sins are weighed, so are they punished:
> Greater pain for greater sins, and lesser for lesser.
> Therefore copulation performed by members of the same sex,
> A crime less serious than none, is punished above all others.[79]

Equally indignant and perhaps equally conflicted, Hildebert of Lavardin also wrote poems that expressed fascination with the beauty of young men, though in others he delivered the familiar objections to homosexual acts (as might be expected of a man who in 1125 became Archbishop of Tours). Hildebert notes in one poem that "when Jupiter seeks a boy and Iphis seeks Ianthe, / The council of heaven says 'It is a crime.'" Hildebert disagrees: "I say this is a mistake," for "neither of the men was made into a woman. / If it were really a crime, the sentence of the gods would have transformed one of the men."[80] Yet it is also Hildebert who attacks the "plague of Sodom" and finds "countless Ganymedes" usurping the rightful place of wifely Juno at the family hearth.

> *People sleep together in any combination, with no rules.*
> *Venus can scarcely set her weapons in motion to increase the race.*
> *More common than any other lewdness is the plague of sodomy.*
> *Men pay what they owe their spouses to other men.*
> *Countless Ganymedes tend countless hearths,*
> *And Juno grieves to have lost the duty she used to claim.*
> *Both boys and men, pimps and old men defile themselves*
> *With this vice and no class escapes it.*
> *All of you who turn nature's honor to this practice*
> *And neglect legitimate love for the forbidden,*
> *Shouldn't you remember the lesson of Sodom's example—*
> *To beware this sin and shun it lest you perish in brimstone?*
> *You Who rule all things, through*
> *Whom law's power stands firm,*
> *May the hearth of a man pleased by this game become his Hell,*
> *Or, sparing him, but avoiding what displeases You,*
> *Fill these hearts, emptied of their own concerns, with Yours,*
> *And, with things turned around, let the flesh, which now dominates*
> *The power of mind, become the master of itself!*[81]

This complaint, as old as Juvenal, adds what Juvenal would not have imagined, the Christian hope and conviction that sodomites will perish in flames. Hildebert also emphasizes the danger sodomites pose to the institution of marriage. The ancient situation of Juno, rejected by Zeus for Ganymede and representing all dutiful wives, reflects the tragedy that has befallen all women deprived of their husband's support, solace, and sex. The "countless Ganymedes" tending countless hearths suggest not only a large homosexual population but also homosexual unions and households. These profane couplings, Hildebert argues, can only lead to a kind of hell as the temptation of the flesh triumphs over the power of the mind, leading the sinner to reject rationality as well as God.

. . .

Marbod and Hildebert expressed some doubts—if not about the truth of received antihomosexual doctrine, then at least about how that doctrine might apply to friendship and its often tempting pleasures. Not so Bernard of Morlaix, a twelfth-century friar at the Benedictine abbey of Cluny who was apparently untroubled by temptation—unless his vitriolic diatribe conceals what modernity describes as latent homosexual desire. In *De contemptu mundi* (c. 1140) Bernard enumerates sodomitical horrors, repeating imagery used by Marbod and Hildebert and common by now to expressions of medieval homophobia:

> *Alas! wickedly public are the fire and heat of sodomites.*
> *No one suppresses this sin or hides it or sighs that he is sinful.*
> *Close your eyes to this beastly sin, all of you here;*
> *Unholy rage rises where someone is aware of it or witnesses it.*
> *Unnaturally, outrageously, he becomes she.*
> *Juno and even Petronilla are abandoned.*
> *Bemoan the world and everything in it, which are full of sin;*
> *Men forget what is manly; O madness! O terror! how like hyenas!*
> *Look how many are buried beneath this unnatural filth.*
> *What category, what name does this abomination have?*
> *The horror of this sin, alas! resounds even to the stars.*
> *Act and outcry are naked; groan, O chastened mind!*
> *Men become each other's helpers, this one with that one.*
> *Your law, your voice, your providence, Christ, are half-dead.*
> *Sodom's law spreads openly; countless Ganymedes arise, alas!*
> *As long as he shows signs of the sin, this beast tends any hearth he*
>   *pleases.*
> *The choicest seats and all the bedrooms belong to Ganymede.*
> *Juno has been deserted, and billy goats,—O madness!—replace the*
>   *female.*
> *You demand to know the number of this flock. I'll quickly announce it,*
> *Broadcast it, proclaim it at once like a tragic actor:*
> *They're as plentiful as barley in a field, oysters at sea, sand on a shore,*
> *Islands in the Adriatic, incense in India, or reeds along the Tiber.*
> *Castles, outskirts of towns, and even our churches are overrun*
> *By this filthy plague. O for shame! horrors overflow.*
> *The lazy world dies; it desires the horrid and does even worse.*
> *It feasts itself on sulfur; it looks like old Gomorrah.*

O ultimate madness! There are now far too many hermaphrodites.
Husbands recite meaningless marriage vows.
Moderation is in mourning as unnatural sins persist;
This leprosy clings to the lesser and the worse. The law of nature
Is perishing, acknowledged customs ruined by this plague.[82]

Literary homophobia received its fullest expression in an anonymous twelfth-century poem that debates the question whether the desire represented by Ganymede or by Helen is superior. Familiar in form from late classical times, employing classical imagery, and enlisting the Olympian gods as characters, this debate is infused with Christian moral ideology. In classical debates, the advocate of homosexual desire, while always aware of sex, stressed the traditional exalted view of such relations; the medieval version focuses unabashedly on sex and seems to assume that the desire of Ganymede and the desire of Helen are mutually exclusive—establishing what might be called in modern terms two opposing versions of sexual orientation. Classical debates were willing to allow that all men could enjoy homosexual sex at one time or another without sacrificing desire for women. The medieval "Debate Between Ganymede and Helen" argues, however, that men who love men despise women and are as a result unnatural, impure, and heretical.

Like so many battles, the debate begins with thwarted desire. The Phrygian boy and the Spartan maid are arguing about which is the more beautiful. Ganymede "compares himself to a female" but Helen, ignoring this clue, tries to seduce him. Ganymede, "not knowing the role expected of him / presses himself against her as if he wishes to be passive." Helen is outraged and curses both Ganymede and nature "that a monster should be given so fair a face." Beneath Ganymede's beauty, the sodomitical monster dangerously lurks. Ganymede's narcissistic attention to his own looks plays upon a cliché perhaps as familiar then as now: the beauty of the homosexual male imperfectly hides a narcissist, indifferent to women and devoid of "natural" heterosexual instincts, who unfeelingly and stunningly rejects the legendary Helen, the preeminent example of irresistible female beauty.

Helen's anger leads to a declaration of war and a battle—not only of the sexes but, as it were, of sexual orientations—in which she praises the sexual pleasures of women and Ganymede those of males. Having determined to appoint Nature and Reason to decide the argument, they make their way to the "house of Nature," Jove's palace. The sympathies of the poet now become clear. Nature, the symbol of creation and generation, works together with Reason to "mingle the unequal sexes, and from this mingling / Springs a brood of diverse species." Nothing less than the union of male Reason and female Nature supports the central role of procreation.

The gods gather in the palace of Jupiter, where, in accord with the various directions of divine sexual desire, "Helen attracts some, and Ganymede others." Ganymede is the picture of arrogant and provocative sexuality: "He seems to disdain everything with his eyes, / Arrogantly refusing to cover his face or his manhood. . . . His mouth, as if it were asking, invites a kiss; / His whole face smiles, seducing the seducer." Helen modestly enters, blushing becomingly, head bowed, and in contrast to Ganymede, virginal: she is "still ignorant of men." The beauty of the pair is so inspiring that "the gods everywhere are restless": "Apollo grows hot"—apparently at the sight of Ganymede— and "Mars plays wantonly, / Venus is yelping as if in someone's arms"; Jupiter "without any shame, summons Ganymede." As Ganymede sits next to Jupiter, it is Nature's turn to be outraged. She pointedly prepares a seat for Helen, but denies Ganymede any part in her domain, declaring him to be "neither son nor heir."

The gods wait in breathless silence as the two, now bitter antagonists, arise. Helen begins the debate by saying that she pities Ganymede: "You openly despise having sex with a woman" and thus "through you, the order of things is overturned and laws perish." His desire is emotionally incomplete since "no love of a boy ever truly touches the heart," and inauthentic because there is no procreation: "When one bed unites a man and a woman / This is a bond that's productive, that follows the right order." It is also unnatural for a male to be, like Ganymede, more beautiful than the female; when the creator made men and women, "he made sure to make the female more lovely than the male, / So that he would lure a man to a bond with woman, / And never would a man love a man more than her." However, Helen asserts, even though it is unnatural, inadequate, and sterile, homosexual desire is irresistible. So powerful is the attraction that Venus "lets men join in sterile union," and boys like Ganymede sell themselves for money. She attacks Ganymede as a prostitute and a particularly vicious representative of what she defines as a type and a sexual class, asserting that Ganymede and his kind are either frenzied and obsessed sexual deviants or greedy sexual merchants. Helen argues that those who engage in homosexual acts, if passive like Ganymede, are sexually inverted; if active, the agents of pollution. Indeed, Ganymede is no man at all, since Nature has turned him "into a girl," while men who "lie on top of other men, / monstrously un-man other men, and shamefully pollute yourselves and boys." When "one man submits to another" and pretends to be a woman, both are "harmfully unjust to women." Homosexual activity, in short, harms everyone: it demasculinizes the passive male and transforms the active male into a vicious sinner; it declares war on that symbol of virtue and of the natural order, the woman as wife and mother.

Ganymede answers each of Helen's objections. Sex between men is justified, he asserts, because it is a game invented by the gods and is still being played by the "highest people." "Honorable men approve of this act, / For men who have ruled the world and held highest offices . . . don't shun the silky crotches of boys." In answer to Helen's assertion that animals do not engage in homosexuality, Ganymede responds that man should not imitate the animals, because "man has been given reason," which convinces him not to "stain himself with women."[83] Ganymede insists that it is not opposites but "like with like" that attracts. Women cannot be loved, because they are naturally immoral, always unfaithful, and promiscuous. When Helen asserts that Ganymede has declared war on Nature and on women, he agrees: "I reject women because I hate them, / For what's the difference between a woman and a she-ass?" Helen is revolted by this insult, but Ganymede overrides her objections and insists that they should put "religion and shame" behind them. By this rejection he becomes the very image of the godless and promiscuous sodomite.

All of Ganymede's bravado crumbles as Helen makes her last and most telling point: when a man "squander[s] Venus' liquid between male thighs . . . the loss of a man is there." Wasting semen is tantamount to murder. Ganymede is struck dumb. So convincing is Helen's argument that Apollo and Jupiter themselves vow to change their promiscuous ways, while Ganymede repents and asks for Helen's hand in marriage. Accompanied by a chorus of virgin voices, Reason celebrates with Nature as the "age-old heresy is put to flight." The poem concludes with the poet's exhortation, "Let everyone guilty of this sin be converted."[84]

Drawing upon the familiar tradition by which the name "Ganymede" was synonymous with an effeminate male homosexual, both Hildebert and Bernard had spoken generically and contemptuously of "countless Ganymedes." In the "Debate," too, Ganymede becomes "a Ganymede," negatively reshaping the classical legend. Though Ganymede, speaking in support of homosexual practice, initially employs antiquity's defense of homosexuality—that it is engaged in by great, learned, and brave men—he does not insist on the nobility of love between men, but rather argues that sex between them is acceptable and defends what had always been indefensible, male prostitution. He quickly abandons all reasoned debate to launch a vulgar diatribe against women, revealing a hatred of them as hysterical as that of some Christians for sodomites. Rather than the attractive figure of classical myth whose masculine and youthful beauty bewitched Zeus, this Ganymede is petulant, arrogant, promiscuous, and vicious. His shallow self-regard is exceeded only by the venom of his discourse, so at odds with his spectacular if effeminate beauty. "Ganymede and Helen" employs classical elements for a thoroughly homophobic end.

Perhaps the most disturbing picture of a sodomite is that drawn by Geoffrey Chaucer (c. 1342–1400) in the General Prologue to the *Canterbury Tales*. His Summoner and Pardoner are a repellent ecclesiastical pair whose presence constitutes a specific condemnation of a sexually dissolute and corrupt clergy and of sodomites as diseased and abominable outcasts. The Summoner's face is hideously scarred by disease, which he has vainly treated with mercury, sulfur, borax, and everything else in the medieval pharmacopoeia:

> *A Somonour was ther with us in that place,*
> *That hadde a fyr-reed cherubynnes face,*
> *For saucefleem he was, with eyen narwe.*
> *As hoot he was and lecherous as a sparwe,*
> *With scalled browes blake and piled berd.*
> *Of his visage children were aferd.*
> *Ther nas quyk-silver, lytarge, ne brymstoon,*
> *Boras, ceruce, ne oille of tartre noon;*
> *Ne oynement that wolde clense and byte,*
> *That hym myghte helpen of his whelkes white,*
> *Nor of the knobbes sittynge on his chekes.*

We have seen that Arnald of Verniolle feared that the people seeing him might think he had leprosy, a disease long associated with sexual excess. Chaucer's audience would certainly have recognized the Summoner as a victim of a hideous disease, a sexual one. Whether it is leprosy or syphilis—or, as has recently been suggested, scabies—is not clear; it was not until the sixteenth century that syphilis was recognized as a disease separate from leprosy.[85] But leprosy was long believed to be a punishment for sexual promiscuity, and its physical ravages were a symbol of spiritual and moral corruption: the Council of Ancyra had early on declared sodomy a leprous—that is, abominable—sin.[86] Whatever his malady, the Summoner's hideous countenance reveals the sinner within and hints at the nature of the sin.

It is the duty of the Summoner to bring sinners into ecclesiastical courts for sins such as the ones he himself has evidently committed. Furthermore, he is addicted to drink and in exchange for a bribe of money or wine will ignore the promiscuity of other men:

> *He wolde suffre for a quart of wyn*
> *A good felawe to have his concubyn*
> *A twelf month, and excuse hym atte fulle.*

Chaucer also says of the Summoner that "ful prively a fynch eek koude he pulle." That is, he could engage in surreptitious promiscuity—pulle a fynch—though with which sex Chaucer does not say. And if the Summoner "foond owher a good felawe, / He wolde techen him to have noon awe / In swich caas of the ercedekenes curs." Like Arnald of Verniolle, he would assure a similarly lecherous sinner that he need not fear the censure of the archdeacon, whose court dealt with sexual sins. Just as Arnald preyed upon the young men of his parish, so the Summoner "in daunger hadde he at his owene gise / The yonge girles of the diocise / And knew hir conseil, and was al hir reed." The "yonge girles"—in Middle English "girles" can signify both male and female—are, Chaucer implies, in the Summoner's power, "in daunger." Since he knows their "conseil"—their secrets—he is able to exercise influence over them. While it is clear that the Summoner's primary interest is in money, there is a sexual overtone here of a particularly unpleasant kind, especially since he is described as "hoot and lecherous." What sexual sins others might commit, or he himself engages in, are of little moral concern to him, as are his evident attempts at sexual intimidation. The Summoner is the agent of the archdeacon, into whose presence he hales those who have committed any sin. As such, he ought to be incorruptible. Instead he is corrupt both in spirit and in flesh, a loathsome exemplar of the consequences of sexual and fleshly excess and an equally vicious representative, Chaucer intends us to see, of a corrupt Church and clergy.

The Summoner's traveling companion is the Pardoner, whose ecclesiastical job it is to sell indulgences, written pardons for sins past or future. Chaucer declares them to be friends but he also implies an unnatural intimacy between them, for as they ride they sing a popular love song:

> *With hym ther rood a gentil Pardoner*
> *Of Rouncivale, his freend and his compeer,*
> *That streight was comen from the court of Rome.*
> *Ful loude he soong "Com hider, love, to me!"*
> *This Somonour bar to hym a stif burdoun;*
> *Was nevere trompe of half so greet a soun.*

It is curious that an ecclesiastic should sing a love song, besides which the Pardoner's voice is "as smal as . . . a goot," that is, weak and falsetto. As for the Summoner's "stif bourdon"—a strong bass accompaniment—there's not much doubt what Chaucer intends us to see: to the Pardoner's seductive song the Summoner responds with a masculine and stiffly phallic bass.[87]

Unsuitably concerned about his appearance for a cleric, the Pardoner wears his hair long and artfully arranged over his shoulders.

> *This Pardoner hadde heer as yelow as wex*
> *But smothe it heeng as dooth a strike of flex*
> *By ounces henge his lokkes that he hadde*
> *And therwith he his shuldres overspradde,*
> *But thynne it lay, by colpons oon and oon.*
> *But hood, for jolitee, wered he noon,*
> *For it was trussed up in his walet*
> *Hym thoughte he rood al of the newe jet*
> *Dischevelee, save his cappe, he rood al bare.*

Diatribes about the effeminate implications of long hair form an extensive subset of homophobic literature, as familiar in the writings of pagans and early Christians as in Chaucer's time. In the writing of Philo Judaeus in the second century, as in those of Ordericus Vitalis in the early twelfth, long hair was associated with effeminacy and sexual deviance, and medieval science had it that yellow hair especially suggested thin and inadequate blood, lack of virility, and weakness and effeminacy of mind and spirit. The Pardoner, whose demeanor ought to reflect his holy mission, carries himself like a court dandy. A hood is part of normal clerical costume, but he rides hoodless and disheveled "for jolitee," for fun, and because he imagines it to be "of the newe jet," in the latest fashion. His dandified and effeminate appearance were, to the medieval audience, the familiar outward signs of the inward perversion.

But most telling in Chaucer's portrait is the association he makes between the Pardoner and various animals with dubious sexual connotations:

> *Swiche glarynge eyen hadde he as an hare.*
> *A voys he hadde as smal as hath a goot*
> *No berd hadde he, ne nevere sholde have—*
> *As smothe it was as it were late shave.*
> *I trowe he were a geldying or a mare.*

He has the eyes of a hare, long a symbol of sexual irregularity and effeminacy in medieval zoology. Alexander of Neckham, an encyclopedist writing in the early thirteenth century, opined that "the hare of the nobler [male] sex bears the little hares in the womb. Can it be that a bizarre nature has made him a hermaphrodite? Effeminate men who violate the law of nature are thus said to imitate the hare."[88] The Pardoner has the voice of a goat, the medieval emblem of lechery; hence even his voice resonates with indiscriminate sexual desire. The beardless Pardoner resembles not only beardless Ganymedes, but the *cinaedi* described in Greek and Roman satire, who plucked out their hair in order to counterfeit youth and attract men. Chaucer categorically states that the Pardoner will never have a beard, and thus hints that he is that other sexual anomaly as well, the hermaphrodite. Yet, almost as a second thought, Chaucer opines that the Pardoner must be a gelding—a eunuch—or perhaps a mare, a female of whatever species he may be. Indeed to the knowing medieval audience, the term "mare" may have denoted one who engaged in homosexual activities.[89]

The profligate Summoner and the effeminate Pardoner form a pair of corrupt sodomites. The Summoner can be seen as a sodomite in the older sense: an indiscriminate sexual debauchee. The Pardoner is a more elaborated figure, in whom effeminacy and homosexuality join to create the monster who had, by Chaucer's time, become the dominant image of sexual deviancy.

8 The Burning Question

It is well to remember that much of what we know about medieval sodomy is derived from sources more suggestive than definitive: from the annals of civil laws that may not have been passed, or may not have been strictly enforced; from penances proposed but perhaps never imposed; from the deliberate exaggerations of literary satire. Such documents may be the archives of legal theory or public alarm rather than a mirror of daily life. What the Church, the state, or the satirist felt ought to done about sodomites suggests a ferocity perhaps not reflected in what was actually done. The persecutions of the Albigensians and the Templars and the trial of Arnald of Verniolle support the opinion that both Church and state actively suppressed sodomy and sought out sodomites for exquisite punishment, but do not prove it. Evidence is lacking that sodomites were especially persecuted in large numbers between the millennium and the middle of the thirteenth century; how many people were actually executed for heresy and sodomy is not known. The earliest legal record of a European execution for sodomy, as has been shown, dates from 1292, and Venice recorded seven deaths for sodomy between 1338 and 1358.[90] Save for the prosecution of the Templars, the reigns of Louis IX (1226–1270) and Philip IV (1285–1314) have left records of only a few executions solely for sodomy.[91] Before the end of the thirteenth century, in fact, there is little written evidence that executions specifically for sodomy did take place.

This may be explained in part by the relative newness of the capital laws. Another factor is that such crimes were deemed so horrible that no legal record of sentence and execution was kept. In France, for example, records of sodomy trials were sometimes burned with the guilty sodomite, since the sin was "so hideous that it should not be named."[92] Sentences commonly condemned a sodomite to be "burned alive together with the records of his trial."[93] Thus, the lack of evidence for executions is not a clear indication that they did not take place. Where an antisodomy law existed, the crime could be prosecuted and punished without leaving a record. If the passage of such laws means anything, it is that Church, state, and public were increasingly anxious about the prevalence of sodomy and increasingly intolerant of the sexually deviant creature by then defined as the sodomite. Contempt for the actor and the act, and fear that both would undermine the stability of society and call down the wrath of God upon cities and nations—a belief seemingly supported by recurrent plagues, earthquakes, and other natural disasters—produced an intolerant and anxious climate in the late Middle Ages.

While the anxiety spread, its focus narrowed: though sodomy had long been defined as any nonprocreative sexual act between human beings, by the end of the thirteenth century it was increasingly taken to mean sexual acts between persons of the same sex—especially the most forbidden act of all, anal intercourse between men, called by some commentators more terrible than homicide. Sodomy conjured a catalogue of horrendous images: excremental filth, pagan pederasty, passive effeminacy, and the indignity of male penetration—framed by the promise of eternal damnation for its practitioners and the threat of destruction for those even marginally touched by it.

These terrors were on display in the common adjectives attached to sodomy—"foul," "stinking," "abominable," "unnatural." What had once been a forgivable sin was now an unredeemable spiritual condition and an unchangeable condition of nature as well. There is little available evidence that sodomites had yet identified themselves as having a special sexual nature—Arnald of Verniolle not withstanding—but society had clearly begun to identify them in just that way, and often as *exclusive* practitioners of homosexual sex. "Sodomite" was an accusation leveled by class against class, by laity against clergy, by Christian against heretic, Muslim, and Jew. Charges of sodomy increasingly came to be employed against anyone whose politics, religion, or social status was deemed worthy of attack and even of extirpation.

The zeal for religious and moral reform in the thirteenth century intended to root out sin, but it also succeeded in creating sinners and made it possible to imagine that the sinner existed independent of what he did, and whether or not his sin was discovered, proved, or punished. In this climate, the authorities, rather than wait for sodomites to reveal themselves by their acts, felt it was urgent to find them, prosecute them, and punish them—whether they had actually committed the now-criminal sin, or were simply suspected of doing so.

Burning of the sodomite Richard Puller and his page, Zurich, 1482. Manuscript illustration from Diebold Schilling, Die Grosse Burgunder-Chronik, *c. 1483, Ms. A5, p. 994. Reprinted by permission of Zentralbibliothek, Zurich*

PART FOUR

Lighting Bonfires

Sodomy and Anxiety in the Renaissance

Chapter Nine

Reinventing Sodomy

During the early Middle Ages, the Church introduced a powerful new word—"sodomy"—to name any nonprocreative sexual act. By the end of the Middle Ages that definition, derived from Scripture, the writings of the Church fathers, and the records of early Church councils, was simplified; "sodomy" came especially to signify sexual relations between persons of the same sex. And since sodomy offended against God, nature, and the Church, many believed it to be a kind of heresy. What had once been a remediable sin was now unforgivable. The Church therefore defined and judged it, though leaving the secular state to carry out the punishment the Church demanded.

As heir to the sexual attitudes of antiquity and the Middle Ages, the Renaissance rewrote sodomy once again, and in the process invented a sodomite of its own. What the Middle Ages had seen as a sexual aberration that might be renounced, the Renaissance began to define as an irremediable vice. The secular Renaissance state demanded and took the right to judge and convict sodomites as well as to execute them, and brought sodomy fully out of the cloister and into the public square, construing the sodomite as not only a sinner but a criminal. Worse, he was a sexual deviant, different morally and sexually from his fellow human beings and present at every level of society; his various roles included the habitual debauchee, the effeminate, the corrupter of youth, the heretic, the traitor, the foreigner. The sodomite was an enemy of the state, the Church, and society, an individual whose very presence might call down upon the innocent disease and catastrophe. He might even, subversively, assume the guise of a friend.

Against such a complex menace, rigorous action was called for: new laws were passed, gruesome punishments mandated; rights were abrogated; trials were held and executions carried out; fear and suspicion were translated into repression and oppression. Reaction to sodomy real and imagined made the detestation of homosexual behavior and those who engaged in it more intense than ever. And yet, even as a new and rigorous structure of legal and social prohibition aimed at the control and punishment of sodomy appeared, homoerotic desire unexpectedly flourished. As Bruce Smith argues, "the one salient fact about homosexuality" in early modern Europe is "the disparity that separates the extreme punishments prescribed by law and the apparent tolerance, even positive valuation, of homoerotic desire in the visual arts, in literature and . . . in the political power structure."[1]

1 Sodomy and Friendship

During the Renaissance, two traditions influenced attitudes toward love and sex. The first was the vernacular literature of courtly love produced in the late Middle Ages, the second the equally fervent religious proclamations of the Church in support of celibacy and sexual abstinence. Courtly love theorized a highly romanticized sexual desire between men and women, almost always outside of wedlock. The Church, however, had long taught that human desire ought to be mediated by and directed toward God alone, thus radically subordinating sexual lust to spiritual love. In theory valuing chastity more than marriage, the Middle Ages also accepted the possibility of chaste affection between men or women in a celibate religious context, so long as that, too, was mediated by devotion to God and regulated by the careful supervision of superiors and by strict adherence to monastic rules.

However, this Christian tradition was challenged, in the Renaissance, by the rediscovery of classical writings, which prompted a cautious reexamination of male eros. Classical legends depicting love between men, classical theories that linked male love and friendship to the proper conduct of life and the true perception of the divine, and erotic texts that described sex between men—all influenced poets and scholars to reevaluate male friendship and love. Though few in the Renaissance would have doubted that sodomy was a sin, a heresy, and a crime, there was a perceptible shift: what had been a forbidden act was now seen as a possibly acceptable feeling; what had been unspeakable was increasingly spoken. While largely retaining old definitions of homosexual behavior, then, the Renaissance began to invent new ways to interpret it positively. Although treatment of sodomites themselves was ever more cruel and uncompromising, literary sodomy resurfaced, more pleasingly called "masculine love," *amor Socraticus,* or "special friendship," or concealed by euphemisms like "the art of Ganymede."

   In Renaissance literature the homoerotic model most often celebrated was the classically sanctioned relationship between an adult male and a youth. The figure of Ganymede emerged as the most visible image in writing and the arts, deployed to express homosexual desire. The most accessible source for the Ganymede story was Ovid's retelling in his *Metamorphoses* (10:151–61). But Virgil's version of the rape of Ganymede in the *Aeneid* (5:250–57) and Statius' in the *Thebiad* (1:548–51) also provided supporting models. Renaissance satirists and sodomites were no doubt pleased by Martial's epigrams, wherein Ganymede is specifically a symbol of sexual relationships between men. In one poem Martial had observed that neither Jove nor Ganymede will enjoy himself so much as will he and his friend after drinking wine and making love (2:26); in another (2:43) he complains more coarsely that his "own hand must do for me as a ganymede." From the fourteenth to the mid-sixteenth century, as James Saslow points out in *Ganymede in the Renaissance: Homosexuality in Art and Society,* "Ganymede was the single most appropriate, if not the exclusive, symbol for male-male love as it was then understood."[2] In his *Genealogy of the Pagan Gods,* Boccaccio retells the story with no attempt at Christianizing or concealment, while references to Ganymede in a homoerotic context are found in the writings of Castiglione and Aretino. In Poliziano's *Stanze per la giostra del Magnifico Giuliano de' Medici* (1475–78), an erotic Ganymede is carried into heaven by Jupiter and described as "so fair / all nude / his golden locks with cypress bound, / And with naught else but ivy girdled round." In Poliziano's *Favola d'Orfeo,* Orpheus renounces women and in Ganymede finds the ideal symbol for the male love he vows to pursue exclusively: "Great Jupiter bears witness to this creed, / Who, by the knot of sweet love held in thrall, / Enjoys in heaven his fair boy Ganymede." Orpheus allows this example to draw a moral: "I urge all husbands: seek divorce, and flee / Each one away from female company." Poliziano also invokes Ganymede as a symbol of homosexual behavior in his *Greek Epigrams,* when he declares that a certain youth is as dear to him as Ganymede was to Jupiter: "For truly I have kissed, and truly I kiss again your mouth, O delightful youth! . . . Intertwine your tongue with mine O youth!"[3]

Ganymede fills the same metaphoric role in English literature of the period. In Marlowe's *Edward II,* the relationship of Jove and Ganymede is called upon as both precedent and justification for that of Edward and Gaveston, while in *Hero and Leander* the poet allows Leander to be mistaken for Ganymede by Poseidon, who leaves no doubt as to the nature and intention of his desire. Rosalind, in Shakespeare's *As You Like It,* takes the name Ganymede when she masquerades as a man. The narrator of Richard Barnfield's *The Affectionate Shepherd,* the youth Daphnis, addresses his love poems to the boy he calls "sweet Ganymede" and asserts: "If it be a sinne to love a lovely lad, O than sinne I."

Tacit approval of homosexual desire sometimes became explicit approval of homosexual behavior, in the arts at least. In a story by the sixteenth-century monk-soldier-writer Matteo Banello, one character asserts that "to divert myself with boys is more natural to me than eating and drinking."[4] At the end of the Renaissance, the genially pornographic *L'Alcibiade fanciullo a scola* ("The Young Alcibiades at School") by Antonio Rocco, a seventeenth-century work set in a comfortably distant ancient Greece, offers exact descriptions of male-male sex as Philotimus, a pederastic pedagogue, welcomes his new pupil, young Alcibiades:

> Philotimus: "I shall fill the vessel of thy mind with the seed of doctrines plentiful and pleasant. . . . That eloquence thou wishest to learn from me . . . my devotion will impart to thee, but thou shalt not possess it truly until thy tongue be joined to mine. For the hand helpeth the hand, the mind assisteth the mind, the tongue aideth the tongue. Come here, come here, my ruby . . ." and folding him against his bosom, he punctuated each word he spake with a lingering kiss.

Alcibiades asks his teacher whether pleasure is keener with lads or with women, and why. Philotimus answers: "So vast is the cunt's capacity 'tis frightening. . . . Mark, on the contrary, that pretty declivity leading to the flowered garden of a boy. . . . Certain lads find such delight in being mounted that they become mad with desire, begging and praying and even forcing their lovers to do the thing to them. These are keener and quicker than all others."[5]

Perhaps the most influential defender of male friendship was Marsilio Ficino (1433–1499). In his *Commentarium in convivio platonis* (1469), a discussion of Plato's *Symposium*, Ficino set Platonic ideals of friendship within a Christianized framework that attempted to explain the homoerotic implications of the *Symposium* as allegorical; Ficino was at pains to disassociate friendship as Plato envisioned it from the sodomy Christianity proscribed. He reads Plato as proposing a view of friendship in which male loyalty is associated with that chaste and virtuous love that is properly given to the Christian God. He argues that Plato's depictions of love between two men are allegories of the spirit, not of the flesh. Such love—in which both partners are enriched by intellectual sympathy and strengthened by chaste affection—becomes the means to apprehend the divine and receive God's grace. Ficino's attempt to desexualize such relations and to dehomosexualize Plato's philosophy rewrites the concept of the Platonic, deleting not only the imputations of *paederastia* but any hint of the physicality of sex.

But however eager Ficino may have been to establish Plato within the safe precincts of a nonsodomitical discourse, he is finally unable to do so with absolute conviction. He comments, for example, that "some men" are better suited than others to produce "offspring of the soul," and that "some men" "naturally love men more than women." Like other Renaissance proponents of masculine love, Ficino defined relationships between men in spiritual terms, placing them within the context of a chaste love. But these writers also implied that for some men—those who "naturally" preferred men to women—masculine love included the physical consummation of desire.

2 Sodomy and Satire

This glossing-over of sex with a veneer of philosophy did not convince everyone that the ancient sin was any less vicious. Beneath the new reading of Plato, some thought, sodomy still lurked. Some writers—devout Christians, as well as satirists who mocked both clerics and philosophers—set out to demonstrate that on this vexed subject the pagan philosopher had little of value to say to Christians. Dante, in the fourteenth century, placed sodomites in the Seventh Circle of his Inferno, in a fiery desert among those guilty of violence against God and nature. Blasphemers, violent against God, share the circle with sodomites, who have violated the order of nature; both are condemned to run constantly backward, in circles, while being bombarded by fiery rain. Among them Dante finds his former teacher Brunetto Latini—a sodomite. Their meeting is affectionate, and the poet's portrait of Latini is approving, yet Dante has placed his teacher among the damned.

Yet there is some evidence that Dante was less than completely persuaded by religious opinion that demanded this judgment. Francesco da Buti, who knew Dante in the poet's later life, noted that he honored the virtue in Latini and ignored the sin.[6] Other writers, asserting that philosophers were especially prone to sodomy, condemned the dissemination of classical texts as a project sponsored by those who simply wanted to justify their own sodomitical indulgence. In the early Renaissance, Domenico da Prato insisted in his *Condemnation of Philosophy* that philosophy and sodomy were fatally and even inevitably linked. A notary rather than a poet, da Prato had neither the wit nor the ingenuity of a satirist, as his verse makes plain: "Whoever directs his mind toward this vice / is breaking the law of God, / Doing damage to himself and Nature." Sodomy is not "some debatable thing" to be brought into philosophical discourse in the guise of friendship. Predictably, da Prato found that "now more than ever people seem to transgress," more even than in that "certain country that perished entirely with Sodom and Gomorrah." He notes that God "didn't give Adam a boy—no, he gave Eve / For companionship under decent laws. / And that's the way everyone should act. / Let all the rest of them"—sodomites—"weep and be miserable."[7] Finally, da Prato demands that the "decent laws" that defend the family values represented by the "companionship" between Adam and Eve be strictly enforced.

Artists and intellectuals were also sometimes accused of being sodomites, especially those whose interest in and care for promising young students and apprentices was believed to mean only one thing. Such speculation, of course, was supported by the public personae of artists like Giovanni Antonio Bazzi (1477–1549), who called himself Il Sodoma and surrounded himself with effeminate and dandified young men, and by the homoerotic writings like those of the Florentine Poliziano. Gossip urged that Leonardo, Benvenuto Cellini, and Michelangelo were all sodomites as well. In 1476 Leonardo was indeed brought to trial for sodomy, though (perhaps through the influence of his father) no verdict was rendered. In 1557, Cellini received a four-year sentence for the offense.

Entire cities were sometimes charged with harboring sodomites. The pseudonymous poet L'Acquettino accuses early-fifteenth-century Florence of being infected with "damnable sodomy, / which vilely offends nature / and annoys Him who sent us here." Even though the world "is full of such filth"—the repeated complaint of the sexual moralist—it is especially appalling that sodomy should be so rife in "you Florence, who have risen so high." One Stefano Finiguerri, who wrote under the name of Lo Za, named many Florentine men as sodomites. In his satirical poem "La Buca di Montemorello," cast as a vision reminiscent of Dante's, Lo Za is led by his guide to a mountain in search of buried treasure. On the way he encounters a group of Florentine sodomites. Among the several he names are "the sodomite Corso Cei," and Doctor Giorgio, who "examines the sick minutely. / And gives excellent treatment to any who bend over."

Some satirists were willing to extend the accusation to all of Tuscany. In a poem dedicated to one Mamurianus, Antonio Panormita notes that "you're Tuscan, and all Tuscans are drawn to cock." Born Antonio Beccadelli, Panormita wrote a collection of verse called *Hermaphroditus* (1425). Some of the poems adopt the voice of a sodomite as narrator. In one, a dead pederast speaks to the traveler reading his epitaph: "When you have a young man that you want to bugger, / Do it, I beg you, right here on my tomb." In this way "Achilles placated the ashes of Chiron"; "blond Patroclus, your bottom experienced this rite," just as "Hylas knew it when Hercules pierced him on his father's grave." The homosexualization of homoerotic myths shattered the romance of those stories and reduced them, as Panormita intended, to tales of lust rather than love. Sodomy does not admit of noble passions or high romance; instead, it is an infectious passion, impossible to cure: "If anyone by chance bends over the back of a young'un / it's extremely hard for him ever to abandon the task."[8]

Perhaps the most complete picture of the sodomite monster—molester of boys and corrupter of youth—was drawn by Pacifico Massimo, who wrote a number of Latin elegies in the fifteenth century warning of the dangers posed to young men by the predatory sodomites of Florence. In one of them, "Advice to Paulinus," he recounts his own experience as a cautionary tale:

> *The only taint on my morals came from the tutor*
> *That my father and mother unwittingly wished upon me.*
> *He was the king of the pederasts; no prey ever*

Escaped his hands, since he was a master of that art.
Oh yes, I learned a lot of things I'd have preferred not to.
  I learned a lot about using my mouth—and my asshole.
Now you, my Paulinus—don't you want to avoid all this?
  Don't you see the appearance of that man you associate with?
I'm wondering in fact if you're not being sucked down in the same
    filth,
  Because, as we know, like is attracted to like. . . .
If a pederast once gets a young kid in his clutches,
  He knows how to drill the recruit in his art.[9]

Friendship between men was often the real and hidden subject of Renaissance poetry, the lesson of heroic and epic poems, and the subject of celebration in drama. It was implicated in a web of fascinated speculation, for though sodomy could not be friendship, friendship might be sodomy. While some writers extolled intimate male friendship as the highest form of human affection and the road to God's grace, others satirized it and condemned it as the path to sodomy. Although the satirists who asserted that friendship really meant sodomy exaggerated the iniquity of their targets to make their satire more pointed, they surely reflected what their audience believed and wanted to hear: sodomy was a sin, not an acceptable kind of love. During this period, however, sodomites would suffer consequences far more severe than the mere sting of satire.

3 Sodomy and the Black Death

Since Old Testament days, sodomy had been implicated as a cause of natural calamity, and antisodomitical rhetoric had also consistently described sodomy as pestilential and sodomites as sources of infection. In the fifth century, Justinian insisted that "because of such crimes there are famines, earthquakes, and pestilences"; in the eleventh century, Peter Damian described sodomy as the vice that "pollutes the flesh"; in the thirteenth, Albertus Magnus defined *sodomia* as a contagious disease. Texts from the twelfth and thirteenth centuries describe Paris as "infected" by sodomy, which is "more common than any other lewdness"—so common that "even our churches are overrun by this filthy plague." In a poem of the same period, sodomy is described as "leprosy." Arnald of Verniolle said his bishop would be hard put to catch all those "who had been infected with the crime of sodomy."

Images of plague, infestation, and disease became the primary metaphors for sodomy and its effects. Beginning in the 1340s, the terrible Black Death, bubonic plague, carried from China by rat-borne fleas, devastated Europe and England. In repeated visitations over the next century it killed anywhere from a third to a half of Europe, causing economic and social disorder from which the continent did not recover for generations. A French surgeon in Auvergne observed that "so contagious was the disease, especially with the blood spitting, that no one could approach or even see a patient without taking the disease. The father did not visit the son nor the son the father. Charity was dead and hope abandoned."[10] Seeking someone to blame for this manifestation of divine displeasure, the panicked populace accused heretics, sodomites, and Jews. The latter were accused of spreading the plague by contaminating Christian wells and by anointing people with plague-ridden potions. In 1348 two thousand Jews were hanged in Strasbourg, and all the Jews of Freiburg were burned alive in retribution for their supposed villainy.

Even before the arrival of the Black Death, the citizens of Florence had attributed disasters to the sodomites in their midst. By the early 1400s the Florentine Officers of the Night were seeking out sodomites and punishing them so that "in this way the city and its upright citizens may be freed from all commotion, wars ended, plague abolished, enemy plots curbed, and cities turned toward good government and praiseworthy conduct."[11] Sodomy and sodomites were the cause of all manner of evils, the worst of which was the plague.

4 Sodomy and Religious Factionalism

The Protestant Reformation, one of the great cultural ruptures of the Renaissance, challenged the authority and moral hegemony of the Roman Church. But though Protestants and Catholics were bitterly divided on almost all areas of doctrine, neither group found any reason to abandon the ancient animosity toward sodomy. In the brutal and unending sectarian religious strife of the sixteenth and seventeenth centuries—an era of doctrinal disputations, anathemas and excommunications, wars and massacres, heresy trials and executions—accusations of sodomy were wielded by both factions. Catholics sought to prove that Protestants' confessions of faith were only a thin veneer intended to hide the extent of their sodomitical practice; they even went so far as to accuse John Calvin of pederasty.[12] Protestant sermons, for their part, presented papists and sodomites lasciviously walking hand in hand; the French Calvinist Pierre Jurieu charged in 1685 that even lay Catholics universally practiced the "horrible abomination" because "the foul spirit makes them find in this crime an abominable pleasure that is greater than that which they find with women."[13]

On the other hand, ever since the Middle Ages reform-minded sects declared heretical by Rome—Albigensians, Waldensians, Lollards, and Hussites—had also been charged with sodomy. These sects in turn claimed that one reason for their rebellion was that Rome had sunk so far into sodomitical iniquity that it was incapable of reforming itself. Furthermore, both Catholic and Protestant doctrine linked religious duty with loyalty to secular governors. Hence many Protestants found it easy to imagine that the Catholic sodomite not only offended God but plotted treason against the king; Catholics returned the compliment. In consequence of their rare agreement that sexual and religious deviants threatened both faith and state, Catholics and Protestants also agreed that the sentence of death was the most effective way to purify both.

Lutherans, Calvinists, and other Protestant sects in the sixteenth century especially cited the unscriptural doctrine of clerical celibacy as the cause of sodomy. Martin Luther declared that "the heinous conduct of the people of Sodom is extraordinary, in as much as they departed from the natural passion and longing of the male for the female, which was implanted by God, and desired what is altogether contrary to nature. Whence comes this perversity? Undoubtedly from Satan, who after people have once turned away from the fear of God, so powerfully suppresses nature that he beats out the natural desire and stirs up a desire that is contrary to nature."[14] Luther not only identified sodomy with Satan but defined it as the absolute antithesis of marriage, which he considered essential to the maintenance of Christian society. Though Rome had always declared that sex was licit only within marriage, it had also held up chastity and celibacy as the ideals. Declaring celibacy a pernicious doctrine, Protestantism saw marriage as the primary bulwark against sodomy, and sodomy as an enemy of marriage even more deadly than fornication.

Recognizing the Protestant danger, and lest anyone doubt its purity, the Catholic Church began to invent its own instruments of reform. Between 1545 and 1563 the Council of Trent addressed the doctrinal challenge raised by Protestant ideology and considered strategies to oppose it. This Counter-Reformation moved to set the Church in order and to regulate the activities of its flock. Leaving untouched the matter of clerical celibacy, the council declared absolutely inviolable the sanctity of marriage and focused on preventing and punishing anything that might undermine it—fornication, bigamy, prostitution, masturbation, and of course sodomy. And since sodomy occurred outside of marriage, and by definition produced no children to embrace the faith, the council saw good reason for ecclesiastical and secular authorities to cooperate in rooting it out. The moral reform movement launched at Trent in the sixteenth century produced an unprecedented number of prosecutions and executions for sodomy.

5 Sodomy and Treason

If sodomy could call down plagues, it could also endanger the state by corrupting even the most loyal citizen. The Florentine Officers of the Night indicated that swift prosecution of sodomy would effectively curb "enemy plots." In Venice, responsibility for the prosecution of sodomy was transferred from the Signori di Notte, local patrols that found and arrested sodomites, to the Council of Ten, which heretofore had dealt only with conspiracy and treason against the Serene Republic.[15] In the Protestant city of Geneva, foreign sodomites, especially Catholic sodomites, were suspect; their presence prompted a wave of trials and executions. The antisodomy laws passed in England were justified, not as punishment for religious infractions, but as necessary to preserve the peace of the king's realm. The English jurist Edward Coke defined treason as "*crimen laesae majestatis,* a sin horrible committed against the King: and this is either against the King Celestial or Terrestrial in three manners: by heresy, by buggery, by sodomy."[16]

The pairing of sodomy with treason surfaced not only in law but in literature. Several Renaissance writers examined the relationships that Edward II of England had with various favorites. The *Polychronicon* of Ralph of Higden notes that Edward "was ardently in love with one of his friends, whom he exalted, enriched, advanced, and honored extravagantly. From this cause came shame to the lover, hatred to the beloved, scandal to the people, and harm to the kingdom."[17] Michael Drayton's *Piers Gaveston* (1593) retells the story of Edward and Gaveston and focuses on the deleterious effects of private passion on the fortunes of the state.

Gaveston recounts the beginnings of his affair with the prince:

My youth the glasse where he his youth beheld,
Roses his lipps, my breath sweete Nectar *showers,*
For in my face was natures fayrest field,
Richly adornd with Beauties rarest flowers.
My breast his pillow, where he laide his head,
Mine eyes his booke, my bosome was his bed.

Edward is besotted with Gaveston, and Gaveston—whom Drayton portrays as a scheming sodomite—erotically plays out his role:

My bewtie was the Load-starre of his thought,
My lookes the Pilot to his wandring eye,
By me his sences all a sleepe were brought,
When with sweete love I sang his lullaby. . . .

Though Drayton paints the relationship between Edward and Gaveston in affecting terms, his tale is a moral one, meant to show the consequences of uncontrolled desire, which even Gaveston describes as the "roote of our woe":

And thus like slaves we sell our soules to sinne,
Vertue forgot by worldes deceitfull trust,
Alone by pleasure are we entred in,
Now wandring in the labyrinth of lust,
For when the soule is drowned once in vice,
The sweete of sinne, makes hell a paradice.[18]

After the death of Gaveston, Edward took as his next favorite Hugh Le Despenser. That this relationship also threatened the state is suggested by how Hugh and Edward died, a death that does not name but pictures sodomy. Hugh's genitals were cut off and he was hanged. Edward, imprisoned and humiliated, was, so the chronicles report, murdered by a repetition of the act that characterized his presumed sin: a hot iron was forced up his anus.

Marked as heretics and bringers of plague, effeminates, sorcerers, and traitors, those who were apprehended in sodomitical acts were branded as sexual outlaws, sinners, traitors, and criminals, and often, though not always, executed. The suspicion that had largely been directed against individuals was, during the Renaissance, increasingly directed at groups of men whose common sexual activities seemed to mark them as a league of sexual deviants, and whose existence threatened the state, the Church, and the populace.

Chapter Ten

A Continental Epidemic

I t was a common jibe that the Italian cities and states were especially rife with sodomy; indeed, St. Bernardino of Siena (1380–1444) described Italy as the mother of sodomy. Florence was reputed to be so infected with the vice that Germans called a sodomite a *Florenzer* and to sodomize someone was *florenzen*.[1] With a sort of nationalist homophobia, such assertions were made by the English about the French, by the French about the English, by Germans about almost all non-Germans, and by Christendom against Islam. The nations or individuals who condemned others were, of course, free of sodomitical tendencies—that was the other tenet of this faith.

Indeed, accusations were hurled on such a grand scale that one may speak of a European pandemic of homophobia. One cause of this widespread fear was certainly the plague, which appeared to justify the conviction that the presence of sodomites threatened the very existence of European cities. In Florence, for example, the plague had reduced the population from more than 125,000 in 1348 to fewer than 40,000 by 1427.[2] As had been the case for some time, sodomy was equated with heresy; moralists charged that sodomites deliberately set out to corrupt youth and undermine marriage and the family.

1 The Italian Panic

Whether Italy really could claim more sodomites than other nations cannot be known. However, in 1324 the governing council of Siena appointed special officers to "ensure true peace, [and] maintain the good morals and praiseworthy life of the people of Siena" by pursuing sodomites and bringing them to trial; since this crime offended both God and nature it was the city's duty to prosecute it, lest God visit her with dire calamity. In Perugia in 1342 a similar law instituted a force of forty men, eight from each of the city's five districts. A number of Italian cities—Florence, Venice, and Bologna among them—established such institutions, charged with searching out heresy and its companion, sodomy. Indeed, it was in the cities of Italy that the most "widescale persecution of homosexual behavior in European history" was carried out.[3]

Under statutes passed in Florence in 1325, anyone convicted of pederasty was castrated, and youths under fourteen who willingly submitted to homosexual advances were driven naked from the city. Investigations were conducted in secret; anyone might denounce anyone. If two witnesses attested to the actual commission of sodomy, prosecution would quickly follow; torture was employed to extract a confession. The convicted sodomite could then be displayed in the pillory, to be abused and beaten by righteous citizens. If he survived this ordeal, he was, at last, burned at the stake. Any site where sodomy was supposed to have been performed was deemed to be polluted. Even referring to sodomy was actionable—a fine was imposed for singing or writing songs that mentioned sodomy.[4]

By the fifteenth century, the fear of sodomy had turned to panic in some cities. In Venice in 1458, the Council of Ten prefaced legislation that established patrols to search out sodomites with this assertion: "It is clear from Divine Scripture that our omnipotent God, detesting the sin of sodomy and wishing to demonstrate that fact, brought down his wrath upon the cities of Sodom and Gomorrah and soon thereafter flooded and destroyed the whole world for such horrible sins, our most wise ancestors sought with all their laws and efforts to liberate our city from such a dangerous divine judgment."[5] To carry on the ancestors' work, the Ten instituted prosecutions of suspected sodomites; they looked for sodomy everywhere. Believing that teachers might be too interested in their students, the Ten decreed that teachers of music, gymnastics, and fencing could not keep their schools open after dark or have private rooms for instruction, lest students who went there "might commit some prohibited deed." Apothecary shops were also suspect, since the barber-surgeons who ran them were heavily represented among those prosecuted for sodomy. The Ten believed that "in the shops of pastrymakers in this city many youths and others of diverse age and condition come together day and night; there they hold games, drink, and commit many dishonesties and sodomy."[6] Gatherings of men and youths at private dinner parties were deemed even more dangerous, since sodomitical temptation might be fueled by the heat of all-male conviviality.

Seeing sodomy rampant, the Ten resolved to punish it severely. The passive partner in a homosexual act—after a confession often extracted by torture—could be punished by lashing, public humiliation, physical mutilation, including the loss of hands or feet, and exile; the active sodomite would be tortured and put to death, either by being burned alive or by decapitation; if by decapitation, his corrupted body was consigned to the cleansing flames.

In Florence, the Officers of the Night charged with finding and prosecuting sodomites were so effective that between 1432 and 1502, when they were disbanded, they tried some fifteen thousand men and boys and convicted over two thousand.[7] Yet despite these efforts, the authorities seemed to believe that sodomy could not be eradicated, only kept in check. In 1436 they wrote that the Officers of the Night

> are watching with unceasing diligence so that the horrible crime of sodomy might be rooted out of the city and its territory, and they devote themselves to almost nothing else. Yet after all their labors, words, threats, and punishments against many persons, they believe that, in effect, it is nearly impossible for any good to come about, so corrupt and stained is the city. Nonetheless, they prudently reason that if despite every sort of punishment these men are still not restrained, at least some might control themselves, and perhaps those defiled by such ignominy will not do it so openly; and if out of a thousand sodomites the authorities punish even one well, all of them experience fear. Although their crimes may not be completely prevented, they may in part be contained.[8]

The scope of the problem had been memorably stated a decade earlier. In 1424, St. Bernardino of Siena delivered a series of Lenten sermons to the Florentines calling upon them to rise up, reform, and cleanse their notorious city in which sodomy was epidemic and youth in daily danger of corruption. Referring to Florence as a modern-day Sodom, sure to be laid waste, Bernardino reminded his congregation of the judgment rendered by the angel in the Apocalypse who "put the trumpet of sodomy" to his mouth and "trumpeted: stink, stink! fire, fire!" The trumpet summoned "a large hailstone mixed with fire and with blood, and the whole land was covered with hailstone and it burned a third of the land and a third of the trees. Of green hay nothing remained." Bernardino's denunciation recalls the atmosphere of infected cities and evokes the most dreadful aspects of the plague: the bloody bodily purges it produced, the stench of burning bodies and rotting flesh, the sulfurous fumes that pervaded the infected atmosphere, the land laid waste.

Sodomy had several causes, according to Bernardino, but the most fearful was the unnatural lust that impelled men to desire boys: "You know well that God sent fire and sulfur above Sodom and Gomorrah, sulfur for the stink of sin, fire for the lust against nature." Three things make "the fire of sodomy" grow: "eating, gorging, drinking and stuffing"; "the full purse, gambling"; and "secret places where a public brothel of boys is kept." Bernardino demanded of his audience, "Wherever you hear sodomy mentioned, each and every one of you spit on the ground and clean your mouth out well. Spit hard! Maybe the water of your spit will extinguish their fire."[9] Bernardino's eloquence was so convincing that masses of Florentines contemptuously spat on the ground. Two days later, goaded by another sermon in which he urged that all sodomites should be consigned to the fire, the Florentines threw wigs, cosmetics, elegant clothing, and other frivolities on a huge bonfire in an orgy of representative destruction, burning sodomites in effeminate effigy to purify their city.[10]

Bernardino whipped up new heights of homophobic frenzy, arguing that not only was sodomy an obvious evil, a chief cause of the plague, but that also the sodomites were actively spreading their poison throughout the city. The target of these sinister activities, Bernardino charged, was the very hope of the city: its youth. How could Florentine youth not be defiled when the daily life of the city was rife with sodomy? Sodomites consorted openly with one another in the streets. Sodomy was a constant topic of conversation, the subject of bawdy jokes in the shops where young apprentices labored. Even in the schools, teachers and mentors were sodomites.

Bernardino saw sodomy even in the bosom of the family, whose values had been destroyed by the machinations of unscrupulous sodomites. Some fathers were sodomites who corrupted their own sons. Careless parents consorted with known sodomites, inviting them into their homes. Ambitious parents connived with sodomites in the sexual corruption of youth, for the sake of advancing themselves or their sons. (A century later, Michelangelo reported in a letter of 1518 that a parent too eager for his son to become an apprentice to the artist had slyly suggested that Michelangelo could have the boy "not only in my house, but also in my bed." Michelangelo says he rejected "this consolation, not wanting to deprive" the father of it.)[11] Parents, Bernardino raged, sent their sons out into the city wearing "fine shirts, with doublets exposing their bodies, with frilly clothes and open tights on their legs, with their hair in buns. Of the soul they do not think at all," but instead have their sons "show a lot of flesh for the sodomites."[12]

Once young men were corrupted by the dissolute Florentine atmosphere, and especially by the laxity of their parents, it was inevitable, Bernardino charged, that they should eagerly turn to sodomy themselves and even urge others to engage in it: "I've heard of boys who dress themselves up and go around boasting about their sodomizers, and they make a practice of it for pay, and go about encouraging others in the ugly sin."[13] Once a young man had reached sexual maturity—the age of fourteen—it was nearly impossible for him to be saved from sodomy, so alluring was the temptation and so lucrative the rewards: "Whenever youth are seized by this baleful ruin, only by force are they ever cured."[14] There was only one definitive cure—marriage. But it had to be undertaken before a man reached his mid-thirties, after which no hope remained.[15] The man who does not take a wife by thirty, Bernardino warned, is probably already a confirmed sodomite or well on the path to being one. "Woe to him who does not take a wife when he has the time . . . for remaining single they become sodomites. . . . When you see a man the right age who doesn't take a wife . . . take it as a bad sign for him, if he hasn't been practicing chastity for spiritual reasons."[16]

Bernardino's association of bachelorhood and sodomy gets some support from Florentine judicial records: three-quarters of the men convicted in Florence between 1478 and 1483 were married. Of the fifty-eight men between the ages of eighteen and thirty who were convicted, fifty-five were single. Among the thirty men between forty and sixty—men well beyond the expected marriageable age—only thirteen were married. In a group of men who voluntarily turned themselves in to take advantage of a clause that allowed a man to accuse himself of sodomy and be absolved, 80 percent were single.[17]

Though Bernardino held out hope that the youthful sodomite-in-the-making might be saved by marrying, some married men were nevertheless sodomites, insensitive to the healing presence of a wife. How could such a married sodomite be discerned? Only a close look at the domestic situation sufficed. The age of the husband and the duration of the marriage were clues, for sodomites often married late in life. And "as a general rule," Bernardino cautioned, "the greater a sodomite he is, the more he hates his wife."[18] Such a marriage could not be happy; no matter what a woman did, she could not deflect the sodomite from his desire. "O women, get it into your head that you will never be able to satisfy your husband if he is caught up in this vice."[19]

Indeed, the indelible mark of the sodomite was that he hated women. At once echoing ancient homophobic notions of homosexual psychology and foreshadowing modern ones, Bernardino insisted that sodomy was so powerful a lure and so obsessive a vice that sex with women could not turn men from it. Just as women naturally hate sodomites, Bernardino said, so "there are men so completely wrapped up in sodomy that they don't esteem a single woman, so base do they consider them."[20] In fact, sodomites are so blind to feminine sexual allure that "no matter how beautiful a woman is, to him she stinks and isn't pleasing, nor will he ever want to yield to her beauty."[21] It might be better for a father to murder his daughter rather than have her marry a sodomite, because "by murdering her you would save her soul, whereas in marrying such men . . . she loses both soul and body."[22] Thus Bernardino affirmed another tenet of homophobia: sodomites cheat women of their proper function, which is to satisfy men and bear their children.

Bernardino's characterization of Florentine sodomites contributed to the terms of Renaissance homophobia. His sodomite is a lascivious creature, obsessed with sex and boys, willing to go to any lengths to obtain his pleasure, even brazenly infiltrating the family in pursuit of his prey. Sodomites denigrate the role of women and mock the institution of marriage itself. To the ancient stereotypes of effeminacy, passivity, and unbridled promiscuity, Bernardino added another: confirmed bachelorhood.

Yet Bernardino seemed to believe that nature itself created the sodomite. It is demonstrable, he asserted, that the psychological mark of the sodomite—hatred of women—is not learned but is a part of his nature. Still, Bernardino was in no doubt about what penalty the sodomite would suffer in eternity: he "will be burned and consumed by the wrath of God."[23] "To the fire," he exhorted the people of Florence in his sermon against sodomy. "They are all sodomites! And you are in mortal sin if you try to help them!"[24]

During the rule of the Medicis—Cosimo the Elder, who governed Florence from 1434 until his death in 1464, and his grandson Lorenzo the Magnificent, who died in 1492—Florence saw much of the intellectual ferment that revived classical literature, and some Florentine writers found support for homoeroticism in Neoplatonism. But the Medicis were no more lenient toward sodomites than the Republic had been; prosecutions continued, as did the activities of the Officers of the Night.[25]

After the fall of the Medicis in 1494, Florence was dominated for a few spectacular years by Fra Girolamo Savonarola, a Dominican reformer. Sodomy prosecutions dramatically increased, in large part because of Savonarola's fiery denunciations. In one sermon, he demanded that "the Signoria must make a law against that cursed vice of sodomy, for which Florence is defamed throughout all of Italy. . . . I say make a law that is without mercy, that is, that such persons be stoned and burned."[26] The priors of the newly restored Florentine Republic announced in December 1494 that "because of the evil government of the past regime"—the Medicis—there had been for some time "much injustice and little fear of God . . . concerning the repression and extinction of this vice." Therefore, they determined to strengthen the antisodomy law "as is necessary in a Christian and religious Republic."[27] They abolished the fines that had heretofore been levied against convicted sodomites, while retaining the severest corporal and capital penalties. A first offender was to be barred from holding public office and exposed in the pillory. For a second offense, he was to be marched through the city, fastened to a pillar in the central square, and branded on the forehead. For a third, he was to be burned.[28] Savonarola was successful in stirring up ever greater popular hostility to sodomy; in the winter and spring of 1495–96 a huge number of accusations were made against suspected sodomites, followed by an equally large number of convictions.

Despite Savonarola's denunciations, the government was not always as eager as he was to burn those convicted, and the friar's attempt to root out sodomy gained him many enemies. Organized groups of youths demonstrated against his measures, interrupted his sermons, and attacked his followers, the "reformed" boys whom he had recruited in an attempt to protect them from the enticements of older sodomites.

Savonarola intensified his campaign. During the Carnival of 1497, in a fiery repetition of the burnings incited by Bernardino three-quarters of a century earlier, he decreed that the frivolous indecencies of the city must be burned in a bonfire of the vanities. Citizens burned their carnival masks, indecent books and pictures, and dandified raiment, while artists consigned nude paintings to Savonarola's cleansing flames. "Abandon, I tell you, your concubines and beardless youths," Savonarola exhorted Florence. "Abandon, I say, that unspeakable vice, abandon that abominable vice that has brought God's wrath upon you, or else: woe, woe to you."[29]

But Florence soon wearied of Savonarola's hectoring. During his Ascension Day sermon on May 4, 1497, bands of youths rioted and the riot became a revolt against everything the friar stood for. The taverns reopened, men gambled in public, and it is said that a high public official gleefully declared, "Thank God now we can sodomize again."[30] In June Savonarola was excommunicated by Pope Alexander VI and arrested. On May 23, 1498, on the platform to which he had condemned so many, Savonarola was himself hanged and burned. As the executioner was preparing to burn the lifeless corpse, an eyewitness records that a citizen of Florence seized a torch and lit the flame, crying, "The one who wanted to burn me is now himself put to the flames."[31]

Even after the Officers of the Night were disbanded in 1502, subsequent Florentine regimes, both republican and ducal, continued to try to repress sodomy, which flourished as before. The last and most stringent law, passed in 1542 by Cosimo de Medici—the first duke of Florence, descended from the elder Cosimo's brother—declared that sodomy was an affront to God and an offense to the duke, "who was appointed to the care, government, and rule of the people."[32] The commission of sodomy thus became a form of treason. The law not only sought to punish men who had sex with youths, but unlike most earlier laws, made a point of assigning special punishment to adult men who allowed themselves to be sodomized by other men.[33] Finally, the law took notice of how often and with how many partners a man had committed sodomy, punishing the habitual sodomite more severely than the single offender; in effect, it asserted that true sodomy was the act of a confirmed sodomite, not merely the lapse of an occasional sinner.

Though Florence may have offered the most dramatic instance of homophobic persecution, other cities throughout Italy also took action. Bernardino, rousing the Florentines against sodomy, had gleefully recounted the burning of sodomites in Venice and Genoa, and described the death of a man convicted of sodomy in Verona: his body was quartered, the severed limbs hung above the city gate.[34] A particularly detailed law from Treviso, dating from 1574, is notable in that it is directed expressly against both male and female offenders.

> If any person (leaving the natural use) has sexual relations with another, that is a man with a man if they are fourteen years old or more, or a woman with a woman, if they are twelve or more, by committing the vice of sodomy—popularly known as "buzerones" or "fregatores"—and this has been revealed to the city magistrates, the detected person, if a male, must be stripped of all his clothes and fastened to a stake in the Street of the Locusts with a nail driven through his male member, and shall remain there all day and all night under a reliable guard, and the following day be burned outside the city. If however, a woman commits this vice or sin against nature, she shall [also] be fastened naked to a stake in the Street of the Locusts and shall remain there all day and night under a reliable guard, and the following day shall be burned outside the city.[35]

2 Spanish Sodomy

Spain was as vigilant as Italy. As early as 1265, *Las Siete partidas*, the legal code compiled by King Alfonso X, prescribed the death penalty for males who committed the *pecado nefando*, the unmentionable sin. Long known for ferocious piety, by the fifteenth century Spain was the center of one of the most active branches of the Inquisition. The Inquisition's aim when it was established in 1232 was simply to seek out heretics, admonish them, and obtain their penance, but it soon adopted stronger measures; in 1252, Pope Innocent IV authorized the use of torture to gain admissions of heresy. In 1451, Pope Nicolas V decreed that sodomy was a proper object of investigation by the Inquisition, though in fact it had long been under scrutiny. In 1478, Queen Isabella of

Castile and her husband, Ferdinand of Aragon, with the approval of Pope Sixtus IV, established the Inquisition in Spain. Originally intended to discover and persecute Jews who had ostensibly converted to Christianity but still practiced their faith in secret, the Spanish Inquisition soon turned its attention to all forms of heresy and sin, including sodomy. In 1483, Ferdinand and Isabella appointed Tomás de Torquemada grand inquisitor of Spain; his merciless persecution of heretics and sodomites was made more terrible by a change in the old Castilian law that had punished sodomy with stoning and castration but now decreed burning. By the end of the sixteenth century, the Inquisition operated in Spain, in Portugal, and in the Italian provinces of the Spanish empire, including Sicily, Sardinia, and Naples, and in Spain's holdings in the Americas, including Mexico and Peru.

During its more than three-century-long history, the Spanish Inquisition has been estimated to have tried and sentenced more than 300,000 people.[36] Though the vast majority of these victims were not sodomites, records of trials in Spain—under the auspices of both the Inquisition and secular courts—during the sixteenth and seventeenth centuries show the extent of the punishment for sodomy.[37] In Barcelona, Valencia, and Saragossa, over sixteen hundred persons were prosecuted for sodomy and bestiality between 1540 and 1700. About 20 percent were actually executed; there are records of 150 executions in those cities in the eighty years between 1560 and 1640.[38] In Seville, seventy people were burned for sodomy between 1567 and 1616.[39] There were three waves of sodomy persecutions in Seville, in 1580, 1585, and 1600, probably in response to three historical events.[40] In 1579 Seville suffered shortages of food—it had been diverted to help provision a royal fleet—and a powder mill exploded, destroying forty houses and killing more than fifty people. In the 1580s the forced resettlement of more than four thousand Moriscos—Spanish Muslims—from the mountains to Seville created a wave of popular feeling against this group, which had long been accused of homosexual practice. In 1599 and 1600 an epidemic of plague—always seen as a sign of God's wrath concerning sins like sodomy—devastated the region. Very likely these events prompted the authorities of Seville to look for those responsible among the sodomites of Seville.[41]

Though "pecado nefando" could denote anal intercourse between a man and a woman, it seems clear that the term was usually used to denote homosexual relations. The jurist Gregorio López, who prepared the standard gloss on the *Partidas* in 1555, argued that the law against sodomy ought to apply not only to men but to women. López cited St. Paul's condemnation of women "who changed the natural use into that which is against nature," as well as fourteenth- and fifteenth-century legal opinions that interpreted Roman laws against homosexual acts as applying equally to women and to men.[42] But charges against women were rare, against men numerous, as is borne out by contemporary sources such as records of confessions made to the Inquisition, various histories of Seville, and documents related to the royal prison where sodomites were held. The most extensive of these records were compiled by Pedro de León, a Jesuit who between 1578 and 1616 was chaplain at the royal prison of Seville. His ministry included fifty male sodomites ranging in age from their late teens to their middle fifties; all were eventually executed. He records no instance of women being imprisoned for sodomy with other women, though another source from the same period, the description of the royal prison by Cristóbal de Cháves, mentions two women imprisoned for lesbian relations, one of whom was whipped and the other hanged. The offense of the latter was apparently thought worse because she confessed to using a false penis in her homosexual relations.[43]

De León mentions a large number of clerics, and though the Church attempted to shield its own from the most severe penalties, many were burned. One of these was Pascual Jaime, chaplain to the powerful Duke of Alcalá. Jaime's elegant appearance and retinue of handsome, painted youths unsurprisingly brought him under suspicion; a law officer entered Jaime's house and found him engaged in sex with a young man. Jaime's partner was sent to the royal prison and Jaime placed in the custody of his archbishop. Under torture, Jaime confessed that all his life he had engaged in sodomy with males, beginning when he was only eight. As a man he searched the streets of Seville for willing but poor and hungry young men; he brought them home, fed them, and dressed them in better clothes than they had ever known. When he had taken his pleasure with a young man and tired of him, he would again begin his hunt. Horrified at this tale, and fearing that a clerical court would exculpate one of its own, the archbishop ordered Jaime to be expelled from holy orders so that he could be tried before a secular court, which, as expected, imposed a sentence of death. Standing on a platform before a crowd that de León reports was huge, Jaime was ceremonially expelled from his orders and as a sodomitical layman was burned alive. A few days later Jaime's most recent sexual partner, Francisco Legasteca—who said Jaime had seduced him with offers of fine clothes and other vanities—also stood before a crowd that had come to watch him die. De León notes that he was very young and "cried as a boy," but like his paramour he was burned alive.[44] These executions were cautionary spectacles serving to terrorize sodomites and satisfy their enemies that God's natural order was restored.

Sodomy in Seville, de León makes clear, was practiced by every class. Among men charged and executed were teachers, soldiers, and even a sheriff who kept a gambling house that also supplied boys to sodomites. Influential nobles were involved; Don Alonso Girón, who like Jaime had been in the service of the Duke of Alcalá, was accused of committing sodomy with one of his servants. He was prosecuted, found guilty, and burned along with the young page who had served him too well. Nor were foreigners exempt from accusation and judgment. Two Frenchmen were burned in 1588, and in 1581 a Neapolitan was burned for what de León describes as "a habit of Italy."[45]

Of the fifty-four men listed by de León who were executed, nine were "mulattos, Negroes, Turks or 'Berberiscos.' "[46] Some may have been prostitutes or procurers; one Muyuca, who de León notes was "famous for his dealings with men," was burned in 1585. Francisco Bautuista was burned in 1596 for committing sodomy with boys from a charitable home; his fourteen-year-old partner was given two hundred lashes. In 1610 Juan Pérez de Mansilla and Antón de Morales, who may have engaged in sodomy together, were executed, as were two unnamed men of color in 1616. A man named Hamete noted in his confession that he and other men of color were especially sought after in the active role because of the size of their genitals.

Several groups of men were prosecuted together. De León reports that one Diego Maldonado was the ringleader of a small group of sodomites—de León calls them a *quadrilla*—who were executed together in 1585. Also in 1585 a group of eight men who were known to gather in an area outside the city walls were burned at the same time. In 1600, fifteen men were burned together, perhaps simply for convenience.

Did these men see themselves as individual sexual seekers or as members of a group that defined itself by what it desired? Some clues exist. When Hamete specifies large genitals as a particular object of desire, he indicates a specific sexual taste, which in turn suggests that there were particular men who shared that taste. Shared desires suggest groups that seek to satisfy them. The sodomites of Seville may have met at the sheriff's gambling house, where they could find attractive boys or engage Muyuca to arrange a meeting with the "handsome painted gallants" who sought male sexual partners. The group that apparently met outside the city walls would have found some privacy among the groves of trees.

Costume and manner often indicated sexual taste. One Francisco Galindo, later executed, walked with "charm" and "appeared more woman than man."[47] That Galindo is thus described, that Jaime the priest dressed "curiously" and with elegance, that Muyuca's clients are noted to be "handsome painted gallants," suggests a swaggering, dandified, effeminate style, and de León seems to associate it with sexual nonconformity. When Muyuca was burned, he appeared before the crowd wearing a ruff, cosmetics, and a wig.[48] It is tempting to imagine that this display was an act of defiance, a deliberate statement of how Muyuca saw himself. More likely, as Elizabeth Perry suggests in her study of sodomy in early modern Seville, the costume was intended by his captors to humiliate Muyuca and to emphasize the iniquity of his acts by caricaturing him as effeminate.[49]

In Spain as in Italy, effeminacy and sodomy were mocked by means of the same items of sodomitical frippery—wigs, ruffs, cosmetics—that fueled the bonfires lighted by Savonarola and Bernardino a century earlier. Some Spanish grandees who watched Muyuca burn were heard to suggest that all such dandified apparel ought to be consigned to the purifying flames along with those whom Francisco de León called "men converted into women."[50]

3 A Portuguese Sodomite

The Inquisition in Portugal was more industrious than that in Spain, but more lenient, too.[51] The *Repertorios do nefando,* a catalogue of sodomy listing all those who had confessed to the crime or had been denounced for it, was kept for over two centuries and includes 4,419 names. Of those listed, only about 10 percent were put on trial, and of those, less than 10 percent—thirty people—were actually executed by the secular authority. However, it is not likely that the Portuguese Inquisition was officially any more tolerant of homosexual activity than the Spanish.[52]

That so many were named in the *Repertorios do nefando* suggests that Portugal, and especially Lisbon, had a substantial number of men who engaged in sodomy. Many of these men represented themselves as effeminate homosexuals—*fanchonos,* which is what they called themselves as well.[53] Like Seville, Lisbon had places known for homosexual assignations. *Fanchonos* frequented a rooming house very near the palace of the Inquisition, and men dressed as women attended a *dança dos fanchonos*. One Portuguese *fanchono,* perhaps ironically or defiantly, conflated his personal and sexual identity by naming himself Rafael Fanchono. Others had the equivalent of modern-day drag names, like "Francisquihna," the diminutive feminine form of "Francisco." One well-known sodomite priest called himself Paula de Lisboa; another priest, who was tried for sodomy, Padre Joao Mendonca de Maia, surrounded himself with *fanchono* friends, giving them names like Miss Turk and Miss Galicia.[54]

A remarkable series of letters, recovered by Luiz Mott and Arnoldo Assunção, provides a unique portrait of a particular *fanchono,* one Francisco Correa Netto. Correa, sacristan of the cathedral of Silves, in 1664 wrote to Manoel Viegas, an instrument maker and guitarist with whom he apparently had a brief affair.

In the first letter Correa invites Viegas to engage in a sexual relationship with him, but bluntly notes that "if men sleep with me, it is not to find a pussy. They place their cock between my legs and have their way. I do not achieve it."[55] Viegas will not have committed the technical crime of sodomy by engaging in anal penetration. The distinction made in canon law between anal penetration—true sodomy—and "sins of the senses" like masturbation and interfemoral sex has not been lost upon Correa.[56] He offers to allow Viegas to "do the same," but he also hints at something more: he tells Viegas that he is "at your service" to do "what is needed," noting that whatever may happen, "the losses are mine."[57]

By the time Correa writes his second letter to Viegas, something has happened. Correa recalls "your arms and the kiss that you gave me," and laments that Viegas "did not want to do what comes so naturally" even though, in a moment of intimacy, Correa had aroused his ardor: "You know this subject well, in that heart of your loins, it was that which desired me, with its craving to fly up. There was no Lent in that heart of your loins, when I touched it with my fingers and it instantly sprang up!"

If Viegas rejected Correa's sexual advances, he apparently was willing to lead him on, for Correa complains that "I would have said that by Easter you would be betrothed to me. You implied that often, and you gave your word on it." In a later letter he promises Viegas gifts. Correa is determined to have Viegas even when he learns that Viegas has become betrothed to a local woman. He offers an arrangement:

"Even though you are married, you do not have to break your promise to be the betrothed of your devoted Francisquinha," that is, Francisco Correa. He begs his paramour simply to pay him heed: "I see that not even with my best argument will my pledge serve you." And again: "Do as you please: in spite of this I shall not stop doing what I can to be at your service." And again: "Here is paper to answer; now you have no excuse not to write."[58]

Correa repeatedly attempts to sway Viegas with gifts, even offering them, incredibly, to his fiancée, Marie Nunes. Though Viegas has publicly mocked him, Correa still swears to remain his friend—"Not even for this will I become your enemy." He does ask that Viegas destroy Correa's love letters, and promises to destroy those Viegas wrote in return. His entreaties have no effect, and after a tirade accusing Viegas of infidelity—with Marie—a thoroughly humiliated Correa breaks off the "engagement," again demands the return of his letters, and sends back the ring that Viegas gave him, ending with, "Do not ever speak to me or look at me again."

To write such letters was brave but foolhardy, since Correa condemns himself of all the vices associated with the sodomite. Unwisely he gives Viegas written evidence that he has had sex with men, and he reveals himself to be a *fanchono*. Correa's letters also show him to be a talented correspondent, and certainly more honorable than the object of his passion. Correa describes Viegas as "a tender gift to me" and as "the mirror of my sight and joy." He invents erotic descriptions of arresting metaphoric quality, as when he notes that in Viegas' loins "there was no Lent." Master of the pathetic and extravagant language of romantic betrayal and loss, he mourns his "heart wounded to death, heart never to be released from my affection for you"; "my destiny is wretched," he says, and he promises to "leave [his] heart afar and look at the ground when you pass."[59]

These letters also reveal the homophobe, in the persons of Viegas and his fiancée Maria. Correa recounts their open contempt of him, their public mockery of his sexual obsession. Against his lovesick deviance they smugly and comfortably set the normality of their own relationship. However seriously Correa took the promises of betrothal Viegas made, apparently Viegas feels that a promise made to a sodomite is not worth keeping. If Viegas had had sex with Correa, he sees him merely as a sexual convenience, to be cast off once he is betrothed. Correa charges that Viegas has gossiped about him to other men in the town, trying to scuttle any imputation that he had a sexual relationship with Correa. Viegas told one Manoel da Costa, Correa alleges, that "if I complied with your whims, even then you would not come to me, because you do not care, and it was all a sham." Not only has Viegas distanced himself from Correa by insult and public humiliation, but he has buttressed his own masculine credentials by seeing to it that his affair with Maria is public knowledge. Stung to anger, Correa rails against Viegas: "False Traitor! False deluded love: with what words can I express this sentiment? After Your Grace left, news came to me that Your Grace intended to possess Maria Nunes, who does not conceal this from anyone, not even from me. . . . My destiny is wretched." Now the once treasured ring that Viegas gave Correa becomes a sign of his own outcast status and a token of the real danger in which he has been placed by Viegas and Maria: "If she goes around telling everyone that she saw what you gave me on my finger, my heart will burst within my chest, and I had to excuse this by saying that I had purchased the ring from Your Grace."[60]

Viegas' public boasting about his mistreatment of Correa suggests the panic said to afflict some heterosexual men in the face of homosexuality. But the final indignity came when Viegas turned over Correa's incriminating letters to the vicar of the cathedral where Correa was sacristan. In his letter to the Inquisition accompanying Correa's letters, the vicar gloated: "We have long had a clandestine sodomite in this city who by God's will is now discovered."[61] As he read Correa's stricken epistles, the vicar annotated them; the attitude of the age is summarized in a single sentence: "Observe that fatuity of this whore of a sodomite."[62]

Apparently Correa was not tried for sodomy; the evidence against him was inadequate, even though the vicar was ready to bring the mayor, other inhabitants of Silves, and another priest of the cathedral to testify to his sacristan's unnatural predilections. To convict for sodomy, the Inquisition required proof that anal penetration had actually occurred not once but twice, and that it had been accompanied by the emission of semen. This proof Correa had carefully avoided offering in his letters, and Viegas, now presumably married, was not likely to provide it. Moreover the vicar's testimony was suspect, since he had previously charged Correa with being one-quarter Jewish and with committing sacrilege by improper administration of the sacred Host.[63]

Francisco Correa Netto was mad with love for a member of his own sex. He effeminized his desire and his own practice by calling himself Viegas' betrothed and his ever-faithful "Francisquinha." And his desire induced fear, loathing, and active animosity in its object. Viegas seemed willing to engage in sex with Correa, but then attempted to destroy him. This cache of seventeenth-century Portuguese letters reveals to us several enduring aspects of homosexual life—and of homophobia.

4 Effeminacy in France

In 1589 the French king Henri III was assassinated by a Dominican monk. This act was celebrated by those who saw in it the punishment by a Catholic God of a king who refused to exterminate French Protestants. The wars of religion that convulsed France in the last decades of the sixteenth century had placed an extreme Catholic party, the Holy League, in opposition to the more tolerant king, and religious fervor worked against him.

But there was an even better reason for God to punish Henri III: sodomy. The king's rumored sodomitical tendencies were the subject of pamphlets and poems. The contemporary poet Théodore-Agrippa d'Aubigné, in Book II of his epic *Tragiques,* written in 1616, excoriates the king:

> *Henri was suited to appraise the arts,*
> *The finery and passion of court tarts*
> *What with his barbered chin and whitened face,*
> *His pathic eye and falsely girlish grace*
> *Indeed, once on a Twelfth Night, this queer beast,*
> *Low-browed and brainless, decked the wonted feast*
> *With pearl tricked ribbons in his flowing hair*
> *Which 'neath a brimless bonnet debonair*
> *Was done up in two arcs. He'd plucked his beard*
> *While's face with powder and with rouge besmeared*
> *Made every courtier shudder and grimace:*
> *A painted whore usurped their prince's place.*
> *Think what a sight this was, how good to see*
> *A king in corsets, satin finery*
> *All black, cut Spanish fashion, slashes made*
> *To cunningly reveal the golden braid;*
> *While, to ensure an over-all effect*
> *His half-sleeves with white satin were bedecked*
> *These, mingling with others slashed and meet*
> *Were lost in frothing fancy round his feet!*

> Day-long sporting in this monstrous fashion
> (The sickly costume equaling his passion)
> For some long time all wondered if they'd seen
> A womanly king or a male queen.[64]

From the royal court came even more pointed attacks. One official, Pierre de L'Estoile, compiled what he called *Registre-journal d'un curieux,* an *Account Book and Journal of a Curious Man*—a combination of his observations about the events of the time and a scrapbook in which he collected pamphlets, broadsides, and satires that were apparently widely distributed in the court and among both educated and popular audiences. As the historian Joseph Cady observes, L'Estoile's compilations are "among the frankest and most extensive depictions of Renaissance homosexuality."[65]

The journals transmit rumors about the king's sexual interests and about the group of young men with whom he surrounded himself, the *mignons,* whose dress and manner apparently suggested sodomy to everyone. Henri was married but childless, and L'Estoile includes in his collection a poem that asserts that "the actual reason he doesn't have any [children] is that he really doesn't tend that way."[66] Which way did he tend? Another poem remarks that the king "has chosen our Good Lady"—the Virgin Mary—as his patron, but "he likes a blond young man better." If that was not clear enough, the king's preference for males is asserted unequivocally in a poem called the "Courtier's Libel," which charges that "the king fucks his *mignons,* makes them his bedmates" ("Le Roy estoque"—thrusts—"ses mignons"). The descriptions of the *mignons* leave no doubt about how they were viewed at court and in the streets of Paris. In "The Virtue and Purity of the Mignons" they are bluntly called "effeminates" and "vile effeminates." In another entry, L'Estoile cites a poem that associates effeminacy with sexual activity, describing the *mignons* as "perfumed poofs, active and passive."[67] He comments that the *mignons* roused the detestation of the people because of their "effeminate lewd make-up and dress"; indeed, they dress like the "whores of the brothels." Another poem not only charges the *mignons* with buggery but describes them as women: "I'm as horrified of these hated cunts [*cons*] / As I am of fucking a common whore," asserts the poet. "The thought of being a bugger disgusts me. / . . . I'm afraid of being swallowed up by these ravenous cunts." The *mignons'* effeminacy is explicitly linked to their promiscuity and to male homosexuality when they are called "shameless Ganymedes."

"The Virtue and Purity of the Mignons" asserts that "they practice among themselves the art of lewd Ganymede" and describes them as a "herd of Ganymedes."[68]

Most of these items, however, were only collected, not written, by L'Estoile. The authors, members of the extreme Catholic faction, were opponents of the king; their animosity was prompted as much by religious politics as by sexual deviancy. One of the poems, called "A Courtier's Libel"—L'Estoile gives this generic name to several anonymous antisodomite poems circulated during the 1580s—charges that at the French court "one man marries another" and "women mate similarly." Here political bias is served by sexual innuendo.[69] L'Estoile himself, however, fearing the chaos of civil war, supported the monarchy.[70] He classes the various Courtier's Libels with other "libels describing the Court of Sodom," but nevertheless notes that it reflects "our courtiers' and ladies' vile affections, against nature, such as we read about in the first chapter of St. Paul's Epistle to the Romans."[71] He follows that comment with his own translation of Paul, as if to point up the iniquity of the court: though L'Estoile supported the king he could not approve of the sodomy he saw around him.

Whatever L'Estoile's motives, his collection indicates that the Renaissance court of Henri III was aware of a "type" of what we would now call a homosexual.[72] Certainly the entries in L'Estoile suggest that the king and his *mignons* were viewed as a distinct kind of sexual debauchee. When Henri established a special order, the Order of the Knights of the Holy Spirit, to which he and all his *mignons* belonged, L'Estoile comments that many saw the order simply as "a cover for [their] love affairs." A description of the gorgeous investiture ceremony provoked one writer to wonder if "beneath it all" there lay "the irregularities that inflame our heroic citizens against Masculine Love, the loves that dominate today."[73] Whether motivated by politics, by disgust at sexual deviancy, or by both, the materials L'Estoile collected reflect the homophobia produced by a particularly public and spectacular display of the outward signs believed to signify sodomy.

5 Counting Sodomites in Geneva

In 1541 John Calvin established a strict Protestant theocracy in Geneva, and the city soon became known throughout Europe for its religious zeal and its strict prosecution of lawbreakers of every sort. Like Florence under Savonarola and Spain under the Inquisition, Geneva maintained that the state ought to prosecute irregular sexual conduct, just as it prosecuted heresy, homicide, infanticide, and witchcraft.[74]

The Genevan authorities kept careful records of sodomy trials, both before and after the Reformation. In 1444 there were two executions for sodomy; over the next century five more trials for sodomy were recorded, but not their outcomes. But beginning in 1555 the numbers dramatically increased, paralleling the trend across Europe at that time. The twenty years between 1556 and 1576 saw twenty trials, which resulted in eight executions, nine banishments, and two whippings (one outcome was unknown). After a brief respite, the seventy-odd years between 1590 and the early 1660s saw thirty-nine trials, resulting in twenty-one death sentences, twelve banishments, one fine, a single release, and four cases in which no decision is known—which might mean anything from an acquittal to an execution whose record was somehow lost.[75]

Of the nearly eighty people tried for sodomy (which in Geneva included bestiality) between 1444 and 1789, around thirty are listed as having been Genevan. Of the Genevans, only eight are known to have been executed; thirteen were banished and eight decisions are unknown. Three trials involved "schoolboys"—one in 1555 (the schoolboy was whipped), another in 1563 of three Genevan schoolboys, who were also whipped, and one in 1672 of two schoolboys, decision unknown.[76] Of the eight Genevans executed, the first, listed as the "partner" of a Greek cook, was hanged in 1444. The second, a woman accused of lesbian activity, was drowned in 1568. Another Genevan citizen was drowned in 1600, along with his partner, a "local peasant."[77]

The most spectacular trials took place in 1610, and involved the circle around Pierre Canal, a Genevan official. Arrested for treason and homicide, he confessed under torture to having committed homosexual acts with more than twenty men. His punishment for treason was to be broken on the wheel. His sentence for sodomy sealed his fate; he was burned. Eleven men implicated by Canal were brought to trial. One, apparently an influential city official, was merely fined and deprived of all political privileges. Three more, including a gatekeeper, confessed and were executed by drowning. The others, however, refused to confess to the crime of sodomy and so were banished. In the following decades, Geneva burned or banished seven more people for crimes of sodomy. No trials were recorded between 1623 and 1633. In the next century and a half—the record ends in 1789, when the last trial was recorded—seven Genevans were tried for sodomy or bestiality; of these one was burned, five banished, the other unknown.

The city was harsher with foreigners. More than half of the trials were directed against foreigners, mostly Catholic or non-Christian, some of them nationals of countries hostile to Geneva. While only about a quarter of the Genevans tried were executed, more than half of the foreigners were. Those tried included one Greek, nineteen Frenchmen—among them a journeyman printer, a student, and two valets—seven Italians, two non-Genevan Swiss, three Turkish galley slaves, two Germans, and four listed simply as Catholic. Of these, twenty-two, including three of the four Catholics, were executed. Thirteen were banished and four decisions remain unknown. The manner of execution included three hangings, one beheading, five drownings, and twelve burnings. Executions were most numerous between 1590 and 1620—the thirty trials that took place led to fifteen executions. This period saw the most intense antisodomitical activity, in part because of the panic occurring during and in the aftermath of the Canal trial in 1610 and also because of xenophobia attending Geneva's war with the Duke of Savoy in the 1590s. The duke's captured soldiers account for some of those executed for sodomy. But all sodomy trials and executions in Geneva reflect the religious fervor of the Protestant Reformation, especially harsh and uncompromising in that city. The theocracy determined to root out sexual dereliction and to especially punish sodomy, which was in their eyes not only the most heinous form of sexual deviance but a pernicious heresy as well.

Of course, these dry statistics do not reveal the tragedies that fell upon individual lives. Among those tried, the records list fourteen pairs as being partners, whether for life or for a night is not known. In 1444 a Greek and his Genevan partner were hanged for their crime. The Greek was a cook for the bishop; the occupation of the Genevan is not known. Though most sodomy trials list only a single defendant, a few passed judgment on both participants. In 1590, for example, a French soldier aged twenty-five was burned along with his "French valet," who was eighteen. Some years later a Genevan boy of fifteen, the sexual partner of a Genevan citizen, was banished, and the citizen was burned. Burned also was a Neapolitan, whose French valet was banished.[78]

The Genevan Consistory, the body that regulated the city's political, religious, and sexual life, heard the testimony of learned jurists in the sodomy cases brought before it. The proceedings offer insight into the changing understanding of sodomy and sodomites. In 1556, a young Frenchman was accused of attempting to rape his roommate at an inn. The crime was attested to by a number of witnesses. The three jurists involved offered similar opinions about the case, invoking both Roman law and scriptural arguments. "This sin," the first jurist observed, "ranks among the most execrable, prohibited by both divine and human laws, such that the Lord showed the rigor of his judgment . . . by burning five cities for it." His opinion was that even attempting such a "grave and atrocious" crime, perhaps even only contemplating it, ought to be punishable by death. The other two jurists concurred, citing Roman law in support of the notion that attempt of the act equaled its completion. "Sodomy" could exist in intent, they asserted, being as much a form of desire as an actual deed. And if "sodomy" could include desire, then even those who never committed sodomy but only desired it could be sodomites.

To prove that the defendant was a true sodomite, and that what he desired but had not achieved nevertheless defined what he was, one jurist—Germain Collodon—recommended that the young man be tortured again before execution to discover if he had ever engaged in sodomy before. Though another jurist pointed out that this was the defendant's first known sodomitical offense and that his recent conversion to the Reformed faith ought to move them to pity, yet he agreed with his colleagues that the offender deserved death. Two urged the defendant's burning, but the judge, perhaps swayed because this was a first offense, or perhaps feeling it was inappropriate to inflict upon a new convert a punishment usually reserved for the confirmed sodomite, instead sentenced him to hang.

Some years later, a woman being tried for fornication also confessed, under questioning, to a single lesbian offense four years earlier. The homosexual crime was described as "unnatural fornication" (to distinguish it from the "natural" crime of heterosexual fornication). The woman was also accused of blasphemy because she insisted that she was a virgin, although physical examination had proved otherwise. And since she was capable of blasphemy, Germain Collodon concluded, she was capable of sodomy as well. Referring to the law code of the Holy Roman Empire, which in 1532 had made sodomy a capital crime, Collodon insisted that "such a detestable and unnatural case deserves the punishment of death by fire." But in the prisoner's sentence the dread word "sodomy" was not mentioned. The transgression was labeled "a detestable and unnatural crime, which is so ugly that, from horror of it, it is not named here."[79] Collodon's recommendation that the woman be burned was ignored; she was simply drowned.

During the Renaissance, between 1450 and 1650, some of the most ferocious laws against sodomy were promulgated and more sodomites were executed than at any previous period in European history. It is sometimes argued that in comparison with the number of sodomy *prosecutions* during this time—or in comparison with the numbers of people executed for other crimes or for their membership in other groups—this "violence against sodomites" was "brief and sporadic."[80] In terms of numbers this is true. In Spain, Portugal, France, Italy, and Geneva from 1450 into the 1700s, nearly sixteen thousand people were tried for sodomy, which by this time generally meant exclusively homosexual acts. Only about four hundred men and women are known to have been executed. Four hundred deaths, however, is not an inconsequential number in the annals of judicial homophobia. What the four hundred executions and sixteen thousand prosecutions represent, after all, is the judicial repression of sexual and social deviance. These were legally instituted persecutions of a sexual minority, persecutions approved by popular opinion. Yet, except in cases of rape or unwilling seduction, homosexual passion was a victimless act, condemned only because it was feared.

Chapter Eleven

England's Abominable Vice

In 1533, the twenty-fifth year of the reign of Henry VIII, Parliament noted that as yet England had no "sufficient" punishment for "the detestable and abominable vice of buggery committed with mankinde or beast." The term "buggery," as we have seen, originally referred to a species of heresy and by this time had come to mean sodomy. The law passed to address the problem made no mention of the usual trio of offenses against God—heresy, sorcery, and witchcraft; it was concerned solely with deviant sexual acts performed "with mankinde or beast."[1]

1 Sodomy and Criminal Law

English legal opinion had long recommended the execution of sodomites and heretics. Both *Britton* and *Fleta,* earlier English treatises, as we have seen, linked sodomy with heresy, an association by this time firmly established in both law and the popular mind.[2] In another law-book of the period, *The Mirror of Justices,* sodomy is defined as a form of treason against God and also specifically allied with heresy and apostasy as manifestations of the crime of *laesa majestas.*[3] In all of these works, sodomy, defined as a religious offense, is included in a list of crimes that grievously affront God and Christian doctrine.

The 1533 law secularized both the crime and the punishment. The new law demanded that the offense be made a felony, and that "such order and form of process therein be used against the offenders, as in cases of felony at common law." That is, convicted offenders were to suffer "pains of death and losses, and penalties of their goods, chattels, debts, lands, tenements, and hereditaments."[4] Like other felons, sodomites were to be hanged. That the convicted lost all their worldly goods may have mattered little to them once dead, but their sons inherited the sins of their fathers and nothing else.

The passage of the law was only one of many tactics employed by king and Parliament in the conflict between Henry and the Roman Church. In the same year, defying the authority of the pontiff, Henry asserted that his marriage to Catherine of Aragon was void. He secretly married Anne Boleyn, and appointed as Archbishop of Canterbury Thomas Cranmer, who had performed the ceremony. A year later, Henry broke with Rome entirely and established himself as head of the new Church of England.

However, while Henry might ignore the pope and appoint his own archbishop, there remained a significant obstacle to his supremacy: the ancient monasteries throughout England, whose wealth was vast and whose loyalty to Rome remained unshaken. Such politically dangerous opponents could be destroyed only by dissolving them and seizing their wealth. What better means to this end than the new law against sodomy, a vice to which clergy had long been believed to be especially prone? Once the law was passed, Henry's commissioners began to inspect the monasteries; within a year Henry declared them dissolved and their goods forfeit to the state.

Just how useful accusations of sodomy had been is evident from a letter Henry sent to the regent of Scotland in 1543, urging him to dissolve the Scottish monasteries as the English ones had been dissolved. To achieve "the extirpation of the state of monks and friars," Henry instructed, the regent ought to send commissioners who "must have secret commission . . . to examine . . . their [the monks'] behavior . . . whereby if it is well handled, he shall get knowledge of all their abominations." A letter by one of the commissioners spelled out the tactic: "This morning," he wrote, "I will objecte against divers of them bugrie . . . wiche I have learned of others but not of them, what I shall fynde I cannot tell."[5] Whether or not he found it, it is clear that the commissioner was ready to use an accusation of "bugrie"—of which in this case he had only hearsay evidence—as a means to achieve the end he sought.

The law of 1533 had wider implications. The parliamentarians who framed the law no doubt knew that buggery was considered a sin, yet the law calls it not a sin but a vice—a significant marker in the history of homophobia. By declaring this vice criminal, the law placed it in another, more fatal category of culpability. A sin *could* be repented and the sinner forgiven. Vice, considered as a moral fault, *could* be rejected, and the vicious could reform. But the criminal's repentance was irrelevant, reform useless. Once discovered and convicted, he inevitably faced punishment. Further, the law promised rich rewards for the removal of troublesome subjects, thus encouraging prosecutors, and, indeed, everyone, to find or manufacture evidence against anyone who might best be undone by an accusation of sodomy.[6] Though clearly intended to help destroy the power of the Church, the law, by declaring sodomy a crime, made it a useful weapon against any number of opponents.

The shift of authority from Church to state had other consequences for England as well. Before the passage of the law of 1533, prosecution for the sin of sodomy—understood to mean not only homosexual behavior but bestiality and any other nonprocreative sexual act—had been the sole prerogative of the Church. Trials were held by ecclesiastical courts, and convictions remained their province. Only execution was the duty of the secular authority. In transferring adjudication of sodomy to civil magistrates, the English Parliament turned a religious offense into an exclusively secular crime.[7] Thus the state claimed the right to judge the sexual activities of its subjects and also the right to define what was "natural" in terms of secular law, thus giving it unprecedented power over the bodies and behavior of its subjects.[8] By politicizing and secularizing sodomy, Henry allowed English legal and popular opinion to construe sodomites themselves as enemies of the state, and sodomy as treason.

After Henry's son Edward VI inherited the throne in 1547, a new antisodomy law repealed some of the harshest penalties of Henry's law. Convicted sodomites were still to be adjudged felons and hanged. But the incentive to accuse an enemy of sodomy was removed: no one who bore witness against an accused felon could profit from a successful conviction. Nor would a vague accusation of buggery committed in the distant past do: accusations and indictments had to occur within six months of the alleged offense. Nor would the convicted felon lose his lands and goods—a matter of keen concern to his heirs, since it not only secured their material well-being but cleansed them of the sins of their father. With the felon died the taint. As a crime, sodomy was now inherent in the body of the individual.[9] Now there could be no doubt in English law about the existence of a criminal called a sodomite.

Mary ascended the throne in 1553 after her half-brother's brief reign and repealed many of his laws and their father's in her attempt to restore the Catholic faith in England. Among these were the sodomy laws, which the language of Mary's repeal described as too harsh. Bloody Mary burned Protestant heretics with as much dispatch as Henry had hanged papist sodomites; her failure to pass laws against sodomites during her reign was due not to tolerance but to her intention to return these sinners to Church jurisdiction.

Mary Tudor died, however, after four years on the throne. In 1558 Elizabeth I reinstated the antisodomy laws, not in Edward's tempered version, but in Henry's original harsh formulations. Her Parliament introduced a bill in 1559 alleging that sodomy had to a frightening degree increased since Mary repealed the sodomy law: "Divers evil disposed persons have been more bold to commit the said most horrible and detestable Vice of Buggery aforesaid, to the high displeasure of almighty God."[10] In addition to reintroducing the language of religious condemnation, the bill also linked sodomy with the traditional horrors of heresy, magic, and witchcraft. In 1563, however, the bill was divided into two parts, one addressing sodomy only, the other black magic and witchcraft, and it was passed in that form.[11]

Thus the sodomy act of 1563 completed the process in English law that made sodomy solely a sexual and a civil crime. In 1607 one H. Stafford was prosecuted for having anal intercourse with a sixteen-year-old boy. His crime is described as the "detestable and abominable sin of Sodom," a "thing displeasing to almighty God and a crime to all mankind, against the peace of the . . . king, his crown, and dignity."[12] In his systematic discussion of English law, the *Institutes* (1644), Sir Edward Coke confirmed the opinion that sodomy as a crime against the king was treason.[13]

The antisodomy law of Elizabeth I remained in effect for two hundred and sixty-five years, until its strict provisions, though not the death penalty, were repealed in 1828. The death penalty for sodomy instituted by Henry VIII remained in force in England for more than three hundred years, until a law passed under Queen Victoria reduced the punishment for those convicted of the "abominable crime of Buggery" to penal servitude for life.

2 Redefining Sodomy

After the passage of Henry's law, the definition of the English word "sodomy" gradually narrowed, coming to mean homosexual acts, especially between men. In his *Bibliotheca Eliotae* of 1552 Thomas Cooper defined "sodomito" as "to use or commit the sinne of Sodom agaynste naturae."[14] Though presumably the reader already knew what the sin of Sodom was, neither sexual nor homosexual activity is specified, so the definition could include all sorts of debauched, riotous, unnatural activity. By 1565, in his *Thesaurus Linguae Romanae et Britannicae,* Cooper individualizes the sin, defining "Catamitus" as "a boy abused contrary to nature." At the end of the century, in *A World of Words: or Most Copious and Exact Dictionarie in Italian and English* (1598), John Florio curiously defines "sodomia" as "the naturall sin of Sodomie," that is, native to Sodom, and perhaps intending to suggest that the sin was also natural to Sodom. He adds to the definition the actor: "a sodomite, a buggrer." By 1670, Thomas Blount in his *Glossographia: Or a Dictionary Interpretting the Hard Words of Whatever Language, Now Used in our refined English Tongue* does not find it hard to interpret sodomy, which he also calls "buggery": "so called from the City of *Sodom* in *Judaea,* which for the detestable sin was destroyed with fire from heaven." The "detestable" sin's scope was now narrowed to bestiality or homosexual behavior, as the cross-reference to "Buggerie" makes clear: "Buggerie (Fr. *Bougrerie*) is described to be *carnalis copula contra naturem* . . . a man or a woman with a brute beast . . . a man with a man, or a woman with a woman." Here there is no general debauchery, no anal intercourse performed on a woman, no extramarital adventure, no heterosexual behavior at all.

So, too, with definitions of Ganymede. In the fourteenth century Peter Berchorius in his *Reductium Morale* rewrote Ovid's Ganymede and Jupiter as an allegory of the soul in its service to God.[15] In Cooper's *Bibliotheca Eliotae* (1552), Ganymede is identified simply as "a Trojan chylde, which feigned to be ravyshed of Jupiter, and made his butlar." But in John Marston's *Scourge of Villanie* (1598), a passive male sexual object is described as "you effeminate sanguine Ganimede," and one gallant has "his Ganimede" who engages with his keeper in "Sodome beastliness."[16]

Eventually Ganymede had come to stand for sodomy itself: in Blount's dictionary of 1670 the entry for "Ganymede" says "any Boy, loved for carnal abuse, or hired to be used contrary to Nature to commit the detestable sin of *Sodomy,* is called Ganymede."[17] Blount's definitions are circular: He defines a "Ganymede" as an "ingle." An "ingle" is "a boy kept for sodomy," cross-referenced to "Ganymede." When Blount defines "catamite" as "a boy abused contrary to nature," "a Ganymede," the circle is closed.[18] A sodomite is now everything: a "Ganimede," an "ingler or a buggerer." These definitions require that sodomy and buggery, Ganymedes and catamites, sodomites, ingles, and buggerers all name a single thing: homosexual acts between males.

3 Literary Sodomites

Despite the criminalization of homosexual relations, the English Renaissance prized and celebrated intimate male friendship. While the literature depicted women as offering sexual pleasure, their love was also known to be a powerful and even disruptive force; women were often cruel and inconstant. For constancy, unselfish affection, and even dedicated love, male friendship far surpassed the love of women.

In the English as in the continental Renaissance a variety of writings attempted to define masculine love and friendship. If "friendship" as a broad general category could include intimacy between men, homosexual relations required specific terminology, such as "masculine love" or "Socratic love" or "special" or "unique" friendship, or were indicated by images of Ganymede or of David and Jonathan. Certainly an understanding of the Renaissance positions on homosexuality and friendship must take account of both the general proscription of sodomy and the substantial presence of homosexual desire. Homoeroticism pervades Shakespeare's intense sonnets to the still unidentified "Mr. W.H." Love between men is wittily mythologized in Marlowe's *Hero and Leander* (1598), where the apparently "heterosexual" Leander—"I am no woman," he cries, as Poseidon tries to rape him—is taken by Poseidon to be the available Ganymede. Familiar classical allusions to same-sex romance appear in Spenser's *Faerie Queene*. In Richard Barnfield's *Affectionate Shepherd,* Daphnis addresses his love poems to the youth he calls Ganimede, while in Thomas Heywood's *Jupiter and Ganimede* there is no doubt about Ganimede's sexual availability, since Jupiter importunes him for kisses. The pastoral—a form derived from Virgil's *Second Eclogue* and exemplified in Spenser's *The Shepheardes Calendar,* Marlowe's "The Passionate Shepherd to His Love," and Barnfield's *The Affectionate Shepherd*—suggests an Arcadian realm outside Christian law where men are allowed free play of homoerotic feelings. Androgyny and homoeroticism surface not only in depictions of Ganymede but in Shakespeare's transvestite characters—young men who adopt the dress of the other sex, or women who dress as boys and are wooed by men. Homosexual attraction is the key to the tension of the text, and it provides the opportunity for either satire or more serious explorations of homoerotic relationships—between Marlowe's Gaveston and Edward, for example, or Shakespeare's W.H. and "Will." Homoeroticism is suggested in prose as well: Sir Philip Sidney's *The Countess of Pembroke's Arcadia* (1590), though ultimately celebrating heterosexual marriage, nevertheless portrays the attachment between Pyrocles and Musidorus in terms that suggest passion as well as friendship. Sir Francis Bacon's celebrated essay "Of Friendship" argues that friendship between men is the most noble of all relationships, while his essay "Of Beauty" constructs ideal beauty in all-male terms.

However, "special" friendships and "masculine love" often threatened darker possibilities. That friendship between males might proceed to sex between them was an almost constant subtext of Renaissance writing, a secret that no one revealed and no one kept. Some English writers insisted that friendship and sodomy were necessarily irreconcilable; since the former ought to be chaste, if passionate, the latter was necessarily promiscuous and depraved. Others feared and asserted that friendship and sodomy were the same terrible thing. While certain writers justified the use of classical models as material for literature, subjects for pictures, and texts for songs, many insisted that this was simply a pretext to justify sin and crime. There were writers who went to some lengths to assure their readers that they did not mean what they seemed to mean.

All this anxiety emerges vividly in the discussions generated by a pair of texts. The first is in a contemporary commentary by one "E.K." on "Januarye" in Edmund Spenser's *The Shepheardes Calendar* (1579). The poem presents a trio of lovers: Hobbinol, who loves Colin Clout, who spurns Hobbinol and is besotted by Rosalind. "It is not Hobbinol wherefore I plaine," explains Colin:

Albee my love he seeke with dayly suit;
His clownish gifts and curtsies I disdaine,
His kiddes, his cracknelles, and his early fruit.
Ah, foolish Hobbinol! thy gyfts bene vayne;
Colin them gives to Rosalind againe.

E.K. addresses the vexed question of just where sodomy and friendship intersect. He fears that the reader will misunderstand the nature of the relationship. Hobbinol may seem to be Colin's "very speciall and most familiar freend, whom he entirely and extraordinarily beloved," and the reader may discern an unpleasant "savour of disorderly love, which the learned call *paederastice*." He hastens to assure readers, however, that such an interpretation is "beside his [the author's] meaning."[19] Determined to save not only Hobbinol's reputation but that of classical philosophy, E.K. moves from the "learned" who justify "disorderly love" by cloaking it in allusions to idealized classical pederasty, to readers of Plato's dialogues, who "may easily perceive, that such love is muche to be alowed and liked of, specially so meant, as Socrates used it: who sayth, that in deede he loved Alcybiades extremely." However, it was not "Alcybiades person, but hys soule" that Socrates loved, E.K. asserts, and in the best homoerotic tradition of the Renaissance he points out that *"paederastice,"* which he construes as male friendship, is "much to be preferred before gynerastice, that is the love whiche enflameth men with lust toward woman kind."

Having said this, E.K. becomes anxious about how the reader may perceive *him:* "But yet let no man thinke, that herein I stand . . . in defence of execrable and horrible sinnes of forbidden and unlawful fleshlinesse, whose abominable errour is fully confuted" by various writers. E.K. no longer seems to fear what his readers may think of Hobbinol or Spenser. Instead he worries that his comments might seem to express even the faintest approbation of sodomy—worse, that others may read him as a sodomite.

The second text, Richard Barnfield's pastoral *The Affectionate Shepherd* (1594), tells the conventional story of the shepherd Daphnis, infatuated with a younger man named Ganimede. Daphnis' rival for Ganimede's affections is the "faire Queene Guendolen," and the comparison of the youth's beauty with the woman's voracious sexuality elaborates a misogynistic theme commonplace in Renaissance texts. Sexual language and homosexual puns abound: when Daphnis sees the "faire boy" who "had my hart intangled" he reacts passionately: "Cursing the time, the Place, the sense, the sin: I came, I saw, I view'd, I slipped in." He also flaunts his fall: "If it be a sinne to love a lovely lad, O than sinne I."

But Barnfield too found it necessary to aver that what he said was not what he meant. In the preface to a second miscellany of poems,

Cynthia, with Certain Sonnets (1595), Barnfield takes great care to clear up any misunderstanding *The Affectionate Shepherd* might have occasioned: "Some there were that did interpret *The Affectionate Shepherd* otherwise than in truth I meant, touching the subject thereof: to wit the love of a shepherd for a boy; a fault the which I will not excuse because I never made. Only this will I unshadow my conceit: being nothing else but imitation of Virgil in the second Eclogue, of Alexis." His poem is merely an imitation of Virgil; no reader should mistake his intention, for he was only following that source. Writing poems about sodomy, Barnfield insists, does not make the poet a sodomite. But about the shepherd the poem's opening verses are unequivocal:

> *Scarce had the morning starre hid from the light*
> *Heavens crimson canopie with stars bespangled,*
> *But I began to rue th' unhappy sight*
> *Of that faire boy that had my hart intangled;*
> *Cursing the time, the place, the sense, the sin;*
> *I came, I saw, I view'd, I slipped in.*
>
> *If it be sinne to love a sweet-fac'd boy,*
> *Whose amber locks trust up in golden tramels*
> *Dangle adowne his lovely cheekes with joy,*
> *When pearle and flowers his faire haire enamels*
> *If it be sinne to love a lovely lad,*
> *O then sinne I, for whom my soul is sad.*

Sodomy stands boldly between the lines, concentrated in the single word "sinne," incessantly heard in the Renaissance whenever sodomy is described. The sight of the boy is "unhappy." But why? Because it is inevitable that the poet's heart will be entangled, and once he is committed, he cannot escape. Why is his soul sad? Because he has sinned, not because he has loved. Whom does he love? A lovely lad. What is this love? It is sin. It is sodomy. But he cannot help himself. The entire event is cursed because he cannot help but succumb to the lure of beauty and the call of sodomy, and because sodomy—the sin that is enacted by "slipping in"—is the sin most cursed by God.

In E.K.'s gloss upon Spenser his subject is friendship, but the subject is so unstable that he finds himself suddenly falling into the abyss of sodomy. He sets out to prove that Hobbinol is not a sodomite, but his project comes to ruin when sodomy precipitately overwhelms his objections even as he tries to distance himself from it. Barnfield too is unable to prevent sodomy from advancing from the perimeter into the heart of the poem. In Barnfield there is no doubt that the shepherd is a sodomite, and what is invented in fiction might well be possible in real life.[20] Barnfield protests that he is misunderstood, but his protest, like E.K.'s, shows that both were well aware of the issues at stake. Sodomy was no arcane subject, far removed from the minds of author and reader as they innocently contemplated friendship and delighted in skilled imitations of a distant classicism. On the contrary; friendly intimacy between males threatened to erupt into desire and passion; sodomy always hovered as a sinful possibility. The cult of all-male friendship was perpetually shadowed by the specter of the sodomite lurking behind the glorious image of the ideal friend.

4 Inventing Homophobia

Though the Renaissance celebrated homoerotic feelings, it also hanged or burned people who acted on those feelings.[21] Plague, war, civil strife, and threats of treason or heresy often provided an excuse for state-sponsored persecutions of sodomites. But despite such attacks, sodomites seemed to be more visible and more numerous than ever before. Moralist preachers revived age-old assertions that sodomy was on the increase, and the state acted to find out if it was true. Coteries of sodomites were discovered by new policing groups such as the Florentine Officers of the Night. Satirists charged that sodomites were organized into bands of dangerous sexual deviants.

By the end of the Renaissance, the abominable sin of sodomy had become an abominable crime throughout Europe. Laws had criminalized sodomy in France and Spain in the early thirteenth century, in Italian cities like Florence, Siena, Perugia, and Venice in the fourteenth century, in the Holy Roman Empire in 1532, in England in 1533, in Prussia in 1620, and in Denmark in 1683; in the Netherlands, capital sentences against sodomites were carried out in the late seventeenth century. Most laws against sodomy demanded the death penalty, sometimes for a single infraction; the usual means of execution was burning, or sometimes hanging.

From the fifteenth to the seventeenth centuries in Europe and England, civil authority occasionally prosecuted sodomy so much more severely than any other crime that the prosecutions could more fairly be described as persecutions. As the seventeenth century drew to a close, "sodomy," a category invented by religious prohibition and civil proscription, had become indistinguishable from the individual who practiced it—the sodomite, to whom state, Church, and citizenry responded with fear, hatred, contempt, and disgust.

THE MAN-WOMAN

A "man-woman" from an eighteenth-century print. Collection of the author

PART FIVE

Sodomy and the Enlightenment

Unmasking and Punishing Sodomites, 1700–1860

Chapter Twelve

Societies of Sodomites

During the eighteenth and early nineteenth centuries, sodomy became a concern for a far broader section of the public, which was by now convinced that sodomites were a curious and probably dangerous species essentially different from other men. The wide public concern was due in part to the clamor for moral reform that swept England after the fall of the Stuart monarchy in 1688 and found an echo in the Netherlands, France, and Prussia. Curiously, in Italy and Spain, where much of the persecution had begun, sodomites were no longer persecuted with anything like the vigor of the fifteenth and sixteenth centuries. But "sodomy paranoia" continued unabated elsewhere.[1] Reform movements, born within the growing and vocal middle class, often passed harsh judgments about what was sexually permissible for men and women. In England, for example, Societies for the Reformation of Manners were created in the 1690s to hunt down blasphemers, drunkards, whoremasters, and—the group that most inflamed and alarmed them—sodomites.

Sodomy's threat to the immortal soul was of less interest to those reformers than was the danger it posed to the social and political body. Consequently, the social control of sodomites—even their extirpation—was seen as a necessary task of the state. Extirpation was the choice of Jeremy Collier (1650–1726), a clergyman bent on reforming an England that he believed to be mired in all manner of wickedness, the chief of which was sodomy. In his 1720s essay "Whoredom," Collier noted that "in ancient Times, these Criminals were burnt by Common Law. Indeed such Monsters ought to be the Detestation of Mankind, pursued by Justice, and exterminated from the earth."[2] A French commentator of 1724 feared that if sodomites were not punished, "there will be great disorders" and "all kinds of people will take off their masks, believing everything is permitted, and they will organize leagues and societies, which will be disastrous."[3]

Indeed, throughout Western Europe, sodomites seemed to present a danger to the state. The German Protestant theologian Johann Michaelis (1717–91) wrote in 1770:

> If one considers how dreadfully damaging sodomy is for the state, and how much this disgusting vice spreads secretly, the death penalty does not seem too hard. Once this vice develops a hold, [not only adults but] striplings begin to seduce striplings. It knows no rest; indeed once its shamefulness and ugliness are lost and it becomes a mark of gallantry and pride in the nation, it will become the greatest force of depopulation and weakness, not in its initial stages but three or four generations later. Not only does sodomy weaken marriage . . . and aid and abet him who refuses to raise a family . . . [it brings] the nation . . . to the brink of destruction.[4]

If marriage bonds and families are destroyed because men find sodomy more compelling than domestic virtue, then there is only a short distance to the destruction of civilization itself.

Indeed, attitudes toward sodomites in the eighteenth century, the age of the Enlightenment, were only occasionally enlightened. Montesquieu, speaking as both a jurist and a philosopher, wondered why each of the three great crimes, "magic, heresy, and the crime against nature"—the first of which can be proved not to exist, the second difficult to define, and the last, he says, "obscure"—are all punished by burning. Nevertheless, while objecting to the punishment, Montesquieu still condemned sodomy. Voltaire argued that homosexual behavior ought to be regarded as an aberration and a personal taste rather than as a crime; but in his article "Socratic Love" in his *Philosophical*

Dictionary (1764) he describes homosexual behavior as an "outrage" against nature, clearly despising what he hoped to decriminalize.[5] While some Enlightenment thinkers could not countenance the idea that homosexual behavior was a sin, and even urged that it ought not be classed as a crime, few were willing to allow it full admission into respectable society.

1 Effeminate Weaklings

The activities and publications of the English reform societies of the 1720s indicate that popular perceptions about the existence of a homosexual underworld might be correct. The reform societies claimed that sodomites frequented certain places—parks, latrines, public arcades, and certain taverns—that they used special codes, signs, and gestures to recognize one another and to indicate sexual interest; and that they sported a distinct language, mannerisms, and dress. "If one of them sits on a bench he pats the back of his hands; if you follow them, they put a white handkerchief through the skirts of their coat, and wave it to and fro; but if they are met by you, their thumbs are stuck in the armpits of their coats, and they play their fingers on their breasts."[6] By the 1730s, London had networks of men (almost never of women) who were involved with one another for both sexual and social reasons, as is documented by raids on sodomite establishments that continued into the nineteenth century.[7]

London was not alone. The Hague and other Dutch cities had special sites frequented by sodomites. In Amsterdam, these included the town hall; certain taverns, such as the Serpent; toilets and parks; and the private houses of known sodomites. In Paris, the Tuileries gardens were a well-known site for sodomite trysts, and in 1724 complaints were made about the "libertine men" who swam nude in the Seine and on its banks committed "abominations with their own sex."[8] In the 1780s, sodomites practiced "vile acts and horrors" at the Café Alexandre in the Boulevard du Temple, according to one antisodomite pamphlet.[9] During the reign of Louis XV, the Paris police organized *patrouilles de pederastie* to survey and report on known sodomites. The *mouches,* as these police patrols were called, both informed on men and entrapped them into illicit homosexual acts.[10] Now the police knew the identity of such men, where they met other men, and what strata of society—as it turned out, all strata—were touched by sodomy.

232 Sodomy and the Enlightenment

Police surveillance established *pederastes* as a class whose criminality lay in their sexual inclination. Arrest or the threat of it was used to instill fear, but rarely now to convict or execute.

Effeminacy was seen as the primary mark of the sodomite. In 1724, a Dutch journalist, Justus van Effen, described sodomites as "hermaphrodites in their minds" and "effeminate weaklings." A pamphlet described sodomites as having a "feminine mind in a man's body."[11] An English antisodomite pamphlet of 1749, "Satan's Harvest Home," detailed the "Reasons for the Growth of sodomy in England," offering the opinion that "men of a tender Constitution" were likely to be sodomites and suggesting that "the Effeminacy of our Men's Dress and Manners, particularly their Kissing each other," was both cause and symptom. Indeed, these "enervated effeminate animals" had "sucked in the Spirit of Cotqueanism ["cotquean": a housewife, or a man who acts like one] since infancy."[12]

In England, effeminate sodomites who cross-dressed in private and sometimes in public were called mollies. "Molly" came to be applied to all sodomites, and molly-houses were where they gathered. The word may have been imported into English from the Latin of the New Testament (where *mollis*—"soft"—was translated in the King James Bible as "effeminate.")[13] Richard of Devizes' *Chronicle of the Times of King Richard the First* (c. 1192) mentions the existence in the London underworld of "molles"—again from Latin—presumably "effeminate" males, since they are conflated with catamites.[14] "Molly" was also, of course, a feminine name. In English slang a molly-cull was the female accomplice of a thief, a denizen of the English criminal underworld in which sodomite mollies also inevitably moved. Certainly by the early eighteenth century "molly" had come to mean an effeminate male with a predilection for sexual activity with other men, a preference for the passive role in anal intercourse, and an interest in practices like transvestitism and gender-role reversal. The word has remained in modern English as "mollycoddle."

In *The London Spy* (1698–1709), Ned Ward exposed the city's sexual underworld; his description of its sodomite subculture both ridiculed and demonized it:

> There are a particular Gang of Sodomitical Wretches in this Town, who call themselves the Mollies, [who] . . . tempt one another, . . . to commit those odious Bestialities, that ought for ever to be without a Name. At a certain Tavern in the City, whose sign I shall not

mention, because I am unwilling to fix an Odium upon the House . . . they have settled a constant Meeting every evening in the Week, that they may have the better Opportunity of drawing unwary Youth into the like Corruption.

The evenings followed a set pattern, Ward reports:

No sooner had they ended their Feast, and run through all the Ceremonies of their theatrical Way of Gossiping, but having wash'd
away with Wine, all fear of Shame, as well as the checks of Modesty, then they began to enter upon their beastly Obscenities, and
to take those infamous Liberties with one another that no Man
who is not sunk into a state of Devilism, can think on without
Blushing, or mention without a Christian Abhorrence of all such
heathenish Brutalities. Thus, without Detection, they continu'd in
their odious Society for some Years, till their sodomitical Practices
were happily discover'd by the cunning Management of some of
the under Agents to the reforming Society; so that several were
brought to open Shame and Punishment; others flying from Justice
to escape the Ignominy, that by this Means the Diabolical Society
were forc'd to put a Period to their filthy scandalous Revels.[15]

In 1748 in Paris, a witness described a house in the Marais "at the sign of the Six Sparrows in the rue aux Juifs" where men "with napkins on their heads imitate women and mince about like them. Any new young man in their midst is called a bride, and they all try for him. People pair off to touch and perform infamous acts."[16] In The Hague, in the Netherlands, a man described in a trial report as one of "that sort of people" ran an inn where it was known that one could spend the night with a fellow sodomite, while the house of Willem van Schalen came to be known as a kind of social center for sodomites, welcoming as many as fifty at a time.[17]

Such outsider descriptions of this subculture most often emphasized its effeminacy. Obviously, effeminate men would be easiest to spot; sodomites who were not effeminate would simply blend in with the majority. Indeed, probably most sodomites were not mollies; trial records show that many were married—a status some used as a defense since it was widely believed that a married man could not be a sodomite.[18] Many sodomites indignantly rejected effeminate practices and role-playing; in 1748 one man, a painter, "withdrew from these gatherings [of mollies] because they were too scandalous. Several members imitated women and made gestures which showed what they were." The painter admonished them: "Can't you adopt men's mannerisms rather than women's?"[19]

Molly-houses provided safe places where mollies could meet and have sex with one another or with "masculine" men who sought homosexual sex. They may also have served as clearinghouses for procuring boys and young men for sex, and as sites for elaborate social rituals that involved feminine roles and dress, such as mock marriage ceremonies followed by sex in special rooms sometimes called chapels. More unusual was the staged "birth" of a baby—a mock labor attended by crowds of well-wishers, midwives, and godparents attired in their finest. On these "festival nights," the man elected to play the mother gave birth to his baby, sometimes represented by a doll—though on the occasion of the lying-in of one "Mrs. May" it is recorded that she was "brought to bed of a Cheshire cheese."[20]

Dress and ritual provided a context for social activities, but sex was what drove the subculture. Sex—between men, between men and boys, between exclusive sodomites, and between sodomites and non-sodomites, whom we would call straight men—is fully and precisely documented in journals, court records, and literature. In 1725, Samuel Stephens, a constable, infiltrated Mother Clap's well-known molly-house: "I found between 40 and 50 Men making Love to one another, as they call'd it. Sometimes they would sit on one another's Laps, kissing in a lewd Manner, and using their hands indecently. Then they would get up, dance and make Curtsies, and mimick the voices of Women. . . . Then they'd hug, and play and toy, and go out by Couples into another Room on the same Floor, to be marry'd, as they call'd it."[21]

Sexual activities between men mostly involved anal penetration, masturbation, and intercrural intercourse; fellatio was seemingly rare though not unknown, and kissing, which in the seventeenth and early eighteenth centuries was a common form of greeting between men, had by the late eighteenth century increasingly become a sure sign of sodomitical tendencies.[22] The paradigm of man-boy sodomy was very much part of this sexual subculture, and anal penetration was what most seemed ultimately to desire. For example, in 1698, Captain Edward Rigby met nineteen-year-old Charles Minton in London's St. James's Park. In the darkness—the park was illuminated only by the fireworks being set off to celebrate Guy Fawkes Day—Rigby took Minton "by the hand, and squeez'd it; put his Privy Member Erected into Minton's hand; kist him, and put his tongue in Minton's mouth." Minton agreed to meet Rigby a few days later at the George Tavern in Pall Mall, where the captain had engaged a private room. There Rigby told the younger man that he had "raised his lusts to the highest degree." He sat on Minton's lap and "kissing him asked if he could fuck him." Minton protested that such a thing could only be done by men and women, but Rigby volunteered to show him how to do it and after pulling down Minton's breeches "put his Finger to Minton's fundament, and applied his body close to Minton's."[23]

John Cleland's 1748–49 novel *Memoirs of a Woman of Pleasure* offers a graphic portrayal of sex between men, neither of whom is a molly. If the reader had any doubt about just what sodomy was, Cleland's book dispelled it. Meanwhile, the narrator, Fanny Hill, who secretly watches the event, utters all the conventional horrifics.

> For presently the eldest unbuttoned the other's breeches, and removing the linen barrier, brought out to view a white shaft, middle sized, and scarce fledged, when after handling and playing with it a little, with other dalliance, all received by the boy without other opposition than certain wayward coynesses, ten times more alluring than repulsive, he got him to turn round, with his face from him, to a chair that stood hard by, when knowing, I suppose, his office, the Ganymede now obsequiously leaned his head against the back of it, and projecting his body, made a fair mark, still covered with his shirt, as he thus stood in a side view to me, but fronting his companion, who, presently unmasking his battery, produced an engine that certainly deserved to be put to a better use, and very fit to confirm me in my disbelief of the possibility of things being pushed to odious extremities, which I had built on the disproportion of parts; but this disbelief I was now to be cured of, as by my consent all young men should likewise be, that their innocence may not be betrayed into such snares, for want of knowing the extent of their danger, for nothing is more certain than that ignorance of a vice is by no means a guard against it.
>
> Slipping, then, aside the young lad's shirt, and tucking it up under his cloaths behind, he shewed to the open air those globular fleshy eminences that compose the Mount Pleasants of Rome, and

which now, with all the narrow vale that intersects them, stood displayed and exposed to his attack, nor could I without a shudder behold the dispositions he made for it. First, then, moistening well with spittle his instrument, obviously to make it glib; he pointed, he introduced it, as I could plainly discern, not only from its direction, and my losing sight of it, but by the writhing, twisting, and soft murmured complaints of the young sufferer; but at length, the first straits of entrance being pretty well got through, everything seemed to move and go pretty currently on, as on a carpet road, without much rub or resistance . . . and thus continuing to harass his rear, the height of the fit came on with its usual symptoms, and dismissed the action.[24]

By the end of the century anxiety was so great that in 1784, the *Mémoires secrets* of a French aristocrat named Moufle d'Angerville warned that "there is no order of society, from dukes on down to footmen, that is not infected" by sodomy.[25] A Parisian document on the subject reported that the police had discovered "dangerous inclinations in certain souls which may promptly lead them to misdeeds." There was only one remedy: sodomites must be "sequestered from society" without respect to rank or status.[26] In the annals of persecution, the call to separate sodomites from society indicates their continuing marginalization and the popular panic.

2 Persecution in the Dutch Republic

In the provinces of the Dutch Republic between 1730 and 1811, this widespread panic led to a spectacular series of trials for sodomy, which resulted in more men being arrested, tried, convicted, and executed than at any other time in the previous history of the nation. The proximate cause was once again a sense of peril. Many felt that the Dutch nation at the time was in grave danger—its commerce declining, its populace enervated by foreign luxuries, its religion unheeded. As a broadsheet poem of the period complained, "God stages wrath in the midst of this our country, submerged as it is in seas of wicked sins, / Befouled by bands of dogs and dirty swine / Whose poison spreads though its entrails like pestilence."[27] In January 1730 a complaint was registered that sodomites were meeting in the cathedral in Utrecht and engaging in sodomitical acts there. Two soldiers were arrested and executed. Their confession implicated one Zacharias Wilsma, who confessed that a network of sodomites stretched from one to another of the great cities of the republic. Further investigations led to arrests and convictions in both large cities and small towns. Several months later, in July, an edict was promulgated that directly ascribed a variety of catastrophes to sodomy: "Some terrible atrocities have been committed for some time past in our dear states of Holland. . . . Offending Nature herself . . . many of our subjects have turned so far away from any fear of God as audaciously to commit crimes which should never even be heard of, on account of which God Almighty had in earlier times overturned, destroyed and laid waste Sodom and Gomorrah."

> Since we could never imagine that such atrocities could be committed in this land, no special laws have been provided for them. Because we feel a just abhorrence towards this execrable crime of sodomy, and wish to employ our full power and all efficacious means to stamp out, lock, stock, and barrel, this sin that cries to heaven, so that God Almighty might not—as he used to threaten at such abominations—punish the iniquity of our land with his terrible judgments, and spew forth the land and its inhabitants, thus bringing to an end his forbearance to our dear Fatherland, it is decreed . . . that, in order to obliterate such a terrible evil from our midst:
>
> First: The crime of sodomy henceforth must always be punished in public, like other crimes, as a deterrent and warning to everyone.
>
> Second: The same crime, according to Divine Scripture, must be punished with death, and the type and manner of death shall be at the discretion of the judge, according to the more or less serious circumstances of this abominable crime.
>
> Third: Everyone who is convicted of having tried repeatedly to debauch others to the crime mentioned, or of having induced others to offer their homes for money for the commission of this crime, shall also be punished with death, even though he has not been convicted of having defiled himself in this manner.
>
> Fourth: The corpse of the executed must, immediately after the execution, be burned to ashes, thrown in the ocean, or exposed as unworthy of burial.

Fifth: The judgments on the above-mentioned crime, with sentences of contempt of court against any fugitives who have been convicted, must be printed and publicly posted in the usual places.

And Sixth: The magistrates, judges, and criminal courts in their respective cities, shall be specially authorized and commanded to investigate thoroughly the reason for the absence of any persons within their jurisdictions, who, since the first of May [1730], when the investigation of those guilty of the above-mentioned crime began, until the first of August next, have secretly, without apparent good cause, absented themselves from their positions, professions, occupations and homes and have thus made themselves extremely suspect of having been guilty of this crime. And if the investigation reveals no reason that would counter the strong suspicion aroused by clandestine departures when they have become matters of common gossip, the authorities shall summon these persons by an explicit edict to give reasons for their suspect absence in person, or through a representative, and those who do not answer after the appearance of the third monthly notice will be exiled under the threat of more severe punishment, should they have the temerity to return to this province.

Zacharias Wilsma seems to have become the source of numerous allegations; he was kept alive so as to incriminate others, many of whom were later executed. One of those he implicated was Caspar Abraham Berse, a servant who was eventually executed by being strangled and his body then burnt. The charge said that "the prisoner has led during many years an immoral and impious life, committing many wicked and abominable deeds with . . . Zacharias Wilsma and other persons. The prisoner has even committed with the same Zacharias Wilsma during the years 1723 and 1724 on three different occasions really the most horrible, the unnatural sin of sodomy; all this in circumstances the mere thought of which makes one shudder and [be] frightened."[28]

Fear became hysteria in the small village of Faan, where the local squire presided over what can only be described as a witch-hunt. Villagers were haled into court on charges that even then seemed to be so circumstantial as to be unprovable—charges made by one villager against another on account of old animosities, or based on hearsay or suspicion. Confessions obtained by intimidation and torture brought convictions; sentences were informed by neither mercy nor justice. Rudolphe de Mepsche, the village judge who began the persecution, presided over the trial of more than thirty of his fellow villagers, of whom twenty-four were first strangled and then burned at the stake.[29]

In the rest of the Dutch Republic, rumors of sodomite networks proved as self-fulfilling as in Faan. Sodomy trials occurred during most of the eighteenth century, with the persecutions at their most intense between 1730 and 1737, in 1764, in 1776, and between 1795 and 1798. Convicted sodomites implicated others, and so the panic spread. In 1730, for example, Pieter Marteyn, who had been implicated by Zacharias Wilsma, incriminated more than forty other men. By the end of the century, over six hundred people had been prosecuted for sodomy throughout the republic.[30]

A list of the executed mentions a decorator, a chief of detectives, numerous household servants, an embroiderer, a grain carrier, a glove launderer, a tavernkeeper, a fishmonger, a teacher, and a churchwarden.[31] Aristocrats, aldermen, bailiffs, the burgomaster of Leiden, and a city father of Haarlem were charged, but men of status or influence were not as likely to be prosecuted as their less prominent partners in sodomy. Even when prominent people were implicated, they were often sentenced to exile, not death. If the case seemed hopeless, they fled the country; having fled, they were condemned in absentia and exiled by default.

Over time, all aspects of the persecutions became more virulent. At first only men were prosecuted. But after 1792 women, too, were tried. In that year Bets Wiebes was exiled for six years because of her "dirty lust"; at trial she was said to have had sex with another woman "in the way a man is used to do when he has carnal intercourse with his wife."[32] Proof of actual sodomy had been needed in the earlier trials, but after 1795, the mere attempt became a sufficient reason for arrest, torture, trial, and conviction. Sentences for attempted sodomy ranged from two years of solitary confinement, to imprisonment for life, to execution. The latter sentence was brutally imposed. In Amsterdam, sodomites were killed by garroting, after which their faces were scorched. Some were drowned, held under water in a barrel placed upon a platform, as the populace watched their struggles. To make sure that their bodies no longer polluted the nation, they were then burned to ashes or weighted down and thrown into the sea. Some corpses were exposed so that others of God's creatures could collaborate in the destruction of the flesh.

A roll of executed sodomites, the "Disclosure of Those Summoned and Executed for the Detestable Misdeed of Sodomy. Presented as a Warning to the Good and a Deterrent to the Bad in the Most Important Cities of Holland," lists the names, the occupations, and the manner of death of sixty men who were executed in 1730 and 1731. A few entries are excerpted below.

Amsterdam
—Pieter Marteyn Janes Sohn and Johannes Keep, decorator, strangled and burnt, June 24, 1730.
—Maurits van Eeden, house servant, and Cornelis Boes, 18, Keep's servant, each immersed alive in a barrel of water and drowned, June 24, 1730.
—Laurens Hospuijn, Chief of Detectives in the Navy, strangled and thrown into the water with a 100-pound weight, Sept. 16, 1730.
Groningen
—A drummer and an "orphan," names unknown, beheaded, Sept. 22, 1731.
The Hague
—Frans Verheyden; Cornelis Wassernaar, milkman; Pieter Styn, embroiderer of coats; Dirk van Rooyen, and Herman Mouilliont, servant, hanged and afterwards thrown into the sea at Scheveningen with 50-pound weights, June 12, 1730.
—Antonie Byweegen, fishmonger, hanged, then burnt to ashes, July 21, 1730.
—Cornelis Palamedes, teacher, 56, half strangled, then burnt to ashes, Oct. 19, 1730. For 20 years a teacher in the village of Veen near Heusden. He confessed in prison that 18 years earlier he had seduced Dirk van Rooyen, who was executed in The Hague on June 12 and that he had likewise seduced several of his pupils.
Kampen
—Jan Westhoff and Steven Klok, soldiers, strangled on the scaffold and buried under the gallows, June 29, 1730.
Rotterdam
—Leendert de Haas, 60, candlemaker; Casper Schroder, distiller; Huibert van Borselen, gentleman's servant, strangled, burnt, and their ashes carried in an ash cart out of the city and then by a ship to the sea and thrown overboard, July 17, 1730.

Zuidhorn [All the executions in this village were carried out on a single day, September 24, 1731.]

—Gerrit Loer, 48, farmer, scorched while alive and then strangled and burnt to ashes. Had committed the sin often both actively and passively with several persons and in several places, even on the way to church, both before and after the sermon.

—Hendrick Berents, 32, scorched while alive and then strangled and burnt to ashes. Had often committed the sin of sodomy actively and passively.

—Harmen Arents, 41, farmer, committed the sin with his brother Sikko Arents, churchwarden. Remained silent when sentenced.

—Mindelt Jansz Rol, 32, strangled and burnt. On hearing the sentence, he swayed back and forth and bowed to those present on departing.

—Jan Jacobs van Donderen, 30, strangled and burnt. Cried out, "Oh! oh!" when his sentence was read.

—Jan Egberts, 19, strangled and burnt. When the sentence was read in which it was stated that he was 20 years old, he cried out, "That is incorrect, Sir, I am only 19 years old." Bowed his head when going away and said, "It is all right, Sir."

—Peter Cornelisz, 20 or 21, strangled and burnt. As the sentence was read he behaved as if he were about to faint, and sighed when leaving.

—Hendrik Cornelisz, 21, strangled and burnt. He said, "I forgive you and thank you gentlemen for the sentence which I shall receive."

—Tamme Jansz, 14, strangled and burnt. Remained silent when sentenced.

Most of those sentenced remained silent, but not all. Cornelis Jansz, aged eighteen, sentenced to be strangled and burnt, "looked in all directions and at everyone and said: 'See how you have judged me.'" When Jan Ides, also eighteen, heard that he was to be strangled and burnt, he said, "I forgive you for the sin which you have committed against me."[33] Thus he demonstrated the Christian charity that had been denied him.

The waves of persecution in the Dutch Republic marked the beginning of a new form of homophobia. Sodomy was now almost always conflated with effeminacy, and the act was thought of as a crime. But sodomites were a special kind of criminal, guilty of fearsomely dislocating nature itself. As everyone knew, they transformed themselves from one sex to another and desired their own sex. Donning disguises, denying their sex, sodomites disturbed the accepted order of male and female, husband and wife, father and son, mother and daughter. It was not surprising that David Hume—not the philosopher but the Scottish jurist—could assert in 1797 that the sodomite deserved the death penalty because his "very presence is a pollution to the society of his fellow creatures."[34]

3 Imagining Sodomites

In England, too, public ideas about sodomy and sodomites had undergone a pronounced change. The profligate rake so common in Restoration comedy, who might have been called a sodomite in the 1680s and whom we might call a lapsed heterosexual, was often described as having a boy on one arm and a whore on the other. This indiscriminate debauchee was a disappearing breed. A new kind of sodomite began to emerge: a male who would willingly take the passive role in sex with other men and who had sacrificed manliness not only thus but also by adopting effeminate ways and even wearing women's, or at least effeminate and dandified, clothing. His passivity, however, might merely disguise a seducer of the innocent young, a ruiner of naive married men, and a perverter of marriageable bachelors. Posing as a weakened and passive quasi-man, such a sodomite would cause unhappiness to both married and marriageable women and bring about the destruction of the family. These depraved denizens of a sexual underworld were united in trying to destroy the moral foundations of Christian society. In books and newspapers, poems and pamphlets, the sodomite was depicted as both monstrous and contemptible; he was at once the object of anxiety and the target of jest, at once weak and dangerous. If weak and effeminate, sodomites were scorned and derided, considered legitimate prey for homophobic violence. But when practicing their "infectious vice," they were dangerous.

Vanity and effeminacy were staples of antisodomite satiric diatribe. The anonymous poem *Mundus Foppensis, or, The Fop Displayed* (1691) skewers the vain dandies who "must more time . . . Waste / E'er their soft bodies can be drest / The Looking Glass hangs just before / And each o' th' Legs requires an hour."[35] A pamphlet of 1703 satirizes effeminacy from a woman's point of view:

> The Men, they are grown full and Effeminate as the Women: we are Rivall'd by 'em even in the Fooleries peculiar to our Sex: They Dress like Anticks and Stage Players, and are as ridiculous as Monkeys: they sit in monstrous long Periwigs . . . and esteem themselves more upon the Reputation of being a Beau, than on the Substantial Qualifications, of Honour, Courage, Learning, and Judgment. . . . If you heard 'em talk, you'd think yourself at a Gossiping at Dover.[36]

A few years later Ned Ward wrote in *The London Spy* that London's sodomites are "so far degenerated from all masculine deportment or manly exercises that they rather fancy themselves women, imitating all the little vanities that custom has reconciled to the female sex, affecting to speak, walk, tattle, scold, and to mimick all manner of effeminacy."[37] The title of a 1729 pamphlet will represent many: "A Hell upon Earth, or, the Town in an Uproar . . . Occasion'd by the late Horrible Scenes of . . . Sodomy . . ." In "Satan's Harvest Home" (1750), the pamphleteer asserts that sodomy is a "Damned Fashion! Imported from Italy amidst a train of other unnatural vices." He plays upon fears of sodomite conspiracy and of an increase in sodomy: "We have much Reason to fear, that there are Numbers as yet undiscover'd, and that this abominable Practice gets Ground ev'ry Day." One of sodomy's chief and most monstrous effects is that "those, who in Contradiction to the Laws of God and Man, to the Order and Course of Nature, and to the most simple principles of Reason, preposterously burn for each other, and leave the Fair, the charming Sex, neglected."[38]

Few eighteenth-century texts present the popular conception of a sodomite as fully as Tobias Smollett's *Roderick Random* (1748). Captain Whiffle and Lord Strutwell respectively represent the effeminate and the monstrous aspects of sodomy. It falls to Smollett's picaresque hero, Roderick Random, a naive, innocent, and handsome lad, with all the prejudices of his English middle-class birth, to make his way through the dangers these two pose.

Random, having squandered his small fortune, goes to sea in hopes of recouping his losses. On shipboard he has his first encounter with sodomites. The commanding officer, Captain Whiffle, together with Simper, his surgeon, and Vergette, his valet, are full-blown stereotypical sodomites. Whiffle arrives in "a ten-oared barge, overshadowed with a vast umbrella."[39] He is a "tall, thin young man," dressed in extravagant and dandified fashion: "His hair flowed upon his shoulders in ringlets, tied behind with a ribbon." He wears a coat of "pink-colored silk lined with white" that "by the elegance of the cut retired backwards," and a "white satin waistcoat embroidered with gold, unbuttoned at the upper part to display a brooch set with garnets." His thinness suggests the weak constitution attributed to sodomites. The luxurious fabrics, the unmanly pink fabric, the wanton and coy ringlets—these leave little room for doubt.

But "the most remarkable parts of his furniture were a mask on his face and white gloves on his hands, which did not seem to be put on with the intention to be pulled off occasionally, but were fixed with a curious ring on the little finger of each hand." One such ring indicates effeteness, but two suggest perversion, while the gloved hands—never bared in labor—indicate overluxuriousness. The mask—a stylish item often worn by women wishing to make assignations, and also associated with libertine masquerades at which sodomites were allegedly engaged in sexual escapades—places him entirely beyond the pale. In addition, Whiffle is surrounded by attendants who share their master's "disposition," a perfumed entourage recalling Ned Ward's "Gang of Sodomitical Wretches" and the "leagues and societies" of sodomites so anxiously featured in popular texts. Smollett's readers would surely recognize Whiffle as emblematic of a crisis of masculinity.

Presumably such a creature would not be concerned with manly and emphatically nonsodomitical subjects like "Honour, Courage, Learning." Indeed, Whiffle is ill suited to his task as captain. He is found "reposing on a couch with a wrapper of fine chintz around his body and a muslin cap bordered with lace about his head." When the ship's mate makes an abrupt entrance, Whiffle reacts by screaming in horror, "I am betrayed," and calling him a "monster." Then the captain "sunk down upon the settee in a fit" while his valet "plied him with a smelling bottle, [and] one footman chaffed his temples with Hungary water." Against Whiffle's effeminate hysteria, Smollett places the rough, healthy, if crude mate, whose tirade against Whiffle recalls the language of the antisodomite pamphlets: "I do affirm . . . that I have no smells about me but such as a Christian ought to have, except the effluvia of tobacco. . . . [A]s for my being a monster, let that be as it is: I am as Cot [God] was pleased to create me, which, peradventure, is more than I shall aver of him who gave me that title, for I will proclaim it before the world that he is disguised, and transfigured, and transmogrified with affectation and whimsies, and that he is more like a papoon [baboon] than one of the human race."

When Whiffle's surgeon, Simper—a "young man gaily dressed, of a very delicate complexion, with a kind of languid smile on his face, which seemed to be rendered habitual by a long course of affectation"—enters his cabin, Whiffle flies "into his arms, crying, 'O! my dear Simper, I am excessively disordered.'" Simper diagnoses this disorder as "entirely nervous"; Whiffle bars from his cabin everyone but Simper and his servants, thus establishing an exclusive community of sodomites in the midst of the larger nonsodomite community of the ship. In doing so, he gives ship's gossip the opportunity to "accuse him of maintaining a correspondence with the surgeon not fit to be named." Of course sodomy is meant: the vice not to be named among Christians.

Although Whiffle's appearance recalls both the Restoration rake and the dandified beau, he is not precisely either one. Nor is he exactly a molly, for his habits of dress—at least those that Smollet lets us see— are not a transvestite's, though his chintz wrapper and lace cap strongly hint that in private moments he may adopt even more effeminate attire. The true London molly was a cross-dressing effeminate, very nearly a third sex.[40] Whiffle is a new type of sodomite, both man and molly, who seeks out his own kind, in the person of Simper, his true confederate.

Random realizes that he will make no fortune on this ship. After several unsuccessful attempts to get rich, he finds himself in London again, still unemployed. He meets two rascally noblemen. Lords Straddle and Swillpot, who, after taking what little money he has, in return take him to the levee of the wealthy and influential Lord Strutwell, the daily audience where those looking for favors await a chance to meet the lord. If he catches the eye of the nobleman and impresses him, Random is told, Strutwell might find a position for him. What Random does not know is that Strutwell's levees provide the nobleman an opportunity to meet handsome young men to seduce.

As Strutwell passes through the crowd of position-seekers, he does indeed catch sight of the handsome Random, and favors him with "a particular smile, squeeze of the hand, and a whisper, signifying that he wanted half an hour's conversation" the next day. When they meet, Strutwell identifies himself as a sodomite, for once again "he frequently squeezed my hand." ("Satan's Harvest Home" had warned that "tho many Gentlemen of Worth, are oftentimes, out of pure good *Manners*, obliged to give into" squeezing of the hand, "yet the Land will never be purged of its *Abominations* till this Unmanly, unnatural Usage be totally abolish'd; for it is the first Inlet to the detestable Sin of Sodomy.")[41] Strutwell immediately offers Random employment; Random is so touched that he cannot "help shedding tears at the goodness of this noble lord." Strutwell, taking the tears as an opportunity for close physical contact, "caught me in his arms, and hugged and kissed me with a seemingly paternal affection." Random is "confounded at this uncommon instance of fondness for a stranger," and "remains a few moments silent and ashamed," aware perhaps that kisses between men and especially between strangers are hardly innocent demonstrations of affection.

Strutwell continues his campaign of seduction, flattering Random by speaking to him as an equal, appealing not to his lust but to his intellect. "Among other topics of discourse," Random says, "that of Belles-lettres was introduced." Strutwell gives Random a copy of Petronius Arbiter's *Satyricon,* in which homosexual lovers play a central role. Strutwell assures Random that even though its subject may offend "narrow minded people," the *Satyricon* will always be admired by "every person of wit and learning." When Random comments that the work is "lewd and indecent," Strutwell replies that this opinion is founded upon "prejudice and misapprehension" and notes that the "passion" has an ancient history. By treating sodomy as a historical subject initially, Strutwell seems to defuse the immediate sexual threat, but in fact he creates a seductive context. By mentioning various forbidden practices, Strutwell sets up a sexual atmosphere that he knows well how to turn to advantage, especially if the object of his discourse shares his inclinations, as he believes Random does.

Strutwell's disquisition on the *Satyricon* is at once satiric and serious. He echoes the popular objections to sodomy, turning them to his own use. Where antisodomite polemicists condemn sodomy as a fashion and a vice, Strutwell asserts that the condemnation is founded upon prejudice. Where they say that sodomy is opposed to the principles of reason, Strutwell asserts that the lack of "true reason and deliberation" on the subject of sodomy violates the principles of reason and thus leads to prejudice. Strutwell sanctions sodomy on two counts. First, the most illustrious men of the past practiced it: "The best man among the ancients is said to have entertained that passion; one of the wisest of their legislators has permitted the indulgence of it in his common-wealth; the most celebrated poets have not scrupled to avow it." Second, the practice is widespread in modern times: "At this day it prevails not only in the East but in most parts of Europe; in our own country it gains ground apace, and in all probability it will become in a short time a more fashionable vice than simple fornication." And for good reason: sodomy is socially desirable, since it incurs no increase in the population, prevents infanticide, and does not burden the state with the support of illegitimate children, who are deserted "to the utmost want and wretchedness, or bred up to prey upon the commonwealth." Even more important, the practice of sodomy "prevents the debauchery of many a young maiden, and the prostitution of honest men's wives, not to mention the consideration of health, which is much less likely to be impaired in the gratification of this appetite than in the exercise of common venery, which, by ruining the constitutions of our young men, has produced a puny progeny that degenerates from generation to generation."

Here is another traditional antisodomitical argument that Strutwell has turned on its head. He, too, invokes virtue, the health of the populace, and the sanctity of marriage, but asserts that sodomy is in fact useful and valuable to them all. Offering his own gloss on the Enlightenment calculus that an act is useful and good if it produces happiness, Strutwell muses: "I have been told that there is another motive, perhaps more powerful than all these, that induces people to cultivate this inclination, namely, the exquisite pleasure attending its success." Of course, this cleverness is just another sign of his nefarious character, another step in his attempt to seduce Random.

Random's response to Strutwell's polemic is predictable: he is at once obtuse and appalled. Not really understanding either Strutwell's intent or the intricacies of his argument, Random fears that Strutwell might take him for a sodomite: "I began to be apprehensive that his lordship, finding I had traveled, was afraid I might have been infected with this spurious and sordid desire abroad. . . . Fired at this supposed suspicion, I argued against it with great warmth, as an appetite unnatural, absurd, and of pernicious consequences, and declared my utter detestation and abhorrence of it." To cap his defense, Random quotes the "lines of the satirist": "Eternal infamy the wretch confound / Who planted first the vice on British ground! / A vice! that, 'spite of sense and nature, reigns, / and poisons genial love, and manhood stains."

Smollett has put in Roderick's mouth lines from his first published work, "Advice," a satire in verse that is in large part an attack on sodomites. The extract usefully summarizes the homophobic discourse of the period.

When, earlier in the book, Smollett depicts Whiffle and his attendants as men of similar "disposition," he suggests that to a certain extent their sexuality leveled social distinctions. His portrayal of Lord Strutwell confirms this by adding aristocracy to the social mix: Strutwell's attempt to seduce Random displays just how desire could, at least for the temporary purpose of sexual satisfaction, erase social boundaries. Smollett portrayed Whiffle as weak and also as laughable; he offends, in Smollett's eyes, by his style and by his pose—his disguise. He is trivialized at the same time that he is satirized. Strutwell is different. His effete surface style may seem to be as vulnerable to trivializing satire as Whiffle's, but he is what Whiffle is not: the sodomitical monster, representing both incarnate evil and dangerous intelligence. Strutwell represents a new sodomitical type: the sodomite apologist and activist who seduces not only by arousing sexual desire or offering material advantage, but by perverting the intellect. Strutwell is not only a practitioner of sodomitical acts but a spokesman for a sodomitical style of life.

One could construe Strutwell's defense as an early salvo in a debate over homosexual rights. His argument—and his character—are firmly founded in a particular and emerging view that the sodomite is a creation, not an accident of nature. For while the author of "Satan's Harvest Home" described sodomy as a "fashion"—a matter of choice—Strutwell, more modern, sees it as an "inclination," that is, an expression of one's nature. He conceives of his identity in terms of sexual desire, identifies sodomites as a discrete group, and advocates social tolerance and legal reform of the proscriptions against them.

It is possible, if anachronistic, to admire Strutwell as a kind of activist. Indeed, with just a shift of the lens, Strutwell may seem no monster but instead a sober, intelligent, and clever apologist, preferable to the callow Random. However, Smollett's transposition of anti-sodomite arguments into a prosodomite polemic probably affected his readers in quite a different way. Strutwell advocates what Smollett's readers abhor, and it is unlikely that Strutwell's positions are Smollett's own. If Strutwell's commentary is meant to be read as absurdist satire, it is also intended to inspire horror that such a monster can so convincingly and persuasively exist.

Still, by providing a podium for Strutwell, who is a persuasive advocate for the humanity of sodomites, Smollett's work cannot help but give pause to homophobes—albeit unwittingly. When Strutwell says that he is glad to find Random's opinion "so conformable to his own," he can be understood as a wicked satirist, not simply as a humiliated seducer. Though Strutwell has not seduced Random, his cogency has bested Random intellectually. Strutwell's triumph is not only over Random but over the forces of moral and social bigotry. Nevertheless, for Smollett's readers, Strutwell has deceived the innocence of England and demonstrated that he is no weak effeminate, but rather a dangerous foe.

4 A Detestable Race

Anxious as they were about sodomites, the public was also fascinated, and demanded to know more. One new force in the spread of homophobia was the popular press, which provided daily accounts of the trials and executions of the "miscreants" or "wretches" or "monsters," emphasizing any evidence of a widespread sexual underworld. During the Dutch trials, English newspapers offered daily "Accounts of the Proceedings against the Sodomites of that Country"; at mid-century, during a single two-year period, England published over two thousand newspaper reports of trials, arrests, and speculations about sodomites. The intense homophobia of late-eighteenth-century England manifested itself in approving newspaper stories about attacks on sodomites, their public punishment and execution, and even their suicide.

Reports of the entrapment of sodomites became the favorite reading of a self-righteous public. The same Minton who had allowed Captain Rigby to toy with him in the park in 1698 was, as it turned out, an informer. Unfortunately for Captain Rigby, he had alerted the constables hidden next door to the site of their assignation. Rigby's transport of passion was all Minton needed. Taking hold of Rigby's erect "privy member," Minton shouted the code word "Westminster," and the constables rushed in. Minton piously exclaimed to Rigby: "I have now discovered your base Inclinations, I will expose you to the world, to put a stop to these Crimes."[42] Entrapment was seen as an appropriate response to the crime; to bait the trap, police employed the very youths who were deemed to be victims of sodomites.[43] English sodomites could be sentenced to death or imprisonment, or absent adequate proof that sodomy was actually committed, to stand in the pillory. There the

wrathful mob would throw offal, dung, mud, and rocks. Some sodomites did not survive the pillory; others were blinded or had bones
broken. Newspaper accounts of these events were lurid, usually condemning the "monster" who was thus assaulted.

One of the most sensational of the sodomite trials described at
length in the press was that of the so-called Vere Street Club. In 1810,
the White Swan, a tavern in Vere Street, was raided by police who
posed as sodomites. The *Alfred and Westminster Evening Gazette*
described the raid: they "gained admittance by some finesse to the back
parlor, which was the principal rendezvous for these miscreants; and
after being at first a little suspected of coming as spies, they were at last
considered as persons of the same propensity, and treated without
reserve."[44] Nearly thirty men were arrested and taken to prison for
examination. Most were eventually set free because of insufficient
proof, but six men were found guilty of attempted sodomy, the charge
preferred when no proof of penetration or emission could be obtained.
The men, William Amos, Robert Aspinall, Philip Kett, William Thom-
son, Richard Francis, and James Done, were sentenced to stand in the
pillory and to prison terms ranging from one to three years.[45]

Such was the popular indignation excited by the press against these
wretches, and so great the eagerness to witness their punishment, that
the streets around the Haymarket were rendered impassable. "The Trying and Pillorying of the Vere Street Club," a pamphlet from 1810,
described the scene:

> Shortly after 12, the ammunition wagons from neighboring mar-
> kets appeared in motion. These consisted of a number of carts
> which were driven by butcher's boys who had previously taken
> care to fill them with the offal, dung, &c appertaining to several
> slaughter houses. Hucksters . . . carried on their heads baskets of
> apples, potatoes, turnips, cabbage-stalks, and other vegetables,
> together with the remains of divers dogs and cats. The whole of
> these were sold to the populace at a high price, who spared no
> expense to provide themselves with the necessary articles of
> assault. A number of fishwomen attended with stinking flounders
> and the entrails of other fish which had been in preparation for
> several days. These articles, however, were not to be sold, as their
> proprietors, hearty in the cause, declared they wanted them for
> their own use.

The crowd waited for the sodomites to appear.

> The gates of the Old Bailey Yard were shut, and all . . . were then
> brought out and all placed in the caravan. Amos began a laugh,
> which induced his vile companions to reprove him, and they all
> sat upright, apparently in a composed state, but having cast
> their eyes upwards, the sight of the spectators on the tops of the
> houses operated strongly on their fears, and they soon appeared
> to feel terror and dismay. At the instant the church clock struck
> half-past twelve, the gates were thrown open. The mob at the
> same time attempted to force their way in, but were repulsed. . . .
> About 60 officers, armed and mounted . . . went forward with
> the City Marshals. The caravan went next, followed by about
> 40 officers and the Sheriffs. The first salute received by the offend-
> ers was a volley of mud, and a serenade of hisses, hooting, and
> execration, which compelled them to fall flat on their faces in
> the caravan. The mob, and particularly the women, had piled up
> balls of mud to afford the objects of their indignation a warm
> reception. The depots in many places appeared like pyramids of
> shot in a gun wharf. These were soon exhausted, and when the
> caravan passed the old house which once belonged to the notori-
> ous Jonathan Wild, the prisoners resembled bears dipped in a stag-
> nant pool.[46]

Four of the men were then stood together in the pillory—a central
post and four revolving wings. The men's heads were clamped in the
extended wings and they were then required to walk slowly in a circle
while the mob hurled at them the revolting objects they had earlier
acquired. Pride of place in front of the pillory was granted to a group
of women, many of them prostitutes, who it was said excelled all the
others in ferocity. The celebratory nature of the event was emphasized by several newspapers and by a general distribution of "gin and
beer, procured from a subscription made upon the spot." When the
other two men were brought to the pillory they were greeted with an
even more violent demonstration, fueled now by alcohol. It was only
when the men were returned to prison that they were sheltered, one
witness reported, "from the further indignation of the most enraged
populace we ever saw." Indeed, it was generally agreed that "it is
impossible for language to convey an adequate idea of the universal

expressions of execration, which accompanied these monsters on their journey."[47]

Rather than face a trial and the pillory, many apprehended sodomites attempted to take their own lives, like the man described in this 1836 report from the London *Ledger:*

> An inquest was held at Brighton on Tuesday on the body of Mr. Stanley Stokes, a proctor of Doctor's Commons, who cut his throat in East Street in that town on Saturday night. Sunders, the landlord of the New Ship Hotel, on Saturday night laid a plan to intercept him, and accompanied by a crowd of fellows, after charging him with an indecent assault upon a boy's person, they simultaneously mobbed him, smeared his face with tar, gave him severe blows on the head with fists, sticks, etc., until he fell down. Whilst undergoing this persecution, the unhappy man, in the open street, drew a penknife from his pocket, and inflicted a severe wound in his throat. He was immediately conveyed to a hospital . . . but the nervous excitement under which he labored, and the blows which he had received, producing fever, he gradually sunk and expired.[48]

Many antisodomites urged that even attempted sodomy should be punished by death. The author of the "The Trying and Pillorying of the Vere Street Club" asserted that such "monsters must be crushed," and demanded "annihilation to so detestable a race" by "instant death."[49] The London press agreed; in reporting the brutal death of some sodomites in the pillory, the *General Evening Post* for September 1810 echoed what was probably the general opinion: "Some of them cannot survive the punishment; and should it prove their death, they will not only die unpitied, but justly execrated by every moral mind throughout the universe."[50]

Such attitudes were reflected in the law, which maintained the death penalty for proven sodomy and prosecuted attempted sodomy with increasing rigor. Indeed, much eighteenth- and early nineteenth-century opinion advocated the extermination of sodomites. Matthew Bacon's *New Abridgement of the Law,* a collection of British law that was reprinted often between 1736 and 1832, offered a rationale for the horrors; according to Bacon, sodomy constituted *the* most terrible crime that could be committed against society. The crime lay not in a willful decision to commit such heinous criminal mischief, but in the being of the sexual criminal, whose tendencies might appear in his sons:*

> If any crime deserve to be punished in a more exemplary manner this does. Other crimes are prejudicial to society; but this strikes at the being thereof: it being seldom known that a person who has been guilty of abusing his generative faculty so unnaturally has afterwards a proper regard for women. From that indifference to women, so remarkable in men of this depraved appetite, it may fairly be concluded that they are cursed with insensibility to the most ecstatic pleasure which human nature is in the present state capable of enjoying. It seems a very just punishment that such wretches should be deprived of all taste for an enjoyment upon which they did not set a proper value; and the continuation of an impious disposition, which then might have been transmitted to their children, if they had any, may be thereby prevented.[51]

In his influential *Commentaries on the Laws of England* (1765–69) William Blackstone explained that sodomy was a personal threat to each and every Englishman; "the voice of nature and reason, and the express law of God determine [sodomy] to be capital. Of which we have a signal instance, long before the Jewish dispensation, by the destruction of the two cities by fire from heaven: so this is universal, not merely a provincial precept. And our ancient law in some degree imitated this punishment by commanding such miscreants be burnt to death."[52]

This view was put into practice not only by the government but by the mob. In 1780 William Smith and Theodosius Reed, a coachman and a plasterer, were pilloried for attempted sodomy. The *Daily Advertiser* for April 11, 1780, described the scene: "A vast Concourse of People had assembled upon the Occasion, many by Seven O'clock in the Morning, who had collected dead Dogs, Cats, &c in great abundance, which were plentifully thrown at them; but some Person threw a Stone and hit the Coachman on the Forehead, and immediately he dropped on his Knees . . . dead." In Parliament Edmund Burke responded to the incident by proposing to abolish the pillory. The

---

*Bacon, like Smollett's Strutwell, implies that sodomy is not chosen but arises from the sodomite's nature.

Morning Post objected: "Every man applauds the spirit of the spectators, and every woman thinks their conduct right. It remained for the patriotic Mr. Burke to insinuate that the crime these men committed should not be held in the highest detestation. And that it deserved a milder chastisement than ignominious death."[53]

5 A Cry for Reform

Few in England spoke up for sodomites, and sodomites rarely defended themselves. One who did was William Brown of London. In 1726, strolling in the area of Moorfields Park known as the Sodomites' Walk, Brown caught sight of a handsome young man leaning over the wall that bordered the lane. As he passed, Brown gave the youth a look, and then made a sexual overture to him. The young man, unfortunately for Brown, was Thomas Newton, a hustler who preyed on sodomites and entrapped them for the police, two of whom, Constables Willis and Stevenson, were hiding in the bushes nearby. Newton's version of the meeting completes the scene:

> A Gentleman passes by, and looks hard at me, and a small distance from me, stands up against the Wall, as if he was going make Water. Then by Degrees he sidles nearer and nearer to where I stood, till at last he comes close to me. —*'Tis a very fine Night*, says he. Says I, *and so it is*. Then he takes me by the Hand, and after squeezing and playing with it a little (to which I showed no dislike), he conveys it to his Breeches, and puts [his penis] into it. I took fast hold, and call'd on Willis and Stevenson, who coming up to my Assistance, we carried him to the Watch house.

When Brown was asked "why he took such indecent Liberties with Newton" he answered: "I did it because I thought I knew him, and I think there is no Crime in making what use I please of my own Body."[54] Brown's startling declaration of sexual independence challenged a millennium of legislation that asserted precisely the opposite.

Also convinced that sodomy ought to be legal was the English utilitarian philosopher and advocate of law reform, Jeremy Bentham (1748–1832). Bentham had long been convinced of the need to apply European arguments for criminal law reform to the English criminal code, which listed over two hundred offenses as punishable by death.[55]

Bentham was also apparently long fascinated by the specific question of the culpability of sodomy. In 1774, at the age of twenty-six, Bentham had begun to write about homosexual behavior—he used the term "paederasty"—and social and legal attitudes toward it, compiling nearly fifty pages of notes. In 1785, concerned by "the persecution they [sodomites] meet with from all quarters" and by "the severity with which it is now treated by the laws and the contempt and abhorrence with which it is regarded by the generality of the people," he turned these notes into an essay, "Offences Against One's Self: Paederasty."[56] His radical arguments for the decriminalization of sodomy put him in opposition to other thinkers of his age.

Bentham first takes up Montesquieu's assertion that sodomy "ought to be proscribed . . . for its giving to one sex the weakness of the other." To answer this, Bentham appeals to history, pointing out that in Athens and ancient Rome "everyone practiced it; nobody was ashamed of it," and no one thought it enervating unless carried to excess. History also shows—here Bentham cites a list of Greek and Roman heroes—that scores of men not only practiced sodomy without shame but were evidently not feminized by it. "If there is any ground derived from history for attributing to it any such enervating effects it is more than I can find."[57]

Bentham next considers Voltaire's argument that homosexual practice, if allowed to flourish, would eventually endanger the reproduction of the species. Such an objection can only be theoretical, he points out, since "before this can happen the nature of the human composition must receive total change" and the "propensity of the male for the female" must "have come to be an altogether unnatural one." He notes that Italy, "in which the prevalence of this practice is most conspicuous, happens to have been remarkable for its populousness." Homosexual behavior is surely no more dangerous, he wryly notes, than celibacy; if it "were right that pederasts should be burned alive" as endangering population growth, then logically "monks ought to be roasted alive by a slow fire."[58]

To a third objection—that homosexual behavior "produce[s] in the male sex an indifference to the female and thereby defraud[s] them of their rights"—Bentham counters: "What are the number of women who by the prevalence of this taste would . . . be prevented from getting husbands?" In European society, "if a women has a husband she is permitted to receive it [sex] only from her husband; if she has no husband she is not permitted to receive it from any man without being degraded into the class of prostitute." No matter how prevalent the taste, Bentham argues, married women whose husbands are not sodomites are unlikely to be affected by the existence of men who are sodomites. This large group must therefore be deducted from "the number of women who would be sufferers by the prevalence of this taste."[59] So too must prostitutes, because no matter how reprehensible or unhappy their lot, they are by definition women to whom men go for sex, and so they, too, are untouched. The only women who might suffer because of sodomy are those who might have married had sodomy not deprived them of a prospective spouse. But that man would in any event have been a sodomite and thus an inappropriate husband in the first place. The number of such women, Bentham argues, is small. The likelihood that a taste for sodomy will prevail among males seems to him equally small.

Having disposed of the "practical" objections, Bentham proceeds to analyze the ethics of pederasty. By utilitarian principles, the "ethical value of an act" is to be tested by whether it "increased pleasure and diminished pain."[60] It is hard to argue that homosexual behavior increases pain in those who already find it pleasurable or in those who do not practice it at all: "The act is disgusting and odious ... not to the man who does it, for he does it only because it gives him pleasure, but to the one who thinks of it."[61] And the abhorrence of the act quickly shades into hatred of the actors: "From a man's possessing a thorough aversion to a practice himself, the transition is but too natural to his wishing to see all others punished who give in to it."[62]

Bentham believed that hostility to sodomy and to sodomites was rooted in religious asceticism and in the associated fear of sexual pleasure.[63] This fear is manifest in popular suspicion and antipathy to difference, but antipathy to difference ought not to be a reason for punishment: "A man's own feelings, tho' the best reason in the world for abhorring the thing, are none at all for abhorring the man who does it—how much less then are they for destroying him." Indeed, "to destroy a man there should certainly be some better reason than mere dislike to his taste, let that dislike be ever so strong."[64]

England seemed to Bentham unique: "The propensities in question have, in the British Isles, beyond all other countries, been the object of violence" inflicted by those who can be satisfied by "nothing less than the heart's blood of the victims marked out for slaughter."[65] When Bentham calls sodomites "victims," he recasts violence against them as a crime in itself. Underlying most attacks on homosexual behavior was the assumption that the hostility was instinctive, that sodomy was self-evidently an abomination. But Bentham attributes the attacks to a "dissocial appetite," a phrase suggesting that he sees homophobia as a social dysfunction, not as an instinct.[66] That is, he invents a nearly modern definition of homophobia.

Bentham was well aware of the possible consequences of seeming to advocate sodomy: "If you let it be seen that you have not sat down in a rage you have given judgment against yourself at once." He continues: "I am ashamed to own that I have often hesitated whether for the sake of the interests of humanity I should expose my personal interest so much to hazard as it must be exposed to by the free discussion of a subject of this nature," for "when a man attempts to search this subject it is with a halter"—a noose—"about his neck. On this subject a man may indulge his spleen without control. Cruelty and intolerance . . . screen themselves behind a mask of virtue."[67]

> A hundred times have I shuddered at the view of the perils I was exposing myself to in encountering the opinions that are in possession of men's minds on [this] subject. As often have I resolved to turn aside from a road so full of precipices. I have trembled at the thoughts of the indignation that must be raised against the Apologist of a crime that has been looked upon by many, and those excellent men, as one among the blackest under Heaven. But the die is now cast, & having thus adhered with that undeviating fidelity [to] the principles of general utility I at first adopted, I will not at last abandon them for considerations of personal danger. I will not have to reproach myself with the thought that those principles which my judgement has approved, my fears have compelled me to abandon.[68]

But despite the courage and uniqueness of his arguments, Bentham did not publish the essay. Given the brutality aimed at convicted sodomites, even seeming to advocate their acts might have opened him to equally brutal reprisal or raised the suspicion that he himself was guilty. Or he may simply have been unable to find a printer willing to risk his neck and livelihood to publish such a work. Whatever the reason, "Paederasty" had to wait two centuries before it finally appeared, in 1978.

6 Risking Their Necks

In 1811, Charles Skinner Matthews wrote to his close friend George Gordon, Lord Byron, then in Malta, about some current London scandals:

> The grand feature, I take it, in the last year of our history, is the enormous increase of *paiderastia* (that damn'd vice). Good God! were the good old times of Sodom & Gomorrah to return, fire not water wd be the Englishman's element. At no place or time, I suppose, since the creation of the world, has Sodomy been so rife. With your friends the Turcomans to be sure, its value (compared with fornication) is as 5 to 2. But that what you get for £5 we must risque our necks for; and are content to risque them.[69]

Matthews' flippant tone should not disguise the sharp edge in this communication between intimates, both of whom were familiar with the desires that brought the Vere Street prisoners to the pillory.

But while Matthews seems to have no doubt about the nature of his friend's sexuality, Byron's indiscretions had long been a matter of anxious speculation. Upon the poet's death in 1824, his close friend John Cam Hobhouse burned his memoirs, fearing what might be recorded there. Byron's first biographer, Thomas Moore, carefully avoided the specific question of Byron's homosexuality and portrayed his relationships with male friends as chaste romantic attachments of a platonic kind.

Speculation about the intimate details of Byron's life continued for decades after the poet's death and ultimately inspired *Don Leon,* an anonymous long poem written in 1833 and perhaps circulated in manuscript, though not published until 1866.[70] Half a century after Bentham's "Offences Against One's Self," *Don Leon* was a well-reasoned plea for sanity, the first and most direct challenge yet sounded in English literature to the persecution that is a consequence of homophobia. It imitates Byron's hugely popular *Don Juan,* in which the famous Spanish libertine tells of his (that is, Byron's, fictionalized) exploits; *Don Leon* is a mouthpiece for the author's mordant commentary on England's treatment of sodomites. The exploits and opinions of Don Leon are clearly meant by the anonymous author to be taken as

Byron's. The narrative of a secret homoerotic life gives the author a way to consider the opposition of homosexual desire and the laws that forbade its expression. The narrator observes:

> *Though law cries "Hold!" yet passion onward draws;*
> *But nature gave us passions, man gave laws;*
> *Whence spring these inclinations, rank and strong?*
> *And harming no one, wherefore call them wrong?*
> *[ll. 241–44]*

Don Leon cites and condemns religious, moral, legal, and social opinions, all of which, he argues, are founded upon ignorance and irrational hatred. In the process he identifies what we now call homophobia as the cause of the unjust persecution of sodomites.

The *Don Leon* poet argues that sodomites, far from being isolated and individual sinners, are an identifiable minority bound together by what he calls a "predilection." The poet insists, repeatedly, that the sexual desire of male sodomites for other males is as natural to them as is the desire of male nonsodomites for women. Furthermore, he asserts that the emotional and literary manifestations of such desire are praiseworthy. A call for the rights of sodomites in an age that conceived of them as monsters of depravity, the poem intends nothing less than to redefine sodomy as a legitimate sexual identity.

Clearly, the poem's anonymous author had intimate knowledge of Byron's life, such as only a friend might have; he reveals information about Byron's homosexuality that would not be substantiated until modern biographers began to examine this aspect of his life. Who was this poet? The most likely candidate may be William Bankes, an antiquarian, art collector, member of Parliament, and longtime friend of Byron's who was arrested in 1833, the year the poem was written, for having sexual relations with a guardsman. Much of *Don Leon* details Byron's homosexual experiences in Greece and Turkey in 1809–11; after returning from a trip to the East in 1821, Bankes had visited Byron in Italy and "may have exchanged confidences with him."[71]

Whoever its author, the poem may have been prompted by Bankes' arrest, and by the execution for sodomy two weeks later of one Captain Henry Nicholls. The latter event was described in the London *Courier* for August 1833:

Captain Henry Nicholas Nicholls, who was one of the unnatural gang to which the late Captain Beauclerk belonged . . . was convicted on the clearest evidence at Croyden, on Saturday last, of the capital offense of Sodomy; the prisoner was perfectly calm and unmoved throughout the trial, and even when the sentence of death was passed upon him. . . . The culprit, who was fifty years of age, was a fine looking man and had served in the Peninsular war. He was connected with a highly respectable family; but since his apprehension not a single member of it visited him.[72]

As the poem begins, Don Leon appeals to an "ermined judge" to look at his "work"—the corpse of a sodomite hanged on the gallows. Leon asks: "What had he done?" He urges the reader to "ask Beckford and Courtenay," who were hounded into exile upon the public revelation of their sodomitical affair. William Beckford was the richest man in England, author of the novel *Vathek,* which was infused with a subtle homoerotic ambience, and master of Fonthill Abbey, a vast Gothic mansion where he maintained an all-male household of handsome servants. He was also the despised object of a particularly public homosexual scandal. He was accused of having unnatural relations with the young and aristocratic William Courtenay, an allegation never adequately proved and perhaps even fabricated. The consequence of the scandal for both men was ostracism from English society. In 1787, three years after the scandal broke, Beckford wrote: "How tired I am of keeping a mask on my countenance. How tight it sticks—it makes me sore."

The hanged man, Leon insists, had committed no robberies, no rapes, no murders; he had broken no bonds of "social safety." Indeed, he kept his activities secret. But his "secret haunts" are discovered when the judge sends his "myrmidons to prowl," to entrap the sodomite in molly-houses and other gathering places. Leon insists that neither convictions gained by entrapment nor sentences meted out for a "crime" that violates no social compact can be described as justice. Moreover, the judgment only confirms the sexual hypocrisy endemic in England, a "land where every vice in full luxuriance flowers." The sexual underworld flourished openly, yet "one propensity," which if "left unheeded would remain unknown," is hounded until "the poor misogynist [sodomite] is hung" and his reputation destroyed.[73]

Since no one will protest this injustice, it remains for the poet to speak out. Even though his laurel wreath might wither, and torment might "rack my body here, my voice I'd raise insensible to fear," since "silence now were tantamount to crime" (23–28). In opposition to the Church's teaching that sodomitical acts and desires perversely negate "natural" inclination (110–24), Don Leon insists that nature herself proves otherwise. For just as "the tree we plant will, when its boughs are grown, produce no other blossoms than its own," so "in man some inborn passions reign / Which, spite of careful pruning, sprout again" (125–28).

If this is so, then it is legitimate to inquire "was I or nature in the wrong, / If, yet a boy, one inclination, strong / In wayward fancies, domineered my soul, / And bade complete defiance to control" (130–32). He notes that "the charms of women first my homage caught," not because of desire, but because his response was "by early education taught" (135–36). His potent observation that his "youthful instincts, forced to brood / Within my bosom seemed awhile subdued" (134–35) supports the proposition that sodomy is not a choice but an instinct.

After early homosexual experiences that "presage / The predilections of my riper age," his recognition of the nature of his desire leads the philosophic lover to further inquiry: "What lights this fire? / Maids not boys were wont to move desire." To answer, Don Leon argues that sodomitical emotions "harm no one" and that they are consonant with Christian ethics—for homosexual desire agrees with "virtue's touchstone," namely "Unto others do, / As you would wish that others did to you." He rings a musical change upon Plato's image of the eternal union of ideal friends: "The chords, when struck, vibrate in harmony." Homosexual acts protect domestic and social harmony, for the sodomite neither deflowers virgins nor commits adultery: "I plough no field in other men's domain." Nor does the sodomite bring unwanted progeny into the world: "Where I delve no seed shall spring again" (244–52).

Not fully satisfied with his own cogent arguments, Don Leon goes on to seek an explanation in literature, to call upon the "volumes of the dead" to justify his passion (254–88). His authorities include Plato, Socrates, Plutarch, Virgil, and Horace—and Shakespeare, whose "sonnets to a stripling's praise" would "damn a poet now-a-days" (315–18). He asks, not unreasonably:

I love a youth; but Horace did the same;
If he's absolved, say, why am I to blame?

When young Alexis claimed a Virgil's sigh,
He told the world his choice; and may not I?
. . . . .
Then why was Socrates surnamed the sage,
Not only in his own, but every age,
If lips, whose accents strewed the path of truth,
Could print their kisses on some favored youth?
Or why should Plato, in his Commonwealth
Score up tenets which I must note by stealth?
[ll. 271–74, 277–82]

That examples of homosexual desire appear in ancient writings is
hardly an original finding, and the poet admits as much: "These are . . .
samples musty grown." But modern times, too, yield examples of "pious
men," kings, saints, scholars, jurists, and captains, many of whom,
unable to resist the imperatives of a sexually "omnipotent" nature,
"found solace in a minion's arms" (289–314). Nature, he insists, cannot be changed by moral or legal fiat. Since the practice exists universally "in every caste and every clime," it cannot logically or rationally
be called immoral, sinful, or criminal. The proscription of sodomy, he
asserts, is derived not from natural fact but from social prejudice; and
it is inconsistent to condemn "wise men . . . whose deeds and sayings
history records" because they "ate of the fruit of that forbidden
tree / Which prejudice denies to you and me" (319–24). He supports
his conclusion by a utilitarian appeal to happiness that is "man's pursuit through life." Happiness has been achieved by the actions of wise
men, ancient and modern, who have found solace as nature, not law,
prompted them to do.

To the common argument that the young learn sodomy only by
example, Don Leon asserts that homoerotic desire is innate: "In vice
unhackneyed, in *Justine* unread, / See schoolboys, by some inclinations
fed: / Some void, that's hardly to themselves confest, / Flying for solace
to a comrade's breast" (349–52). The poet lets no opportunity pass to
insist that such desires are natural—"Imperious nature's sensual prick-
ings goad, / they own her dictates" (360–61)—not a crime against
nature. He urges teachers and parents to allow "truth" to find the way
"through fogs of prejudice" and to "shut your eyes" to the sexual
experiments of the young rather than teach them that what they do is
sinful. And if sodomy is not a crime against nature, then abhorrence of

it cannot be a natural reaction. On the contrary, pedagogues and parents are responsible for the fogs of prejudice: " 'Twas ye who roused the latent sense of shame, / And called their gambols by an odious name" (375–85).

Since England offers no freedom to announce or satisfy his desire, Don Leon seeks a sexual Arcadia where he can find "clandestine" love, a place where "Cupid's wings were free, his hands unbound, / Where law had no erotic statutes framed, / Nor gibbets stood to fright the unreclaimed" (425–27). He finds it in Turkey, where sodomy is not forbidden and youths "with their blandishments inveigle man, / As does in Christian lands the courtezan." In Constantinople he seeks out the brothel where "the black-eyed boy his trade unblushing plies." But because he is accompanied by a disapproving companion to whom he "dared not own / How much the sight had touched some inward sense," he desists from indulging: "Deep in the dark recesses of my mind / I hid my thoughts." Nonetheless he "resolved to do what yet I feared to tell." Surrounded by companions who are shocked by Turkish sexual morality—John Cam Hobhouse had accompanied Byron to Turkey and had responded thus—he is forced to recognize the difference between them and himself: "I found no kindred leaning in the breast / Of those around me, and I felt opprest" (458–70).[74]

The poet determines to leave his companions (as Byron did Hobhouse), for "mental freedom is to think alone." He sets out on a "different course" to Greece, where he hopes to lie down "beneath the shady plain, / Where Phaedrus heard grave Plato's voice complain." There, "another Phaedrus may perchance go by" and his "fond dreams become reality" (486–500).

In Greece Don Leon encounters Nicolo Giraud, a youth whom the historical Lord Byron had loved. He takes the youth as his page and "with culture stirred his mind, and in it choice instruction poured" (575–76). Giraud becomes to Leon what Phaedrus had been to Socrates: a younger man loved and taught by an older lover.

With scholarly delicacy, in 1830 Thomas Moore described this relationship in quite other terms: "In Greece we find him forming one of those extraordinary friendships . . . in which the pride of being the protector, and the pleasure of exciting gratitude, seemed to have constituted to his mind the chief, the pervading charm. . . . In [Giraud] he seems to have taken the most lively, and even brotherly interest."[75] In a letter to Hobhouse written the same day as one mentioning Giraud, Lord Byron reports: "I have employed the greater part of today in conjugating the [Greek] verb [to kiss]. . . . I assure you my progress is rapid."[76] In *Don Leon,* the poet offers a far more precise explanation of the relationship. His desire for Giraud effects the wedding of inspiration and passionate sexuality: "Oh how the happy moments seemed to fly, / Spent half in love and half in poetry! / The muse each morn I wooed, each eve the boy, / And tasted sweets that never seemed to cloy" (618–21).

Despite his success with Giraud and the pleasure it brings, Don Leon is still unsure about the nature of his desires; he attempts the presumed curative of heterosexuality, wooing three daughters of an aging widow. But he finds them, by comparison with Giraud's "ardent passions," intellectually vapid and spiritually dead: "Felt I their charms? I felt them not." The experience teaches him that "women as women, me had never charmed, / And shafts that others felt left me unharmed." By contrast, his affair with Giraud awakens him to a new life—the boy's beauty has unlocked "the gates of prejudice," the narrator's own lingering doubt about homosexuality. The affair gives him the courage to "mock the sober fears that timid minds endure." Before coming to Greece, he had only "resolved to do what yet I feared to tell," but now he is able at last to combine action with speech: "So boldly I set calumny at naught, and fearless utter what I fearless wrought" (676–91).

The narrator's passage from sexual doubt to sexual acceptance, his triumph over homophobia, is complete. The verbal affirmation of his desires—that "fearless utterance"—is the first published assertion in English that homosexual sex is both a political act and a mark of sexual and social rebellion. He carries the argument one step further when he speculates: "Is there an idiosyncrasy prevails / In those whose predilection is for males?" Thus homosexuality is inscribed within nature rather than outside it, for "idiosyncrasy" as used here denotes a special temper or a constitution—a "rooted bent."

Don Leon concludes with a plea to Moore, as Byron's biographer, to "be true to nature, paint me as I am" (1309). As a sodomite Don Leon places himself within the circle of the natural, outside which nothing—not even homosexuality or the sodomite, as he has now defined himself—can exist. Since the poem exemplifies the salutary effects of fearlessly uttering what he had discovered about his sexual nature, he urges Moore to "let my example one great truth unfold": that there are those "whose words and deeds are never understood," especially if they are guilty (as the world sees it) of sexual deviation. "Don Leon"'s real purpose in telling his story is to offer himself as an example: "I stand a monument, whereby to learn / That reason's light can never strongly burn / Where blear-eyed prejudice erects her throne, / And has no scale for virtue but her own" (1383–86). It is not only the poem that is an effective attack on homophobic prejudice, but the example of the poet himself.

7 The End of Sodomy?

The Enlightenment and the French Revolution had consequences for sodomites, the most important of which was the decriminalization of sodomy in many European nations. A call for reform was sounded by the Italian criminologist and jurist Cesare Beccaria in 1764, in his treatise *Dei deletti e delle pene* ("Essay on Crimes and Punishments"), where he called for the decriminalization of numerous crimes, including sodomy, on the grounds that false confessions were often obtained by torture, that such crimes were too difficult to prove, and that they were ultimately harmless. Beccaria's work was applauded by many Enlightenment thinkers, including Voltaire, who attacked the existing code of criminal law with its cruel and barbaric punishments for even minor infractions, and also opposed the death penalty for sodomy.[77] The ideas of Beccaria and Voltaire swept through Europe and were adopted first in France, when the Revolutionary Constituent Assembly decriminalized sodomy in 1791. There had been earlier intimations of change: the Parlement of Paris, which had convicted so many in the sixteenth and seventeenth centuries, executed only a handful of persons for sodomy in the eighteenth, the last in 1783.[78]

The example of France was followed by other European nations influenced by the Enlightenment. Though Prussia under its absolute monarchy continued to execute sodomites for most of the eighteenth century, it finally abolished the death penalty in 1794, as did Russia and Tuscany by the end of the century. In 1810, the Napoleonic Code eliminated all penalties for homosexual practice throughout Napoleon's European empire. Spanish law eased restrictions on sodomy in Spain and in Latin America, and by the end of the nineteenth century "criminal prohibition of consensual homosexual acts in private between adults" was gone from the laws of Belgium, France, Italy, Luxembourg, Monaco, Portugal, Romania, Spain, and even the Netherlands.[79]

In England, though, the pace of persecution dramatically increased. Between 1749 and 1804, executions averaged only one every ten years.

But between 1806 and 1836, sixty men were hanged for sodomy.[80] Among all the nations of Europe, England was the last to abandon (in 1861) its ancient statutes demanding death for the commission of sodomy, and homosexual acts remained criminal in England until well into the twentieth century.

The decriminalization of sodomy in the late eighteenth and early nineteenth centuries did not mean that intolerance of sodomites also disappeared. Only a few years earlier (in *The Decline and Fall of the Roman Empire* [1776–78]), Edward Gibbon had voiced the era's virulent disapprobation of sodomy: "I touch with reluctance and dispatch with impatience, a more odious vice, of which modesty rejects the name, and nature abominates the idea." Sodomy, for Gibbon, was an "infection," a "disease," and a "mortal pestilence." The abolition of the death penalty may have convinced those who most especially detested homosexuality that even more vigilance was necessary to prevent the wholesale infection of society and to expose, control, and "cure" the fearful "disease."

It was left to the Marquis de Sade to extend the Enlightenment values of reason and toleration to the lives of sodomites. In 1795 he asked: "But sodomy, that alleged crime which will draw the fire of heaven upon cities addicted to it, is sodomy not a monstrous deviation whose punishment could not be severe enough?" His answer was no:

> Ah, sorrowful it is to have to reproach our ancestors for the judiciary murders in which, upon this head, they dared indulge themselves. We wonder that savagery could ever reach the point where you condemn to death an unhappy person all of whose crime amounts to not sharing your tastes. . . . What single crime can exist here? . . . Is it possible to imagine Nature having allowed us the possibility of committing a crime that would outrage her? Is it possible that she consent to the destruction by man of her own pleasures, and to his thereby becoming stronger than she? It is unheard of—into what an abyss of folly one is hurled when, in reasoning, one abandons the aid of reason's torch! Let us abide in our unshakable assurance that it is as easy to enjoy a woman in one manner as in another, that it makes absolutely no difference whether one enjoys a girl or a boy, and as soon as it is clearly understood that no inclinations or tastes can exist in us save the ones we have from Nature, that she is too wise and too consistent

to have given us any which could ever offend her. The penchant for sodomy is the result of physical formation, to which we contribute nothing and which we cannot alter. . . . Regardless of how it is viewed, it is her work, and, in every instance, what she inspires must be respected by men.[81]

M. Vasdaz, "Les p'tits jeun' hommes." Crapouillot, 1954, no. 30, p. 40.

PART SIX

Victorian Secrets

Uranians, Inverts, Perverts, and Homosexuals, 1850–1910

Chapter Thirteen

Inverting Perversion

Long after the rest of Europe had abolished the death penalty for sodomy, England kept it in place. In 1836 a commission on the reform of criminal law made recommendations concerning capital crimes but noted that "a nameless offense of great enormity we, at present, exclude from consideration." In 1841 a bill to abolish the death penalty for rape and sodomy passed the House of Commons but was defeated in the House of Lords on the grounds, as one member argued, that if it passed, the Lords would appear to sanction "what the people of the country would never confirm—that sodomy and rape were not crimes of so heinous a character as to deserve death."[1] Finally, in 1861, during the reign of Queen Victoria, the death penalty for sodomy was at last abolished. However, sodomy—still called buggery—remained a criminal offense, punishable by "penal servitude for life, or for any term not less than ten years." Attempted sodomy could be punished with a term of up to ten years. In 1885, all mention of sodomy and buggery was removed from the law; now the abominable crime became simply—but vaguely, and therefore dangerously—"gross indecency." The bill of 1885 read:

> Any male person who, in public or private, commits or is a party
> to the commission of, or procures or attempts to procure the

commission by any male person of, any act of gross indecency with another male person, shall be guilty of a misdemeanor, and being convicted thereof shall be liable at the discretion of the Court to be imprisoned for any term not exceeding two years, with or without hard labour.[2]

This legislation actually expanded the range of prosecutable offenses: it explicitly criminalized *any* form of homosexual activity, not simply sodomy. Thus the state assumed the legal right to police, control, and investigate any act by a person suspected of homosexual inclinations. Blackmailers, always a threat, were given a much wider scope, since they could use even the imputation of homosexuality—a careless word, an insinuating letter, an unsubstantiated accusation—as a weapon. Entrapment was another threat; men were often caught in compromising positions, frequently with the collusion of the police. The implications for English homosexuals were tragic. One consequence of the law was that it fanned the smoldering fires of homophobia; another was that secrecy became even more imperative for homosexuals, for the public and the press often seemed as intent as the police on ferreting out homosexual infractions. The law eventually made a martyr of England's most prominent sodomite, Oscar Wilde.

Nonetheless, writers in particular chafed against these repressive conditions. In December 1894 an Oxford undergraduate magazine called *The Chameleon* published its only issue. In it, Lord Alfred Douglas' poem "The Two Loves" provided perhaps the most famous description of homosexual love: "the love that dare not speak its name." The poem was not as revolutionary as Douglas may have thought. Rather it belonged to a tradition of prohomosexual polemic that, in England, began with Bentham. By the 1890s England had a substantial body of writings that advocated resistance to homophobia in the law, in social attitudes, in religion, and in literature, and that expressed an identity created by homosexuals themselves, not by those who despised them.

Their desire fascinated homosexual writers, but it perplexed moralists and scientists, who tried to explain homosexuality even when they opposed it. In the middle of the nineteenth century, just as homoerotic texts started to proliferate, homosexual behavior began to undergo a major reinterpretation. The terms "homosexual" and "homosexuality" came into use as the act came to be seen less as a sin or a crime than as a pathology.

Medicine, heeding the findings of the new theories of human sexual behavior and psychiatry, invented the terms "invert" and "pervert" for types of "sexual abnormality," distinct from the normality of most men and women. To make these distinctions, medicine began to consider the simple mechanics of sex as an all-encompassing and all-determinative description of the individual, called sexuality. The invention of sexuality in the last decades of the nineteenth century contributed to the continuing growth of homophobia by adversaries of homosexuality who could now both moralize and medicalize sex and homosexuality.

1 The Invention of Abnormality

Eighteenth-century mobs threw offal at pilloried sodomites; nineteenth-century homophobes, deprived of that possibility, attacked with deadly verbal ferocity. Douglas' poem, for instance, drew a quick response from Jerome K. Jerome, a guardian of respectable culture, writing in his own newspaper, *To-Day:*

> The publication appears to be nothing more nor less than an advocacy for indulgence in the cravings of an unnatural disease.... This magazine is an ... outrage on literature.... It can serve no purpose but that of evil. It can please no man or woman with a single grain of self-respect left in their souls. Let us have liberty; but this is unbridled license. Let all things grow in literature which spring from the seeds of human nature. This is garbage and offal.[3]

A year earlier, a poem by Theodore Wratislaw that appeared in the *Artist and Journal of Home Culture* praised the "exquisite breasts and arms adorable" not of a woman but of a Sicilian boy. Cyril M. Drew matched Jerome K. Jerome in censoriousness: "Mr. Wratislaw is an apostle of 'the new cult,' *i.e.,* a small body of unimportant and opinionated young men who fancy that they can invert Nature and the human passions." Wratislaw's poem referred to kissing the boy; Drew reacted thus: "For one man to kiss the lips of another is a positively repellent idea.... The love of a man for a woman, of woman for man, is the axis whereon the universe revolves.... It is more natural to ... sing of kissing a woman's hair than to advocate the composition of amatory sonnets addressed to members of their own sex."[4]

Jerome's phrase "unnatural disease" encapsulated the history of homophobia: "unnatural" brought the most familiar and most ancient indictment against Douglas' unnameable love, just as "disease" brought the most modern. As for Drew, he used fashionable psychiatric terminology when he accused homosexual writers of intending to "invert" human passions.

As early as 1852, some medical theorists distinguished between "innate" and "acquired" sexual characteristics, and applied the distinction to define the new sexual creature, the "invert." As a scientific term, "invert," signifying a reversal of the direction of sexual desire from the opposite to the same sex, was new in the nineteenth century, though the notion of sodomy as a reversal was as ancient as the Roman phrase "posterior Venus." Some theorists asserted that if desire was reversed, then in inverts, gender roles—believed to be immutably established in nature—must also be reversed. Inverts must think, feel, and act like members of the other sex—men attracted to men, effeminate; women attracted to women, masculine.[5]

The distinction between innate and acquired homosexuality raised the question whether "sexual inverts" could be held responsible for their acts, and thus whether they should be subject to punishment or to medical "treatment," which could be equally brutal. Some joined the debate in defense of the new invert, advocating the abolition of antisodomy laws and insisting that inverts were genetically different from the majority of men. In 1868, the sexologist Karl Heinrich Ulrichs, a homosexual writing in Germany under the name of Numa Numantius, began to publish a series of pamphlets advocating homosexual rights and describing what he believed to be a separate sexual entity, a third sex. Indeed it was in a letter to Ulrichs that the German-Hungarian journalist "Károly Mária Kertbeny" (Karl Maria Benkert) first proposed the terms "homosexuality" and "heterosexuality." Benkert himself published two pamphlets in 1869 which advocated the abolition of antisodomy laws in Prussia on the grounds that the state ought not to interfere in the private life or sexual behavior of its citizens.[6]

However, most medical opinion saw inverts in a darker light. In 1870, Karl Westphals' "Contrary Sexual Feeling" argued that homosexuality was a kind of moral insanity resulting from a congenital reversal of sexual feeling.[7] For Paul Moreau (1877), pederasts and sodomites were a class of people whose emotional constitution wavered between sanity and insanity, and whose "malady" was hereditary. Benjamin Tarnovsky, a Russian researcher, insisted (1886) that homosexuality was "incurable" and that homosexuals could not help being what they were, since the condition arose when parental genes were damaged

by epilepsy, alcoholism, or a number of other psychological or physiological traumas. Cesare Lombroso (1836–1909) in Italy placed homosexuals in a class of moral and psychological criminals, concluding that
they were insane and should be committed to asylums. In 1886 Dr.
Richard von Krafft-Ebing published *Psychopathia Sexualis,* containing the "autobiographies" of more than two hundred "inverts." Echoing Westphals, he defined homosexuality as an absence of "normal
sexual feeling" but saw its cause as mental "degeneration." For him,
homosexuality, or inversion, could be inborn or acquired, but since it
did not further procreation it was in either case abnormal, unnatural,
and perverse.

Almost all of these studies asserted their "objective" approach to the
issue. *I pervertimenti dell'amore* ("The Perversions of Love") (1886),
by the Italian physiologist and anthropologist Paolo Mantegazza,
reveals the strength of bias behind such objectivity by arguing that the
disease of homosexuality can be cured if studied with the pitying and
indulgent eye of the physician. The term "perversion," for most
nineteenth-century theorists, meant simply an involuntary change in
the direction of the sexual instinct. But the word had long been associated with willful moral degeneracy. As science and morality collabo-
rated to define and to judge sexuality, the scientific and the moral terms
were increasingly conflated. In *Sexual Inversion,* his 1897 study of
homosexuality, Havelock Ellis used the terms interchangeably in his
description of Krafft-Ebing's *Psychopathia Sexualis* as containing histories "not only of sexual inversion but of all other forms of sexual perversion." It was not long before sexual inversion and sexual perversion,
in popular discourse and often in scientific discourse too, came to be
understood as one and the same.[8]

Turn-of-the-century medical texts seemed increasingly obsessed with
the topic of sexual inversion; over a thousand articles appeared on
the subject between 1898 and 1908 alone.[9] Conceptions of homosexuality as a medical "problem" found their way from the circumspect
pages of professional journals into the popular press and thus into popular perceptions. By 1892 the word "homosexual" was coming into
common use. Imported from the German, it was perhaps first used in
English by John Addington Symonds in his 1883 study of Greek homosexuality, *A Problem in Greek Ethics.* The term made it possible to
imagine a group of sexually different creatures, both men and women,
but also to imagine them in the darkest terms. When in 1893 an American, Dr. C. H. Hughes, classed all homosexual acts as "eroto-pathia or

erotomania," or "perversions of the proper and natural human passions," he confirmed what Jerome and Drew already clearly believed: that "normal" human passions are "the ardent affections of the heart," which are "chaste and honorable" and lead to reproduction. Abnormal passions—those entertained by the young men who wrote for *The Chameleon*—are "strange morbid perversions" that can "destroy both body and mind."[10]

The urge to define what was perverse or "abnormal" and what was "normal" in human conduct was especially strong among those studying what was coming to be called sexuality. First, of course, it was necessary to define the "proper" relation between the sexes—indeed, to invent a definition of the sexes themselves. The "true woman" was to be submissive socially and sexually, focused on domestic life, pious, and morally pure. Men were assertive both socially and sexually; they ruled the patriarchal family and were active providers of material goods. Victorian theorists inevitably assumed that these roles were dictated by biology, that they were "naturally" associated with the biological female or male. A biological woman was naturally "feminine," a biological male naturally "masculine," and gender was defined as having fixed and immutable natural characteristics. Nineteenth-century sexual theorists further presumed that males and females "naturally" engaged in sex respectively as active and passive partners; this opposition, they believed, was written into the structure of sex itself.

Included in these definitions was the insistence that "love" was the only proper channel in which these roles might be emotionally expressed. Marriage manuals and social-purity tracts declared that love was truly possible only between men and women. When the American Thomas Wentworth Higginson reviewed Walt Whitman's poetry in 1892, he observed a "curious deficiency" in him "of anything like personal and romantic love. Whenever we come upon anything that suggests a glimpse of it, the object always turns out to be a man and not a woman." Confronted with social or literary examples of male-male sex or affection, readers like Higginson balked: since there was no woman involved, this could not be love. What, then, of love between men? It was not just suspect but impossible. The pervert, not motivated by the natural imperative to procreate, still desired sex, to be sure, and his desire must express some sort of feeling. But since natural, procreation-oriented sex could not exist outside the emotional context called love, the pervert, who acted outside of normality, obviously could not feel love. Only lust was available to him. And since sex-as-procreation was the driving force behind human nature, the pervert's desires could only be abnormal, antisocial, and therefore dangerous.

The possibility of sex between two men, was, to use Drew's word, "repellent." Such deviant sexual acts were generally assumed to be of one kind only, anal penetration. But a man who wished to penetrate another male presented a special problem for Victorian sexual theory. What he wanted to do seemed active, aggressive, and hence masculine. Since his desires were not directed toward women, their natural object, his activity was abnormal and his actions perverse. Nonetheless, his urge was to be the active partner, that is, to take the manly role ordained by nature. In light of this natural inclination, Victorians considered his desire to penetrate another man a willful pursuit of abnormality, an "acquired" and "vicious" perversion rather than an inborn compulsion. It was the passive male, the one who liked to be penetrated, who was the "real" homosexual; his desires were congenital and hence involuntary. Sexually passive, such men were appropriately described as "effeminate" and their physical mannerisms were presumed to mirror a sexual and psychological deficiency.

Various writings reveal that some homosexuals took on the prevailing notion of what they were, and described themselves in medical terms. In E. M. Forster's novel *Maurice,* the hero presents himself to a doctor as "an unspeakable of the Oscar Wilde sort."[11] In consulting his doctor and not his priest, Maurice accepts the nineteenth-century medical definition of homosexuality as a pathology, a "condition" deviating from the "normal," a perversion of sexuality. But where early medical theorists had believed such people to be rare anomalies, it was popularly suspected—and this suspicion was often articulated by the press— that homosexuals, passive and active, had created a social organization in which their practices flourished and even a literature that advocated abnormality. As individuals, homosexuals were disturbing but could be trivialized as objects of pity or contempt. In groups, however, they were a threat to morality, love, health, and the family.

2 A Flourishing Literature

Drew and Jerome were, in one way, right: the young men who wrote such scandalous literature did indeed advocate the possibility that one man might "kiss the lips of another." Moreover, a number of them were no longer willing to agree that their desire was "indulgence in the cravings of an unnatural disease." They aimed to mount a counterattack.

Between the mid-1860s and 1895 in England and Europe, several hundred titles of prose fiction, poetry, and essays that dealt with homosexuality were published or printed privately, in tandem with the proliferation of scientific studies, though with different agendas. Many of the most important writers wrote on homosexual themes or were themselves homosexual: Alfred Tennyson, John Addington Symonds, Gerard Manley Hopkins, Walter Pater, Algernon Charles Swinburne, Edward Carpenter, Oscar Wilde, A. E. Housman, and Havelock Ellis in England; on the continent, J.-K. Huysmans, Charles Baudelaire, Arthur Rimbaud, Paul Verlaine, Théophile Gautier, and Alexander Pushkin, to name only the most well known. Across the Atlantic, Walt Whitman had begun to experiment, dramatically and far less evasively than many of those in England, with homoeroticism in texts. Other American writers—Bayard Taylor, Herman Melville, Henry Thoreau, Theodore Winthrop, and Charles Warren Stoddard—had also begun to sound in their writing significant if cautious homoerotic themes. By 1895, in both England and America, homosexuality had found not only a name but a literature that began to define its identity.

By the end of the century, names for the not-to-be-named condition had begun to proliferate. But, as J. A. Symonds wrote in 1891, "the accomplished languages of Europe in the nineteenth century supply no terms for this persistent feature of human psychology, without importing some implication of disgust, disgrace, vituperation."[12] Homosexual writers looked for a term to describe themselves that, unlike "invert" and "pervert," did not reflect hostility. They found one in the writing of Ulrichs, the German sex researcher. In *Vindex* (1864), the first of a series of pamphlets exploring aspects of same-sex relationships, Ulrichs coined the term *Uranismus* to describe male homosexuality. He drew from Plato's *Symposium,* where the goddess who presides over love between men is the daughter of the god Uranus. Ulrichs also coined the term *Urning* to mean a class of individuals "in whom alongside a male physique a female sexual drive is inborn, a particular subspecies of male in whom male love is inborn."[13] English homosexuals often used "Uranian" to describe themselves, and writers on the subject called it Uranian love. Homosexuality did dare to speak its name—or, by the 1860s, its many names—and writers freely made use of new, nonpejorative terms: "the third sex," "inverts," "similisexuals," and the new invention, "homosexual."

At first, writings confronting homophobia were quite tentative. In 1858, William Johnson published a small book of poems, titled *Ionica.* Interspersed among the conventional verses—tributes to Queen Victoria, and to Tennyson, praises of childhood, bravery, and the beauty of young women—are several poems that deal in one way or another with relationships between the speaker and persons whose names and gender remain ambiguous. Johnson (who later took the name of William Cory) was dismissed from his teaching post at Eton in 1871 on suspicion of too-intimate relations with his pupils, a suspicion that may have seemed justified by the vaguely dubious reputation of his book. But at the end of the 1880s and into the early years of the twentieth century, a number of books revealed homosexuality's newly assertive voice: Sir Richard Burton's "Terminal Essay" (1888), appended to his translation of the *Arabian Nights,* was, in effect, a history of homosexuality—the first to be published in English. Oscar Wilde's story "The Portrait of Mr. W.H." (1889), a speculation on the relationship between Shakespeare and the Mr. W.H. of the sonnets, was one of the first stories to depict romantic homoeroticism. J. A. Symonds' essays exploring homosexuality in ancient Greece and modern Europe—*A Problem in Greek Ethics* (1883) and *A Problem in Modern Ethics* (1891)—had been much circulated privately, and the latter was published in Havelock Ellis's *Sexual Inversion* (1897). Edward Carpenter delivered his essay "Homogenic Love" as a public lecture in Manchester in 1894.

As homosexuality became an increasingly legitimate subject for writers, the challenge was how to describe a practice that had only a pejorative lexicon. In the 1860s some writers had hinted—with classical allusions, foreign-language titles, sensual phrases, and erotic but coded language—at what they were really about. Swinburne's "Hermaphroditus" (1863) and Roden Noel's "Ganymede" (1868) are examples of the genre. Hints about homosexuality also appear in Walter Pater's essay "Winckelmann" (1867), which proposed that the German aesthete's "affinity with Hellenism was not merely intellectual" but derived from "his romantic, fervid friendships with young men." Pater's essay marks the beginning of a literary process that would eventually introduce sexual difference as a component—and perhaps as a basis (indeed, for Pater and some other writers, perhaps the only basis)—of an "aesthetic" sensibility.

Edward Carpenter's *Narcissus and Other Poems* (1873) and Symonds' *Lyra Viginti Cordarum* (1875) with allusions to Hylas, Ganymede, and "Uranian Love," left little doubt as to what the poets intended. But Symonds could also be more explicit. In "Midnight at Baiae" he pictures a youth whose "naked form supine" is described as "very white and smooth and fine." Gerard Manley Hopkins' "The Bugler's First Communion" (1879) celebrates a "limber liquid youth" breathing "bloom of chastity in mansex fine"—which might alert certain readers to a subtext concealed from the less discerning by the religious primary text. Lord Alfred Douglas' publication of "The Two Loves" (1894) outraged the moral establishment with its personification of both heterosexual and homosexual love. When homosexual love famously responds, "I am the love that dare not speak its name," to the assertion by heterosexual love that his true name is "shame," it is clear that "shame" means "homosexuality": in the same issue of *Chameleon,* Douglas insisted in a poem called "In Praise of Shame" that "of all sweet passions Shame is loveliest."

Homoerotic and antihomophobic references began to appear in fiction as well. John Francis Bloxam's "The Priest and the Acolyte" (1894) told of the doomed love between a priest and his altar boy, and a pederastic ambiance pervades Frederick Rolfe's *Stories Toto Told Me* (1898). In *Tim* (1891), Howard Sturgis depicted homoerotic attachments in the sanctum of the all-male boarding school—a popular setting for both homoerotic and homophobic writing. Walter Pater's *Marius the Epicurean* (1885) praised similar homoerotic relationships in classical times. Even such popular books as Thomas Hughes' *Tom Brown's School Days* (1857), Dean Farrar's *Eric, or, Little by Little* (1858), and Hall Caines' *The Deemster* (1887) suggested that extremely close relationships between boys—and sometimes between men and boys, especially between tutors and their students—were a feature of both academic and public life.

Pornographic novels like *Teleny* (1890), sometimes attributed to Oscar Wilde, and *The Sins of the Cities of the Plain* (1890s), both anonymously published, provided detailed pictures of homosexual life and practices. Indeed, *Teleny* was the first novel in English to focus exclusively on homosexuality, not only presenting explicit sexual descriptions but also using its subject as an occasion for sensitive exploration. *The Sins of the Cities of the Plain*—the cities referred to, of course, are Sodom and Gomorrah—purports to be a factual presentation of the world of the London male prostitute; as explicit as *Teleny,* it is not nearly as well written.

A. E. Housman published *A Shropshire Lad* in 1896; generations of Englishmen have read the poems as a nostalgic mirror of British rectitude. But the homoerotic ambiance its homosexual author intended can be appreciated when Housman's evocation of English "lads" is read in company with John Gambril Nicholson's *A Garland of Ladslove* (1911) and John Barford's *Ladslove Lyrics* (1919). Already, Aleister Crowley's poems published in *White Stains* (1898)—including one that ends, "Ah! You come—you kill me! / Christ! God! Bite! Bite! Ah Bite! Love's fountains fill me!"—had explosively and explicitly brought the century, though not the literature, to a close.

3 Fictive Strategies

To some writers it seemed that the best way to valorize love between men might be to build a new world where there was no homophobia. To this end, they began to define locales of their own, protected sites, whose language, myths, manners, and ethics would define them and them alone. Though the walls had been built by society, homoerotic literature began to furnish the enclosure with a special style and artifacts. Writing about a young man of whom he was enamored, J. A. Symonds said that he shared "my Arcadian tastes."[14] Arcadia, the pastoral haven of Greek literature, became understood as a code for a homosexual sanctuary.

Gerard Manley Hopkins' "Epithalamion" of 1888 locates the refuge at a secret pond where his speaker bathes in communion with a group of young men and, having done so, finds himself transformed. E. M. Forster sends Maurice and his lover, Alec, to the "greenwood," which he defines as "big spaces where passion clasped peace, spaces no science could reach, but they existed forever, full of woods some of them, and arched with majestic sky and a friend." Maurice determines to go into the greenwood because, as a homosexual, he is "an outlaw in disguise." Perhaps, he muses after his affirmation of his homosexuality, "among those who took off to the greenwood in old times there had been two men like himself—two. At times he entertained the dream. Two men can defy the world."[15] In Arcadia men could cast off their outlaw status, homosexuality could be revealed without reprisal, homosexual love could be consummated without fear of punishment or scorn.

While the vision of Arcadia offered freedom, it also implied isolation and segregation; the young men in their sylvan glades had no part in society and could not influence its opinions. Another strategy was to accentuate rather than deny homosexuals' differences, and so force acceptance in heterosexual society. Indeed, some nineteenth-century homosexuals emphasized effete characteristics, employing languid dandyism—"aesthetic" behavior, as they called it—to signal their defiance. In turn, Victorian homosexual poetry described men and boys in terms that deliberately mimicked the notion of the effeminate homosexual. Some writers cultivated an effete homosexual literary style that undermined orthodox gender expectations. Thus two poems yield the words "rapturous," "exquisite," "tremulous," "delicate," "yearnings," "sinuous," "heavenly," "adorable," "enchanting," "tenderest," "bliss," and "divinest" to describe male beauty and love for males. Late in the century, the poet Marc-André Raffalovich urged that homosexuals ought to assume an effete manner on purpose to offend "men like that," that is, the homophobic public. In "Put On That Languor" (1889) he argues that the effete pose itself is far more honest than the dissimulation and secrecy that homophobia enforces.

> Put on that Languor which the world frowns on,
> That blamed misleading strangeness of attire,
> And let them see that see us we have done
> With their false worldliness and look up higher.
> Because the world has treated us so ill
> And brought suspicion near our happiness,
> Let men that like to slander as they will;
> It shall not be my fault if we love less.
> Because we two who never did them harm,
> And never dreamt of harm ourselves, find men
> So eager to perplex us and alarm
> And scare from us our dove-like thoughts, well then
>   Since 'twixt the world and truth must be our choice,
>   Let us seem vile, not be so, and rejoice.

Of course, effeminate homoeroticism is only one side of the nineteenth-century literary homosexual identity. John Addington Symonds had no patience with the effete or the effeminate. Harking back to the teaching of his idol Walt Whitman, Symonds preferred to speak of manly friendship and to define homosexuals as, if anything, even more manly, masculine, athletic, and sexual than heterosexual males. In "Eudiades" (1868), a poem about star-crossed Greek male lovers, Symonds describes Melanthias as possessing "wide shoulders, knitted arms, and narrow waist." But he also mentions that the "wavy down" on his "smooth white thighs and perfect breast / Lay soft as sleep."

Edward Cracroft Lefroy's "A Palaestral Study," from his *Echoes from Theocritus and Other Sonnets* (1885), is set in the palaestra—the Greek gymnasium—and is ostensibly a meditation on beauty and art. The beauty under discussion is specifically male. A reference to wrestling—a primary activity in the palaestra—allows manly images of sexual struggle to come to the fore:

> *The curves of beauty are not softly wrought;*
> *These quivering limbs by strong muscles held*
> *In attitudes of wonder, and compelled*
> *Through shapes more sinuous than a sculptor's thought,*
> *Tell of dull matter splendidly distraught,*
> *Whisper of mutinies divinely quelled—*
> *Weak indolence of flesh, that long rebelled,*
> *The spirit's domination bravely taught.*

The invocation of an almost hypermasculine sexuality is frequent in the literature of this period. Reginald Brett, Viscount Esher associates athletic activity with sex in a poem describing a player: "He moves Titanic 'mid the strife of games, / So fleet of foot, so sure of eye, so glorious, / With stately youth, and beauty which enflames / Desire for him."[16] Walter Pater, writing about the Greek sculptor Myron, waxes lyrical about the youths who were his subjects: "When [Myron] came to his main business with the quoit-player, the wrestler, the runner, he did not for a moment forget that they too were animals, young animals, delighting in natural motion, in free course through the yielding air." The title of Pater's essay, "The Age of Athletic Prizemen," provided a term—"athletic"—that was to become another coded allusion to homosexuality. In *Maurice*, E. M. Forster describes Maurice's feelings for Clive as "athletic love." If glorious athletic images revealed homosexual passion, how could such passion be weak, effeminate, and diseased?

Another antihomophobic literary strategy was to claim that homosexual sex was superior to heterosexual. Symonds asked: "What is the charm of barren joy? / The well-knit body of boy / Slender and slim, / Why is it then more wonderful / than Venus with her white breasts / And sweet eye dim?"[17] When Edwin Barford published *Passing the*

Love of Women and Other Poems in 1913, he recalled the tradition
that valorized men's emotional capacities over women's. His title
derives from the biblical story of David and Jonathan in 1 Samuel; their
relationship, described there as "passing the love of woman," gave
homosexual writers an unimpeachable citation justifying male-male
desire. In his notorious "To a Sicilian Boy" (1893), Theodore Wratislaw insists that homosexual men excelled in sex itself:

> *I love thee, sweet! Kiss me, again, again!*
> *Thy kisses soothe me, as tired earth the rain;*
> *Between thine arms I find my only bliss;*
> *Ah, let me in thy bosom still enjoy*
> *Oblivion of the past, divinest boy,*
> *And the dull ennui of a woman's kiss!*

A number of writers directly confronted the effect of homophobia
on homosexual life. In Symonds' poem "What Cannot Be" (1861), the
speaker shouts his "rebellious scorn" against "high heaven." What he
rebels against is not only the sexual conventions of society, represented
by "high heaven," but the "doom" he believes is inevitable for himself
as a homosexual in a homophobic world. A young man passes the
speaker's house and with a glance invites him to a life of erotic bliss, a
life of love and "the brotherhood of strength" that seems to be "of all
convention free." But the chance to achieve happiness in a homosexual
relationship is blighted by the speaker's own doubts and fears, his self-
disdain, and his inability to ignore homophobic conventions. The
speaker ends the poem alone, racked by "sharp self-disdain" and afraid
that the apples of love might hide "dust within."

In "The World Well Lost IV," Marc-André Raffalovich indicates the
difficulty of daily confrontation with homophobic society—"They":

> *Because our world has music, and we dance;*
> *Because our world has colour, and They gaze*
> *Because our speech is tuned, and schooled our glance,*
> *And we have roseleaf nights and roseleaf days,*
> *And we have leisure, work to do, and rest;*
> *Because They see us laughing when we meet,*
> *And hear our words and voices, see us dressed*
> *With skill, and pass us and our flowers smell sweet:—*
> *They think that we know friendship, passion, love!*

Our peacock Pride! And Art our nightingale!
And Pleasure's hand upon our dogskin glove!
And if They see our faces burn or pale,
   It is the sunlight, think They, or the gas,
   —Our lives are wired like our gardenias.

Raffalovich not only anatomizes the cost of difference in a world where sexual conformity is prized, but also details a particular kind of homosexual identity, in which the effete homosexual style is highly developed. Raffalovich asserts that this fabulous creature, who drifts on the surface of a world of elegance, costly objects, and witty badinage, has invented himself, his manner, his "tuned" speech and his "schooled" glance as a defense against the social disapprobation "They" represent. But the text also highlights another price of the collision between the aesthetic/erotic pose and homophobia: the need for a constant masquerade that conceals the real beneath an invented identity. The speaker's life, like the gardenia in his buttonhole, is a careful contrivance supported against collapse by a hidden wire. The damaging effects of homophobia are profound: the speaker doubts the possibility of "friendship, passion, love." But even though the text paints a grim picture of a world in which social difference is predicated upon sexual difference—"our" world as opposed to the one "They" inhabit—the title of the poem nevertheless suggests that the world of sexual conformity is well worth losing.

John Francis Bloxam's short story "The Priest and the Acolyte," written in 1894, is an especially powerful account of the effects of homophobia. The acolyte is the ideal friend that Ronald Heatherington, the priest of the title, has long sought. But having found him, Heatherington is accused by the rector of the church where he serves of harboring improper affection for the boy. The rector asks for an explanation, and Heatherington's reply speaks of the need for an ideal friend, but also of the process of self-discovery and of the attraction of the eroticized aesthetic ideal. "I was always different from the other boys. I never cared much for games," he says. "My one ambition was to find the ideal for which I longed. . . . I always sought for love: again and again I have been the victim of fits of passionate affection: time after time I have seemed to have found my ideal at last." Attracted by sin— "my whole early life is stained and polluted by the taint of sin"— Heatherington reflects that "there are vices that are bound to attract almost irresistibly anyone who loves beauty above everything." In fact,

his love of beauty, the "aesthetic tendency" of his soul, drew him to
"the wonderful mysteries of Christianity." And his "exquisite delight"
in religion continues in the aesthetic beauty of the services, the ecstasy
of devotion, the "passionate fervour that comes with long fasting and
meditation." But it has brought him no respite: "Ever since my ordina-
tion I have been striving to cheat myself into the belief that peace had
come at last . . . but all in vain. Increasingly I have struggled with the
old cravings for excitement, and . . . the weary, incessant thirst for a
perfect love."

When the rector observes that he ought to have married, Heatherington replies angrily:

> I have never been attracted by a woman in my life. Can you not see
> that people are different, totally different, from one another? To
> think that we are all the same is impossible; our natures, our tem-
> peraments, are utterly unlike. But this is what people will never
> see; they found all their opinions on a wrong basis. How can
> deductions be just if premises are wrong? One law laid down by
> the majority, who happen to be of one disposition, is only binding
> on the minority legally, not morally. What right have you, or any-
> one, to tell me that such and such a thing is sinful for me. . . . For
> me, with my nature, to have married would have been sinful: it
> would have been a crime, a gross immorality, and my conscience
> would have revolted. . . . Conscience should be that divine instinct
> which bids us seek after that our natural disposition needs. . . . To
> the world, to Christians in general, conscience is merely another
> name for the cowardice that dreads to offend against conven-
> tion. . . . I have committed no moral offense in this matter; in the
> sight of God my soul is blameless; but to you and the world I am
> guilty of an abominable crime—abominable because it is a sin
> against convention. . . . I met this boy; I loved him as I had never
> loved anyone . . . he was mine by right; he loved me, even as I
> loved him. . . . How dare the world presume to judge us? What is
> convention to us? Nevertheless, although I really knew that such a
> love was beautiful and blameless, although from the bottom of my
> heart I despised the narrow judgment of the world . . . I tried to
> resist. I struggled against the fascination he possessed for me. . . . I
> would have struggled on to the end: but what could I do? It was he
> who came to me, and offered the wealth of his love. . . . How
> could I tell to such a nature the hideous picture the world would

paint? . . . I knew what I was doing. I have faced the world and set myself against it. I have openly scoffed at its dictates. . . . In God's eyes we are martyrs, and we shall not shrink even from death in this struggle against the idolatrous worship of convention.[18]

Heatherington's remarkable *cri de coeur* is not only an apologia for same-sex love and a condemnation of homophobia, but also an insistence on the natural and irreversible fact of sexual difference. Significantly, he reverses the role of the Church and religious proscription. No longer the defiling sinners, homosexuals are now martyrs in God's eyes. The Cities of the Plain and their inhabitants are no longer guilty of transgression; the new idolators are those who worship convention.

Writing in a climate of prohibition, yet responding to the discourses that were beginning to redefine sex and sexuality, these writers produced one of the most significant bodies of literature concerned with homosexuality and homophobia to have been published in English, or any language, up to that time. By their very existence they defied homophobia, just as they enraged homophobes.

Chapter Fourteen

Modern Ethics

Three men stand out above all others for the spirited battle they waged against homophobia. John Addington Symonds, historian, essayist, and poet, was among the most vigorous defenders of the social value of homosexuality. The poet and social theorist Edward Carpenter forged a new path in claiming equality for homosexual men and women and calling homosexual love "a very important factor in society" because "its neglect, or its repression, or its vulgar misapprehension, may be matters of considerable damage to the common-weal."[1] Oscar Wilde, in his writing and in the way he lived his life, mounted perhaps the strongest challenge to homophobia—and paid the greatest price.

1 The Social Value of Homosexuality

At his trial for gross indecency in 1895, Wilde was asked to define "the love that dare not speak its name." He described it as "such a great affection of an elder for a younger man" as "Plato made the very basis of his philosophy." This appeal to Greece drew upon the presumption that the arts and literature of ancient Greece had become woven into the texture of Western cultures. Indeed, the idea of Greece had been incorporated into the cultural poetics of nearly every age since. A model for systems of education, ethics, and government, Greece stood for all that was original and estimable in Western thought, a source for ideals of democracy and individual freedom. Of course there were Victorians unwilling to believe that the Greek heroes they so admired could have practiced what they themselves despised as "the sin not to be named among Christians." In *Maurice,* E. M. Forster portrays one teacher who urges his students in their translation of a Greek text to "Omit: a reference to the unspeakable vice of the Greeks." The Greek scholar and translator of Plato Benjamin Jowett maintained that what Plato had to say about pederasty in the *Symposium* was only a figure of speech and a "matter of metaphor."[2]

Nonetheless, Greek studies offered homosexuals a source of hope and personal vindication. Greek texts celebrated homosexual desire, not finding in it any taint of the criminal, the sinful, or the unnatural. And appeals like Wilde's to the Greeks attempted to secure a site in history without homophobia. If Greece embodied all that was noble, humane, and manly in Western culture, while at the same time the makers of that culture engaged in behavior that Christian culture condemned, perhaps logic demanded that homosexuality be reevaluated in light of the lessons the Greeks taught about love and sex. Thus Greece came to be seen by some writers as a place where love between men had been accepted and sanctified, and even deemed to be of spiritual value.[3]

Among the founding texts of modern gay studies is an essay on Greek homosexuality by John Addington Symonds, one of the most eminent English men of letters of the late nineteenth century, the author of several volumes of poetry, criticism, and literary history, including a two-volume study of Greek literature. Symonds was also intimately familiar with the effects of homophobia. In 1858, having just entered Balliol College at Oxford, he discovered Plato, an intellectual and spiritual revelation he describes in his autobiography:

> It so happened that I stumbled on the *Phaedrus.* I read on and on, till I reached the end. Then I began the *Symposium;* and the sun was shining on the shrubs outside the ground-floor room in which I slept, before I shut the book. . . . That night was one of the most important nights of my life. . . . In the *Phaedrus* and *Symposium*—in the myth of the soul and the speeches of Pausanias, Agathon, and Diotima—I discovered the true *liber amoris* at last, the revelation I had been waiting for, the consecration of a long cherished idealism. . . . Here was the poetry, the philosophy of my

own enthusiasm for male beauty, expressed with all the magic of unrivaled style. And what was more, I now became aware that the Greek race—the actual historical Greeks of antiquity—treated this love seriously, invested it with moral charm, endowed it with sublimity. For the first time I saw the possibility of resolving in a practical harmony the discords of my instincts. I perceived that masculine love had its virtue as well as its vice, and stood in this respect upon the same ground as normal sexual appetite.[4]

But even this epiphany did not erase Symonds' sense of alienation, as his own case history—anonymously presented after his death in Ellis and Symonds' *Sexual Inversion* (1897)—so eloquently testifies:

He has suffered extremely throughout life owing to his sense of the difference between himself and normal human beings. No pleasure he has enjoyed, he declares, can equal a thousandth part of the pain caused by the internal consciousness of pariahdom. The utmost he can plead in his own defense, he admits, is irresponsibility, for he acknowledges that his impulse may be morbid. But he feels absolutely certain that in early life his health was ruined and his moral repose destroyed owing to the perpetual conflict with his own inborn nature, and that relief and strength came with indulgence. Although he always has before him the terror of discovery, he is convinced that his sexual dealings with men have been thoroughly wholesome to himself, largely increasing his physical, moral, and intellectual energy, and not injurious to others. He has no sense whatever of moral wrong in his actions, and he regards the attitude of society toward those in his position as utterly unjust and founded on false principles.[5]

To do battle against those false principles Symonds turned his critical attention to the question of homosexuality. In 1871 he wrote *A Problem in Greek Ethics* (it appeared in 1883 in ten privately circulated copies). In this first sustained attempt to reclaim Greece as the lost fatherland of homosexuals, Symonds cites it as an example of a tolerant, unprejudiced society that valued rather than condemned homosexual desire and argues that the Greeks' "genius"—the source of their unparalleled achievement—lay precisely in the passion that his own age condemned:

For the student of sexual inversion, ancient Greece offers a wide field for observation and reflection. Its importance has hitherto been underrated by medical and legal writers on the subject, who do not seem to be aware that here alone in history have we the example of a great and highly developed race not only tolerating homosexual passions but deeming them of spiritual value, and attempting to utilize them for the benefit of society. . . . What the Greeks called *paiderastia* or boy-love, was a phenomenon of one of the most brilliant periods of human culture.[6]

At the end of *A Problem in Greek Ethics* Symonds invokes his heroes, who "regarded humanity as a part of a good and beautiful universe, nor did they shrink from any of their normal instincts." The aim of Greek ethics was always to realize the full potential of human nature, to "find the law of human energy, the measure of man's natural desires, the right moment for indulgence and for self-restraint, the balance which results in health, the proper limit for each several function which secures the harmony of all":

Their personal code of conduct ended in "modest self-restraint" not abstention, but selection and subordination ruled their practice. They were satisfied with controlling much that more ascetic natures unconditionally suppress. Consequently, to the Greeks there was nothing at first sight criminal in *paiderastia*. To forbid it as a hateful and unclean thing did not occur to them. Finding it within their hearts, they chose to regulate it, rather than root it out.[7]

Symonds' argument that the Greeks considered homosexual passion a normal instinct and a natural desire confronts homophobia itself. Greek morality, he observes, was "aesthetic and not theocratic," unlike the repressive heritage of his own time. For the Greeks "the sensual impulses, like the intellectual and the moral, were . . . held void of crime and harmless." By comparison, Christianity had produced a "separation of flesh and spirit," with unhappy results: "the abhorrence of beauty as a snare and the sense that carnal affections were tainted with sin, the unwilling toleration of sexual love as a necessity, the idealization of celibacy and solitude." Just these are what Christian doctrine proclaims as central virtues, and so Symonds' assertions were not only dangerous in their muted advocacy of an officially illegal homosexual love but could seem heretical as well.

Though Symonds' text pledges an uneasy allegiance to Christian doctrine, the focus of his desire is clearly elsewhere. We must, he says, imitate the Greeks "by reproducing their free and fearless attitude of mind"; we must acknowledge "the value of each human impulse" and aim at "virtues that depend on self-regulation rather than on total abstinence and mortification. To do this in the midst of our convention-alities and prejudices . . . is no doubt hard. Yet if we fail of this, we lose the best the Greeks can teach us."[8]

In his history of the Greeks, Symonds paused on one of his favorite themes: the difference between effeminacy and "manly love," the former a characteristic of "savage tribes," the latter of civilized man. Only the Dorian Greeks, he believed, had practiced "the distinctive fea-tures" of comradeship, "tolerating no sort of softness," while "barbar-ians"—among whom he includes the native peoples of Madagascar, North America, Mexico, and Peru—esteemed "effeminate males who renounce their sex, assume female clothes, and live either in promiscu-ous concubinage with the men of the tribe or else in marriage with chosen persons." He reports that such effeminacies were considered "pathological by Herodotus"—presumably also by Symonds himself, whose preference was for young strapping soldiers. Symonds is at his most culture-bound here; still, in putting a premium on masculine com-radeship and manliness he does attempt to extricate those concepts from the exclusive claims of the heterosexual world. Symonds recog-nized that effeminacy—according to his own age the essential charac-teristic of the sodomite, the molly, and the new "homosexual"—was a social construction. What his research proved was the "universality of unisexual indulgence in all parts of the world." It was the Greeks' sig-nal achievement to "moralize and adapt this practice to social use" and to "elaborate it into the region of romance and ideality."[9] It was Europe's great failure to follow suit.

A few years later, Symonds took up the battle once again, in *A Prob-lem in Modern Ethics* (1891). Now his concern was with his own time, and his purpose frankly polemical: to correct "vulgar errors," point up the inaccuracies of current studies, and propose a theory of his own.[10] *Modern Ethics* offers a historical argument for decriminalizing homo-sexuality and changing social attitudes toward it. The essay attempts to rescue the study of homosexuality from the arbiters of sin and crime, from the priests, the state, and the doctors, and return it to those to whom Symonds argues it rightfully belongs, homosexuals themselves. The study of homosexuality and homosexuals had been dismissed on the grounds that any investigation of "the depraved instincts of humanity is unprofitable and disgusting"; Symonds calls for a new kind of scholarship, "a complete history of inverted sexuality in all ages and in all races."[11] Only then will change follow in laws and attitudes.

A Problem in Modern Ethics is written in a tone of withering irony that barely masks Symonds' anger. His is the voice of the advocate, his text a radical brief against oppression. Symonds was no political activist; he stormed no citadels of power. But what he did is amazing enough: for the first time in English prose, he called upon homosexuals not to hide but to resist. *A Problem in Greek Ethics* had argued that in ancient Greece no disapproval attached to homosexuality. In *Modern Ethics* Symonds takes up the "new and stringent morality" of Christian nations, which is "almost universally regarded as a great advance upon the ethics of a pagan world."[12] He will show otherwise and by doing so educate the ignorant.

To begin with, the intellectual foundations of moral disapproval are baseless. Early Christianity possessed no "delicate distinctions, no anthropological investigations, no psychological analysis." It also had "no spirit of toleration" necessary for any objective assessment.[13] No phenomenon, not the laws of physics, nor the psychology of primitive peoples, nor the sexual habits of a minority, can be studied objectively when preconceived notions bias the investigation. Furthermore, no true investigation can ignore historical and cultural contexts. Little wonder that the general understanding of homosexuality teems with errors. Symonds confronts a number of unexamined beliefs—his contribution is precisely to point out that they *are* unexamined—that categorize and stigmatize homosexuals.

One of these is the old belief that homosexuals are in effect heterosexuals gone wrong, men who "originally loved women" but from "a monstrous debauchery and superfluity of naughtiness, tiring of normal pleasures," have pursued other avenues of desire. Symonds counters with evidence amassed by "medical jurists and physicians" to the effect that homosexual desires are "inborn and incontrovertible."[14] If homosexuality is inborn, he implies, no amount of debauchery can produce it.

Another common belief is that homosexuals are "despicable, depraved, vicious, and incapable of humane or generous sentiments." Most people—here Symonds quotes Edward Gibbon's remark about homosexuality in *Decline and Fall*—"touch with reluctance and dispatch with impatience" the study of homosexuality. They "expect to discover the objects of their outraged animosity in the scum of humanity." Even if "Greek history did not contradict this supposition," Symonds argues, "a little patient enquiry into contemporary manners would suffice to remove it. But people will not take this trouble."[15]

Those who study history or contemporary society do so, Symonds argues, with a will to erase homosexuality from the historical and the social records. This omission of the homosexual presence, or its overwhelmingly pejorative presentation, has prevented the formation of any positive attitudes about homosexuality.

Symonds challenges a third common belief, that homosexuality is linked with sickness and "produces spinal disease, epilepsy, consumption, dropsy and the like." If this were so, he points out, then Sophocles, Pindar, and "all the Spartan kings and generals" would be "one nation of ricketty, phthisical, dropsical paralytics." Casting aside irony for anger, he locates the true disease of homosexuality in homophobia: "Under the present laws and hostilities of modern society the inverted passion has to be indulged furtively, spasmodically, hysterically; the repression of it through fear and shame frequently . . . convert[s] it from a healthy outlet of the sexual nature into a morbid monomania."[16]

The remainder of the essay examines contemporary legal, medical, historical, and anthropological texts. Symonds proposes that a positive study of homosexuality ought to be "approached from the point of view of embryology" rather than psychology; in this he echoes Karl Heinrich Ulrichs' recommendation that homosexuals be classified as a separate sexual entity, a third sex with a female spirit or sensibility in a male body. Since Ulrichs' pamphlets were available only in German, Symonds summarizes them for English readers, and soon his summary shades into a platform for his own views. He cites Ulrichs' point that homosexual passions "ought not to be punished except in the same degree and under the same conditions as the normal passions of the majority," and he finds in Ulrichs support for his own contentions: that homosexual passions are "inborn and healthy," that they do not "owe their origin to bad habits of any kind," that they are incapable of being "converted to normal channels," and that men subject to them "are neither physically, intellectually, nor morally inferior to normally constituted individuals." The present state of law "is flagrantly unjust to a class of innocent persons" who have done nothing deserving of punishment. "No social evil ensues in those countries" that have placed homosexuality "upon the same footing" as heterosexual passion, and "toleration of inverted passion threatens no danger to the well-being of nations." Symonds' conclusion is a manifesto of political and sexual radicalism: "If I have taken any vow at all, it is to fight for the rights of an innocent, harmless, downtrodden group of outraged personalities. The cross of a crusade is sewn upon the sleeve of my right arm. . . . We maintain that we have the right to exist after the fashion that nature made us. And if we cannot alter your laws, we shall go on breaking them."[17]

Symonds' attack on unexamined stereotypes is particularly vigorous with respect to effeminacy. This may well reflect his own anxiety about society's demand that a "normal middle-class male" exhibit masculine behavior. But it also reflects an attempt to rewrite homophobic constructions of homosexual identity. Appearance, gesture, and style are social artifacts; they serve homophobia by confirming the belief that "all subjects from inverted instincts carry their lust written in their faces; that they are pale, languid, scented, effeminate, painted, timid, oblique in expression." Such signs are obviously not essential, he insists, since "the majority" of homosexuals "differ in no outward detail from normal men" and are therefore invisible. "Were it not so, society would long ago have had its eyes opened to the amount of perverted sexuality it harbors."[18]

Having destabilized accepted notions of masculinity, Symonds went a step further: by insisting that sex and classical Platonic relations were inextricably intertwined, he argued that the same conjunction existed in the Victorian version of Platonic relations. This was a frontal attack on that other near-sacred and certainly romantic aspect of the normal middle-class male experience—the ardent, presumed pure friendship between men. E. F. Benson (1867–1940), a friend of Oscar Wilde and of Henry James, author not only of the witty Mapp and Lucia novels but of a number of others in which repressed homosexuality occasionally serves as a tantalizing subtext, wrote of such friendships: "To suppose that this ardency was sensual, is to miss the point of it and lose the value of it altogether. That the base of the attraction was largely physical is no doubt true, for it was founded primarily on appearance, but there is a vast difference between the breezy open-air quality of these friendships and the dingy sensualism which is sometimes wrongly attributed to them."[19] Symonds would have agreed that not all homosexual acts and feelings were due to dingy sensualism. But he also knew that a remark like Benson's capitulated to the deliberate homophobia that could insist with the classical scholar Benjamin Jowett that homosexuality in texts must be read only as metaphor. Symonds knew that the animosity that sought to erase sex and homosexual desire from literature could as destructively touch men's lives.

In his memoirs, written in 1889 but not published until 1984, Symonds laments the torments of his masked existence: "It was my destiny to make continual renunciation of my truest self, because I was born out of sympathy with the men around me."[20] Notably, his travails did not prevent him from acting upon his sexual desires; he had a number of involvements with men, including a long if turbulent relationship with a handsome Italian gondolier. Writing of himself in the third person, Symonds offered eloquent testimony to the power of realized desire: "At length, when he has reached the age of twenty-nine, he yields to the attraction of the male. And this is the strange point about the man, that now for the first time he attains mastery and self control. Contemporary with his indulged passion he begins to write books, and rapidly becomes an author of distinction. The indecision of the previous years is replaced with a consciousness of volition and power. . . . Altogether he is more of a man than when he repressed and pent within his soul those fatal and abnormal inclinations. Yet he belongs to a class abhorred by society and is, by English law, a criminal. What is the meaning, the lesson, the conclusion to be drawn from this biography?"[21]

One lesson surely concerned the terrible effects of institutionalized homophobia on an individual torn between the "natural action of his appetite" and the proscriptions of an "acquired respect for social law," daily forced to see his desire "not in the glass of truth to his own nature, but in the mirror of convention." Another lesson was about bravery, about the courage to write and publish in the face of abhorrence and criminalization, and thus to reorient public views of homosexuality. When Symonds began to write, there were no studies in English, and few in any other language, that dealt with the subject scientifically or historically. The writings that existed mostly concentrated on condemning, defining, or explaining homosexual behavior as sin, crime, or sickness. Symonds, however, not only delineated the hatred of homosexuals that we would now call homophobia; he also showed how that hatred shaped the political, cultural, emotional, spiritual, and social lives of homosexuals. He urged the recognition of their contributions to society, and of a separate homosexual identity founded upon a concept of sexual difference.

2 The Panic Terror That Prevails

Symonds sought to move homosexuality out of the realms of sin, criminality, and disease, and to legitimize it as a subject of scholarly study. Edward Carpenter, poet, radical socialist, and open homosexual, added a political dimension to Symonds' project; in his view, homosexuals, like women and the working classes, were essentially involved in a struggle for individual rights. Convinced that society would recognize these rights if it could be educated, Carpenter formulated the qualities that would define homosexual identity into the next century.

In his autobiography *My Days and Dreams* (1916), Carpenter suggests that it was his discovery of Whitman's poetry in 1868, at the age of twenty-four, that led him to see homosexuality as a public problem and not merely a personal one. At the same time he became aware of even wider social issues, the political and sexual rights of women, and the political influence of socialism. To advance his educational mission, he put his ideas into a long Whitmanesque prose poem called *Towards Democracy*, which he published in four parts starting in 1883. *Towards Democracy* presents Carpenter's advanced views on the need for working-class egalitarianism, on the sexual and political rights of women, and on the special place of homosexuals in society. But it was soon clear that poetry was not enough, and that a more powerful polemic was needed to address these topics, especially the one closest to him.

In 1895 he published his pamphlet "Homogenic Love," whose title introduced the term he preferred to the Greek-Latin hybrid "homosexual." The next year brought *Love's Coming of Age* (1896), a volume of essays discussing sexual morality in general, which included an essay on homosexuality, "The Intermediate Sex." He continued his work with *Iolaus: An Anthology of Friendship* (1902), the first English-language collection of homosexual literature. Carpenter continued to write about homosexuality well into the twentieth century, producing *Days with Walt Whitman* (1906); a collection of old and new essays on homosexuality, *The Intermediate Sex* (1908); *Intermediate Types Among Primitive Folk* (1914); and *Some Friends of Walt Whitman: A Study in Sex Psychology* (1924). He died in 1929.

"Homogenic Love" discusses homosexuality in Greece, reviews modern medical discussions, advocates law reform, and invokes Whitman as the source and major prophet of the new erotic era. For Carpenter, the universality of homosexuality is an article of faith: "The passionate attachment between two persons of the same sex" is a phenomenon "widespread through the human race. And once at least in history—in the Greek age—the passion rose into direct consciousness and justified, or it might even be said glorified, itself; but in later times—especially during the last century or two of European life—it has been treated by the accredited thinkers and writers as a thing to be passed over in silence, as associated with mere grossness and mental aberration, or as unworthy of serious attention."[22]

Indeed, he continues, "it may be doubted whether the higher heroic and spiritual life of a nation is ever quite possible without the sanction of this attachment in its institutions." Leveling a broadside against gender and sex roles in England, he argues that "it is not unlikely that the markedly materialistic and commercial character of the last age of European civilized life is largely to be connected with the fact that the only form of love and love-union that it has recognized has been founded on the quite necessary but comparatively materialistic basis of matrimonial sex—intercourse and child bearing."[23]

The essays collected in *The Intermediate Sex,* whose title is indebted to Ulrichs' phrase "third sex," elaborate on Carpenter's views concerning homosexuality's special contribution to the heroic and spiritual life of a nation. Interestingly, Carpenter advances homosexuality as a subject relevant to both men and women and to all kinds of moral natures: "good and bad, high and low, worthy and unworthy—some perhaps exhibiting through their double temperament a rare and beautiful flower of humanity, others a perverse and tangled ruin."[24] The same refusal to think in simplistic categories informs Carpenter's work throughout. Whereas Symonds, for example, believes that homosexuals are *essentially* different from nonhomosexuals, Carpenter proposes a spectrum of sexuality made up of "inner psychical affections and affinities" that "shade off and graduate in a vast number of instances most subtly from male to female, and not always in correspondence with the outer bodily sex." Concerning "facts of Nature," he writes, we have to "preserve a certain humility and reverence and not rush in with our preconceived and obstinate assumptions." For example, if homosexuals fall outside social expectations concerning gender, it is possible that sex roles are not immutable facts of nature, but instead are derived from culture and society.[25] Indeed, in matters of sexual behavior, "the law, the Church, and the strong pressure of public opinion interfere, compelling the observance of certain forms; and it becomes difficult to say how much of the existing order is due to the spontaneous instinct and common sense of human nature, and how much to compulsion and outside interference: how far, for instance, monogamy is natural or artificial."[26]

Intent on dismantling stereotypes, Carpenter directly challenges conventional views. Homosexual attachments, far from being "necessarily sexual, or connected with sexual acts," are "often purely emotional in their character."[27] Nor are homosexuals motivated solely by lust and devoid of "normal" human love and kindness. The notion that homosexual men are effeminate and lesbians masculine is equally indefensible. Carpenter posits two types of male homosexual: the "extreme" and the "normal." The extreme type is the effeminate homosexual or manly lesbian familiar from homophobic texts. "This type is not particularly attractive, sometimes quite the reverse. In the male of this kind we have a distinctly effeminate type, sentimental, lackadaisical, mincing in gait and manners, something of a chatterbox, skillful at the needle and women's work, sometimes taking pleasure in dressing in women's clothes; his figure not infrequently betraying a tendency towards the feminine, large at the hips, supple, not muscular, the face wanting in hair, the voice inclining to be high-pitched. His affection, too, is often feminine in character, clinging, dependent and jealous, as of one desiring to be loved almost more than to love."[28]

Popular perceptions of effeminate homosexuals may well be founded in reality, Carpenter acknowledges. Some homosexual males are indeed effeminate, but "effeminate" does not necessarily mean "weak" and "unmanly." Rather, it suggests "sensitive," "artistic," and "intuitive." (Of course, Carpenter was to a degree trapped in preconceived gender-bound concepts. For him, such qualities as the intuitive, the artistic, and the sensitive were aspects of "the feminine sensibility.")

Moreover, the effeminate is not the only or even the preponderant type of homosexual. The "normal" homosexual male is one who, "while possessing thoroughly masculine powers of mind and body, combines them with the tenderer and more emotional soul-nature of the woman." Such men, often muscular and well-built, are "not distinguishable in exterior structure" from others of their own sex; "but emotionally they are extremely complex, tender, sensitive, pitiful and loving." While their logical faculty may not be well developed, their intuition is always strong. They are artists by nature, possessed of peculiar inborn refinement: "Such an one is often a dreamer, of brooding reserved habits, often a musician, a man of culture." They are also "the faithfulest friends, the truest allies, and most convinced defenders of women."

Women, too, can achieve the ideal. The normal homogenic woman is

> a type in which the body is thoroughly feminine and gracious, with the rondure and fullness of the female form, and the continence and aptness of its movements, but in which the inner nature is to a great extent masculine; a temperament active, brave, originative, somewhat decisive, not too emotional; fond of out-door life, of games and sports, of science, politics, or even business; good at organization, and well-pleased with positions of responsibility, sometimes indeed making an excellent and generous leader. Such a woman, it is easily seen, from her special combination of qualities, is often fitted for remarkable work, in professional life, or as manageress of institutions, or even as ruler of a country. Her love goes out to younger and more feminine natures than her own; it is a powerful passion, almost of heroic type, and capable of inspiring to great deeds; and when held duly in leash may sometimes become an invaluable force in the teaching and training of girlhood, or in the creation of a school of thought or action among women. Many a Santa Clara, or abbess-founder of religious houses, has probably been a woman of this type; and in all times such women—not being bound to men by the ordinary ties—have been able to work the more freely for the interests of their sex, a cause to which their own temperament impels them to devote themselves *con amore*.[29]

If Symonds implied a homosexual superiority when he associated homosexuality with the highest standard of Greek civilization, Carpenter goes him one better: he asserts that the very elements of civilization are the special possession of homosexuals, who, in his formulation, are very nearly a race apart: their "double nature"—"the instinctive artistic nature of the male of this class," his sensitive spirit, his "hardihood of intellect and body"; "the frank free nature of the female, her masculine independence and strength wedded to a thoroughly feminine grace of form and manner"—gives them a "command of life in all its phases, and a certain freemasonry of the secrets of the two sexes." Some of the world's great leaders and artists, he points out, have been dowered with "the Uranian temperament."[30]

For Carpenter, homosexuals are privileged possessors of affections, talents, and intuitions that are more refined, more profound, more complex than those of "normal" men and women. He suggests that they represent a "new form," "new types of humankind." Far from being socially dangerous, homosexuality is essential to the common-weal. In certain primitive societies, Carpenter points out in a later essay, homosexuals performed ritual social roles—prophet, priest, magician, and inventor—for which they are especially suited. In contemporary life, homosexuals have most to contribute in the "domain of love," because of their "immense capacity" for attachment, which could allow them to become "reconcilers and interpreters of the two sexes."[31] Indeed, a new form of social organization is necessary. Just as marriage is "of indispensable importance to the State" for the breeding and rearing of children, "another form of union is almost equally indispensable" for other social activities, such as the maintenance of democracy (by drawing "members of different classes together") and the creation of the artifacts of culture. Homosexuality forms "an advance guard of that great movement that will one day transform the common life by substituting the bond of personal affection and compassion for the monetary, legal and other external ties which now control and confine society."

Before the importance of homosexuals can be recognized, argues Carpenter, certain truths must finally be accepted: that homosexuals exist in considerable numbers, rather than being rare accidents of nature; that there is "nothing abnormal or morbid" in their constitutions and they are not necessarily emotionally or medically damaged; that their temperament is inborn and ineradicable, not to be changed by an embrace of "normal" sexuality. They "suffer a great deal from their own temperament"—not because of what they inherently are, but because of the way society has defined them and marginalized them. "How hard it is," he comments, "that a veil of complete silence should be drawn over the subject, leading to the most painful misunderstandings, and perversions, and confusions of mind; and that there should be no hint of guidance; nor any recognition of the solitary and really serious inner struggles they may have to face!"[32]

Carpenter makes clear that the obstacle to homosexual liberation is "the panic terror which prevails" whenever affection is expressed between members of the same sex. The most effective way to remove that terror is "by the spread of proper education and ideas."[33] Homosexuality has its own valid history, its own distinct identity, and a useful social role. In Carpenter's writings homosexuals emerge as a special, even superior, species, whose talents make them standard-bearers of a new age, in which there will be no panic terror, no homophobia.

3 Sexual Inversion

In 1897, a study of homosexuality called *Sexual Inversion,* which the year before had appeared in a German-language edition bearing the names of its co-authors, was about to be published in England. The authors were Havelock Ellis and John Addington Symonds. Ellis, a doctor, had achieved a reputation as a scientist and liberal thinker through his study of male and female sexuality, *Men and Women* (1894), and through an earlier book of essays, *The New Spirit* (1890), intended, Ellis said, to apply the scientific method "to all the problems of life."[34] Symonds had died in 1893. His family, fearing scandal in the aftermath of the Wilde affair and wishing to protect his reputation, attempted to suppress *Sexual Inversion* by buying up all the copies and destroying them; only a few escaped.

Later that year Ellis succeeded in publishing the book, without Symonds' name, as the first volume in *Studies in the Psychology of Sex.* The book comprised a brief history of homosexuality over the ages and a summary of the most recent medical studies, both supplied by Ellis; case histories of "sexual inversion in men and women" contributed by Ellis and Symonds equally; and Ellis' analysis of the cases and the "theory of sexual inversion" he derives from them, that homosexuality is congenital. Appendices included Symonds' *A Problem in Greek Ethics* and a portion of his *A Problem in Modern Ethics,* as well as various articles on homosexuality contributed by Symonds and by his and Ellis' correspondents in the medical community. Ellis published two more editions of the work, revising it and adding more histories, in 1901 and 1915.[35]

Out of thirty-six histories in the 1897 edition, only six concerned women, though more (about inverts of both sexes) were added in the later editions. Ellis points out that "we know comparatively little of sexual inversion in women." The reason, he theorizes, is that men are indifferent to it, it has not been illegal, and it is less easy than male homosexuality to detect; a woman may "feel a high degree of sexual attraction for another woman without realizing that her affection is sexual," because of the "extreme ignorance and extreme reticence of women regarding any abnormal or even normal manifestation of their sexual life."[36] The case histories display that reticence, not only on the part of their subjects, but on the part of Ellis himself. Miss S., an American, has found her life to be "glorified and made beautiful by the friendship with women," though "her friends are not aware of the nature of her affections." Miss M., fascinated from her earliest years with women, cannot recall a time when "I did not feel different from other children." For her, "love is a religion" and "the very nature of my affection for my friends precludes the possibility of any element entering into it which is not absolutely pure." As Ellis observes, "physical gratification plays no part." Miss M. has "many boyish tricks of manner and speech which seem to be instinctive; she tries to watch herself continually, so as to avoid them, affecting feminine ways and feminine interests, but always being conscious of an effort in so doing." Until she came across a treatise on homosexuality, Miss M. had no idea that "feelings like mine" were "under the ban of society," or were considered "unnatural and depraved."[37]

Two other histories of women in the 1897 edition are those of Miss B. and Miss H. Miss B. "has no repugnance to men," though she "never felt any sexual attraction" to them. She finds sexual pleasure in "kissing and embracing," but "there appears to be no orgasm." Miss H., like Miss M., idealized women when she was young, and has continued to do so; her several intense relationships with various women have included experiences that "became vaguely physical." Like Miss B., she has found sexual satisfaction in "tenderly touching and caressing and kissing the loved one's body." She has sometimes "resisted the sexual expression of her feelings" but "always in vain." For her, like Miss M., who expresses similar sentiments, the effect "of loving women is distinctly good" both "spiritually and physically."[38]

Ellis' generalizations echo clichés about gender roles, but also reflect real sexual attitudes imposed upon women in the late nineteenth century. He asserts that "the chief characteristic of the sexually inverted woman is a certain degree of masculinity." She is an "enthusiastic admirer of female beauty," and "she may become shy and confused in the presence of attractive persons of her own sex." In her sexual habits "we rarely find the degree of promiscuity which is not uncommon among inverted men." Though the movement for women's emancipation—the campaign "to obtain the same rights and duties, the same freedom and responsibility, the same education and work" as men—is "wholesome and inevitable," it may also cause "an increase in homo-sexuality" among women. "I do not say," he observes, that the "influ-ences of the modern movement can cause inverted sexuality." But there is "a tendency for women to carry this independence still further and find love where they work."

The case histories of men are much more detailed. They describe the growth of the tellers' homosexual feelings and give details of their homosexual experience. Some contributors were English, some Ameri-can; their ages, like their professions, covered a broad range—the youngest is twenty, the oldest in his seventies—but most were in their middle years. Sometimes an identifying profession is supplied—"Physician," "Engaged in business," "Now at University," "Artist," "Government official," "Employed in a workshop," "Of Independent means," "Clerk." Several accounts are given in their subjects' own words, others in paraphrase. The narrators typically describe their youth, their first intimation of attraction to their own sex, mastur-bation, their first homosexual experience. They disclose their erotic fantasies, imagine ideal friends, and describe real ones. They reveal their sexual prejudices and preferences, analyze their attitudes toward women, and theorize about the morality and nature of homosexu-ality. They muse on the connections between homosexuality and the arts; they speculate on the possibility of long-term homosexual relationships.

All were affected by homophobia. Many of the accounts report the hostile climate. Case 2 describes a boarding school where "the idea was held in abhorrence by an enormous majority, and public opinion is a strong factor." Case 13 agrees: "All these things were treated by mas-ters and boys alike as more or less unholy . . . a kiss was as unclean as fellatio." Doctors were unsympathetic. Troubled by his affections, one subject sought medical help. Upon hearing his confession of homosexu-ality, the doctor "walked out without a word. He would not see me again." A second doctor "would hardly listen. He at once said that such inclinations were unnatural, and evidently made up his mind that I was insane." The young man concludes, "It is really a matter of psy-chology, not of medicine, and poets know more about such matters than doctors."[39]

The effects of social condemnation could be severe. In his own anonymous case history, Symonds reveals that he had "always before him the terror of discovery."[40] Another man believes that "I was a rebel from the law, natural and divine, of which no instinct had been implanted in me" (Case 25). The silence imposed by homophobia caused many of these men to feel that homosexuality was unique to themselves, and though they declared it the central fact of their lives, they also describe a profound alienation. As one man says, "My own sexual nature was a mystery to me. I found myself cut off from the understanding of others, felt myself an outcast. . . . I was . . . on the brink of despair and madness with repressed passion and torment" (Case 7).

Many men found validation in relationships, however. Case 26 had met "a companion to love me in the way my nature required. Under sexual freedom I have become stronger." Another reported that "a young man some years younger than myself and of lower social class, whose development I was able to assist," succeeded in lighting up "the gold of affection that was within me and consumed the dross. It was from this that I first learned that there was no hard and fast line between the physical and spiritual in friendship . . . everything in life began to sing with joy, and what little of real creative work I have done I attribute largely to the power of work that was born in me during those years" (Case 13). Despite social prohibition, one after another these men affirm themselves. Although he suffered much "from unsatisfied homosexual desires," C.M. insists that he would not "be prevented from being an invert by any consideration." Carpenter's own history concludes: "I cannot regard my sexual feelings as unnatural or abnormal, since they have disclosed themselves so perfectly naturally and spontaneously within me" (Case 7). "To me," T.W. says, "what other people call unnatural is the most natural of all conditions" (Case 10). This theme is repeated: "I am an absolute believer in the naturalness of my inclinations" (Case 15). And again: "I believe that affection between persons of the same sex, even when it includes the sexual passion and its indulgence, may lead to results as splendid as human nature can ever attain to" (Case 4).

These men are, in composite, "the homosexual" who was so often, by homosexual and homophobe alike, coming to be described as a species. Attracted to men early in life, they confess to being dreamy or indolent in youth; their dreams developed into rich fantasy lives populated by handsome, available, and muscular young men—roughs, shepherds, workingmen, soldiers, sailors—or by more passive and effeminate youths. In life as well as fantasy, they ardently pursue friendship, love, and sex. Some of them enjoy an active and adventurous sexual life.

They respond to women as social, but rarely as sexual, beings; often they express abhorrence of the notion of heterosexual union, and an equally absolute conviction that homosexual love is nobler, more passionate, and more profound than heterosexual love. Almost none of them express any desire to be other than what they are, even though many of them keenly feel that they are outcasts in a world that condemns what to them seem natural and imperative emotions. With remarkable unanimity, they celebrate homosexuality and consider it natural, elevating, and the source of creative power. Many of them suspect that they are a discrete and physiologically unique group.

Their language is heavily freighted with conventional homoerotic imagery. They subscribe to Arcadian ideals, appeal to classical examples, celebrate mythical and historical lovers, fantasize sexual dominance and submission by conjuring up wrestlers and youthful Ganymedes, create wishful fantasies of bands of devoted lovers and cities of friends. All of them, without exception, look for the ideal friend.

The concealed but substantial fact of homosexuality colors every aspect of their lives. Its presence is exciting and yet threatening, tantalizing and impossible. The men sometimes feel themselves society's adversaries, sometimes its victims; usually they are anxious about their relationship with society. Nearly all suffer a deep sense of alienation from the common expectations of male sexual conduct, generally represented by stern fathers, teachers, doctors, or priests. In their own words they demonstrate both the unconscionable effects of homophobia and their triumph over it.

4 Symbolic Sodomite

In 1895, barely a year after Alfred Douglas published the poem that so dramatically focused attention on the love that dare not speak its name, the unmentionable love seemed to be on everyone's lips. In the same year, Oscar Wilde was accused of being a sodomite by Douglas' father, the Marquess of Queensberry. Wilde mounted a libel suit against Queensberry and lost. After the trial a London newspaper rejoiced:

> There is not a man or woman in the English-speaking world
> possessed of the treasure of a wholesome mind who is not under
> a deep debt of gratitude to the Marquess of Queensberry for
> destroying the High Priest of the Decadents. The obscene impos-

tor, whose prominence has been a social outrage ever since he transferred from Trinity Dublin to Oxford his vices, his follies, and his vanities, has been exposed, and that thoroughly at last. But to the exposure there must be legal and social sequels. There must be another trial at the Old Bailey, or a coroner's inquest—the latter for choice; and of the Decadents, of their hideous conceptions of the meaning of Art, of their worse than Eleusinian mysteries, there must be an absolute end.

Wilde's failed suit had brought out evidence of his involvement with Douglas and his relations with a number of male prostitutes, and had aired an interpretation of some of his writing as advocating "perversion." All this was sufficient to allow the government to try Wilde under the 1885 Criminal Law Amendment Act, which penalized the commission of "gross indecency" with another male. He was brought to trial on that charge in April 1895.

During the trial, Wilde was asked to explain the meaning of the phrase "the love that dare not speak its name." He responded:

> "The Love that dare not speak its name" in this century is such a great affection of an elder for a younger man as there was between David and Jonathan, such as Plato made the very basis of his philosophy, and such as you find in the sonnets of Michelangelo and Shakespeare. It is that deep, spiritual affection that is as pure as it is perfect. It dictates and pervades great works of art like those of Shakespeare and Michelangelo. . . . It is in this century misunderstood, so much misunderstood that it may be described as "the love that dare not speak its name," and on account of it I am placed where I am now. It is beautiful, it is fine, it is the noblest form of affection. There is nothing unnatural about it. It is intellectual, and it repeatedly exists between an elder and a younger man, where the elder has intellect and the younger man has all the joy, hope, and glamour of life before him. That it should be so, the world does not understand. The world mocks at it and sometimes puts one in the pillory for it.[41]

Wilde cited all the classical texts commonly used to justify and celebrate homosexual desire. He may well have felt that these citations overwhelmingly spoke against homophobia. Nonetheless, he was convicted and sentenced to two years' imprisonment at hard labor. The London *Daily Telegraph* commented upon the verdict:

> We have had more than enough, of MR. OSCAR WILDE, who has been the means of inflicting upon public patience during this recent episode as much moral damage of the most offensive and repulsive kind as any single individual could well cause. If the general concern were only with the man himself—his spurious brilliancy, inflated egotism, diseased vanity, cultivated affectation, and shameless disavowal of morality—the best thing would be to dismiss him and his deeds without another word to the penalty of universal condemnation.

But the real import of the verdict was much greater:

> It will be a public benefit, compensating for a great deal that has been painful in the reports of this trial, if the exposure of a chief representative of the immoral school leads to a clearer perception of its tendency and a heartier contempt for its methods. There is nothing difficult to understand in the principles of such people or in the results to which they lead. . . . The superfine "Art" which admits no moral duty and laughs at the established phrases of right and wrong is the visible enemy of those ties and bonds of society—the natural affections, the domestic joys, the sanctity and sweetness of the home. . . . A nation prospers and profits precisely by those national qualities which these innovators deride and abjure. It goes swiftly to wreck and decay by precisely that brilliant corruption of which we have just had the exposure and the demonstration.[42]

The episode ended Wilde's brilliant career as the master practitioner of nineteenth-century aestheticism. It silenced him as an accomplished poet, a controversial novelist, and the most brilliant dramatist of his age. The timing of his criminal trial, indeed, suggests a connection between the flourishing literature of the 1890s, the increasing visibility and boldness of homosexuals, their efforts to speak out, and this massive act of retribution. Wilde's trial remains the most celebrated example of homophobia directed against an individual. Wilde stood for all that England detested.

After serving his sentence, Wilde left England, driven out by its homophobia; he became a wanderer, a sexual exile from the nation he had spectacularly ornamented. He lived in France for the few years left to him. There, in penury, he wrote almost nothing, sank into alcoholism, and received occasional visits from friends, including Alfred Douglas. He was buried in Paris, at Père Lachaise, under a monument that carried the epitaph he himself had written in Reading Gaol:

> *And alien tears will fill for him*
>   *Pity's long-broken urn,*
> *For his mourners will be outcast men,*
>   *And outcasts always mourn.*

5 Outlaws

In the aftermath of Oscar Wilde's conviction, a dark shadow descended on advocates of homosexual rights. The major works challenging homophobic law and opinion—the works of Carpenter, Symonds, and Ellis—were suppressed. After Symonds' death, at the insistence of his family, his name was removed from *Sexual Inversion* and the book was effectively banned from publication in England. Carpenter's *Love's Coming of Age* was refused by his publisher, though it was soon brought out by the more radical Labour Press. And when Carpenter looked for *The Intermediate Sex* in the British Museum in 1911, he was told that it had been expunged from the catalogue because of its subject matter. (The ban was lifted two years later.)

In 1913, E. M. Forster—already, in his mid-thirties, the successful author of five novels—began his novel *Maurice,* finishing it the next year. But though he showed it to a few friends, he did not publish it. It finally appeared in 1971, the year after his death. Forster said that *Maurice* was directly inspired by a visit to Edward Carpenter and Carpenter's lover, George Merrill. Carpenter was, Forster recalls, "a rebel appropriate to his age." He was not only a socialist and a poet but "a believer in the Love of Comrades, whom he sometimes called Uranians. It was this last aspect of him that attracted me in my loneliness. For a short time he seemed to hold the key to every trouble. I approached him . . . as one approaches a saviour." After his visit—during which, Forster also recalled, George Merrill "touched my backside," thereby uniting Carpenter's idealistic homoerotic theory with direct homosexual sensation—Forster "immediately began to write *Maurice*."

In *Maurice,* a respectable member of the upper-middle-class establishment becomes a rebel against birth and class, entering into a love affair with a social inferior, a gamekeeper. The union of this "unsuitable" pair ends not in disaster but in idyllic happiness. This outline might describe D. H. Lawrence's *Lady Chatterley's Lover* except that the lovers are men, and rather than a mere social indiscretion their love is a revolution. As Forster puts it in the "Terminal Note" he wrote for *Maurice* in 1960: "A happy ending was imperative. I shouldn't have bothered to write otherwise. I determined that in fiction anyway two men should fall in love and remain in it for the forever and ever that fiction allows."[43]

Maurice is in every way a solid representative of English probity. But into his psychology Forster "dropped an ingredient that puzzles him, and wakes him up, and torments him, and finally saves him." This ingredient is Maurice's sexual desire for men. Maurice is emblematic of what Forster calls "suburbia"—the middle, not the upper class. He is neither effete nor effeminate; nor is he possessed of that alleged "sympathy" or "sensibility" that nineteenth-century myth ascribed to homosexuals. But the unconscious world of this very English youth is filled with dreams in which a half-understood image constantly reappears: the ideal friend. "He could die for such a friend . . . they would make any sacrifice for each other."[44] When he discovers a friend in his classmate Clive Durham, then his heart "[lights] never to be quenched again, and one thing in him at last was real" (40).

The Platonic romance between Maurice and Clive derives from the wishful texts of nineteenth-century homoerotic poetry, from Pater's Epicurean Marius and his friend, from the passionate realities of schoolboy romance in any English public school, from Tennyson, Whitman, and Carpenter, and not a little from the classical trope of selfless male love that dominated English school life and literature. In Clive's company Maurice reads Plato, encounters the *Symposium,* and then faces homophobia when the Greek master "observed in a flat toneless voice" during translation class: "Omit: a reference to the unspeakable vice of the Greeks." The unspeakable love, however, turns out to be something well known to his classmates. "He hadn't known it could be mentioned, and when Durham did so in the middle of a sunlit court a breath of liberty touched him" (51). It does not take very many innocent embraces from Clive before Maurice realizes that "he would not deceive himself so much. He would not—and this was the test—pretend to care about women when the only sex that attracted him was his own. He loved men and always had loved them. He longed to embrace them and mingle his being with theirs" (62).

They are not destined to stay together. Clive takes a trip to Greece, home of all homoerotic imaginings; when he returns he is out of love with Maurice and changed from one "who loved men" to one who will "henceforward love women." Forster allows Clive to explore the spiritual home of his presumed homosexuality; there he discovers that his love for Maurice was a blend of unrealized lust and the condescension of an upper-class man for the middle-class youth he sought not to love but to change.

But Maurice, too, has changed. He has recognized his position in society as untenable and his life as a lie. In one of their last conversations he says to Clive: " 'You and I are outlaws. All this'—he pointed to the middle-class comfort of the room—'would be taken away from us if people knew.' " When Clive is gone, Maurice embraces ever more determinedly his outlaw status: "He grew more bitter, he wished that he had shouted while he had the strength and smashed down this front of lies. . . . He was an outlaw in disguise. Perhaps among those who took to the greenwood in old time there had been two men like himself—two. At times he entertained the dream. Two men can defy the world" (135).

Exasperated by the "very normality" of his life and by his respectability—his comfortable job, his comfortable home—Maurice turns to social action. He teaches arithmetic to working-class youths and gives up golf to play football with them at a settlement house in south London. He discovers himself admiring the youths he teaches and very nearly attempts to seduce a handsome boy. Horrified by his desire, he resorts to answers drawn from received social attitudes. He attributes his admiration for the handsome youths solely to "lust" and reminds himself that "the feeling that can impel a gentleman towards a person of lower class stands self-condemned." His solution is equally conventional: abstinence and hard work. "He had only to keep away from boys and young men to ensure success" (151). When success does not come, he consults a doctor, who refuses to believe his assertion that he is "an unspeakable of the Oscar Wilde sort," refuses even to discuss it. He assures Maurice that when "you get the right girl, there'll be no more trouble" (161).

An uneasy reconciliation with Clive brings Maurice to Penge, Clive's estate. Having married and taken his place in society as squire and politician, Clive is the very picture of upper-class heterosexual responsibility. As for Maurice, he has become a wary inhabitant of a world that he now sees as dangerous to men like himself: "There was now a complete break between his public and his private actions" (170). But at Penge Maurice meets at last the ideal friend, Alec, who works as a gamekeeper on the estate. The relationship begins with glances and comes to first fruition when, one night at Penge, in the midst of a dream about "big spaces where passion clasped peace, spaces no science could reach, but existed for ever, full of woods some of them, and arched with a majestic sky and a friend," Maurice suddenly awakens and with a sure sense of destiny about to be fulfilled, opens the window and cries, "Come!" In response, the "head and shoulders of a man rose up" at the window: Alec, the young god come to lead Maurice at last into sexual revelation.

Their desire turns to love, no less powerful for being outlawed. As Maurice says to Alec: "All the world's against us. We've got to pull ourselves together and make plans while we can" (229). Many pages later, after quarrels and reconciliations, after Alec determines to leave England but then remains for Maurice's sake, after Maurice recognizes that the gulf of class that yawns between them has been bridged and indeed abolished by love, they meet at last in the abandoned boathouse at Penge, and Alec answers him: "And now we shan't be parted no more, and that's finished."

Maurice has one more task to perform. In a final interview Clive—determinedly blind and equally determined to ignore what passed between him and Maurice and what it signified—imagines that "the core of blackness" he discerns in Maurice comes from an unhappy relationship with a woman. He urges Maurice to consult his wife, since "where a woman is in question I would always consult another woman." Maurice defies the entire edifice of heterosexist prejudice when he answers: "It's miles worse for you than that; I'm in love with your gamekeeper." Clive, appalled, reacts with horror—not only because of Maurice's admission that he is, after all, not "normal," but because "intimacy with any social inferior was unthinkable to him." Then Maurice strikes the final blow to Clive's complacency: " 'I have shared with Alec,' he said after deep thought. 'Shared what?' 'All I have. Which includes my body.' Clive sprang up with a whimper of disgust. He wanted to smite the monster and flee, but he was civilized." He resorts to the only cliché he knows: "But surely, the only excuse for any relationship between men is that it remain purely platonic" (242–43).

But there is no answer: Maurice has disappeared into the night, returning to his Alec, who waits for him next to the path to the greenwood,
ready to defy the world. Forster leaves Clive alone in the darkness with
nothing but the "petals of the evening primrose" that Maurice had earlier plucked, fallen in a little pile at his feet.

Heir to those who tried to dispel the panic terror, Forster completes
what Symonds had begun. *Maurice* is the first modern homosexual
novel: aiming to change society, constructing a positive identity for
homosexual readers, rejecting imputations of sickness, insanity, perversion, and universal effeminacy, while retaining the essentiality of difference. Forster, a major writer, attempts to confront crucial questions
raised by sexual difference and same-sex desire and to resolve them, as
he puts it, without recourse to "a lad dangling from a noose or with a
suicide pact." Moreover, this novel is infused with Carpenter's awareness that the inequities of class must be defined in sexual as well as
social terms, and it proposes that sex between men can erase class
inequality. Finally, Forster's book may be the earliest homoerotic text to
directly advocate a kind of revolutionary action in order to eradicate
sexual and social oppression. This revolutionary advocacy is expressed
not only in Maurice's love for Alec and their subsequent rejection of
society, but in Maurice's confrontation with Clive, the embodiment of
English homophobia.

But Forster had no illusions about the difference between art and
life. In the "Terminal Note" he assures us that "Maurice and Alec still
roam the greenwood" in that forever world of fiction. For the rest of us,
Forster fears, social attitudes toward homosexuality have done no
more than change "from ignorance and terror to familiarity and contempt." What the "public really loathes about homosexuality is not the
thing itself but having to think about it."[45] Convinced that the greenwood was the only place where men who loved men, and books written
by and about them, could find a safe haven, Forster specified in his will
that *Maurice* was not to be published until after his death.

Forster's delay may have been due to personal caution. When he
wrote *Maurice* in 1913 homosexual acts were still criminal—the British
law of 1885 remained in force until 1967. There were no public organizations in England advocating homosexual reform, and homosexuality was rarely spoken of in public or mentioned in the press. King
George V was of the opinion that homosexuals should shoot themselves,
and "decent" society agreed with Clive that relationships between men

should not include sex. That Forster felt he had to keep his dangerous book hidden, just as Ellis' respondents felt the need to maintain their anonymity, testifies to the continuing power of homophobia in England during the six decades before *Maurice* was published. Forster's personal caution may well have been amplified by the recognition that he might not have been able to publish the novel even if he had wished to do so. In 1918 the British government tried, though unsuccessfully, to suppress a novel by the pseudonymous A. T. Fitzroy called *Despised and Rejected,* a novel with an openly homosexual theme. The British Museum Library kept its copy locked in a "private case" and did not include the title in its general catalogue. In 1928, Radclyffe Hall's *The Well of Loneliness,* the first novel about a lesbian relationship, was declared by the British courts to be an "obscene libel," and copies of it were ordered destroyed. *Lady Chatterley's Lover* was banned until 1960 because of its explicit sexual content. Forster felt, and probably rightly, that *Maurice*—openly advocating homosexual love and with scenes of homosexual intimacy—would have been suppressed and that he might have been prosecuted.

By the time *Maurice* was published in 1971, homosexual activity between adult males in private had been decriminalized in England. Where it had been the obsessive concern of a coterie of mostly minor writers and activists, homosexuality was now a preoccupation in modern social life. A gay rights movement had begun, though its achievements were not so immediately spectacular as in the United States. Many of the greatest contributors to modern world literature were English, and many of those were homosexual. Some did not hesitate to reveal their homosexuality and even made the subject central to their work. It is a testimony to the country's oppressive atmosphere, however, that two of the greatest writers, W. H. Auden and Christopher Isherwood, chose to live in America rather than under what Isherwood called the English "heterosexual dictatorship." British homophobia, so long and deeply ingrained in the national consciousness and largely untouched by law reform, continued to dominate public perceptions of homosexual relationships, and British laws against writing about homosexuality remained. The freedom to write about homosexuality or simply to be homosexual is one that England did not, would not, and perhaps still does not, fully afford.

Maurice brings us to the edge of our own times. Ahead lies the rich and vast landscape of twentieth-century English homoerotic fiction, poetry, and drama. Where once a single anthology could represent, a brief bibliography could list, and one or two critical books were adequate to survey pertinent texts, the material is now extensive, everywhere to hand. In life as in art, men like Maurice—not sodomites, not effete or effeminate aristocrats, not dandified or aesthetic decadents, but beneficiaries of all their resistance—would try to do what Maurice had done. Decades of legal reform were necessary before those men would be able to live more freely. Much of the impetus for reform came back to England from the land England had colonized.

More than any other European nation, England exported to America both its humane convictions about the sanctity of individual freedom and its Protestant and overwhelmingly middle-class morality—a morality that was generally suspicious of sex and sexuality, that defended unquestioned certainties about sex and gender, and feared anything that might imply sexual difference, unmanliness, or homosexuality. England colonized the New World not only with its peoples and its ideals, but with its prejudices. The focus must now shift to the New World.

ValboaIndosnefandumSodomiæſceluscom- XXII.
mittentes, canibus obijcit dilaniandos.

"*Balboa Feeding Indian 'Sodomites' to the Dogs.*" *From Theodore de Bry,* America, *Frankfurt, 1590, vol. 4, pl xxii. Reprinted by permission of the Rare Books Division, New York Public Library, Astor, Lenox and Tilden Foundation*

PART SEVEN

New World Homophobia

Sodomy and Persecution in America,
1500–1900

Chapter Fifteen

Colonizing Sodom

The New World held tremendous promise for conquerors in search of lands and riches, as well as for religious dissidents hoping to find refuge from the evils of the Old World. But in at least one way, the unfamiliar cultures reproduced an all too well known vice. Among the Aztecs and among the Iroquois, conquistadores and Pilgrims discovered that sodomy had already established itself—or so it seemed to their horrified eyes. That homosexual behavior was actually practiced is not in doubt; what it meant to the native peoples, however, was not what Europeans thought they saw.[1] Along with the will to conquer native peoples and impose European religion and customs, Europeans imported the myth of Sodom. One of many doctrines used to justify conquest and even extermination, this myth, with its poisonous rhetoric and demand for terrible punishment, played a significant and destructive role.[2]

1 Eliminating Sodom

Many conquerors hoped their feats would redound to the greater glory of God. When Vasco Nuñez de Balboa crossed Panama and saw the Pacific Ocean on September 29, 1513, "never seene before of any man

conmynge owte of owre world," he doubtless fell on his knees to thank
God for the miracle of the new land. But only two days earlier he had
had to take strong action to drive out the godless.

On October 5 Balboa had ordered the massacre of several hundred Panamanian Indians in the village of Quarequa, among them
some forty who, he was sure, had engaged in sodomy. Pietro Martire d'Anghiera's *De Orbe Novo*—published in Latin in 1530 and
translated into English in 1555 by Richard Eden as Peter Martyr's
Decades—describes Balboa's discovery that the house of the king of
Quarequa was "infected with the most abhominable and unnaturall
lechery. For [Balboa] founde the kynges brother and many other
younge men in women's apprarell, smoth & effeminately decked,
which . . . he abused with preposterous Venus. Of these abowte the
number of fortie he [Balboa] commaunded to bee gyven for a pray to
his dogges."[3]

A 1594 engraving shows the naked victims writhing on the ground
as the dogs tear them apart.[4] The Europeans stand watching, fully
armed and dressed in the most dandified contemporary male fashion:
tassels and ribbons and ruffs, feathers and doublets and embroidery.
That these Indians are sodomites in Balboa's eyes—or at least in the
eyes of Peter Martyr and his translator—cannot be doubted: the
"unnaturall lechery" they practice is confirmed by the phrase "preposterous Venus." Peter had written that they were "infected" with
"abominable" lechery—clear enough—but Eden adds the explicit "preposterous."[5] The Latin *praeposterus* means that what comes before,
prae, is confused with what comes after or behind, *posterus;* hence,
the term signifies "inverted" or "contrary to nature" as well as
"ridiculous."

Balboa's quick and brutal punishment impressed an immediate
moral lesson on the other villagers, who brought the explorer "al suche
as they knew to bee infected with that pestilence" so that these "contagious beasts" could also be exterminated. The remaining Indians were
innocent: "This stinking abomination hadde not yet entered among the
people, but was exercised only by the noble men and gentlemen." It
had not yet entered, but (in the way of sodomy) it might soon do so; it
was best, then, to kill those infected before the disease spread. Sodomy
as a special vice of the nobility is a familiar European concept, though
whether the Indians shared it is impossible to know. By killing the king,
his sodomite brother, and his retainers, Balboa liberated "the people"

from the tyranny of sodomy—and provided himself with a useful moral justification for the conquest he achieved and the blood he spilled.

We read that "the people," piously horrified by the sodomy they had just seen so appropriately punished, lifted up "theyr handes and eyes toward heaven, [and] gave tokens that god was grevously offended with such vyle deedes."[6] Translating Peter Martyr's account of newly Christianized Indians, Eden notes in a marginal gloss: "I wolde all men were of this opinion."[7] Martyr made European sodomites out of some Indians, European enemies of sodomy out of others.

Hernán Cortés, whose depredations in Mexico matched the ferocity of Balboa's in Panama, believed that the great Aztec civilization upon which he had stumbled was rife with sodomy; in a 1519 letter, he observed: "We have been informed, and are most certain it is true, that they are all sodomites and practice that abominable sin."[8] Declaring individuals and whole peoples suspect has ancient authority, and the conquistadores' accounts continued the theme. Tomás Ortiz asserted that the Caribs were "sodomites more than any other race," and Gonzalo Fernández de Oviedo was certain that "the Indians eat human flesh and are sodomites."[9] Cortés, concerned about the souls of the people he would soon destroy, made it his practice to try to convert them to Christianity and convince them to renounce sodomy by teaching them "how filthy and unnatural a sin it is."[10] Bernal Díaz, an eyewitness to Cortés' conquest of Montezuma's empire, reports a speech in which Cortés urged the natives of the village of Cingapacinga to "abandon their idols which they mistakenly believed in and worshipped, and sacrifice no more souls to them," and to "give up sodomy, for they had boys dressed as women who practiced that accursed vice for profit."[11] One reason to convert, this account implies, is supplied by the priests. They are monsters: their hair is long and matted with blood, "and they smell of decaying flesh." Worse yet, they were "the sons of chiefs and had no wives, and indulged in the foul practice of sodomy."[12] The priests may indeed have told Cortés that they had no wives, but they surely did not tell him that they engaged in "the foul practice of sodomy," even if they did volunteer (or confess under torture) that they had sex with one another.

Farther north, too, sodomy seemed to be the first thing that Europeans—Spanish, French, and English—noticed upon making contact with Native American populations. Cross-dressing natives—sometimes called and often believed to be hermaphrodites—are mentioned in many European descriptions of Native Americans. In some accounts the word "berdache" (Persian *bardag,* Spanish *bardaxa,* French *bardache:* a passive homosexual male) is used for men who assumed the role of women: working instead of hunting, farming instead of fighting, and being sexually available, it was thought, to men.[13]

White men's descriptions almost always include the disgust with which they viewed the berdache and the acts they imagined he engaged in. They generally conflate the phenomenon with sodomy and effeminacy; some claim that the berdaches were as much despised by their native peers as by the white observer. Other reports, however, suggest that the berdaches served a religious function and were understood by Native Americans to be special individuals with unique spiritual and healing powers. Indeed, while the berdaches are often depicted as effeminate, they are also frequently—sometimes within the same report—described as quite the opposite. Álvar Núñez Cabeza de Vaca, a Spanish explorer who in the 1520s and 1530s spent years wandering among various Native American peoples writes: "In the time I continued among them, I saw a most brutish and beastly custome, to wit, a man who was married to another, and these be certaine effeminate and impotent men [*hombres amarionados impotentes*], who goe clothed and attired like women, and performe the office of a woman; they carry no Bowes, but beare very great and waightie burdens: and among them we saw many such effeminate persons, as I have said, and they are of greater lims and taller than the other men."[14] The English translation dates from 1613 and seems to effeminize the men more than the Spanish original, for whereas in the English text the men carry no bows, in the Spanish they do, and use them.

The Jesuit Jacques Marquette, traveling the Mississippi between 1673 and 1677, discovered that among the tribes of the Illinois "some young men assume the garb of women, and retain it throughout their lives." Marquette found "mystery in this," for the young men "never marry and glory in demeaning themselves to do everything that the women do. They go to war, however, but can only use clubs, and not bows and arrows, which are weapons proper to men." Also mysteriously, these men are actually revered by their people: "They are summoned to the councils, and nothing can be decided without their advice. Finally, through their profession of leading an Extraordinary life, they pass for Manitous,—that is to say, for spirits—or persons of consequence."[15] Marquette can only understand the reverence as "superstition," can only apprehend these men through the rhetoric of effeminacy. Pierre Liette, who traveled among the Miami peoples in 1702, encountered young men who tattooed their cheeks "like women . . . and imitate their accent, which is different from that of the men"; he notes that "they omit nothing that can make them like women. There are men who are sufficiently embruted to have dealings with them on the same footing." Liette is willing to use the word Marquette only implies: "The sin of sodomy prevails among them more than in any other nation."[16]

Most of those who describe Native American cross-dressing males are convinced that such abominations arise from some ingrained perversity of character and from the inadequacy of their religion. In 1721, the Jesuit Pierre-François-Xavier de Charlevoix wrote in *Journal of a Voyage to North-America* that among the Iroquois and the Illinois, "men were seen to wear the dress of women without a blush." These men "debase themselves so as to perform the occupations which are most peculiar" to women, with the predictable result: the "corruption of morals past all expression," for these "effeminate persons never marry, and they abandon themselves to the most infamous passions." Told that the custom had its foundation in native religion, Charlevoix, like Marquette, was scornful: "It was pretended," he contemptuously reports, "[that] this custom came from I know not what principles of religion." Charlevoix has no doubt that native belief is degenerate: "This religion had . . . taken its birth in the deprivation of the heart," he writes. "If the custom I speak of had its beginning in the spirit, it has ended in the flesh."[17]

The French explorer Jean Bernard Bossu would have agreed. His *Travels in the Interior of North America* details his experiences among the Choctaw in the 1750s. He found the Choctaw "of a generally brutal and coarse nature" and deaf to the truth of religion. Indeed, he says in exasperation, "you can talk to them as much as you want about the mysteries of our religion" but "they always reply that all of that is beyond their comprehension." Bossu can conclude only one thing: "They are morally quite perverted and most of them are addicted to sodomy." Bossu may have decided this because the "corrupt" men "have long hair and wear short skirts like women."[18]

Confronted with the religious customs of native peoples, European writers could only react with moral outrage. When they saw effeminacy, they concluded that sodomy must be near, so they dismissed what they saw as brutish, coarse, and perverse, justification for any means to root out the evil. The Spanish Jesuit Pedro Font, visiting California in 1775–76, hinted at what might be in store for the men dressed like women he saw among the native population of California. Upon inquiry he learns that "they were not men like the rest," so he concluded that they were hermaphrodites. But he was soon disabused of that innocent explanation: "From what I learned later I understood that they were sodomites, dedicated to nefarious practices." So "nefarious"—the term used in Spanish law to signify sodomy—are they, Font chillingly warns, that "in this matter of incontinence there will be much to do when the Holy faith and the Christian religion are established among them."[19]

The missionary Francisco Palóu, writing in 1774 about the foundation of Catholic missions in California, describes two men who apparently sought shelter at the house of a convert. One was "dressed like a woman" and was called by the other a *joya*, "jewel," "[the] name they are given in the native tongue." Palóu was shocked to find that "every village has two or three" such cross-dressing males. After catching the couple "in the act of committing a nefarious sin," he was horrified when one described the other as his wife. They were duly punished, though not "with the severity that [the crime] properly deserved." Palóu consoled himself by observing that "this abominable vice will be eliminated to the extent that the Catholic faith and practice and all the other virtues are firmly implanted here." Specifically, "these accursed people will disappear with the growth of the missions."[20]

The ferocity of the Catholic conquerors of Mexico and South America was matched by the new Protestant masters of North America in the eighteenth and nineteenth centuries. Edwin James' *Account of an Expedition from Pittsburgh to the Rocky Mountains in the Years 1819 and '20* is permeated with antisodomitical rhetoric. One member of the expedition, T. Say, remarked of the Konzas, who live near Omaha, that "sodomy is a crime not uncommonly committed; many of the subjects of it are publicly known, and do not appear to be despised, or to excite disgust; one of them was pointed out to us; he had submitted himself to it, in consequence of a vow he had made to his mystic medicine, which obliged him to change his dress for that of a squaw, to do their work, and to permit his hair to grow." Say was unable to disassociate the European "crime" of sodomy from what he was explicitly told is a religious institution apparently not censured by the Konza. Edwin James said of the Omaha: "Among their vices may be enumerated sodomy, onanism and various other unclean and disgusting practices," which he called "abominable traits of character."[21]

Disgusted by what he saw as emasculating effeminacy was Isaac McCoy, who in his *History of the Baptist Indian Missions* described a visit to the Osage in 1828: "Among some of the uncultivated tribes to the north there are instances, though rare, of men assuming the office of women. They put on women's apparel and mingle with them, and affect the manner and appearance of females as much as possible, and continue this folly during life. While I was at the Osage villages, one of these wretches was pointed out to me. He appeared to be about twenty-five years of age, was tall, lean, and of a ghost-like appearance. His presence was so disgusting, and the circumstances of the case so unpleasant, that I spoke not a word to him, and made few inquiries about him. He was said to be in a delicate state of health and certainly his death could not have been lamented."[22]

The artist and explorer George Catlin, recounting his experiences among the Sioux between 1832 and 1839, echoed the general attitude of white settlers. Catlin described a ritual that he called "the Dance to the berdashe":

> a very funny and amusing scene, which happens once a year or oftener, as they choose when a feast is given to the "Berdashe" as he is called in French, (or I-coo-coo-a, in their own language), who is a man dressed in woman's clothes, as he is known to be all his life, and for extraordinary privileges which he is known to possess, he is driven to the most servile and degrading duties, which he is not allowed to escape; and he being the only one of the tribe submitting to this disgraceful degradation, is looked upon as *medicine* and sacred, and a feast is given to him annually; and initiatory to it, a dance by those few young men of the tribe who can . . . publicly make their boast (without the denial of the Berdashe), that [here Catlin transcribes, purportedly in the Sioux language, the "boast" that describes sexual experiences between the "berdashe" and the young men].
>
> Such, and such only, are allowed to enter the dance and partake of the feast, and as there are but a precious few in the tribe who have legitimately gained this singular privilege, or willing to make a public confession of it, it will be seen the society consists of quite a limited number of "odd fellows."

This is one of the most unaccountable and disgusting customs that I have met in the Indian country, and so far as I have been able to learn, belongs to the Sioux and Sacs and Foxes—perhaps it is practiced by other tribes—but I did not meet with it; and for further account of it I am constrained to refer the reader to the country where it is practiced and where I should wish that it might be extinguished before it be more fully recorded.[23]

Just as McCoy tried to forget what he saw by ignoring it, and Francisco Palóu hoped that cross-dressing berdaches might "disappear" and be "eliminated," so Catlin wished that this native custom might be "extinguished" before knowledge of it could be broadcast, perhaps infecting those who heard about it.

The early settlers who colonized America hoped to find a new Eden, free of the sins and ills of old Europe. Instead, almost immediately they discovered sodomy—or so they saw it—not an occasional isolated crime by a degenerate, but the accepted practice of entire peoples. However, Europeans possessed, so they were certain, the divine warrant and the legal right to prescribe a cure. That cure, administered by a Holy Office, a conqueror, a missionary, or a gun, tended largely to exterminate peoples who knew nothing of Sodom. Of course it can hardly be said that colonization was primarily a battle against sodomy. Europeans well knew that what they wanted was land and wealth. But sodomy, the most terrible offense against the Christian god, very often became a useful pretext for demonizing—and eliminating—those whose real crime was to possess what Europeans desired.

2 New English Sodomy

The Puritans especially abhorred sodomy and pursued it vigorously. Indeed, as Michael Warner observes in his essay "New English Sodom," the Puritans "relied on the myth of Sodom in their self-understanding to a degree that is probably without parallel in history."[24] In 1666, the American preacher Samuel Whiting delivered a sermon entitled "Abraham's Humble Intercession for Sodom," which described what punishment awaited the Puritan who committed sodomy. Whiting cited chapter and verse to support his text. Sodomy was

Unnatural Uncleanness: Strange Flesh, as it is called, *Jude* ver. 7, when *men with men commit filthinesss and women with women,*

as the Apostle expresseth it, *Rom.* 1.26, 27, and this makes men
ripe for ruine. *Strange lusts* bring *strange punishment; strange fire*
kindled upon earth, brings *strange fire* from heaven. Fire naturally
ascends, but the fire that destroyed the Sodomites descended, Gen.
19.24, the *sin* was strange, and the *destruction* strange: God proportions the *punishment* to the *sin,* payes men in their *own coin;*
they have *fire* for *fire,* and not onely so, but *strange* fire, for *strange
fiery lusts.*[25]

Whiting's italic munificence emphasizes not only the sin but its strange-
ness, making sodomites outcasts, odd, and queer.

When the Puritans brought their zealotry to America, they brought
as well their antisodomitical ferocity; this crusade became an especially
potent symbol in a theology based on the principle that God had
offered the Puritans a new and special covenant.[26] Like the old covenant between God and Israel, this new one gave the Puritans a
promised land in return for absolute obedience; the story of Sodom
clearly pointed out the consequences of breaking the covenant. There
was no more spectacular example of the price of disobedience.

That New England might become a new Sodom was a constant
source of anxiety to the Puritans. They believed that homosexual
behavior was the essence of the Sodomites' rejection of the covenant.
Sodomy and its terrible partner bestiality stood among the most terrible
sins that an individual could commit, since they polluted not only his
own body but the entire community. So awful was such a sin, the Puritan minister Samuel Danforth warned his New England congregation,
that if they were indeed guilty of sodomitical uncleanness they ought
"not linger or defer thy repentance"; and, lest they corrupt everyone,
they ought to "hasten out of Sodom."

John Winthrop, about to emigrate to America, where he would soon
become governor of the Massachusetts Bay Colony, warned in a 1629
letter to his wife that a heavy scourge and judgment were about to fall
upon England because it was too much like Sodom. Winthrop's friend
Robert Ryece agreed. In a letter to Winthrop, Ryece argued that
England had become a land where "what so ever is evyll is countenanced," and so it were better "to make haste owte of Babylon, and to
seek to dye rather in the wyldernes then styll to dwelle in Sodome."[27]

The "good land" in which they had settled, the Puritans hoped,
would not only be free from sodomy but would stand as a reproof to
it. At least so Winthrop declared in the famous sermon aboard the

Arabella in which he urged that the colonists must view themselves as a city upon a hill upon which the eyes of the world were trained with suspicion and ill-will. If the colonists did not succeed in building the New Jerusalem, Winthrop feared, "Wee shall be made a story and a by-word through the world, wee shall open the mouthes of enemies to speak evill of the wayes of God and all professours for God's sake; wee shall shame the faces of many of God's worthy servants and cause theire prayers to be turned unto Cursses upon us till wee be consumed out of the good land whether we are goeing."[28]

In 1651, the New England preacher Peter Bulkeley made the comparison clearer while stressing the absolutely foreign and unusual nature of Sodom's sin: "The filthinesse of *Sodome and Gomorrah* is known, they were *exceeding* sinners against the Lord, *Gen.* 13.13; their sins were not of the common sort, but exceeded; and therefore they perished not by the common visitation of all men, but their judgment was exemplary, to stand as a warning to all ages; *a fire not blowne by man* (as it is in *Job* 20.26) consumed them, the fire of God fell upon them from heaven."[29] Bulkeley's clear warning helped place Sodom among America's founding myths. The Puritans would suffer the fate of the Sodomites if the uncleanness that destroyed the Cities of the Plain was allowed to flourish in the city upon a hill.

Nonetheless, the spirit of Sodom did flourish in the New World. In 1629—only nine years after the *Mayflower* brought the Pilgrims to the new Plymouth Colony, and the very year the Massachusetts Bay Company and Colony were founded—"5 beastly Sodomiticall boys," passengers on the ship *Talbot* bound for New England, were caught engaging in some version of the nameless sin. As the Reverend Francis Higginson, a fellow passenger, wrote in his journal, the boys "confessed their wickedness not to be named," but "the fact was so foul" that "we reserved them to be punished by the governor when we came to New England." After deliberating, the court of the Bay Colony felt unequal to the task of judging such a terrible crime and sent the boys "to bee punished in ould England as the crime deserved," charging the Massachusetts Bay Company there to "advise what punishment may be inflicted upon them."[30] The boys appear no more in history, but since anyone over fourteen could be hanged for sodomy in England, it may be that once there, they met their end.

In 1635, according to New Hampshire Colony archives, two men "committed sodomy with each other and that on the Lord's day."[31] The next year, responding to a request by the General Court of Massachusetts to draft laws for the colony, the Reverend John Cotton included one decreeing that "unnatural filthiness be punished with death, whether sodomy, which is carnal fellowship of man with man, or woman with woman, or buggery, which is carnal fellowship of man or woman with beasts or fowls."[32] Cotton's proposals were rejected. However, recognizing that the laws of England needed to be reaffirmed, the Plymouth Colony in 1636 drew up a code of laws by which—like treason, murder, conjuration and witchcraft, adultery, and the willful burning of ships and houses—the crime of sodomy was to be punishable by death. The law was passed none too soon, for in 1637 John Alexander and Thomas Roberts were found guilty by the Plymouth court of "often spending their seed upon one another." The record suggests that there was an even more alarming aspect to the case, since Alexander was a repeat offender: "John Alexander & Thomas Roberts were both examined and found guilty of lewd behavior and unclean carriage one with another, by often spending their seed one upon another, which was proved both by witness & their own confession; the said Alexander [was] found to have been formerly notoriously guilty that way, and seeking to allure others thereunto." Apparently it could be proved only that they had spilled their seed, and not engaged in penetration, so the crime was not technically sodomy. Nevertheless, the punishment was painful and humiliating, making Alexander a permanent outcast from society and depriving Roberts of most of its privileges:

> The said John Alexander was therefore censured by the Court to be severely whipped, and burnt in the shoulder with a hot iron, and to be perpetually banished [from] the government [territory] of New Plymouth, and if he be at any time found within the same, to be whipped out again by the appointment of the next justice, and so as oft as he shall be found within this government. Which penalty was accordingly inflicted. Thomas Roberts was censured to be severely whipped, and to return to his master, Mr. Atwood, and serve out his time with him, but to be disabled hereby to enjoy any lands within this government, except he manifest better desert.[33]

Despite such harsh treatment, sodomy continued to surface. William Bradford, the governor of Plymouth Colony, described events of 1642 in his history, *Of Plimouth Plantation:* "Marvelous it may be to see and consider how some kind of wickedness did grow and break forth here, in a land where the same was so much witnessed against and so narrowly looked unto, and severely punished when it was known. . . . But that which is worse, even sodomy and buggery (things fearful to name) have broke forth in this land oftener than once."[34] Bradford suspected that the "corrupt natures" of the colonists may have something to do with so much sin, an opinion shared by Thomas Shepard, the pastor of the church in Newtown, Massachusetts, who only the year before had warned his congregation in a sermon called "The Sincere Convert" that "thy mind is a nest of all foul opinions, heresies, that ever were vented by any man: thy heart is a foul sink of all atheism, sodomy, blasphemy, murder, whoredom, adultery, witchcraft, buggery"—a list nearly identical with the list of crimes Massachusetts had just pronounced capital. For Shepard, sin lurked in every heart "like a nest of snakes in an old hedge" waiting to break forth. The listener should look to his heart, he commanded, for "thou art guilty of heart whoredom" and "heart sodomy."[35]

But even the corrupt heart might not be enough to explain the explosive public presence of so much sin; supernatural causes might be at play, Bradford suggested. The New England churches were noted for their "holiness, purity, and strictness"; because of that the devil himself might "carry a greater spite against the churches" and therefore have cast "a blemish and a stain" upon them. Indeed, perhaps inordinate strictness itself was the cause of the outbreak in New England: "Wickedness being more stopped by strict laws" may break out even more violently, just as water stopped by a dam flows more violently when the dam breaks. Furthermore, "many wicked persons and profane people" had "come into this land" and mixed "among us, unlike those religious settlers who first came here" for "religion's sake." Bradford described the case of one Thomas Granger, a teenage boy executed in 1642 for sexual relations with "a mare, a cow, two goats, five sheep, two calves and a turkey." When asked how he learned about "such wickedness," Granger confessed he had learned it from another, who in turn had heard about such things in England. This showed, as Bradford warned, how "one wicked person may infect many."[36]

Evidence of sodomy's ubiquity came to Bradford's attention in the form of a letter from Richard Bellingham, the governor of the Massachusetts Bay Colony. Bellingham wrote to Bradford in March 1642, asking for advice about the punishment of "heinous offenses in point of uncleanness." (The particular cases involved heterosexual rape of children, and bestiality.) Bradford in turn asked three Plymouth ministers to give their opinions about what constituted sodomy and how it ought to be punished.

In their response, the ministers concentrated on sex between males. The Reverend John Raynor wrote that "carnal knowledge of man or lying with man as with woman . . . was sodomy, to be punished with death." While penetration was certainly definitive, Raynor asserted that "this foul sin might be capital" even if there was no penetration, but only sexual contact that caused ejaculation. He further argued that even the intention to commit "the foulest acts" should be punished with death, for it was the great "foulness of sodomy and bestiality that made them capital." The Reverend Ralph Partridge concurred: "A voluntary effusion of seed" caused by sexual contact between males ought to be punished by death. The Reverend Charles Chauncy widened the definition of sodomy further, to include bestiality, rape, adultery, and incest, all punishable by death in Mosaic law. Referring to ancient authorities, who agreed that even the attempt to commit such sins should be capital, he argued that the biblical phrase "lying with" included "other obscure acts preceding" penetration, so that any act tending to sodomy ought to be capital. He concluded: "The unnatural lusts of men with men, or women with women or either with beasts" should be "punished with death."[37]

In 1646, Governor Winthrop of the Massachusetts Bay Colony described a case of sodomy that offers some insight into the colonists' abhorrence of sex between men. The defendant, William Plaine of Guilford, was accused of masturbating with "a great part of the youth of Guilford" and provoking "others to do so." Plaine, though married, had a past history of sodomy. At his trial it was revealed that he had "committed sodomy with two persons in England." Worse still, he "did insinuate the seed of atheism, questioning whether there was a God." This was adequate to prove the alliance between sodomites and Satan. Though Plaine was tried for *doing* something, he was executed for *being* someone. More than a masturbator, Plaine was a heretic. Winthrop called him a "monster in human shape" whose actions had consequences far greater than the spilling of seed, namely "frustrating of the ordinance of marriage and the hindering of the generation of mankind."[38]

From almost the first years of the English settlement on this continent, sodomy was treated as a major crime against the state, one of the few infractions meriting death.[39] Laws like New England's were adopted in some southern colonies, though in most the English sodomy laws were assumed to be in force, and the death penalty was more often demanded than in the North.[40] After the Revolution, in America just as in Europe, the ideas of the Enlightenment helped to shift attitudes toward sodomy away from moral and theological to legal condemnation. Many of the new states—the first among them Pennsylvania—abolished the death penalty, although Thomas Jefferson recommended castration as the penalty for sodomy between males.[41] But unlike Europe, where many nations were decriminalizing sodomy and private sexual acts, in America the sin remained a crime. Indeed, at the midpoint of the nineteenth century thirty-eight states maintained criminal sodomy statutes in force. Gradually, however, the sodomite who had been hanged in New England became the pervert derided and despised throughout the United States.

Chapter Sixteen

The Discord Young Men Feel

T he warning that sodomy was everywhere was repeated in 1810 at a
trial in Maryland. The offense was, as usual, called "that most hor-
rid and detestable crime (among Christians not to be named)." The
defendant was convicted and the judges observed that "the crime of
sodomy is too well known to be misunderstood and too disgusting to
be defined."[1] What was well known in the courtroom, however, was
not always so well understood outside it. In the nineteenth century, the
condemnation of sodomy was complicated by the existence of a cult of
intense male friendship, so often expressed in the literature of the
period that it has come to be called "the friendship tradition." Shaped
by the sentimental sensibility of the late eighteenth century as well as
by the sexually and psychologically suggestive writings of the early
nineteenth-century Romantics, "friendship" allowed strong, even passionate, emotions between members of the same sex, though the presumption was always that such friendships could not and ought not
include consummation or even desire. Close friendship between women,
too, was accepted, as Carroll Smith-Rosenberg has argued: "deeply-felt
same-sex relationships" between women within a closely structured
"female world" were a key component of American society.[2]

1 Friendship and Anxiety

Although overt sex between males was forbidden, it was suggested in the popular literature of the day. In the Davy Crockett "Almanacs," a series of popular magazine accounts that appeared in the 1830s and 1840s, the handsome young frontiersman lands in implicitly sexual situations. His world is rough, violent, and uninhibited. In one incident, Crockett engages in a wrestling match with a stagecoach driver. To the driver he says: "Take care how I lite on you"; then Crockett tells us, "I jumped right down on the driver and he tore my trowsers right off me. I was driven almost distracted and should have been used up, but luckily there was a poker in the fire which I thrust down his throat, and by that means mastererd him." In another scene Crockett is attracted to an oak tree, which he climbs; he then "slide[s] down to the bottom," making his legs "feel mighty warm and good."[3] The homoerotic implications of the phallic poker that Davy uses to master the coach driver as they wrestle trouserless need not be spelled out. It is hard to know whether nineteenth-century moralists would have been troubled more by that image or by Davy's solitary sport with the oak tree. They might well have pricked up their ears at his mention of being "used up," for it was against the danger of such exhaustion that they warned young men who masturbated.

Young men were special objects of sexual reform, and masturbation, along with its darker shadow sodomy, was the subject most anxiously addressed. The moral purity movement preached the unqualified evil of masturbation and warned of its debilitating effect upon the energies of American youth. Manuals like William Alcott's *The Young Man's Guide* (1833) and Sylvester Graham's *Lecture to Young Men on Chastity* (1834) prescribed dietary and sexual abstinence for those vulnerable to sensual excess. The chief actor in these texts was the adolescent male, beset on every side by the lures of rich food, masturbation, seductive women—and sometimes seductive men. Since sex outside of marriage was a sure path to ruin, young men were counseled to seek the safe haven of the bourgeois home and marriage—even, once the duties of procreation were completed, sexless marriage.

Because private friendship was made problematic by public preaching, both professions of it and doubts about it are fairly common in letters and diaries. In a journal written in 1820, Ralph Waldo Emerson addressed what was apparently an anxiety-ridden collision with homoerotic feelings. He describes his passion—inexplicable even to him, who had explained Nature itself—for a young man named Martin Gay.

Unnerved but fascinated by Gay, Emerson—in the diary—asks of him: "Why do you look after me? I cannot help looking out as you pass." In a poem probably written to Gay, he pleads: "Grant me still in joy or sorrow / In grief or hope to claim thy heart." The friendship remained distant, and Emerson transformed what reality it possessed into fiction. He wrote a small play named *The Friends,* which he credits to one "Frodmer," who is also the hero of the piece. Gay appears in the play as Malcolm, to whom Frodmer confesses: "Malcolm I love thee more than women love."

In a journal entry made fourteen years later, perhaps while thinking about his unsettling experience, Emerson wondered about "the disturbance, the self-discord which young men feel," and concluded that it "is a most important crisis." He located such a crisis in Shakespeare's sonnets, which leads him to speculate on Shakespeare's "unknown self." He observes: "How remarkable in every way are Shakespeare's sonnets. Those addressed to a beautiful young man seem to show some singular friendship amounting to a passion."[4]

Henry David Thoreau also speculated on eroticized friendship. In an 1838 poem called "Friendship," he defined love as the "connecting link between heaven and earth," and lovers as "kindred shapes" possessing a "kindred nature." Such lovers are intended "to be mates, / Exposed to equal fates / Eternally." They are like "two sturdy oaks" whose "roots are intertwined insep'rably." Perhaps intending to reinforce his references to Plato's *Symposium* and its imagery of kindred lovers, Thoreau insisted that "love cannot speak . . . without the help of Greek." In January 1840 he again noted the association of Greece with homoeroticism: "History tells us of Orestes and Pylades, Damon and Pythias, but why should not we put to shame those old reserved worthies by a community of such"—"such" lovers, that is. He conjures a vision of this erotic Arcadia: "Constantly, as it were through a remote skylight, I have glimpses of a serene friendship land." Here is needed only one other: "I would live henceforth with some gentle soul such a life as may be conceived, double for variety, single for harmony,—two, only that we might admire at our oneness,—one, because indivisible. Such a community to be a pledge of holy living."

The relation between love and friendship in an all-male world was a recurring theme of Thoreau's meditations: "I conceive of true friendship when some rare specimen of manhood presents itself," he wrote in 1839. Speaking in the language of marriage, he inquires: "By what degrees of consanguinity is this succulent and rank growing slip of manhood related to me?" (The "degrees of consanguinity" are the limits set by the Church on marriage between kindred persons.) There is a clear disjunction between manly love and "other"—heterosexual—love: "The rules of other intercourse are all inapplicable to this."

Thoreau's young men, nearly divinities, even create the world he lives in: "They make the landscape and sky for us." But the social taboo that enforces separation between male friendship and erotic passion is harmful to both: "Commonly we degrade Love and Friendship by presenting them under a trivial dualism." In an entry written in 1840, Thoreau elaborated on the effects of society's suspicion: "Mean relations and prejudices intervene to shut out the sky and we never see a man as simple and distinct." In June 1852, Thoreau again considered the proscriptions against eroticized male friendship: "Boys bathing at Hubbard's bend, playing with a boat (I at the willows). The color of their bodies in the sun at a distance is pleasing, the not often seen flesh-color. I hear the sound of their sport borne over the water. . . . What a singular fact that . . . men were forbidden to expose their bodies under severest penalty." The distance Thoreau keeps from bathing boys is measured for him by the "prejudices" he earlier mentioned; such sights cannot be "simple and distinct" when what they arouse could be punished by "severest penalties."[5] Perhaps, for Thoreau, the chaste solitude of Walden offered the only acceptable solution.

Thoreau was not alone in being aware of the danger attendant on passionate expressions of love between men. In 1866, the novelist and poet Bayard Taylor wrote to Walt Whitman to say that he found in *Leaves of Grass* what he had found "nowhere else" in literature, "that tender and noble love of man for man which once certainly existed but now almost seems to have gone out of the experience of the race."[6] Taylor himself had tried to put that love back into literature. In a poem called "On the Headland," from *The Poets Journal* (1862), he writes: "I pine for something human, / Man, woman, young or old,— / Something to meet and welcome, / Something to clasp and hold." He confesses: "I have a mouth for kisses. . . . I have a heart in my bosom / Beating for nobody's sake. . . . O warmth of love that is wasted!" So powerful is his desire that "I could take the sunburnt sailor, / Like a brother, to my breast."[7] Even earlier, in *Poems of the Orient* (1855), he had explored sexual affection between men. Set in an exotic locale, "the Orient," legendarily tolerant of homosexuality, the poems intend to display "the unshackled range / Of all experience," especially "the warm red blood that beats in hearts of men." In "A Paean to the

Dawn," Greece is the land where "love was free, and free as air / The utterance of Passion." There "the heart in every fold lay bare, / Nor shamed its true expression." In Greece "men acknowledged true desires" and acted upon them: "Impulse and Deed went hand in hand." Such sexual freedom is a source of power, so Taylor determines to "seek the fountain head / Whence flowed their inspiration, / And lead the unshackled life they led." In this land of friendship, the poet can admit the truth of his desire and renounce "the World's false life."

He can also discover his "native soul," as he declares in "The Poet in the East." He compares what he finds in these homoerotically charged eastern lands with the "familiar visions" that "mocked his quest / Beside the Western streams." The western streams, named in "The Nilotic Drinking Song," are the Schuylkill and Croton, flowing through a land where homoerotic passion must be repressed. In the East, however, the poet stands beside waters where "Ganymede dipped for Jupiter" and is reminded of the poetry of Anacreon and of the "honeyed lips of Hylas," that handsome youth for whose love Hercules pined. He decides to remain "on the lost Arcadian shore." Taylor concludes the Oriental poems with an intriguing comment. In the East, he writes, "I found, among those Children of the sun, / The cipher of my nature,—the release / Of baffled powers, which else had never won / That free fulfillment." Had he remained in America, his true "nature" would not have been realized, and his poetic powers would have remained forever "baffled."

2 Sexual Comrades

Walt Whitman called *Leaves of Grass* a "language experiment." Among the many rich linguistic inventions in that great book must be counted the creation of a language to express comradeship and manly love. In his journal from the early 1850s, five years before he published *Leaves of Grass*, Whitman speculated upon the relationship between language, manly friendship, and desire. "The young men of these states," he wrote, possessed of "a wonderful tenacity of friendship," a "passionate fondness for their friends, and always a manly readiness to make friends," have remarkably few words or names for "the friendly sentiments." Such words "do not thrive here among the muscular classes, where the real quality of friendship is always freely found. Also they are words which the muscular classes . . . rarely use, and have an aversion for;—they never give words to their most ardent friendships."[8]

Whitman's project was to give young men the words to name their desire and even perhaps name themselves. This mission had definite personal ramifications: "As for me, I feel a hundred realities," he wrote, "clearly determined in me, that words are not yet formed to represent. Men like me . . . will gradually get to be more and more numerous . . . then the words will follow."[9]

Over the next few years Whitman invented a language to express the "hundred realities" within himself, among them his homosexuality. In the first poem of the 1855 *Leaves of Grass,* the poem that would eventually be titled "Song of Myself," he underlined the importance of having a word for manly friendship, calling it "the unfolding word of the ages . . . a word of the modern . . . a word en masse . . . a word of faith that never balks." The word is a "password primeval," a key that will allow him to speak in "forbidden voices," strip away veils, and erase the boundaries that keep men who love men outside traditional society.

Whitman recognized that one element of the aversion to naming male friendship was the widespread assumption that men who loved men were effeminate. Effeminacy was despised by the muscular classes that Whitman admired, yet it dominated the literature. In a letter to Emerson in 1856, Whitman explained: "As to manly friendship, everywhere observed in the States, there is not the first breath of it to be observed in print."[10] Instead he finds a literature "without manhood or power," in which only "geldings" are depicted. The "flesh" of such literature "is soft; it shows less and less of the indefinable hard something that is Nature." It reflects its reader and its writer, "helpless dandies" who "can neither fight, work, shoot, ride, run, command"; who are "devout, some quite insane, castrated"; who can be seen "smirking and skipping along," who display no "natural and manly tastes" of their own. These dandies produce writing in which the lives of men and women appear to have been "of the neuter gender": with a change of dress, "the men might easily pass for women, and the women for men." This literature makes "unmentionable" the "manhood of a man" as well as "sex, womanhood, maternity, desires, lusty animations, organs, acts."[11]

Whitman's attack on literary dandyism is filled with the clichés habitually applied to the effeminate homosexual. But if he employs the terms traditionally used to demonize same-sex love, he does so in order to redefine the basis on which a literature of manly friendship can be built. His opposition to effeminacy introduced into American literature a masculine, antiaristocratic, democratic style that is nevertheless informed by a homoerotic aesthetic. To convey "manly friendship," he wrote to

Emerson, muscular words must be found; they in turn would form a language that will make American literature "strong, limber . . . full of ease, of passionate friendliness." He intended to invent a language applicable to "men not fond of women, women not fond of men."[12]

The liberation of homoerotic energies was part of a larger enterprise: literature must repeal the "filthy law" that enforces silence about sex, Whitman insisted to Emerson. What is "important in poems" is to name "in specific words" the "main matter" that "is so far quite unexpressed in poems; . . . the body is to be expressed and sex is." Sex, "avowed, empowered, unabashed," is that on which "all existence, all souls, all realization, all decency, all health, all that is worth being here for, all of women and of men, all beauty, all purity, all sweetness, all friendship, all strength, all life, all immortality depend."[13] In that rush of language, friendship nestles between sweetness and strength, but like all the other items on the list, it "depends" on sex.

In the second (1856) and third (1860) editions of *Leaves of Grass,* Whitman unveiled a full-scale program to liberate same-sex love from the "filthy law" that silenced and condemned it. In 1856 he found the word to name manly friendship: "adhesiveness," a term heretofore used in the popular science of phrenology to describe nonsexual friendship. Whitman used it differently. In "Song of the Open Road" he wrote, "Here is adhesiveness, it is not previously fashioned, it is apropos."[14] It is "apropos" because it signals a free response to the possibilities inherent in the unspoken signs exchanged between strangers, as Whitman says in the next lines: "Do you know what it is as you pass to be loved by strangers? / Do you know the talk of those turning eyeballs?" This "talk" is the language of adhesiveness and of sexual invitation: men like Whitman are fluent in it. In "Proto-leaf," the poem that introduces the third edition of *Leaves of Grass,* "adhesiveness" will "clear one's path" on the road to the "new ideal of manly friendship."

The third edition included Whitman's greatest contribution to the poetry of manly love: the "Calamus" poems, more than thirty of them. They are exclusively concerned with homosexual desire, love, and sex. The first Calamus poem, now called "In Paths Untrodden," was the last of the series to be written. Whitman completed it shortly before he took the 1860 edition to the printer, and it sums up the result of a decade of his growing sexual awareness. "In Paths Untrodden" is a record and celebration of what we might call Whitman's "coming out," a rejection of the sexual conformity imposed by society, and a manifesto of the role Whitman assumed as the apostle of manly love.

In paths untrodden
In the growth by margins of pond waters,
Escaped from the life that exhibits itself,
From all the standards hitherto publish'd, from the pleasures, profits,
    conformities,
Which too long I was offering to feed my soul;
Clear to me now standards not yet publish'd—clear to me that my soul,
That the soul of the man I speak for rejoices in comrades,
Here by myself away from the clank of the world,
Tallying and talk'd to by tongues aromatic,
No longer abash'd, (for in this secluded spot I can respond as I would
    not dare elsewhere,)
Strong upon me the life that does not exhibit itself, yet contains all the
    rest,
Resolv'd to sing no songs to-day but those of manly attachment,
Projecting them along that substantial life,
Bequeathing hence types of athletic love,
Afternoon this delicious Ninth-month in my forty-first year,
I proceed for all who are or have been young men,
To tell the secret of my nights and days,
To celebrate the need of comrades.

By the "margins of pond waters" the poet finds a safe haven, far from the prohibitions against manly love. Here he can escape the "standards" and "pleasures" and "conformities" of traditional social and sexual conduct, which he has too long and unquestioningly accepted as the only moral and spiritual sustenance. Here there are new "standards not yet publish'd." And he will be their publisher.

But first he seeks a solitary place where he can respond as he "would not dare elsewhere." There he hears mystic voices—"tongues aromatic" that inspire him with a vision of "the life that does not exhibit itself, / yet contains all the rest." In this most profound of Whitman's definitions of manly love, he rejects the received opinion that manly love means only sex. On the contrary, it "contains all the rest." It is the poet's responsibility to declare this revelation to history on behalf of "all who are or have been young men." To them he will bequeath "types of athletic love." In the coded world of Whitman's texts, "young men" are icons of homoerotic desire, of "athletic love," a reference not only to strength and prowess, but to manly love itself. But the time for codes is past; he will now "celebrate the need of comrades" and proudly tell the "secret of my nights and days."

3 Unmanly Passions

Despite this brave program Whitman was very much aware that he lived in an exceptionally hostile climate. He had said so as early as 1841. In a short story, "The Child's Champion"—a tale of love between a young man and a boy—Whitman recognized that the "forms of custom" can "smother" the "wish to love and be loved." By the time he wrote to Emerson in 1856, he had already experienced the smothering effect of the forms of custom and discovered just how the "exhibited" life might react to the publication of new standards. When *Leaves of Grass* appeared in 1855, it was immediately treated as a noxious text. In a review of the poems, the journalist Rufus Griswold left no doubt about what he found there. After a general diatribe against writers who disregard "all the politeness and decencies of life," he inveighed against "the tendency of thought in these later years," which allowed in literature "a degrading, beastly sensuality that is fast rotting the healthy core of all the social virtues." Griswold associated Whitman's poetry with the "crime" committed by "monsters" of "vileness," an allusion to homosexuality not difficult to decipher. But if there was any doubt what he meant, in his peroration he is clear:

> In our allusion to this book, we have found it impossible to convey
> any, even the most faint idea of its style and contents, and of our
> disgust and detestation of them, without employing language that
> cannot be pleasing to ears polite; but it does seem that some one
> should, under circumstances like these, undertake a most disagree-
> able, yet stern duty. The records of crime show that many mon-
> sters have gone on in impunity, because the exposure of their
> vileness was attended with too great indelicacy. *Peccatum illud
> horribile, inter Christianos non nominandum.*[15]

Griswold's argument, hardly subtle to begin with, concludes with the Latin legal description of sodomy: "the horrible sin, not to be named among Christians." Griswold had no doubt that his readers were acquainted with sodomy and disgusted by it. His assertion that Whitman's poems "may leave a foul odor, contaminating the pure, healthful air," allies his criticism with contemporary discussions of homosexual behavior in the literature of disease, mental disorder, and pathology.

Though Whitman announced in 1860 his determination to tell the "secrets of my nights and days," by 1870 the homophobic specter summoned in Griswold's review had become so frightening that Whitman seemed less sure his project could be accomplished. That year, a young writer of homoerotic tales named Charles Warren Stoddard sent Whitman a letter in which he invoked "the name of CALAMUS" for "people who are not afraid of instincts." He sent along his novel, *South-Sea Idylls,* in which he describes his affection for an island boy, which Whitman read and described as "beautiful and soothing." However, Whitman cautioned Stoddard that "I do not of course object to your emotional & adhesive nature, & the outlet thereof, but warmly approve them," yet "do you know (perhaps you do,) how the hard, pungent, gritty, worldly experiences & qualities of American practical life also serve? how they prevent extravagant sentimentalism?"[16]

Whitman's veiled warnings to Stoddard sound a tentative note and surely reflect his disillusionment with the progress of his mission. However, he was not yet quite ready to abandon it. In a footnote to his essay *Democratic Vistas* (1871), Whitman argued that a "materialistic and vulgar" American democracy—the same democracy that maintained the "filthy law" of silence about sex and condemned same-sex love—could be transformed only by manly friendship:

> It is to the development, identification, and general prevalence of that fervid comradeship, (the adhesive love, at least rivaling the amative love hitherto possessing imaginative literature, if not going beyond it,) that I look for the counterbalance and offset of our materialistic and vulgar American democracy, and for the spiritualization thereof. . . . I confidently expect a time when there will be seen running, like a half-hid warp through all the myriad audible and visible worldly interests of America, threads of manly friendship, fond and loving, pure and sweet, strong and life-long, carried to degrees hitherto unknown—not only giving tone to individual character, and making it unprecedentedly emotional, muscular, heroic, and refined, but having the deepest relation to general politics. I say democracy infers such loving comradeship, as its most inevitable twin or counterpart, without which it would be incomplete, in vain, and incapable of perpetuating itself.[17]

Religion had long defined homosexual behavior as an activity that prevented the perpetuation of the race; science, by the time Whitman wrote, was describing it as incomplete both sexually and emotionally. Whitman reversed both assertions and declared that without manly affection democracy itself would be "incomplete" and "incapable of perpetuating itself."

Other American literature that addressed the anxiety of intense masculine friendship did not follow Whitman down the path of joyful adhesiveness, but rather confirmed society's faith in heterosexual marriage and its horror of sodomites. In *Cecil Dreeme* (1861), a novel by Theodore Winthrop, the hero is attracted to two men, one a sinister if erotic villain, the other pure and chaste, both handsome. He chooses the purer of the two, but is saved from the imputation of sexual impropriety when his choice turns out to have been a woman in disguise. Bayard Taylor's novel *Joseph and His Friend* (1870) describes a passionate but nonsexual relationship between Joseph and the handsome Philip. Taylor prevents darker suspicions about Joseph from surfacing by having him marry, at the end of the novel, the twin sister of his beloved.

Popular literature expressed a more straightforward revulsion. *A Marriage Below Zero* by "Alan Dale" tells the story of a young woman who competes with a man for the love of her handsome if slightly effeminate husband, who has never consummated the marriage. She loses him to the villainous Captain Jack. When she discovers her husband and the captain alone in a room, she correctly imagines the worst. In one last attempt to salvage her marriage she follows the pair to Paris but arrives too late to save her husband, who has killed himself. She finds his body in a room in which two portraits hang side by side, one of him, the other of the captain, who looks down on the melodramatic scene in triumph. *A Marriage Below Zero* thus introduces the homosexual villain into American fiction.

Ironically, the creator of the American dream—that a young man can reach material comfort and happiness through pluck, virtue, and hard work—was himself an inventor of homosexualized fictions and a victim of homophobia. In Horatio Alger's books, the young heroes are often aided in their enterprise by an older male patron. Before inventing these homoerotic capitalist fictions, Alger may have tried to live them out. In 1866, he was accused of "the abominable and unnatural crime of unnatural familiarities with boys" by the Unitarian church of Brewster, Massachusetts, where he was minister. Two boys of the parish said

he had "practic[ed] on them at different times deeds that are too revolting to relate." The elders of the church, in turn, found his deeds "too
revolting to think of." Worst of all, when confronted with his crime,
Alger "neither denied nor attempted to extenuate it, but received it with
the apparent calmness of an old offender." Not surprisingly, he "hastily
left town on the very next train for parts unknown," fleeing home, job,
and community, the pervert cast out by his righteous peers.[18] Profiting
from adversity, as he would teach millions of young men to do, he went
to New York and began to write books glorifying youth and the American dream, the twin ideals his accusers supposed he was bent on
corrupting.

By the end of the century, intimate friendships between men, and
between women, once unexceptionable, had become the object of per-
plexity. One 1880s diarist is shocked at his discovery that an acquain-
tance is "a C——sucker & that he loves and enjoys that d——d custom
so revolting to every right minded person." Speaking of another friend,
the author says: "I loved to hug & kiss him" but quickly denies that
such behavior shows the "least demonstration of unmanly and abnormal passion." Such a thing, he writes, would be as "revolting" to the
man he hugged and kissed "as it is & ever has been to me."[19] A few
years later, in 1891, J. A. Symonds wrote to Whitman asking directly
whether the "Calamus" poems could be construed to advocate homosexual affections and their physical realization. Whitman's explosive
denial suggests how homophobia had infected the new and manly
world he had tried to build. The poet professed horror that his work
could support such "morbid inferences." His use of the medical term
"morbid" shows that Whitman knew well that the love of comrades he
had celebrated in the 1860s, and hailed as the cure for democracy's ills
in the 1870s, had been defined, by the 1890s, as a sickness and a perversion. In 1895 the German journalist Max Nordau published his
popular book *Degeneration,* in which he ascribed the decline of the
West to homosexuality and sexual promiscuity. Nordau cited Whitman
as "one of the deities to whom the degenerate and hysterical of both
hemispheres have for some time been raising altars." It was not hard to
decipher this: some who suffered from hysteria, a malady believed to be
the especial curse of women, were men, degenerate and effeminate
men—homosexuals, in fact. And of this degenerate cult the homosexual
Whitman, whom Nordau called "morally insane," was the prophet.[20]

Chapter Seventeen

In Fear of Fairies

As we have seen, by the end of the nineteenth century, the study of what many European medical theorists called sexuality included the concepts of homosexuality and heterosexuality, if not yet the actual terms. For nineteenth-century theorists in the United States, as in Europe, an individual's "sexuality" depended not only on biological sex, but also on the biological sex of that individual's object of desire. Then too, while "sexuality" claimed merely to categorize the sexual "facts" about an individual, it was nevertheless subject to moral judgments about mental health and emotional stability. "Normal" sexuality was stable and mentally sound; "abnormal" sexuality unstable and emotionally damaged. Finally, definitions of sexuality relied on the presumption that characteristics of "masculinity" or "femininity"—gender—were an inherent component of every sexual subject. Sexuality was, therefore, the dominating principle that underlay human actions and defined each person's psychological and physical nature. As Dr. William Howard explained it in 1904, summing up the speculations of half a century of scientific discourse: "Every physician should understand the sexual side of life, for it is sexual activity that governs life, permits the continuation of the species and promotes crime and its causes. It is the basis of all society."[1]

If procreational sex was the "basis of all society," then the presence of sexually deviant beings was a threat to that same society, and those ruled by abnormal passions needed to be identified for safety's sake. Dr. George Shrady, writing in July 1884 on the subject of the "perverted sexual instinct," suggested what to look for. Such "debased men have an irrepressible desire to act the part of the opposite sex." They are obsessed by sex, and "they often masturbate while having lascivious images of the male beloved before their imagination." They also evinced specific physical and "mental peculiarities": they "have a mincing gait" and are "of the artistic, poetical, and imaginative temperament, often exhibiting a tendency to rather weak philosophizing," although "sometimes they are of a vigorous understanding."[2]

No doubt, effeminate homosexual men and mannish lesbians were to be seen in society. Indeed, the "fairy"—the effeminate, often cross-dressing male invert—was a well-known denizen of the streets of many American cities, as George Chauncey has documented in *Gay New York: Gender, Culture, and the Making of the Gay Male World, 1890–1940*. Though the fairy and the mannish lesbian were considered standard types by the defenders of "sexual normality," fairies were no doubt vastly outnumbered by those who were not effeminate, just as mannish women were surely outnumbered by women whose lesbianism was not so evident. As Chauncey points out, many men embraced the fairy identity because "it embodied a way of understanding how they, as men, could have feelings their culture ascribed exclusively to women."[3] A parallel dynamic may well have influenced women.

1 Natural Objects of Disgust

Identifying such creatures also meant judging them. In July 1893, Dr. Edward Mann, discussing the case of "one girl, of a faulty nervous organization, in a young ladies' seminary," described her "morbid sexual love for a person of the same sex." This "insane girl" nearly began an "epidemic" by causing "an hysterical tendency among others not insane"; the epidemic was suppressed only by threats of immediate dismissal. The "hysteria" that some medical textbooks saw as recurrent in women of "faulty nervous organization" here also becomes a motivating factor in lesbian desire. The inherent instability of homosexuals, George Shrady noted in 1884, caused by the mental distress evoked by a consciousness of their "unnatural instincts," can bring on "melancholia," insanity, and even suicide.

In 1892, Dr. T. Griswold Comstock lectured readers who might be in doubt concerning how they ought to feel about perverts. He assured them that "perverts" are "natural objects of disgust to normal men and women," but also reassured them that because the sexual relations of perverts are "practiced in an unnatural manner . . . Nature will surely avenge herself upon the offender. Mental disturbance and insanity will often follow." Comstock also proposed that homosexuals possessed a "mysterious bond of psychological sympathy" with one another. "Instances have been authenticated to me," he said, "where such perverts when meeting another of the same sex have at once recognized each other, and mutually become acquainted and have left in company with each other to practice their unnatural vices."[4]

That the homosexual was diseased and abnormal was the message delivered by Dr. C. H. Hughes in 1893. Classing all homosexual acts as "erotopathia or erotomania," he distinguished between proper human passions—"the ardent affections of the heart," which are "chaste and honorable" and lead to reproduction—and abnormal passions, the "strange morbid perversions" that can "destroy both body and mind."[5] Comstock's evocation of homosexuals as sexual monsters with a sinister sixth sense, and Hughes's mix of sentimentality, morality, and jargon each demonstrate homophobia masquerading as objective science.

2 Colonies of Perverts

If the individual deviant was abnormal, groups of deviants were positively dangerous. A lecture by Dr. G. Frank Lydston in 1889 raised the specter of numerous and well-organized colonies of homosexuals. Such clusters were easily recognized by their members' "effeminacy of voice, dress, and manner," and they existed "in every community of any size," he claimed. "They are usually known to each other, and are likely to congregate together. At times they operate in accordance with some definite and concerted plan in quest of subjects wherewith to gratify their abnormal sexual impulses." According to Lydston, there are not just a few such perverts; they are legion. They sponsor subversive "establishments whose principal business is to cater to the perverted sexual tastes of a numerous class of patrons."[6] One such gathering place was the Artistic Club, located at 56 West Thirtieth Street in New York City; the Slide, at 157 Bleecker Street, was another place where "unspeakable" orgies were practiced by "men of degenerate type."[7]

An essay on perversion and insanity written by Dr. Allan Hamilton in 1894 places homosexuals precisely where medicine and the public wanted them to be: in "a class by themselves." To prove how marginal they are to respectable and normal society, Hamilton emphasizes the marginality of "sexual perverts":

> In many large cities the subjects of the contrary sexual impulse form a class by themselves and are recognized by the police. The men have their balls where they dress as women even to the details of dainty underwear. They adopt the names of women, and affect a feminine speech and manner, "falling in love" with each other, and writing amatory and obscene letters. In New York City alone there are not less than one hundred of these, who make a profession of male prostitution. . . . Physically, many of the men who I have examined present the stigmata of degenerative insanity, or else physically approach the female type. . . . The female pervert or *Lesbian* rarely differs from others of her sex, except that the active agent wears gross mannish attire, and cultivates masculine habits.[8]

In the 1880s Lydston had described a "homosexual conspiracy" of "male sexual perverts" plotting to subvert and even destroy society. He thus buttressed the view of homosexuals as dangerous monsters whose antisocial activities ought to be suppressed. A few years later, in 1896, Colin Scott sounded the same alarm in an article for *The American Journal of Psychology*. He described "peculiar societies of inverts," whose members "dress themselves with aprons, knit, gossip and crochet," and he unsettlingly observed that the " 'Fairies of New York' are said to be a . . . secret organization."[9] In 1898, Dr. Francis Anthony warned that such secret organizations of homosexuals might conceal a dreadful purpose: "I have been told that there is [in] nearly every center of importance—a band of Urnings, men of perverted tendencies, men known to each other as such, bound by ties of secrecy and fear and held by mutual attraction." Their purpose was to "draw boys and young men, over whom they have the same jealous bickerings and heart burnings that attend the triumphs of a local belle."[10]

Opinions about just who participated in this subculture differed radically. Dr. F. E. Daniel wrote in 1893 that sexual perversion and "illicit intercourse" were especially prevalent among "the lower classes, particularly Negroes."[11] In 1899, Dr. George Monroe told Americans that homosexuality was more a foreign than an American vice: "bad as the practice is becoming in America," homosexuality was worse in other countries. He further assured his middle-class readers that people like them were safe from infection, since such habits are "practiced to a greater extent among the low and degraded than . . . among the better class."[12] Monroe's introduction of sexual patriotism and class distinctions into the rhetoric of perversion tallies with the racism of accounts like Daniel's, which presumed that "colored men" were more prone than white men to engage in homosexual activities. Such texts exiled homosexuals to the margins of white, male, and bourgeois respectability and relegated them to the "lower classes" or described them as being of some "other" race. Through such generalizations, homosexuals, already seen as sick and insane, were portrayed as outcasts as well.

Another view was less reassuring about the sexual purity of the middle class. Dr. Francis Anthony, who had discovered secret bands of homosexuals everywhere, argued that homosexuals were "not as you might think, the low and vile outcasts of the slums, but men of education and refinement, men gifted in music, in art and in literature, men of professional life and men of business and affairs." The testimony of a European homosexual substantiated Anthony's report: after traveling throughout America, he claimed that "he had never been in any country where the Uranian element was so widely distributed and averaged such high-class moral and intellectual types as in North America."[13] These varying opinions, of course, only fanned the homophobic flames; it was one thing if homosexuals were to be found only among the "outcasts of the slums" or "primarily among Negroes," another if they secretly lived among white middle-class "men of business and affairs." Of course, in Europe, homosexuality had long been considered as much an upper-class vice as a "common" practice.

That there were perverted men was bad enough. That women, too, might be perverts seemed to some almost unimaginable. An article in the New Orleans *Mascot* of October 21, 1893, described the scandalous murder of Freda Ward by her lover Alice Mitchell in 1892. The *Mascot* noted that "for several years past, disgusting stories have been hinted at, in which men were the participants." But now "indignation and astonishment fill the land." "Medical men," the *Mascot* reported, had written about "a feminine mania" like that which existed between Ward and Mitchell. Not to be outdone by medical men, the *Mascot* retailed a "story of love between two women—licentious, horrible love." "One of the most beautiful girls in the city" of New Orleans turned out to be "viler than the most lost harlot." Her "vile passions" were exhibited when she approached a "grass widow," a woman recently separated from her husband, and said, "Oh what a beautiful form you have. I wish I could see you without your clothes." Even more horribly, the paper reported, "the widow consented."[14]

3 Policing Perverts

If groups of dangerous perverts threatened society, it was up to society to control them. But how? Dr. C. H. Hughes offered one solution in 1893. Science must assume the role religion had abdicated, he argued. It must act as a mentor to the state, to "determine for society and for the State, what is restrainable and vicious, and what are the morbid and resistless organic impulsions of these bizarre eroto-sexual states." The "resistless" organic impulsions—"perversions," such as sodomy, pederasty, and masturbation, that are too powerful to be resisted—should be made "crimes or misdemeanors punishable by forfeiture of all rights, including that of procreation." The state "cannot be too careful as a protector of morality," Hughes insisted. "The moral pestilence is in our midst. Sodom and Gomorrah are revived and surpassed."[15] In 1898, Dr. Francis Anthony published a paper entitled "Responsibility in Cases of Sex Perversion" that called for an antihomosexual crusade, to be led by doctors. Anthony urged his colleagues to "show no mercy":

> It may fall to the lot of one of you to be the active means of destroying such a school of vice and perversion. Nay, more than that, it may be your son or the son of your intimate friend whom you are called upon to rescue. If it comes in the line of duty to take a hand in the overthrow of such a circle, I beg of you to let no dread of notoriety, no consideration of position . . . come between you and the fulfillment of such a duty. Exercise all due charity, have the suspected and accused submitted to a most thorough examination to determine his responsibility, and then have him removed from the community to his proper place, be it asylum or be it prison.[16]

At the turn of the century, science promised progress everywhere, and Anthony Comstock, whose business as head of the Society for the Suppression of Vice was "hunting down inverts and haling them off to prison," passed a judgment with which the author of Leviticus, Paul, Chrysostom, and Gregory would have concurred:

> These inverts are not fit to live with the rest of mankind. They ought to have branded on their foreheads the word "Unclean". . . instead of the law making twenty years imprisonment the penalty for their crime, it ought to be imprisonment for life. . . . They are willfully bad, and glory and gloat in their perversion. Their habit is acquired and not inborn. Why propose to have the law against them now on the statute books repealed? If this happened, there would be no way of getting at them. It would be wrong to make life more tolerable for them. Their lives ought to be made so intolerable as to drive them to abandon their vices.[17]

Comstock's words did not augur well for the new century—indeed, they echo in the acts of twentieth-century homophobes, as we shall see.

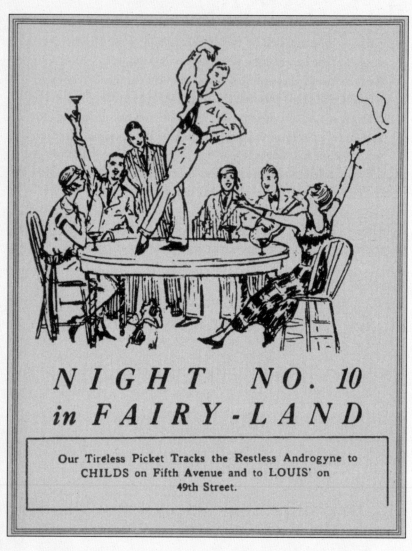

NIGHT NO. 10
in FAIRY-LAND

Our Tireless Picket Tracks the Restless Androgyne to
CHILDS on Fifth Avenue and to LOUIS' on
49th Street.

"Night No. 10 in Fairy-Land." Broadway Brevities, 1924. *From George Chauncey,* Gay New York: Gender, Urban Culture and the Making of the Gay Male World, 1890–1940 *(New York: Basic Books, 1994). Collection of Leonard Fingar*

PART EIGHT

Normal Homosexuals

*Homophobia and Resistance
in the Twentieth Century*

Chapter Eighteen

The Riddle of Homosexuality

I n the new century, American homophobia was challenged by very few. Ellis and Symonds' *Sexual Inversion* included an anonymous letter by "an American of eminence"—thought to be James Mills Pierce—"who holds a scientific professorship in one of the first universities of the world."[1] Homosexuality, the letter's author insists, is not an aberration or "a lamentable mark of inferior development"; it is neither "inverted or abnormal" nor the "unhappy fault [of] a masculine body with a feminine soul," but instead a "natural and pure and sound passion." Homosexual desire "tends when duly understood and controlled by spiritual feeling, to the physical and moral health of the individual and the race"; there is "no breach of morality involved in homosexual love." Passion, too, has been misunderstood: not "naturally" directed by male desire for the female, "passion itself is a blind thing . . . a furious pushing out, not with calculation or comprehension of its object, but to anything which strikes the imagination as fitted to its need. It is not characterized or differentiated by the nature of its object, but by its own nature." Arguing for an undifferentiated sexuality, he insists that it is "unisexual" love (love for one sex only) which is a perversion: "Normal men love both." It is "a travesty of morality" to invest heterosexuality "with divine attributes and denounce the other as infamous and unnatural." If there are "two main forms of sexual passion," then it is clearly an error to extirpate one on the basis that one but not the other reserves "sexual energy for the increase of the race" or that one but not the other gets "the utmost merely fleshly pleasure out of the exercise of passion." Appealing to the classical past, he maintains that contemporary civilization "suffers from want of a pure and noble sentiment which they [the Greeks] thought so useful to the state." In Greece, homosexuality was a "natural, pure and sound passion, as worthy of reverence . . . as the devotion of husband and wife, or the ardor of the bride and groom."[2] Peirce—if indeed he is the author—argues that either homosexuality should be recognized as a normal sexual response, or else the norm itself should be abandoned.

Though Ellis published the letter in the first American edition of *Sexual Inversion* (1901), he deleted it from subsequent editions, perhaps because of the growing hostility to any approval of homosexuality. The strength of American homophobia at the beginning of the twentieth century is demonstrated by another anonymous letter, this one sent by an American in 1907 to the German magazine *Monthly Reports of the Scientific Humanitarian Committee*. The committee, founded in 1897 by Magnus Hirschfeld, a pioneer in sex research, was charged with gathering historical, social, psychological, and autobiographical information about homosexuality. Its activities formed part of the general prohomosexual ferment then taking place in Germany and, as reported in the magazine, they provoked an outburst of hope from an American reader:

> I'm always delighted to hear about even the smallest success you have in vanquishing the deep-rooted prejudices. And here in the United States we really need this kind of activity. In the face of Anglo-American hypocrisy, however, there is at present no chance that any man of science would have enough wisdom and courage to remove the veil which covers homosexuality in this country. And how many homosexuals I've come to know! Boston, this good old Puritan city, has them by the hundreds. . . . [H]omosexuality extends through all classes. . . . There is an astonishing ignorance among the Uranians I've come to know about their own true nature. This is probably the result of absolute silence and intolerance, which have never advanced real morality at any time or place. But with the growth of the population and the increase of

intellectuals, the time is coming when America will finally be forced to confront the riddle of homosexuality.[3]

The letter's writer was prescient. In the new century, homosexuals would gather strength to audibly resist homophobia and correct the intolerance and ignorance of homophobes.

1 Oswald's Story

The riddle of homosexuality, as well as prejudice against it, was addressed in *Imre* (1906), the first openly homosexual American novel, and in *The Intersexes* (1908), the first American history of homosexuality. Both books were written by Edward Prime Stevenson, who, fearful of the homophobic climate, published them under the pseudonym "Xavier Mayne." Little is known about Stevenson, but his entry in the 1901 edition of *Who's Who* notes that he spent much time abroad, "for professional and personal reasons"; the 1908 edition revealed that he "has retired to reside permanently in Europe." Stevenson became a vagabond man of letters; he sent articles back home on European affairs, wrote short stories and music reviews for *Harper's*, and, according to the 1912 *Who's Who,* conducted "important studies in the branch of the psychiatrics of sex." In 1913 he published under his own name a collection of stories called *Her Enemy, Some Friends,* on the title page of which is a quote from *Imre,* an oblique coming out. In one biographical sketch, he coyly hints that he has known many of the "dangerous people" of humanity. Perhaps to avoid dangerous sexual gossips Stevenson lived quietly in Switzerland and published nothing after 1932; he died in Switzerland in 1942, as prime a candidate for obscurity as American letters offers.

Although Stevenson was not willing to face homophobia, Oswald, the narrator of *Imre,* is. In this novel, there is no coded discourse, no pretense that friendship is platonic or that desire is allegorical. *Imre* romantically and passionately defends homosexual love. The story—set in exotic Hungary—concerns a man who falls in love with a handsome Hungarian officer, reveals his secret to him after much agony, and happily finds that the officer, Imre, reciprocates. The book details Oswald's history, his feeling of otherness so familiar from medical cases: "I felt myself unlike other boys in one element of my nature. That one matter was my special sense, my passion, for the beauty, the dignity, the charm, what shall I say, the loveableness of my own sex." Oswald searches for an ideal friend, for he knows that "at the root and fibre of myself, there was the throb and glow, the ebb and surge, the seeking as in a vain dream to realize that passion of friendship, the Over-Friendship, the Love-Friendship of Hellas—which meant that between man and man could exist—the sexual-psychic love."[4] But he is aware as well of the hostility that such love provokes; "from the disgust, scorn and laughter of my fellow men when such an emotion was hinted at, I understood perfectly that a man must wear the Mask."

Perplexed by his emotions, Oswald turns to literature, where he discovers that "tens of thousands of men, in all epochs, of the noblest natures, of most brilliant minds had been such as myself." Life, however, shows him that others "of this same race, the Race Homosexual, had been also trivial, loathsome, the very weaklings and rubbish of humanity." Oswald (like Stevenson, perhaps) is as horrified as any homophobe by "effeminate artists, the sugary and fibreless musicians, the Lady Nancyish, rich young men, the second-rate poets and neurasthenic *precieux* poetasters, the cynical debauchers of little boys, the pederastic perverters of clean-minded lads in their teens; the white-haired satyrs of clubs and latrines."[5] The vehemence of this catalogue is staggering and it includes every homophobic cliché. Beneath the overheated protest, however, Oswald enlists himself in the campaign to erase perversion and effeminacy from the definition of homosexuality. His ideal figure displays an exaggerated Victorian masculinity: "Such human creatures as I am have not in body, in mind, nor in all the sum of our virility, in all the detail of our outward selves, any openly womanish trait! Not one! In every feature and line and sinew and muscle, in every moment and accent and capability we walk the world's ways as men. We hew our ways through it as men, with vigour, with success, honour; our master-instinct unsuspected by society for, it may be, our lives long! We plough the world's roughest seas as men, we rule its states; direct its finances and commerce; we forge its steel; we fill its gravest professions, fight in the bravest ranks of its armies as men, so super-male, so utterly unreceptive to what is not manly, so aloof from feminine essences, that we cannot tolerate women at all as a sexual factor."[6] Protesting too much, perhaps, Oswald insists that weakness, effeminacy, and ineffectuality are found in only a small segment of the homosexual population. In fact, most homosexuals are indistinguishable from others, are the same as heterosexuals in all respects—save for the "master-instinct" that ultimately differentiates them.

Oswald's super-virile masculinity is in the tradition of Benedict Friedländer, a leader in the German homosexual emancipation movement. Friedländer argued in his book *Die Renaissance des Eros Uranios* (1904) that homosexual relationships were the most perfect and highest form of masculine expression and that homosexuality was the highest form of gender development. But no such notion exists in Oswald's America. Once his homosexuality becomes known, Oswald must leave. "I changed my life to avoid gossip. A few months later I started on a long travel-route to the continent. But now I knew that I was to be a refugee, an exile! For so began those interminable and restless pilgrimages, my unexplained and perpetual exile from all that earlier meant home, sphere, career, life." For Oswald, a sexual exile, America represents a dense "blending of popular ignorance, of century-old and century-blind religious and ethical misconceptions, of unscientific professional conservatism in psychiatric circles, and juristic barbarisms; all of course accompanied with the full measure of British and Yankee hypocrisy toward the daily actualities of homosexualism."

Imre has also been touched by homophobia, and it has forced him to don the mask Oswald knows all too well. "He wore his mask each and every instant; resolving to make it his natural face before himself! He bound his warm heart in a chain, he vowed indifference to the whole world, he assisted no advances of warm, particular regard from any comrade." The appearance of Oswald convinces Imre that he has "found the one friend in the world out of a million-million men not for me"; yet Imre's deepest self is different from Oswald's. Within him there is "the psychic trace of the woman. I am not as you, the Uranian who is too much man," he says. "I am more feminine in impulse."[7] Fortunately, Imre considers his "feminine impulse" a weakness and begs Oswald to help him change. Oswald, the super-male, and Imre, the male who conceals the woman within, reflect, of course, heterosexual ideals about "natural" relationships, except that when Imre asks Oswald to help him root out the feminine impulse, he seems to believe that the love of a good man can exorcise the woman within. While this hope may well reflect the misogyny of the time, it also suggests an attempt to challenge homophobia by demonizing the traditional arrangement of domestic heterosexuality.

As a novel, *Imre* is improbable, sometimes ridiculous, but it represents a pivotal and defining moment when American homoerotic fiction comes out, as it were. With Imre's femininity effectively banished, he and Oswald enter into a happy and monogamous relationship, an arrangement that homophobia insists is impossible. Quite remarkably, *Imre* concludes with two men living happily ever after, an ending heretofore reserved for heterosexual romance.

2 The Intersexes

The Intersexes: A History of Similisexualism as a Problem in Social Life is the first American entry in the field now called lesbian and gay studies. Again writing as Xavier Mayne, Stevenson here examines homosexuality—"similisexualism"—in literature, in history, and in political and social life. He catalogues homoerotic literature from ancient to modern times and surveys the lives of homosexual men and women with an emphasis on their contributions to society. Unlike earlier medical texts, *The Intersexes* does not construct homosexuality as an anomaly or as a medical, legal, or social "problem" that must be dealt with by social engineering, punishment, or treatment. It is not the homosexual, Stevenson argues, but the nonhomosexual who must change to accommodate a natural manifestation of human affection.

Stevenson surveys the history of homosexuality in antiquity, in the early Christian era, in Middle Eastern and Oriental cultures, in medieval and Renaissance Europe, and in Europe and England from the seventeenth century to his own time. He finds that the homosexual "instinct is inborn" and is to be found everywhere—in "Military and Naval careers, Athletic Professions and in Royal, Political, or other Aristocratic Life"; in "Distinctively Ethical, Religious, and Intellectual Life and in the Distinctively Aesthetic and Professional Environments." Listing famous homosexuals as proof of homosexuality's superior and eternal nature was a familiar strategy, and Stevenson's chapters are among the most encyclopedic. The section on homosexuals in the military, for example, provides capsule biographies of very nearly every ancient and modern military hero reputed to have been homosexual. Stevenson's purpose is clear: "the notion that the man-loving man is always effeminate in body and temper" must yield before "the fact that in scarcely any other profession—in no other walk of practical life— has the full sexualism of romantic passion been more general than in the ranks of soldiers and sailors."

Such historical facts have been obscured by moralistic judgments, social prejudice, and scientific fallacies. Looking back to the origins of homophobia, Stevenson argues that the episode of Lot and the wicked men of Sodom affords no grounds at all for the assertion that the city was destroyed on account of homosexual practices, or even that such practices were special to Sodom. Further, he continues, "there is no proof that homosexual intercourse ever was or is an offense to God, even to a Jehovistic concept of God," or that the word "sodomy" ever deserved the meaning ascribed to it "in the world's statute-books, and pulpit parlance." A correct reading of the story reveals "a common episode of a suspicious Oriental town." Fearing political treachery, the mob "violated the hospitality that Lot offered to the strangers," demanding that he "bring out the men that we may know them." Going straight to the heart of the matter, Stevenson asserts that "there is no textual or other reason to give the verb *know* a sexual value."[8]

Stevenson's reading of the story as a cautionary tale about "violated hospitality" rather than as an injunction against sodomy was highly original; indeed, it anticipated the scholarship of some seventy years later. His contributions to scientific and social theories were equally original. Rejecting notions of aberration and degeneracy, Stevenson locates homosexuality in a natural system of sexual differentiation: "Nature has always maintained in the human species a series of graduated and necessary Intersexes between the two great sexes that we recognize as distinctly 'man' and 'woman,' i.e., as the extreme masculine and feminine type. These sexes are not physically obvious. . . . Their subtle separation begins at a deeper plane, the psychological, not physical." For centuries "the world has narrowed man down into two sexes," he notes. However, "there are at least two more than our traditional anthropological spectrum has perceived and recognized, each of primary importance," that is, homosexual men and homosexual women. Sex is not determined by physical structure, he insists; that is, biology is not destiny. Instead "sex is determined by the sexual instinct: by desire physical and psychical of one human being for another, no matter what his or her bodily aspects." If homosexuals fall between the extremes of masculine and feminine, then the male homosexual is "outwardly" most masculine, "yet not fully a man," while the female homosexual leans "toward the feminine, yet [is] not fully a woman." They are each "indisputably a blend of the two extreme sexes."[9] Stevenson's theory owes much to Karl Ulrichs' notion of homosexuals as a third sex. Unlike Ulrichs, Stevenson does not conceive of the homosexual male as a woman trapped in a male body. Nor does he accept any formula that stigmatizes homosexuals as less than normal, or mentally or physiologically aberrant. Instead, like Symonds and Carpenter, he argues that homosexuals combine the best attributes of both sexes.

Stevenson targets not only medical but social oppression—the result, he believes, of a fear of difference. "It is true that they [homosexuals] present many traits, claims, theories, impulses, practices, deviations from the more or less normally human. They have sex idioms that repel and terrify us." Homosexual style, in short, includes far more than mere sexual acts, and all of it inspires fear. The resulting intolerance has serious consequences for individuals, to be sure, but also for society as a whole: "The fact remains that a great proportion of Intersexual lives are led under a sexual, social, and moral ban that blots our human civilization."[10] Even though homosexual "love is capable of agreement with the finest and purest social and moral civilization, the most distinct aesthetic superiority, with the strongest religious quality in the race or the individual—these ideas will not be endured for a moment by the average Anglo-Saxon. He refuses them as out of the discussion. He has not found it worthwhile, as a special and ethical problem, to think twice about them seriously in his life."[11]

There is no escaping that homosexuality is "indisputably entitled to recognition as to its individual rights."[12] But Stevenson has no illusions on that score; the law "knows no philosophic questioning attitude toward homosexuality." In the absence of legal reforms, homosexuals, no matter what their position in society, must become adversaries of social orthodoxy: "Each day proves how powerless are legal provisions to lessen the similisexual impulse in humanity the world over: how vain are ethical or religious positions to pit it out of the heart and the life impulses of mankind in each class. Similisexual love flourishes today in every phase of finer or deteriorated character and expression, from binding the master-bond of high souls to being the living of the sordid male prostitutes of a boulevard. It defies clandestinely all penalties, and all social intolerances."[13]

The Intersexes and *Imre,* both radical works, were privately printed in Naples, in editions of fewer than two hundred, and therefore reached few readers. Nevertheless, Stevenson's vision of reform and liberation was beginning to be shared by many homosexuals, and his act of courage gave warning that in the decades to come homophobia would not remain unchallenged.

3 Introducing Jennie June

Another writer who invented a fictional character to tell the story of a real homosexual life was Earl Lind, who also signed himself "Ralph

Werther" and "Jennie June." In two volumes of autobiography, Lind offered the most candid homosexual memoir ever written in America. The first, *Autobiography of an Androgyne* (1918), describes his experience as an active "androgyne"—a male homosexual, sometimes self-identified as a "fairy," who considered himself more female than male—in New York between 1895 and 1905. The second, *The Female Impersonators* (1922), details more of that life, provides case histories of fellow "fairies," many of whom were transvestites, and touches on a variety of relevant subjects, from the crimes committed against homosexuals to the history and causes of homosexuality.[14]

Lind was precisely the sort of person Stevenson's Oswald would have described as "Lady Nancyish." Jennie June, as Lind emphatically prefers to be called (though he also used "Baby June" and "Pussie"), is a character as fabulous as any in fiction, a true fairy godmother to the activists who rebelled at Stonewall. A seeker after sexual experiences, Lind thought profoundly about what he saw as his anomalous position, for he, together with some sexual theorists, believed himself to be a woman trapped in the body of a man.

Lind's books are like overdecorated rooms, filled to bursting with graphic scenes of sexual experiment, perhaps real, perhaps fantasized, embellished with all the trappings of nineteenth-century morality, religiosity, and sentimentality. His life—he would prefer "her" life—is an erotic confessional tale, operatic in its profusion of finely observed sensual detail and breathlessly revealed sexual exploits. Deliberately titillating, the sex is often rendered in Latin for the sake of "scientific" propriety, though not much Latin is required to guess what is being done and to whom. We read, dictionary in hand, descriptions of American sex, of back-street orgies and Bowery love: "Whenever I have encountered *virum* who appeared to me as exceptionally beautiful, a strong desire has immediately arisen *membrum virile in ore recipere.*" We follow Lind's transformation from a "low class fairie" cruising Stuyvesant Park to a high-class drag queen looking for men on Fourteenth Street, New York's "gay Rialto." We watch with incredulity June's seduction of a squad—no, a company, a whole battalion—of the U.S. Army. We are lured into a host of sexual adventures, fascinated and amused as Jennie June in one or another of her various disguises disappears into rooms or back alleys with handsome young men who throw themselves at her feet or, in more violent moments, throw her at theirs.

Yet for all the baroque and effeminate splendor that marks these books, their leitmotif is curiously modern: the quest for liberation,

sexual emancipation, and tolerance for sexual difference. With strik-
ing bravery Lind confronts society's violent response to his person,
his appearance, and his sexuality. He hides nothing, and he makes it
clear that the men he entertains are as eager for sex as he, even though
many of them try to kill him after using him. Not only that, but Lind
takes a very modern pride in his identity, and eloquently argues for the
rights of men like himself. Indeed, he demands that society recognize
not only the sexual but the social and political rights of fairies and
androgynes.

Born in New York, the fourth of eleven children, Lind comes from a
family he describes as "enormously respectable religious people," none
of whom "ever distinguished themselves." Lind asserts that there are no
"bad strains" in his blood to account for his sexuality, though he mentions that a "maternal uncle used to fondle me excessively." Whether
by nurture or by nature, his sexual direction is evident from early childhood: "I had innumerable relations *cum pueris*. The earliest I can
remember occurred when I was three and a half years old. A boy of nine
had myself, a brother of five, and another of fifteen months *sugere
penum erectum*."[15] Such opportunities appeared daily as he grew older:
"While engaged in games with boys, sometimes fellatio would occur
every few minutes." By the time he reached age seven—in 1882—he
recalls, "My thoughts were entirely of boys and of myself as a girl. I
imagined all sorts of flirtations and amours with every good looking
boy with whom I went to school. . . . I would imagine a dozen of them
standing behind a long screen, with *erectis* sticking through the aper-
tures, and myself going from one to another. . . . I would imagine
myself walking on a lonely road and meeting a handsome youth who
would force me to fellatio. . . . I would imagine myself a beautiful girl
skating in the rink, and having a bevy of boys frolicking with me—I
falling down and having several of them pile on top of me."[16]
  Imagining himself as a girl became his idée fixe, but imagining himself as one pales next to his final conviction that, in fact, he is one: "I
have been doomed to be a girl who must pass her earthly existence in a
male body." He even considers castrating himself "in order to bring my
physical form more in accord with that of the female sex to which I
instinctively yearn to belong."[17] He insists that "it was not alone fellatio I craved, but also to be looked upon as a member of the gentler sex,"
a recognition that will eventually transform the uncertain Ralph Lind
into the accomplished Jennie June.[18]

Lind's sexual fears, coupled with his sexual experience, soon create a clear sense of difference and with it the pain of internalized as well as external homophobia. His desire collides first with the religiosity of his upbringing: "[I] developed into a religious prodigy," he writes, "spending a full two hours daily in private religious exercises. . . . I now looked upon fellatio as my besetting sin and until the age of nineteen fought against it as few others have struggled to be freed from lustful desire." To no avail: "The realization that I was differently constituted from all other males, and such an individual as during the whole history of the human race—so far as I was then acquainted with the history of the phenomenon—has been abhorred, reviled, and regarded as . . . an outcast, was accompanied by the bitterest sorrow, causing me about once a week to go forth at night to a lonely graveyard, throw myself on the grass-covered graves, writhe in an agony of tears and moans, and beseech my Creator to . . . take away my perverted instinct. . . . This was the beginning of three such melancholy years as few are called to pass through, and I meditated suicide repeatedly."[19] Perhaps histrionic, this is nevertheless a cry from the heart, one that surely echoed a thousand similar laments rising unheard and unremarked from secret places in other American hearts.

In 1891, Lind entered a university in New York City, where he took up the study of theology, striving to become even more devout. But New York, then as now, displayed a feast of temptations at every turn, and faith provided no defense against desire.

> While walking the street, my gaze would be riveted on stalwart adolescents, and I would halt to look back at the handsomest that passed. If a street car conductor happened to be youthful and good-looking I became almost irrational. . . . When in a crowded car he brushed against me, a tremor would pass over my body. . . . Even in the midst of continuous prayer my delirious imagination brought obscene images before me. . . . I would go raving about the room like an insane person . . . and if it had not been for the lateness of the hour . . . I would have gone in search of fellatio which alone would pacify me. . . . Finally on an evening in June, I arose from my studies and prepared for my first nocturnal ramble.[20]

For his first adventure Lind donned a "cast-off suit" and "placed some coins in my pocket and several bills in a shoe, stuffed a few matches in

one pocket . . . and carefully went through my clothing . . . to make
sure that I had not left by oversight some clue to my identity."[21] Having divested himself of clues to his old self, he proceeds to construct a
new one.

Though his cast-off suit does not mirror the woman within, it is
apparently revealing enough, for he soon encounters one of the stalwart adolescents who people his dreams, a youth "about my own age
seated alone on a beer keg in front of a bar room." Here Jennie June
makes his first appearance, in a scene of homosexual seduction
unprecedented in American letters.

June: What big, big strong hands you have! I bet you are a good fighter.
Stalwart Adolescent: There's a few as kin lick me but not many.
June: I love fighters. If you and I had a fight, who do you think would
  win?
SA: I could lick half a dozen like yer together.
June: I knew you could. I am only a baby.
SA: Hah. Hah. Only a baby!
June: Say, you have a handsome face.
SA: Me hansome! Stop yer kiddin.
June: Really, you are handsome. I am going to tell you a secret. I am a
  woman hater. I am really a girl in a fellow's clothes. I would like to
  get some fellow to marry me. You look beautiful to me. Would
  you be willing to?
SA: How much does it cost yer to git married? Give me V [five dollars]
  and I'll be yourn, or else git out of here.

Despite June's reference to marriage, the young man clearly knows
what is meant. But all does not end with wedding bells, for June's statement that she didn't have five dollars with her "brought the threat of
pummeling." Just as the incorruptible American boy is about to yield to
corruption for less than a fiver, his pals come along and righteousness
prevails. The boy calls out, "I've got a fairie here!" and he and his pals
rob Lind, beat him, and chase him through the streets. He escapes,
exhausted, but draws strength from the biblical words "the way of the
transgressor is hard." So much a transgressor is he that despite having
just been beaten, he feels an "intense desire for fellatio," so he
approaches one boy after another as he makes his way down the Bowery, "staring longingly and beseechingly into the eyes of adolescents."
In the deserted streets he approaches "one or two young dockrats who

were still abroad, but they simply ransacked my pockets, gave me a parting blow, and went on their way."[22]

His first "ramble" fills Lind with shame and guilt. But he warns the reader not to "begin to set his own virtue against the apparent depravity of such as I. If he has not fallen so low as I, it is not necessarily because he is morally good, and I morally bad, but because in him there has been no overpowering impulse to do what mankind regards as unspeakably low." He has, he says, "in my more mature judgment considered myself practically irresponsible for the conduct just described." Lind's assessment of his "overpowering impulse" reflects the contemporary medical judgment that homosexual impulses were indeed irresistible and that those affected by them were in some sense not responsible for them.

Still, Lind tries to find a "cure." He goes to a faith healer, but without success. He throws himself into his work, but study confuses him further, for in his books he discovers that "such a class of males were found among the ancient Greeks." Having encountered homophobic violence in the streets, he discovers a more passive though no less virulent form of it in academia, when a professor assures him that Socrates' "Phaedo had been a slave devoted to unmentionable uses."[23]

With no consolation in sight, the call of the streets is hard to resist, and he searches there for sexually available if nominally heterosexual young men—those whom fairies were beginning to call trade.[24] Finally, he finds some solace:

> If the reader had been on Mulberry Street between Grand and Broome on an evening in November of 1892, he would have seen meandering slowly with a mincing gait, a haggard, tired-looking, short, slender youth between eighteen and nineteen, clad in shabby clothes. . . . As he walks along, whenever he meets any robust, well-built young man . . . he is seen to stop and address him a few words [or] occasionally [halt] near groups of ruffians congregated in front of bar rooms, and then, failing of courage to speak, pass along. Finally he addresses a tall, muscular, splendid specimen (subsequently a member of the New York police force) who continues in conversation with him. . . . The spirits of the little one are visibly heightened. If we watched closely . . . we would have seen the little one throw his arms around the neck of his companion, and kiss him passionately. Finally they pass out of sight down one of the dark covered alleys. . . . When after an

interval the pair emerges again, the smaller is clinging tightly to his companion, as if afraid he might escape.

These reckless approaches to ruffians bespeak an obsession that defies good sense and self-preservation. There is a kind of bravado in Lind's open pursuit of his desire as the "little one" takes one of New York's prospective finest into an alley for love. Remarkably, he finds what he is looking for, and with a respectable representative of the social order to boot. The future policeman says at parting: "You kin find me round this block any time. Just ask any one fur Red Mike."[25]

The midnight triumphs of Jennie June in no way change the daylight torments of Earl Lind as he strives "if possible to be cured of my abnormality." He goes to doctors, who advise him to marry or, as a practical alternative, accept castration on the assumption that the addition of a "good" woman or the subtraction of a "defective" organ will accomplish much the same "cure." One doctor tries hypnotism, another "drugs and stimulation of the brain," for which read shock therapy. Lind undergoes the entire repertory of tortures devised by twentieth-century medical science to treat homosexuality, with the result that after several months "I was rendered almost a physical and nervous wreck by the powerful drugs administered, but my amorous desires showed no change." Indeed, at a convention for missionaries he attempts to seduce his pious roommate, "a rather athletic student from another college." In the dark of night, his roommate apparently yields, but the next day, hearkening to the stern exhortations of the Bible, exposes Lind and humiliates him publicly. Forced to flee the convention, Lind concludes that his "abnormality bars [him] from the ministry."[26]

As life becomes ever more tortured, the streets continue to call him to nightly rambles. Finally, he discontinues medical treatments and, as if to reward him, Red Mike reappears, this time in the company of several chums. Lind joins them. The beer pail is passed around as they lounge in the door of an abandoned warehouse. "I reclined in the arms of one after the other, covering face, neck, hands, arms, and clothing with kisses, while they caressed me and called me pet names. I was supremely happy. . . . At the end of the hour, we adjourned down an alley, where the drinking and love making continued even more intensely." Lind tells them the story of his life and "sang with them in the mock soprano or falsetto that fairies employ, trying to imitate the voice of a woman." However, the tenderness turns to violence; Red Mike and his friends turn on Lind, rob him, and sodomize him: "With my face in the dust, and half-suffocated by one ruffian's tight grip on my throat I moaned and struggled with all my might because of the excruciating pain. But in their single thought for animal pleasure, they did not heed my moans and broken entreaties to spare me the suffering they were inflicting." Half dressed, he flees into brightly lighted Mulberry Street, but is too exhausted to go farther. Two of Lind's assailants follow him, but amazingly they express their regret and assure him of their friendly feelings: " 'You are only a baby' they said, and 'so we will fight for you and protect you.' " Lind is overwhelmed by their "gallantry" and goes back to the gang, who "received me kindly, petted and soothed me . . . and sobbing with happiness . . . I rested my head against their bodies. To lie in the bosom of these sturdy young manual laborers, all of whom were good-looking and approximately my own age, was the highest earthly happiness I had yet tasted."

Though sex is Lind's ultimate goal, he now consorts with other male homosexuals—the "fairies of New York," whom he calls his "brother and sister courtesans." In *The Female Impersonators,* he lets us hear the language of their streets and view the inhabitants of the Bowery and of the more "high class" purlieus of Fourteenth Street. He details the complex choreography of the homosexual demimonde and reveals names, gathering places, cruising sites, sexual practices, even fragments of camp conversation. We meet Frank-Eunice, Angelo-Phyllis, Prince Pansy, and Manon Lescaut. We know that Lind joined the Cercle Hermaphroditos, a club formed to "unite for defense against the world's bitter persecution." For entertainment they frequent Paresis Hall, the Hotel Comfort, or a bar called the Pugilist's Haven, all catering to homosexuals. They meet men in Stuyvesant Square and "cruise" Fourteenth Street, which in "the last decade of the 19th-century" was "as gay as any European bright light district I was fated to explore."[27] (This may be an early use of "gay" to mean "homosexual.") Homosexual men wore red ties to make themselves known to the apparently vast numbers of nonhomosexual men who, Lind asserts, were looking for androgyne love. Some homosexual men brought their female-impersonating lovers to sumptuous drag fêtes with names like the Philhedonic Ball. Others lived together in quiet relationships, envied by the likes of Lind and his confidant Roland Reeves, another member of the Cercle Hermaphroditos. In a conversation about these kinds of friendships, Roland asks Lind: "Do you know of any man-woman who we ought to get into the Cercle?"

"Four," responds Lind:

But they do not realize that anybody is wise outside the young athlete each has selected as a chum. No one but a man-woman or a full-fledged man who has read Krafft-Ebing would suspect them. Their public conduct is always the height of propriety. . . . None of the four ever visits the Underworld. They do not feel the need. Their being so fortunate as to have secured soul mates among their every-day circle has proved their safety-valve. You, Roland, and I have simply been denied by Providence a hero-confidant. . . . One is a university student. The college body refers to his ultra-virile room-mate and himself as X and wife. But no user of the phrase ever dreams of its real significance. . . . Of course they have heard of homosexuality, but think only the scum of mankind could be guilty. Impossible in the case of a high-minded intellectual!

Their conversation is interrupted by Plum. "Two days ago I was fired," Plum reports. "I have hope for the future only in the grave. Some bigot denounced me to the boss. He called me into his private office. As this had never happened before I guessed the reason." Plum's boss lectures him sternly: "The innate feelings as well as the Bible teach that the invert has no rights. I myself have only deep-rooted contempt for him. Every fibre in my body cries out in loud protest against him. He is the lowest of the low." But Plum won't be intimidated. In a passionate outburst, he insists: "A bisexual"—a term then used to mean an individual who combined the attributes of men and women—"has no more reason than a full-fledged man or woman to be ashamed of his God-given sexuality. . . . If your views have any justification in science or ethics I am unable to see it. Although it breaks my heart to be made an outcast and penniless by yourself, I prefer that lot, knowing that I am in the right, than to be in the wrong even if sitting, as yourself, in the chair of the president of the company."[28]

Inspired, Lind determines to "follow Nature's behest" and live "according to the dictates of my peculiar instincts." The result? "I was happier than I ever had been before. . . . I felt that I had come into possession of the earthly *summum bonum,* hitherto denied me, I had arrived at the conviction that while the voice of the world would cry 'Shame' I was acting according to the dictates of reason and conscience."[29] In the course of his odyssey, Lind has been transformed into a sexual activist, speaking for the rights of those whom he clearly sees as his people.

Lind's particular passage may not be that of every homosexual at the start of the twentieth century, but that all of them needed the social mask was a fact, as was the confrontation with homophobic violence. Lind has no doubt about the nature of homophobia: "The sexually full-fledged"—that is, heterosexuals—who constitute "more than ninety-nine percent" of the public "are obsessed with an irrational horror of androgynes."[30] Drawing on the new science of psychology, he perceptively classifies homophobia as a psychological disturbance, levying the charge of "sickness" against those who have defined homosexuality as sick. Like Whitman, who saw comradeship as the sign of a sound democracy, Lind opines in *The Female Impersonators* that "the emergence of androgynism is a sign of national health." An authentic and original American voice, Lind is supremely aware of his mission: "We androgynes who for two thousand years have been despised, hunted down, and crushed under the heel of normal men, have no reason to be ashamed of our heritage." He knows exactly why he is to be valued: "My own is a Herculean task: to be an intellectual iconoclast. To break the last remnant of cultured man's savage, criminal instincts and mores."[31]

Lind's two books were published in editions of a thousand each and were sold, as an advertisement for them notes, "only by mail order to physicians, lawyers, legislators, and sociologists." Whether many of those read the books is difficult to know; their plea for equality seems to have had little effect. The books disappeared, like Stevenson's even rarer volumes, and now only a few copies can be found. Did homosexuals, who, as Lind says, had been despised for two thousand years, actually read Lind's books and take heart that liberation might be at hand? There is no record that they did so. But, like Stevenson, Lind believed that homosexuals must be the agents of their own liberation; as the twentieth century moved toward its midpoint, that same anti-homophobic doctrine would be proclaimed by ever more militant voices.

Chapter Nineteen

Hit Them! Hit Back!

I n 1911 the Chicago Vice Commission issued a report on sexual perversion that echoed and exacerbated public fear, calling the homosexual "community" a "cult" with many members, who engage in
"practices which are nauseous and repulsive."[1] The Chicago report is
one of many writings cautioning people against the dangers of the
newly identified homosexual. In his book of sexual advice *Confidential
Chats with Boys* (1911), Dr. William Lee Howard warned:

> Never trust yourself in bed with a boy or a man. No matter if you
> are so situated that there is only one bed to be had. Sleep on the
> floor. . . . There are things in trousers called men, so vile that they
> wait in hiding for the innocent boy. These things are generally
> well-dressed, well-mannered—too well-mannered in fact—and
> pass as gentlemen. . . . Look out for these vermin, be suspicious of
> any man in trousers who avoids real men, who never takes interest
> in manly sports, who tries to see you alone and prefers to go
> bathing with boys instead of men. They are only waiting to teach
> boys to help them in self-abuse or something far nastier. . . . If you
> should be so situated that you find yourself in bed with a man,

keep awake with your eyes on something you can hit him with. At
the slightest word or act out of the way, HIT him.[2]

Writers like Howard helped perpetuate the dread of effeminate homosexual predators whose special predilection was the molestation of
boys and who had to be destroyed. Howard's particularly blunt exhortation—"HIT him"—was prompted most likely by a widespread sense
that homosexuality was on the increase.

1 Strike

World War I had expanded the sense of homosexual community as
American homosexuals met like-minded men and women in Europe.
But as that sexual community became more open, homophobic studies
of homosexuality, some originating in Europe, entered popular American culture. One of these, Alfred Adler's essay "The Homosexual Problem," which appeared in English translation in 1917, reinforced the
prevailing image of the sinister homosexual. Adler, with Jung and
Freud, was an exponent of psychoanalytic theory, so his assertions that
homosexuals were not simply more visible than formerly but more
numerous carried the weight of the new science. "Like a specter the
condition of homosexuality rises up in society," he warned, and "in
defiance of everything the number of perverts is on the increase." Still,
Adler assured his readers, "the barriers of society against the toleration
of perversion remain unshaken," for these barriers are built upon "the
safeguards and disinclinations of normal feelings."

Homosexuals, Adler explained, deny the "popular will," show "an
active hostility to society," and are ready to take "hostile measures"
against the "requirements of social life," including the "normal sexual
act" and the ideal of the family. The homosexual feels "inferior to
women"; indeed, male homosexuality is a "flight from women." His
other attributes include "low self-esteem," lack of "constraint," and
"cowardice." Although the homosexual attempts to justify his perversion by establishing "the irresponsibility of his conduct," Adler had
personally observed a "sinister often well concealed obstinacy," which
revealed the homosexual's unwillingness to be "cured." The only "con-
cession" that society ought to make to the homosexual is to advocate
"concealment."[3] Adler's diatribe, another example of homophobia
masquerading as science, includes the many pejoratives that would be

leveled against homosexuals after the First World War: inferior, cowardly, hostile, lacking constraint, fearful of women.

The dangerous increase in homosexuality, a problem not only for the doctor in his library but for decent folk on the streets, is a recurrent theme in American writings as well. One Dr. E. S. Shepherd observed in 1918 that "our streets and beaches are overrun by male prostitutes (fairies)." He argued that "intermediates" should not be judged by their "lowest manifestations," for among them may be "a number of valuable citizens." And indeed, science might yet discover a way to "put us in a position to salvage" many homosexuals who are now "socially worthless." Shepherd was rebutting a Dr. William Robinson, who had declared that homosexuality was a "sign of degeneracy" and suggested that society might be better off if homosexuals were eliminated.[4] Shepherd allowed that "one is frequently tempted to agree," except that "such wholesale elimination" might remove "a number of valuable citizens."[5] Shepherd's apparent sympathy did not conceal his presumption that most homosexuals were socially worthless, a notion that prevailed throughout the twenties and thirties.

Following the First World War, the military was especially exercised by the social damage done by inverts. In a 1918 essay, "Homosexuality—A Military Menace," Dr. Albert Abrams pointed out that "in recruiting the elements which make up our invincible army we cannot ignore what . . . will militate against the combative prowess of our forces." That prowess will be adversely affected because "from a military point of view the homosexualist is not only dangerous but ineffective as a fighter." Curiously, although the homosexual is too weak to conquer the enemy Abrams implies, his sexual power will nonetheless gain him an easy triumph over the American fighting man. The danger is compounded by another problem. Unlike civilian homosexuals, who are easy to identify, those in the army "may be like normal individuals"; "months of painstaking psychoanalysis [may be required] before the inversion is discovered."

In 1919 an investigation at the Naval Training Station at Newport, Rhode Island, uncovered cases of homosexual contact between civilians and sailors. A second investigation discovered that "the investigators while acting as decoys to trap perverts, had several times engaged in sodomy" and had "used highly improper and revolting methods in getting evidence," namely seduction and entrapment of known civilian "queers"—as much of the testimony described them—and homosexual sailors. The decoys were asked by their superiors to "use their own discretion and judgment whether they should or should not actually permit to be performed upon them immoral acts." The navy did not prosecute the decoys or any sailors known to have been "serviced" by "queers," even though they may have initiated the sex. They saved their wrath for the men who actually committed the "immoral acts," that is, the "active" homosexuals. George Chauncey, who studied the Newport scandal, reports that those who had sex with known "queers" or "fairies" were themselves not stigmatized by the association: "The sailors believed that their physical sexual contact with queers remained acceptable so long as they avoided effeminate behavior and developed no emotional ties with their partners."[6] The distinction made between getting and giving was central to the popular myth that distinguished the "real" and "practicing" homosexual from the seduced innocent.

2 Counterstrike

While Dr. Howard was urging young Americans to "HIT" homosexual predators, some writers responded with a guarded call for sympathy. In his short story "Hands" (1919), Sherwood Anderson depicts the ugliness of homophobes. "Hands" is a tragedy of the homosexual as an outcast who is nevertheless intellectually and morally superior to the world that condemns him. Wing Biddlebaum is a man "forever frightened," whose "slender and expressive" hands convey what he is unable to put into words. Only in the company of young George Willard does he lose "some of his timidity, and his shadowy personality, submerged in a sea of doubts, [comes] forth to look at the world." With Willard, Biddlebaum is able to express his dream of a world in which "men lived in a kind of pastoral golden age" where "clean limbed young men" gathered "about the feet of an old man who sat beneath a tree." This Arcadian vision so inspires Biddlebaum that while telling it to young Willard he puts his hands on the boy's shoulders. As he raises his hands to "caress the boy" a "look of horror" sweeps over the boy's face and he abruptly hurries away, leaving Willard "perplexed and frightened upon the grassy slope."

The secret of Biddlebaum's hands and the source of his fear lie in his past. Biddlebaum was once a schoolteacher; his real name is Adolph Myers. His intimacy with the boys he taught led him to "talk until dusk upon the schoolhouse steps, lost in a kind of dream. Here and there went his hands, caressing the shoulders of boys, playing about the tousled heads. As he talked his voice became soft and musical. There was a caress in that also. In a way the voice and the hands, the stroking of the shoulders and the touching of the hair was part of the schoolmaster's effort to carry a dream into young minds." But when he caresses a "half witted boy" who has "become enamored of the young master," disaster follows. The boy accuses him of "unspeakable things." Soon "a shiver" went through the Pennsylvania town and "hidden shadowy doubts that had been in men's minds concerning Adolph Myers were galvanized into beliefs." Myers is confronted and beaten by one of the parents and ultimately run out of town by a gang of men: "As he ran away into the darkness . . . they ran after him, swearing and throwing sticks and great balls of mud at the figure who screamed and ran faster and faster into the darkness."[7] (Biddlebaum's expulsion recalls, and may be based on, that of Horatio Alger, who was also run out of town for "unnatural familiarity with boys.") Anderson's anatomy of bigotry is made even more terrible by Biddlebaum's own incomprehension of the source of his obscure impulses and desires.

Though his portrait of Biddlebaum may be intended as sympathetic, Anderson seems to see his character's fate as the only one possible for a homosexual. Biddlebaum knows that he must "keep his hands to himself," and in doing so he symbolically and emotionally imprisons himself. Forced to change his name, he erases his desire and his identity, precisely what homophobia demands. His homoerotic dream of a masculine golden age—that vision of a city of lovers, which Whitman had introduced into American literature—can never be explained or made acceptable to a world that reads a dream of pure innocence as a nightmare of perversion and interprets expressive caresses as the touch of a monster.

Homosexual writers hit back as well with outrageous characters who transgressed against standards of social and sexual propriety. Carl Van Vechten often implied sexual difference, although he did not always specifically name it. In *The Blind Bow-Boy* (1923), homosexuality appears not as a sexual but as a social identity, a surface rich with meaning. Indirection is everywhere; nothing can be proved. But how much proof is needed with respect to a man described thus: "A young man in white flannels, a young man with curly golden hair and blue eyes and a profile that resembled somewhat Sherill Schell's photograph of Rupert Brooke, a young man with slender, graceful hands which he was inclined to wave rather excessively in punctuation of his verbal effects, reclined on a divan upholstered in green taffeta, smoking a cigarette in a jade holder of a green so dark and so nearly translucent that it paraphrased emerald."[8] Van Vechten paraphrased homosexuality here; the signs surround this young man like smoke from his cigarette, though nowhere in the text are we ever told what we already know about him. Paul—that is his name—has vague vices that are intimated by language, by signs of difference, but never revealed.

Fully aware of the punishment homophobia could inflict in real life, Van Vechten made his books into elaborate escapist fantasies of homosexual life. In *The Blind Bow-Boy*, he has his superbly named heroine, Campaspe Lorillard, wittily confront homophobia as she reads Waldo Frank's homoerotic but also homophobic novel *The Dark Mother* (1920), in which the male villain seems to have an erotic interest in the innocent hero:

> She opened the book and read a sentence or two. Then with some impatience, she tossed the volume aside. Why, she wondered, did authors write in this uncivilized and unsophisticated manner? How was it possible to read an author who never laughed? For it was only behind laughter that true tragedy could lie concealed, and only the ironic author who could awaken the deeper emotions. The true tragedies of life were either ridiculous or sordid. The only way to get the sense of this absurd, contradictory, and perverse existence into a book was to withdraw entirely from reality. The artist who feels the most poignantly the bitterness of life wears a persistent and sardonic smile.[9]

The signs of difference are as thick here as around Paul—homosexuality is absurd, perverse, contradictory, and best approached through irony and a pose of sardonic detachment. In short, homosexuality is most effectively communicated by the mechanisms of camp, which focus not on the transcendent or the profound, but on the surface sublime, so as to make real life—life in a homophobic world—unreal and therefore bearable.

Another challenge to homophobia was presented by Robert McAlmon, one of the best writers of the period and among the first to present frankly homosexual characters. His collection, *Distinguished Air* (subtitled *Grim Fairy Tales*), was published in Paris in 1925; its four stories are set in Europe, the bad Old World, where homosexuals are more likely to be found than in the purer—and homophobic—American landscape. McAlmon's characters are blatantly homosexual and even sympathetic; nevertheless, for their portrayal he relies on homophobic clichés (the screaming drag queen in "Miss Knight" and the limp-wristed fairy in "Distinguished Air"), and it is hard to tell where sympathy ends and caricature begins. "Miss Knight" shrieks: "Whoops dearie! What us bitches will do when we draw the veil. Just lift up our skirts and scream."[10] "Distinguished Air" introduces the "fairy" Foster Graham, who walks into the narrative wearing trousers "drawn in at the waist" and a "coat padded at the shoulders, so that the descending line to the waist gave his figure a too obvious hour-glass appearance."[11] "Camping, hands on hips, with a quick eye to notice every man who passed by," Graham looks back to Smollett's Captain Whiffle and ahead to some of the Boys in the Band. Miss Knight, a near relative of Jennie June, though without June's intelligence, pretensions to elegance, or social perspicacity, is representative of the outlandish and exotic homosexuals who had begun to appear in novels of the twenties. "Miss Knight" takes place in Paris, where the raunchy heroine pursues her passion for what she calls "rough trade" (thus siting another bit of homosexual argot firmly at an early point in the century). McAlmon's use of "cruising" and "queer," of "Mary" and "drag" and even "gay" in a sexual context suggests that these expressions were current at an early date. Miss Knight picks up soldiers, sailors, and assorted other uniformed professionals, gloating as she sits with her hand in their pocket, "My god, Mary, I've got my hand on a real piece of meat at last. Oh Mary."[12]

Both stories pinpoint an identity constructed by homosexual and nonhomosexual alike: in fiction and out of it, homosexuals were now "queers." Gay novels of the twenties rejected the masculinized homoeroticism celebrated by Melville, Whitman, Bayard Taylor, Stoddard, and Mayne; effeminacy and the blatant crossing of gender roles now indicate homosexuality. Moreover, these "fairies" and "queers" are not the dangerous monsters of the moral, medical, and criminal literature, but amusing, often endearing, and almost always trivial, sex-obsessed pleasure seekers whose primary activities are bitchy talk, outlandish attire, and a fondness for inventing equally outlandish versions of reality. Of course, this outrageous style only further enraged an unsympathetic public.

Ernest Hemingway, for example, cut to the heart of homophobia in *The Sun Also Rises* (1926), when Jake Barnes says of the homosexuals in Paris bars: "I was very angry. Somehow they always made me angry. I know they are supposed to be amusing, and you should be tolerant, but I wanted to swing on one, any one, anything to shatter that superior composure." Barnes does not care about sin or crime, sickness or insanity; what enrages him is style: that effective, if effeminate, homo-sexual style. Whatever homosexuals are supposed to be in the eyes of middle-class observers like Barnes—lonely, loveless, sexually inade-quate, unfulfilled, unhappy—is given the lie by their public assumption of easy superiority and confident worldliness. When Barnes sees his own life reflected in this highly polished mirror, it seems drab and lack-ing in style. In the presence of homosexuality, heterosexuality becomes invisible. Homosexuals know it, and in *The Sun Also Rises,* Jake Barnes knows they know it. Homosexual panic turns to rage, and homophobia is not far behind.

3 Disgusting Performances

While novelists were busy either drawing sympathetic portraits of homosexuals or trotting out the clichés of homophobia, dramatists, too, began to recognize homosexuality's box office appeal. A 1902 *New York Times* review of a performance of Oscar Wilde's *The Impor-tance of Being Earnest* found the play "inextricably associated with the saddest and most revolting scandal." Anyone who saw it must "dissoci-ate the man Oscar Wilde from the playwright" and "rejoice in the excellence of his quality, while not forgetting its defect." The term "defect" is, of course, freighted with medical implications. The nature of the defect is made clear when the *Times* notes that "the simper of Bunthorne leers from the pages."[13]

Twenty years later, the effeminate homosexual male and the man-nish lesbian still dominated stage portrayals of homosexuals. Alexan-der Wolcott's *New York Times* review of *March Hares* (1921), a play by Harry Gribble, described it as a "curiously effeminate comedy," quite the opposite of a "Red-Blooded Hundred Per Cent American Play" since it invoked Oscar Wilde and featured "odd folk" who "talked a good deal about one another's sex appeal." Among the char-acters was Geoffrey, "an odd young professor of elocution," according to Wolcott, who does the right thing in the end by marrying his fiancée, whom he has tried to make jealous by inviting a young man home.

Odd women in twenties plays fared no better. The plot of *The Cap-tive* (1926), a translation of a French play by Edouard Bourdet, exploits homophobic fears: an innocent young woman becomes infatuated with another woman whose sexual attraction is so powerful that the help-less heroine leaves her male lover for her. Brooks Atkinson described the women's relationship as a "warped infatuation," "loathsome,"

"doomed," and "twisted"; it led the heroine to be "crushed by a fright-
ful tyranny beyond her control."[14] Even when praising the play's honest portrayal of an "abnormal relationship," most reviews reinforced
the by now familiar image of the lesbian as a sexual predator.

So controversial was *The Captive* that a debate about "sexual perversion" on the stage erupted in the press. In 1926, the *Times* reported
that a commission of twelve people—a "play jury"—would meet to
consider whether *The Captive* was "objectionable and salacious." Even
though the "jury" voted not to condemn the play, Mayor Jimmy
Walker warned Broadway producers that "censorship would result
unless they voluntarily cleaned up the stage." The producers' efforts
were halfhearted, and on February 9, 1927, *The Captive,* along with
two other plays, *Sex* (starring Mae West) and *The Virgin Man,* were
raided and their producers and casts arrested. The plays soon reopened
to even larger audiences, but in March 1927, a bill was proposed in the
New York State legislature to outlaw the depiction of "sex degeneracy
or sex perversion" on the stage. The bill passed, and the law remained
in force until 1967.[15]

Despite the closing of *The Captive* and *The Virgin Man,* plays suggesting same-sex love continued to be produced and reviews continued
to condemn them. *The Incubator* (1932), set in a boys' school, alarmed
one reviewer because "for a time" it "threatens to become a shocker
dealing with twisted relationships": "two of the boys develop an unnatural affection" for the hero.[16] In Noël Coward's *Design for Living*
(1933) the *Times* detected "a constant odor of sin." As the reviewer
points out, Leo, talking with Gilda, "succinctly describes the plot: 'I love
you. You love me. You love Otto. I love Otto. Otto loves you. Otto loves
me.'"[17] If this was not enough to provoke disgust, then *The Green Bay
Tree* (1933) by Mordaunt Shairp certainly was. The *Times* reviewer
described it as the story of "a relationship between Mr. Dulcimer, a rich
hot-house sybarite, and Julian Dulcimer, whom he adopted at a tender
age and has reared in emasculating luxury. The relationship is abnormal,
since Mr. Dulcimer with all his petty sensuousness is an abnormal person. But there is nothing in the play to indicate that the relationship is
more than passively degenerate."[18] The language invokes nearly every
cliché associated with homosexuality, from imputations of excessive and
possibly depraved sensuality ("hot-house sybarite"), to the suggestion of
child molestation ("a tender age"), to unmanly weakness ("petty sensuousness and emasculating luxury"), to a depraved but nevertheless inadequate and sterile sexuality ("passively degenerate").

In 1934 Lillian Hellman's *The Children's Hour* depicted not clichéd homosexuals but the destructive effects of homophobia: rumors about the nature of the relationship between two women lead to social isolation and death. But critics were not listening. Stephen Powys' *Wise Tomorrow* (1937), another portrayal of the relations between women, was characterized by the *Times* as "the story of an evil minded and treacherous old actress who falls in love with an attractive young actress and wrecks her life."[19] A 1946 review of Jean-Paul Sartre's *No Exit* once again summoned up the homosexual victimizer of the innocent in its description of one character as a "loathsome homosexual who has poisoned and destroyed the life of a married woman of whom she has been enamored." From the twenties to the mid-sixties, the theater mostly generated such stereotypes, and reviewers confirmed them. Homosexuals could not hope to find positive or tolerant portrayals of their lives in mainstream drama.

4 Rights and Cults

In the first decades of the twentieth century, there was little organized resistance to homophobia. Though Earl Lind's Cercle Hermaphroditos, formed around 1895, was the first known group in America to announce a political agenda to fight the persecution of homosexuals, it was not until 1925 that the Society for Human Rights, founded in Chicago with a similar mission, became the earliest homosexual group in America. Its charter, granted by the state of Illinois, states its purpose: to "protect the interests of people who by reason of mental and physical abnormalities are abused and hindered in the legal pursuit of happiness . . . and to combat the public prejudices against them." Even though the charter enshrined common stereotypes about homosexuals, it stands as a significant achievement, marking the entrance into American social and political life of an organization that officially defined itself as homosexual. Moreover, the society assumed that defining oneself as homosexual entailed oppression, and stated its intention to combat that oppression. To that end, the society determined to provide information for homosexuals. Its newsletter, *Friendship and Freedom*, was probably the first American homophile journal; two issues were published.

From the beginning the group met with opposition. As Henry Gerber, a founding member, recalled in a memoir, "The big fearful obstacle seemed always to be the almost willful misunderstanding and ignorance on the part of the general public concerning the nature of homosexuality." Misunderstanding turned to persecution when Gerber was arrested:

> On Sunday . . . I returned from a visit downtown. After I had gone to my room, someone knocked at the door. . . . I opened up, two men entered the room. They identified themselves as a city detective and a newspaper reporter from the *Examiner*. The detective asked me where the boy was. What boy? He told me he had orders from his precinct captain to bring me to the police station. He took my typewriter, my honorary public diploma, and all the literature about the Society and also personal diaries as well as bookkeeping accounts. At no time did he show a warrant for my arrest. At the police station I was locked up in a cell but no charges were made against me. . . . A friendly cop at the station showed me a copy of the *Examiner*. There right on the front page I found this incredible story: "Strange Sex Cult Exposed."

In court, Gerber was confronted with a copy of *Friendship and Freedom,* which, it was alleged, urged men to "leave their wives and children." In addition, the police produced another incriminating piece of evidence: "The detective triumphantly produced a powder puff which he claimed he found in my room. . . . It was admitted as evidence of my effeminacy. . . . The young social worker . . . read from my diary out of context: 'I love Karl.' The detective and the judge shuddered over such depravity. To the already prejudiced court we were obviously guilty. We were guilty by just being homosexual." The experience convinced Gerber that the society was "up against a solid wall of ignorance, hypocrisy, meanness, and corruption. The wall had won. The parting jibe of the detective had been: 'What was the idea of the Society for Human Rights anyway? Was it to give you birds legal right to rape every boy on the street?' " This, as Gerber said, "definitely meant the end of the Society for Human Rights."[20]

In 1926, Dr. Joseph Collins published *The Doctor Looks at Love and Life.* "The majority of homosexuals are not degenerates," Collins allowed; he even admitted "to have known many well-balanced homosexuals of both sexes." But as to homosexual claims to "superior intellectuality and affectivity," Collins found them without justification. Though he hoped to convince his readers that "Urnings are not monsters in human form," he did so by arguing that "they are to be the most pitied of all nature's misfits." They might assume many forms:

"people think that homosexuals are invariably timid, shy, retiring, fastidious, dainty," but some are "husky, articulate, self-opinionated and even domineering." Still, there is no cause for worry: homosexuals "are not nature's elect, but deviates who will one day disappear from the world when we shall have guessed the last riddle of the sympathetic nervous system and the ductless glands." That, Collins implies, will be for the good of society.[21]

5 Inferior Human Beings

The *New York Times* first used the word "homosexuality" in 1926. "Heterosexual" may have first appeared in the popular press a bit later: a 1930 *Times* review of André Gide's *The Immoralist* refers to a character's move from a "heterosexual liaison to a homosexual one."[22] By then, the perception that homosexuality was the abnormal opposite of normal heterosexuality was fixed in the popular mind and reinforced by the medical profession. Dr. William J. Robinson, in his 1925 essay, "Nature's Sex Stepchildren," affirmed what everyone wanted to believe: "I cannot help regarding homosexuals as abnormal. . . . I insist, homosexuals are mentally, morally, and physically different from normally sexed men and women." Far from being superior to "normally sexed" men and women," they are "with some glorious exceptions, taken all in all, rather inferior human beings."[23] Writing in 1929, Dr. John F. W. Meagher noted "a particularly great increase in morbid homosexuality since the war," and catalogued the symptoms. Homosexuals are "vain, prudish, affected, and prejudiced." What's more, "active male homosexuals are not prone to make sacrifices personal or social." They "like pleasant artistic things, and nearly all of them are fond of music. They also like praise and admiration. They are poor whistlers. Their favorite color is green." Some "aggressive homosexual women wear male attire, and are often very proficient in business or sports. The passive ones are of the clinging type, who like to kiss other girls." They often try to seduce "innocent girls," a seduction likely to be successful, since "homosexual relations, once experienced, produce a craving for repetition."[24]

Perversely, homosexuals do not want to be "cured," Meagher insists. On the contrary, many "have a psychopathic pride in their condition." Dr. Clarence Oberndorff, a psychoanalyst, agreed: the "male homosexual may be annoyed by the social hazards of his perversion and seek some means for escaping from the ostracism and legal jeopardy, but rarely wishes to be cured when he appreciates that the cure involves relinquishing the inversion." Instead of seeking a cure, homosexuals all too often flout their proper roles. Among women, for example, those "who want a career, do not want to be subjected, and so avoid marriage" are egregious examples of perversion. Through therapy the abnormal homosexual can, should he or she wish to, become that exemplary creature, the normal heterosexual, accepting of the proper role. But "if the pervert homosexual insists on not following advice, he knows society's attitude and must bear the responsibility for his conduct."[25]

Society's attitude was made very clear in a *New York Times* story of 1936, concerning an apparent vigilante action by a group calling itself the White Legion:

> A shouting jeering mob, about 100 men and women, severely beat William Haines, former motion picture star, and Jimmie Shields, a companion, near Manhattan Beach, and drove them and nineteen friends out of town. . . . At his antique and interior decorating shop in Hollywood, Mr. Haines declared he did not know the reason for the mob's acts. "It was a lynch mob all right," he said. "Some wild or untrue rumor must have stirred them up. It might have been some sort of clan or secret organization." Several men in the Manhattan Beach area said today they were members of an organization known as the White Legion and that they aided in the demonstration. Others openly boasted on the streets of participating in the disturbance.[26]

The substance of the "wild or untrue rumor" goes unreported (though the incident may have arisen from an unfounded rumor that a friend of Shields had molested a young boy at a party at Haines' beach house).[27] The description of Haines—an antiques dealer and interior decorator with a "companion"—might enlighten even the obtuse reader concerning, if not the nature of the rumor, at least the nature of the men.

Though homosexuals had made some gains in confidence, assertiveness, and community, the heterosexual world had responded with powerful, punitive measures. Dr. Aaron Rosanoff, in his 1927 *Manual of Psychiatry,* compiled an accurate list of what awaited homosexuals who refused to conform: "Conventional society abhors homosexuals and these patients are in dread of detection, social ostracism, blackmail, economic ruin, and legal prosecution."[28]

Chapter Twenty

American Masculinity

After World War I, diatribes against homosexuality were frequently interwoven with the discourse of patriotism; sexual difference was pictured as un-American, and homosexuals as a threat to the purity of the nation's pioneer traditions. Homosexuality, an offense against the family and social expectations about gender, was also coming to be seen as subverting America itself. As Joseph Collins says in *The Doctor Looks at Love and Life*:

> It will probably be difficult to convince the generation succeeding ours that . . . it was improper to utter the word homosexuality, prurient to admit its existence and pornographic to discuss the subject. It was proper to read novels in which it was treated more or less openly if the setting was European; decadent people in decadent countries. Here, if it existed at all, it could not flourish, our soil is unfavorable, our climate prejudicial, our people too primitive, too pure.[1]

As in Europe in earlier years, war—a time of fear and upheaval—produced a virulent, xenophobic strain of homophobia, one that conflated sexual difference with betrayal of the nation's values.

1 Sinister Decadence

In 1933, advertisements for a book by Dr. La Forest Potter called *Strange Loves: A Study in Sexual Abnormalities* luridly warned: "Do you know what really goes on among the men and women of the Shadow World? Do you know that their number is constantly increasing? The strange power they wield over normal people is almost unbelievable." Dr. Potter looked back nostalgically on the impeccable sexual climate of prewar America: "Before the war we used to consider homosexuality as a more or less foreign importation. We regarded ourselves as the true exponents of the sane and uncompromising traditions of our pioneer ancestors." Potter went on to say that "all those foreigners who were fortunate to have been permitted entrance to our shores, so we thought, were leavened by our practical matter-of-factness. The dross of abnormal desire—assuming that they may have been thus infested when they landed in this country—was burned away in the melting pot of our staunch masculine or commendably feminine characteristics."[2]

Should his readers be in doubt about what "staunch masculine or commendably feminine [American] characteristics" ought to be, Potter sketched the "born" homosexual: "The 'girlishness' of the male homosexual, or the 'boyishness' of the female invert" are symptoms that will "bear watching." If after the age of fourteen a boy is "deeply interested in cutting out paper dolls or embroidering his initials on his pocket handkerchiefs," parents should see to it that steps are taken—"the proper kind of suggestion, gland stimuli, endocrine treatment and direction"—to make "men of their boys and women of their daughters."[3] Potter further develops the signs of inversion in a series of chapters that tell how to spot the "female man and the male woman." Lesbians, of course, are mannish, with deep voices and facial hair. Innocent American girls are no match for "the confirmed lesbian [who] is almost invariably a woman in the full maturity of her sexual powers with an uncanny facility in seduction."[4] "There is no question," Potter notes, that the majority of male homosexuals "have a more feminine facial appearance than do heterosexual men of similar age"; "the contours of their bodies are more gracefully rounded than those of a normal male." Their skin is "more delicate," and whereas "square, large-boned shoulders [are a mark] of the average heterosexual man," homosexuals can be discovered by the "peculiar rounding and slope of their shoulders" and the "remarkable whiteness of their skin, even when no powder has been applied." On the question of "why the invert swings his hips," Potter offers nearly a page of explanation and notes that such a "feminine gait" makes its appearance "very early in life and is one of the most constant differences that exist between the homosexual and the heterosexual man."

Psychic differences are as noteworthy as physical ones. The "average homosexual," Potter notes, "is known to occupy a position midway between the psyche of a normal man and that of a woman." The invert "reasons more with his emotions than he does with his understanding," just like "the average intuitive woman." Because of this womanly character, "will-power, perseverance and dogmatic energy" are "lacking" in the homosexual. But even though "inverts are unquestionably more dreamy and more imaginative than the heterosexual person," Potter insists that "abnormals" do not have a superior higher sense of moral values as some of their defenders have claimed. In point of fact, many of these people are "thoroughly unscrupulous and are absolutely untrustworthy in many things that have to do with common honesty and human decency."[5] To give perverts their due, however, Potter notes that "when decked out in an artistically waved wig, and made up in the present attractive mode, many of these homosexual men are positively beautiful."[6]

Potter sees hope for such unfortunates. To the question "Can these abnormals be reformed by marriage?" he answers a resounding yes. Marriage "may help marvelously in restoring normal mental and psychical equilibrium," though only if the invert has "a will to be normal."[7] Marriage is not the only cure, however. There are a number of treatments that may solve the "problem." Some homosexuals, Potter observes, are "neurotic due to unbalanced endocrines, improper diet, or faulty habits of hygiene." Such conditions can be remedied. Others may have become perverts because of "ovarian or prostatic congestion"; these, too, can be corrected. Even a "change of scene" may "yield wonderful results," but for most, "psychic treatment" is required to cure the "biological phenomenon" that is homosexuality. Just what such treatment might consist of remains vague, but the direction is clear: "Those who suffer from curable abnormalities should be institutionalized and cured. The others should be kept in permanent restraint." "Some," Potter observes philosophically, "we would probably kill." The message of Potter's book, which went through six printings, is clear: when "society at large" has "suffered" from "perversion," science, working with the state, "owes it to its citizens to protect them."[8]

Dr. James Segall, perhaps wanting to outdo Dr. Potter, warned in *Sex Life in America* (1934) that homosexuals offered a real danger to the American way: "There are ten million male and female 'queers' in this country," he wrote, and there is "something terribly sinister in this decadence—in this repulsive suggestion of senility and impotence. It is so out of keeping with the lusty traditions, the he-man virility of our country."[9] By the end of the thirties, such clichés demonizing homosexuals had been firmly established in public consciousness and public speech. As Potter pointed out, "today there is scarcely a schoolboy who doesn't know what a 'pansy' is."[10] Indeed, the image of the lesbian as an imitation male, and the male homosexual as a counterfeit woman, had become fixed in the public eye. Even the term "gay" itself—though used by homosexuals since the 1920s—had achieved a certain currency. In the film *Bringing Up Baby* (1938), Cary Grant explains that he is dressed in a woman's housecoat because "I just went gay all of a sudden." "Going gay" may not have been all that sudden for many Americans, but it was too sudden for the *Times* reviewer, who objected that the script was filled with objectionable lines "like the one about the man wearing a woman's negligee."[11]

2 Cataloguing Sex

Some works did try to counter prejudices against homosexuality. Most notable among these were *Sex Variants: A Study of Homosexual Patterns* (1941), by Dr. George Henry, and *Sexual Behavior in the Human Male* (1948), by Dr. Alfred C. Kinsey, popularly called the Kinsey Report. Henry compiled a dossier of "case studies" of homosexual men, and argued that the "rigid standards of human conduct to which we profess to adhere" had hampered the study of sex in general and of homosexuality in particular. Contradicting the stereotypes in vogue, he claimed that no two homosexuals were alike and that homosexuality was associated "with an almost endless variety and complexity of human problems."[12] Though he labels homosexuality a "problem," he considers society, not homosexuals, to blame. Yet though some advances had been made in the study of homosexuality and some "prominent citizens and leaders in public life" had developed "a better understanding of the sex variant," no such enlightenment was evident in general society. To prove his contention, Henry offered a detailed account of the persecution of some thirty homosexuals as the result of a crusade against vice that took place "in a large residential community." Calling it an action "reminiscent of witch hunting," Henry blamed the surveillance, entrapment, and arrest of these men on "ignorance and prejudice."[13]

With the Kinsey Report, homosexuality entered spectacularly into mainstream consciousness. Kinsey claimed that 37 percent of the male population of the United States had some homosexual experience between adolescence and old age, and that between 4 percent and 10 percent of American men were exclusively homosexual. Moreover, he argued that homosexuality, far from being a foreign import, was part of the very fabric of the republic. *Parents* magazine, a conservative supporter of heterosexual American values, felt called upon to respond to these findings. Insisting that "homosexuals are not born—they are made," the magazine claimed further that "homosexuality is not a reflection on sex but only a sign that it has been diverted into the wrong channels, according to our social and cultural standards." These standards, naturally, "are the monogamous ones of marriage and the establishment of a family"; by running counter to them, homosexuals often "find themselves in dark alleys and dead end streets seeking expression for their instinctual drives in socially unacceptable ways." As for what "makes" homosexuals, both instinct and nurture are to blame. On the one hand, *Parents* considered it the responsibility of domestic moms and masculine dads to keep an eye out for telltale signs that their daughters or sons were likely to suddenly go gay. On the other, the article called for pity, not punishment, since homosexuals "through no fault of their own have been unable to fall in love with a person of the opposite sex." Though homosexuals "would like to . . . if they could," they are unable to have "meaningful" adult heterosexual relationships. Homosexuality "is not wicked or unfortunate since it is often sterile instead of creative."[14]

Parents seemed to want it all ways: nodding to older theories that the homosexual's "instinctual drives" make him the irresponsible plaything of a mysterious biological destiny, the article also flirted with popularized psychoanalytic theory that suggested that homosexuals are a product of home, hearth, and excessive motherly love. The writer added to the mix an image of homosexuals as sterile people whose perversions are practiced on the criminal fringes of society. If the theory was unclear, the conclusion was not: if homosexuals were to be pitied, they were also to be feared.

Other magazines also took aim at Kinsey's findings. *Time*—soon to be known for its virulent homophobia—published the opinions of Dr. Lawrence Kubie, a psychiatrist, who asserted that Kinsey's "implication that because homosexuality is prevalent we must accept it as 'normal' or as a happy and healthy way of life, is wholly unwarranted."[15] The next year *Newsweek*—speaking, perhaps, for the majority of Americans whose opinions it professed to represent as well as shape—pointed out that "the sex pervert, whether a homosexual, an exhibitionist, or even a dangerous sadist, is too often regarded merely as a 'queer' person who never hurts anyone but himself. Then the mangled form of some victim focuses public attention on the degenerate's work." Making an obeisance to medicine, *Newsweek* urged that the degenerate—a term under which it conflated all homosexuals—may be "brought to the realization of the error of his ways" by psychiatry. Morality and homophobia walked hand in hand. "A sterner attitude is required if the degenerate is to be properly treated and cured. The sex pervert [ought to] be treated not as a coddled patient, but as a particularly virulent type of criminal."[16] Just behind the homosexual monster conjured up by *Newsweek,* one can make out the leering faces of other monsters from the past: the corrupting sodomite, the effeminate but predatory molly, the mincing fairy, and the well-dressed pervert ever ready to help boys engage in self-abuse—or something far nastier.

3 Gardens of Pansies

The fears stirred by these magazine pieces surely contributed to one of the most appalling episodes of persecution ever to have been seen in America. Between 1950 and 1955, the U.S. government investigated its own employees, members of the armed forces, and others in an attempt to discover Communist agents and sympathizers. One aspect of this investigation was an attempt to link political beliefs with sexual activity, and many suspected of Communist affiliations were also accused of being homosexual. Though these accusations were often simply fabricated, by the time the campaign was finished, the notion that the homosexual was a political menace had been added to all the other imputations of social undesirability.

The *New York Times* started the chase in 1950. Reporting on a government inquiry into the percentage of government personnel who had resigned because they were being investigated as security risks, the *Times* revealed that some of those personnel "were homosexuals." A few weeks later Senator Joseph McCarthy, who headed the investigation of suspected Communists in government, alleged in the Senate that the State Department had a "flagrantly homosexual" employee who was therefore at risk for blackmail. In April 1950, the *Times* reported that Guy George Gabrielson, the Republican National Committee chairman, had claimed that "sexual perverts who have infiltrated our government in recent years" were "perhaps as dangerous as the actual communists." In May, a private study by U.S. senators from Nebraska and Alabama alleged that according to the Washington vice squad more than 3,500 "perverts" were employed by the government. When asked by reporter Max Lerner how he arrived at this figure, Lieutenant Roy E. Blick, the officer in charge of the vice squad, said that his information was a "quick guess" based on his experience. Upon arrest, he noted, homosexuals often implicated others, whose names were then added to the list of known homosexuals kept by the Washington police. Unwilling to accept a guess, Lerner again asked Blick how he arrived at a number. Blick explained that "since every one of these fellows [arrested] has friends," he multiplied "the list by a certain percentage— say three or four percent." Asked if this meant that his list included fewer than 200 names and he multiplied it by 25 or 30, Blick responded: "I multiply my list by five," to which Lerner responded, "You mean you started with a list of one thousand?" When asked how he arrived at the figure of 3,500 homosexuals in government, Blick replied that since his quick guesses had led him to believe that there were 5,000 homosexuals in Washington, "I figured that three out of four of them worked for the government." As Lerner commented: "This was how a statistic got to be born."[17] Despite their element of farce, Blick's imaginary numbers helped to precipitate a Senate investigation. By December 1950 the federal government had issued a document, "Employment of Homosexuals and Other Sex Perverts in Government," that, as the *Times* reported, "labeled sexual perverts today as dangerous security risks and demanded strict control and careful screening to keep them off the Government payroll." The Senate committee issuing the report noted: "The lack of emotional stability which is found in most sex perverts and the weakness of their moral fibre makes them susceptible to the blandishments of foreign espionage agents" and "easy prey to blackmailers."

In "A Garden of Pansies," a chapter in their muckraking book *Washington Confidential* (1951), Jack Lait and Lee Mortimer sensationalized the event even more:

> The only way to get authoritative data on fairies is from the other fairies. They recognize each other by a fifth sense immediately. . . .

Some are deceptive to the uninitiated. But they all know one another and have a grapevine of intercommunication. Since they have no use for women . . . and are uneasy with masculine men, they have a fierce urge . . . for each other's society. They have their own hangouts . . . and cling together in a tight union of interest and behavior. Not all are ashamed of the trick that nature had played on them. They have their leaders, unabashed, who are proud queens who revel in their realm.[18]

Once again the specter of organized homosexuality was invoked to whip up hysteria. The "homintern"—so dubbed as a play on "Comintern"—the authors intimated, had spread its tentacles into every corner of the nation: "With more than 6,000 fairies in government offices, you may be concerned about the security of the country." As substantiation, the authors quoted Congressman A. L. Miller, "author of the District's new bill to regulate homos." Miller had assured them that foreign agents were "given a course in homosexuality, then taught to infiltrate in perverted circles."[19]

By January 1955, more than 8,000 people had been removed from their government jobs as security risks; more than 600 were found to be involved in "sex perversion." It was not reported in the *Times,* or anyplace else, until 1974, that the columnist Drew Pearson mentioned in his diary that Senator McCarthy, whose accusations began the witchhunt, had been linked by rumor to homosexual activity.[20] Roy Cohn, McCarthy's aide-de-camp, concealed his homosexuality throughout his life, denying it even as he lay dying.

4 Demand Our Rights!

Paradoxically, the government investigation of homosexuals helped spur the creation of the modern homosexual rights movement in the United States. Harry Hay, who has been called the founding father of the American homosexual liberation movement, describes what led him to conceive of the gay organization that would be called the Mattachine Society:

The anti-Communist witch hunts were very much in operation; the House Un-American Activities Committee had investigated Communist "subversion" in Hollywood. The purge of homosexuals from the State Department took place. The country, it seemed to me, was beginning to move toward fascism and McCarthyism; the Jews wouldn't be used as a scapegoat this time—the painful example of Germany was still too clear to us. The Black organizations were already pretty successful looking out for their interests. It was obvious McCarthy was setting up a pattern for a new scapegoat, and it was going to be us—Gays. We had to organize, we had to move, we had to get started.[21]

In 1950 Hay wrote out "Preliminary Concepts" for a group he called the International Bachelor's Fraternal Order for Peace and Social Dignity, "a service and welfare organization devoted to the protection and improvement of society's androgynous minority." Hay was the only member. However, he was soon joined by several others, and together they formed the Mattachine Society in April 1951. (The name was derived, rather obscurely, from a French medieval and Renaissance group of masked musicians, the Mattachines, whose masks Hay perhaps saw as a symbol of the enforced anonymity of gay people.) The society announced four goals: to "unify" those "isolated from their own kind" so that "all of our people can . . . derive a feeling of belonging"; to develop an "ethical homosexual culture" paralleling "the emerging cultures of our fellow minorities—the Negro, Mexican, and Jewish peoples"; to encourage "socially conscious homosexuals" to "provide leadership to the whole mass of social deviates"; and to take "political action" to counter "discriminatory and oppressive legislation" and aid "our people who are victimized daily as a result of our oppression."[22] Mattachine asserted that homosexuals made up "one of the largest minorities in America today," a minority defined not by sexual desire alone, but also by cultural sensibility and political responsibility.

In 1951, a pathbreaking book urged homosexuals to take an active and public stand against homophobia. *The Homosexual in America*, by the pseudonymous Donald Webster Cory, was the first examination by a homosexual of the current state of knowledge about homosexuality to appear in America since Mayne's *The Intersexes*. Cory, whose real name was Edward Sagarin, argued that homosexuals were a minority group with concerns similar to those of other oppressed American minorities and that, by the same token, homosexuality should not be discussed in terms of the moral or medical discourse that demonized it, but as part of a larger dialogue about civil liberties and human rights. Cory asserted that "there is no homosexual problem except that created by heterosexual society" and located the root of homophobia in a general fear of sexuality. The only possible course of action for the homosexual, he argued, "is to take the initiative in bringing about change" despite the "pillory and contumelious scorn" that were sure to greet such efforts. "What the homosexual wants," Cory explained, "is freedom—not only freedom of expression, but also sexual freedom" to use his body as he sees fit "so long as he does not use the force of violence, threat, or superior age, so long as he does not inflict bodily harm or disease upon another person; so long as that other person is of sound mind and agrees to the activity." If the homosexual "does not rise up and demand his rights, he will never get them, but until he gets those rights, he cannot be expected to expose himself to the martyrdom that would come should he rise up and demand them."[23]

Chapter Twenty-one

A Panic Close to Madness

In a provocative essay entitled "Preservation of Innocence: Studies for the New Morality" (1949), James Baldwin argued that the American obsession with masculinity was founded on an attitude toward women that joins "the most abysmal romanticism and the most implacable distrust." The American hatred of the (male) homosexual, Baldwin continued, and "our present debasement of and our obsession with him corresponds to the debasement of the relations between the sexes." Baldwin's point, that the ideal of masculinity relies on sexual domination over and social discrimination against women, explains why homosexual men are despised. For in the dark fantasies of the homophobic imagination, homosexuals are believed to enact a hideous parody of American womanhood; their presumed effeminacy challenges domestic femininity as well as staunch masculinity, and betrays both. Women and homosexuals are inferior because they are not "men"; they are threatening because their sexuality is not male. For Baldwin, homophobia, or the "ambiguous and terrible position" assigned to homosexuals in our society, derived not just from hatred of homosexuality, but from sexism.

Baldwin recognized another shared aspect of homophobia and sexism: both cause and condone social and sexual violence against the objects of their loathing. Many novels written by or about homosexuals, Baldwin points out, "are not concerned with homosexuality," but rather "with the ever-present danger of sexual activity between men." In them brutality "rages unchecked." Indeed, the death visited upon so many homosexual characters reflects "a panic which is close to madness."[1] That panic would repeatedly find expression as the century wore on.

1 Narrow Sensibilities

The postwar years saw the appearance of numerous novels, poems, and plays that touched on sex and love between men. Some critics of American fiction and culture were decidedly uncomfortable with this development. One *New York Times* reviewer in the 1950s disdainfully referred to the "groaning shelf" of homosexual writing, and others took it as their special mission to attack the "narrow sensibility" that they felt homosexual literature represented. The central assertion of the attack was that good books and homosexuality were, by definition, mutually exclusive. Books—especially fiction—by homosexuals were denigrated as art, their authors dismissed as mediocre writers whose purpose was special pleading for the immoral and the indefensible, their theme rejected as immature, marginal, minor, and often obscene. An American critic, John W. Aldridge, writing in 1951 about homosexual novels, is typical:

> The importance of homosexuality in the development of a writer is always difficult to determine. At its best it is probably no more crippling than a strong taste for women or dry martinis. It may even be beneficial in so far as it frees the writer from the dangers of premature domesticity and enables him to go on having fresh emotional experience long after his more normal contemporaries have settled into a comfortable emotional fog. But the homosexual experience is of one special kind, it can develop in only one direction, and it can never take the place of the whole range of human experience which the writer must know intimately if he is to be great. Sooner or later it forces him away from the center to the outer edges of the common life of his society where he is almost sure to become a mere grotesque, a parasite, or a clown. The homosexual talent is nearly always a precocious talent, but it must necessarily be a narrow one, subject to all the ills of chronic excitation and threatened always with an end too often bitter and tragic.[2]

For Aldridge, both homosexuality and "racial conflict" (as he also said!) were "simply minor issues. They cannot be other than minor subjects for a kind of writing that operates only on one level." The unwillingness of nonhomosexual critics to make a distinction between desire and text, between difference and its manifestation in the world, perpetuated, at least in the world of literary criticism, one of homophobia's cherished premises: homosexuals are nothing more than sexual actors, lacking the emotional, intellectual, and rational characteristics of the complete human being.

Aldridge may have been familiar with a certain type of novel of the 1930s and 1940s in which effeminate pansies or wicked homosexuals received the recompense that society felt was due such creatures: usually violent death at the end of the book. A number of American novels of the period also managed to demonize homosexuality under the guise of "sympathy" and "compassion." Their titles—*Strange Brother, Twilight Men, Butterfly Man, Shadows Flying, The Divided Path, The Dark Tunnel, Dark Desires*—indicate the melodramas of sexual anxiety and homophobia played out in their pages, and also suggest the psychoanalytic theories that shape them. In these books homosexuality is often ascribed to the absent father and the all-too-palpably present domineering mother. Boys raised in these circumstances usually become effeminate or sensitive—or worse, they turn into villains and sexual predators. All are lonely, self-absorbed, and incapable of love. They frequent a stereotypically lurid gay underworld or live closeted in a state of furtive isolation. Their lives are invariably tragic; their usual end is suicide or violent death. If by some chance they remain alive, they are promised nothing but celibacy, which, many of these books insist, is the only real cure for homosexuality.

Strange Brother, a 1931 work by Blair Niles, exemplifies the genre. The protagonist, a young artist named Mark, can bear his difference no longer. As he explains to a close woman friend, he is "what you might call a half-man." In New York he encounters other "outcasts" like himself; however, fearing that he cannot control his passion, he determines to renounce sex altogether. But no one can escape a fault of such magnitude; when Mark is threatened with blackmail, he kills himself. The book's jacket pictures the Strange Brother: his features are fine, even effeminate, his eyes sloe black and narrowed, darkly shadowed as if made up. He supports his head with a delicate long-fingered hand that rises languorously from a bent wrist. He looks out at the reader with a sensuous if somewhat sinister gaze. A sartorial sign of his inversion, the red tie he wears—identified by numerous observers of the homosexual scene as "the badge of the invert"—picks up the deep but obviously artificial red of his full, slightly pursed lips.

Some novels, probably by homosexual authors, did try to offer a less tragic vision of homosexual life, though they did so in terms that supported what society wanted to believe. In the 1930s, Bruce Kenilworth's *Goldie,* Charles Henri Ford and Parker Tyler's *The Young and the Evil,* and Robert Scully's *A Scarlet Pansy* did not condemn their flamboyant characters. Nevertheless, those men belong to the twilight world of effeminacy, cross-dressing, and sexual promiscuity that by popular stereotype included all homosexuals. Occasionally a novel attempted to reconcile homosexuality with American middle-class domesticity. Richard Meeker's *Better Angel* (1933), for example, allowed its homosexual characters a happy ending. Kurt and David could be mistaken for examples of the ultra-virile male, but they seem about to embark on a happy domestic life together, with no hint of death or retribution awaiting either of them.

Between 1945 and 1950, however, nearly two dozen works of fiction with frank and sympathetic homosexual themes appeared, including Christopher Isherwood's collected *Berlin Stories* (1946), John Horne Burns' *The Gallery* (1947), and Gore Vidal's *The City and the Pillar* (1948). Vidal's novel sets out to prove that effeminacy and homosexuality need not occupy the same conceptual space. Its message was that homosexual men are not women in disguise, nor even very special in any way, and that homosexuality can—almost—be as normal and ordinarily American as football, or as the tennis that the novel's hero plays. *The City and the Pillar* was the most openly homosexual novel yet published in America. "I decided to examine the homosexual underworld," Vidal explained, "and in the process show the 'naturalness' of homosexual relations." As Vidal knew all too well, in 1946 "it was part of the American folklore that homosexuality was a form of mental disease, confined for the most part to interior decorators and ballet dancers. Knowing this to be untrue, I set out to shatter the stereotype by taking as my protagonist a completely ordinary boy of the middle class and through his eyes observing the various strata of the underworld."[3] Nevertheless, Vidal ends his book with a murder: his ordinary American boy, Jim, kills the thing he loves—Bob, with whom he had his first homosexual experience. Vidal had always intended to end the book with violence. In an early version, Jim meets Bob again after many years and tries to make love to him, but Bob, in a fit of homophobic panic and disgust, rejects his former lover. Jim then rapes Bob. Vidal's publisher, however, urged an even more violent ending. Vidal complied, but restored the original in his 1965 revision.

Though Vidal attempted to bring "normalized" homosexuality into respectable fiction, other homosexual writers, even while producing some of the period's best fiction, continued to depict homosexuality as bizarre, abnormal, and vaguely effeminate. Christopher Isherwood's magnificent creation *The Last of Mr. Norris* (1935) features an engaging though predatory homosexual villain. John Horne Burns' story "Momma" (1947) is set in a World War II Italian bar where Allied soldiers gather with swishy queens and lisping fairies. In *One Arm* (1948), a collection of homoerotic stories, Tennessee Williams offered some especially fantastic homosexual encounters, including a scene of erotic but literal cannibalism in "Desire and the Black Masseur." Truman Capote's *Other Voices, Other Rooms* (1948) constructed a sensual, homoerotically charged world of hothouse perversion. Even Baldwin himself, in *Giovanni's Room* (1956), perhaps the most famous of all American gay novels, was unable to avoid either the violence that homophobia breeds or the isolation that it creates. At the end, both men, the American David and his Italian lover, Giovanni, are driven to different kinds of desperation, Giovanni to murder and David to what Baldwin hints will be a lonely and futile life of sexual searching and despair.

By the end of the 1950s and into the 1960s, however, some writers seemed to declare war on the middle-class values represented by critics like Aldridge, flaunting the "gay" carnival of homosexual life in the faces of "straight" Americans. William Burroughs' *Naked Lunch* (1959), a fantasy of sexual sadism and orgiastic homoeroticism, seemed intended to confirm America's worst fears about unbridled homosexual license and the threat it posed to American youth. Works like John Rechy's *City of Night* (1963) and Hubert Selby's *Last Exit to Brooklyn* (1964) also depicted America's nightmares, for in these books transvestite homosexuals, hustlers, sexual predators, and insatiable seducers of boys are offered as a version of homosexual reality, though without apology and sometimes without explanation. *Last Exit* presented an especially grim picture of the homosexual underworld of drugs and drag queens. In *City of Night,* the defining activities of earlier homosexual fictions, like the giddy boys-will-be-girls masquerade of Jennie June or of "Miss Knight," are transformed into the brutal sexual preening of the superstud macho gay male whose clones would come to dominate sixties gay style. Such characters' every act is informed by a politics of sexual power: of dominance and subordination. Some reviewers, homosexual critics among them, argued that such books portrayed an identity steeped in self-hate, that they were as homophobic as the heterosexuality they claimed to challenge. For critic James Levin, *City of Night* "infers that the extremes of gender role playing, hypermasculinity and effeminacy, are just two different sides of a similar pathology." Put differently, the book's ethos was another version of internalized homophobia.[4]

If these works attacked conventional values with humorless and even grim determination, Gore Vidal chose quite different weapons to attack what Adrienne Rich later called "compulsory heterosexuality." Vidal's *Myra Breckinridge* (1968) continued what Jennie June and "Miss Knight" had begun, parading the high-camp spectacle of homosexuality as a sublime affront to American social conventions of manhood and sexuality. In *The City and the Pillar* Vidal had written the first American novel to normalize homosexuality. In *Myra Breckinridge* he went a step further and challenged the canons of "normal" heterosexuality. Myra Breckinridge, once Myron Breckinridge and now postoperative, sets out to avenge the sexual and personal humiliation she suffered as Myron. She chooses as the symbolic object of her revenge the handsome Rusty, a perfect heterosexual male. Myra rapes Rusty with an artificial instrument of truly American proportions, in response to which Rusty eagerly embraces homosexuality, which, Vidal implies, was only awaiting liberation from the compulsory heterosexual role he was forced to play. Myra also takes revenge on an exemplary flower of American heterosexual womanhood, Rusty's girlfriend, Mary Ann. Mary Ann falls in love with Myra even though she fears a sexual encounter with her. When Myra is regendered and once more becomes Myron, Mary Ann marries him, despite his lack of certain key endowments. Rusty's rape and conversion, and Mary Ann's marriage to Myra/Myron, skewer what Vidal sees as a peculiarly American anxiety about sexuality and gender.

These books confront and affront homophobia. All describe sex, graphically and lyrically; and no matter how lurid or tawdry they may have seemed to reviewers, all merit a place in the tradition of American gay fiction. The hustlers, studs, and sexy boys who populate Rechy's and Burroughs' books swear allegiance to the highly masculine image created by American heterosexual values, even as they homosexualize it. The drag queens and transvestites of Selby and Vidal reflect an ideal of American womanhood, even as they parody it. Together these authors invert and subvert those values, insisting on their right to restate them.

2 Good Gay Poets

Poets, too, saw the shattering of stereotypes as a remedy against homophobia. In a 1944 essay, "The Homosexual in Society," the American poet Robert Duncan examined the damaging effects of homophobia on homosexuals. His critique of homosexual oppression took a new turn, however. He had no doubt that homophobia originated outside the community of homosexuals, but he laid some of the blame for it at the feet of that community. He argued that one remedy for the evil effects of homophobia was for homosexuals to emphasize similarity instead of difference. Homosexuality was only one of many common human experiences, and homosexuals should work to eliminate all stereotypes, those fostered by heterosexuals, and by homosexuals as well. Medical as well as popular judgments about homosexuals—too often shared by gay men and women in Duncan's view—emphasized the isolation, bitterness, and tragedy of their lives. Some homosexuals willingly internalized this homophobic view and, accepting myths about the abnormality and inevitable tragedy of homosexual lives, retreated into sexual ghettos. The problem for some homosexuals, Duncan said, was that "far from seeking to undermine popular superstition," they have "accepted the charge of Demonism." Duncan rejected the ghetto mentality that he felt flourished in homosexual enclaves and that produced "a cult of homosexual superiority to the human race." This cult, Duncan notes, was characterized by "the cultivation of a secret language . . . a tone and vocabulary that is loaded with contempt . . . designating all who are not homosexual, filled with unwavering hostility and fear." In his view, the "cult of the homosexual" too smugly assumed homosexual superiority to heterosexuals; the homosexual claim to special knowledge and talents was not a salutary but a pernicious assertion of difference. Even though they sensed the "fear in society" generated by "ignorance of their nature," homosexuals have not sought to "assert their equality and their common aims with mankind." "No homosexual," he charged, has been willing to make "his own persecution a battlefront toward freedom."[5]

Other poets of the 1950s also addressed homosexual identity and the problem of homophobia. In "Homosexuality" (1954) Frank

O'Hara described "the law of my own voice"—a law founded in his sexuality—as the motive power of his poetry. Cruising the subways, men's rooms, and parks of New York, O'Hara depicts homosexuals as remarkable creatures whose "delicate feet" may never "touch the earth again" as they utter a cry "to confuse the brave." Like O'Hara, Allen Ginsberg took to heart Whitman's admonition to infuse poetry with sex; and, like Whitman, he wrote about the "midnight orgies of young men." Indeed, in the 1950s Ginsberg became the essential homosexual poet, the heir of Whitman, a celebrant of difference and of unabashedly homosexual desire. His poem "Howl" (1956) effectively put into poetry Duncan's call to destroy stereotypes even as it asserted that the only way to fight homophobia was to affront the sensibility that supported it. In a moment Ginsberg banished the superior pose of the homosexual cult so despised by Duncan. In "Howl," Ginsberg's fairies ecstatically engaged in sexual experiments; they were "fucked in the ass by saintly motorcyclists and screamed with joy." Ginsberg announced that happiness and enlightenment, not pain and degradation, could be the result of homosexual sex. He argued that sex, not philosophy, was the most powerful weapon against oppression.

However, homophobia's official guardians could not allow such an unabashed and explicit celebration of "perversion." On June 3, 1957, the San Francisco police entered the City Lights Bookshop—owned by the poet Lawrence Ferlinghetti, who had published "Howl"—seized all the copies of the poem, and arrested the clerk. A warrant was issued for Ferlinghetti's arrest. At trial, "Howl" was alleged to be obscene and "not fit for children to read." The obscenity charge did not hold: the judge ruled that "Howl" had social importance and remarked that "life is not encased in one formula where everybody acts the same or conforms to a particular pattern." Such victories, however, did not prevent the police from opening a campaign against the San Francisco gay community, whose presence "Howl" had so spectacularly announced to the nation.[6]

3 Drama Queens

In 1947 Tennessee Williams had allowed the offstage presence of a dead homosexual to motivate Blanche DuBois' breakdown in *A Streetcar Named Desire*. Her description of her lover's death forever fixed in the mythology of the American stage the tortured, doomed homosexual who is destroyed by the conflict between his desire and the world's expectations of real men. Williams also invented that other peculiarly American character, the doomed woman hopelessly in love with a man whose desires lie elsewhere. Blanche says:

> There was something different about the boy, a nervousness, a softness and tenderness which wasn't like a man's, although he wasn't the least bit effeminate looking—still that thing was there. . . . He came to me for help. I didn't know that. I didn't find out anything until after our marriage, when . . . all I knew was I'd failed him in some mysterious way. . . . He was in the quicksands clutching me. . . . Then I found out. In the worst of all possible ways. By coming suddenly into a room that I thought was empty—which wasn't empty, but had two people in it . . . the boy I had married and an older man who had been his friend for years.

Williams' female characters are not homosexuals in disguise, as is often suggested. They are women who want men. Yet when Blanche intones her invitation to the innocent paper boy—"Oh young, young, young man"—homosexual desire echoes in her litany. The men these women want, like Brick in *Cat on a Hot Tin Roof,* Sebastian in *Suddenly Last Summer,* Kilroy in *Camino Real,* and Val Xavier in *Orpheus Descending,* are ultimately unobtainable, and sometimes actually homosexual. The women desire them *because* they are unobtainable, and because they believe that they can save them. Without much success, Williams' women, like Blanche and Maggie, refuse to recognize the truth even as they seek to change the damaged and emotionally emasculated American male hiding beneath the surface of an ostensibly American masculinity; as Blanche says, "he wasn't the least bit effeminate."

Attempts to portray homosexuals onstage seemed unable to escape homophobic stereotyping, even when the playwright was homosexual. In 1953, Robert Anderson's *Tea and Sympathy* gave homosexuals a high-camp line to use at parties—"In years to come when you think of me, and you will, be kind"—but little else, for the sensitive young man who is accused of being homosexual by a schoolmaster (himself probably homosexual) ultimately finds heterosexual salvation in the arms of an older woman. When not stereotyped, homosexuality in 1950s plays is only suggested. William Inge, for example, populates his plays with handsome young men whose ultra-virility and tight jeans are often admired equally by both men and women, and whose sexuality is curiously and sometimes ambiguously presented. Homosexual stereotypes, usually negative, make their appearance in a number of plays of the fifties, from the effeminate drama queens of Wollcott Gibbs' *A Season in the Sun,* set on Fire Island, to the thoroughly hateful homosexuals in *Compulsion,* Meyer Levin's account of the Leopold-Loeb murder case.

By the mid-sixties, though, some playwrights saw drama as a forum in which homophobia could both be dissected and attacked. In 1960, in *The Best Man,* Gore Vidal took up the theme of victimization: his homosexual character is destroyed by rumors about his past. While the commercial Broadway stage was still hostile to such a project, off Broadway and small experimental theaters were more sympathetic venues. Plays like Lanford Wilson's *The Madness of Lady Bright* and Robert Patrick's *The Haunted Host* were among the first to present homosexual characters who tried—if they did not precisely succeed—to break out of stereotypical molds. But stereotypes are, after all, an essential tool of theater, and so in 1968 Mart Crowley's *The Boys in the Band* gathered together in one room several versions of mid-twentieth-century gay identity, and their homophobic doubles.

The play was a textbook study of the sexual categories broadcast everywhere in the 1960s, as gay liberation and sexual freedom, effeminate queens and closeted homosexuals, confronted the old morality. Crowley's version of gay life as campy, bitchy, sexy, and sad was precisely on target; it accurately reflected a certain kind of urban gay sensibility, and could not be dismissed as mere sensational exposé. Gay viewers left the theater convulsed with laughter, but also uncomfortably shocked by recognition and not a little touched by anger. The characters were real. Gay people loved the camp humor, witty repartee, and subversive effrontery of Emory, who had the guts to love a black man; the magnificent bitchiness of Harold, whose Jewish shtick meshed so perfectly with his grand queen malevolence; the sheer all-American reality of Donald; the honest, decent, caring normality of Hank; and the excitingly promiscuous and slightly sinister Larry. Familiar too were the hustler, Cowboy, dumb and hot and the stuff of which dreams, though not relationships, are made, and finally the monstrous, old-style self-hating sickness of Michael, trapped by the twin addictions of religion and booze. With its perfect-pitch rendition of sixties gay talk and gay style, *The Boys in the Band,* more than any other play—probably more than any work of literature to that time—publicized for both straight and gay alike a fully formed catalogue of gay identity. The play invited homosexuality to come out of the closet into the mainstream of heterosexual American life, but out of that closet came a group of men whose identities expressed both old stereotypes and new reality: they were up-to-the-minute sixties gay people, and they looked the way heterosexuals expected them to look.

In that sense, *The Boys in the Band* reinforced homophobia—both the heterosexual and the internalized homosexual varieties—just as it tried to engage and confront it. The play allowed straight America to confirm what it had always suspected, that homosexuals were self-hating, pitiable and pitiful, promiscuous, alcoholic, drug-taking, incredibly funny, but ultimately trivial denizens of a minority culture. If some of them tried to pass as straight, others allowed themselves to be freaks. And those who saw the true nature of their sickness were unable or unwilling, because of their disability, to find a cure for it anywhere, so they responded with drugs, alcohol, or promiscuity.

Straight audiences may have been comforted by the play's suggestion that any harmful impact these creatures might have on society was negated by their irrelevance to anything that America really valued, and perhaps by their occasionally witty or inventive presence in certain artistic professions. The play allowed straights to disapprove even as they laughed. And it provided an appropriate moral conclusion: the young men, each more or less damaged, but none destroyed, disappeared into the morning light to live another day with Michael's grim admonition, "If you show me a happy homosexual I'll show you a gay corpse," ringing in their ears.

4 Pride and Prejudice

Not surprisingly, gay books, plays, and poems did not change the opinions held by American homophobes. For *The Puritan Jungle: America's Sexual Underground* (1969), Sara Harris interviewed a cross-section of "lesbians, homosexuals, hustlers, vice cops, alcoholics, sadists, masochists, transvestites." She also asked some pillars of society for their opinions on homosexuality. "I would rather see any of my children dead than homosexual," responded one John Sorenson, a Baptist church deacon and former head of the Miami vice squad, "[because] I feel there is no cure and because of the complete degeneracy of these people. They appear on the surface to be respectable, but they're the lowest forms of people." Homosexuals should be regulated, Sorenson asserted, because no matter what they do in private, sooner or later "they have to come out of that room and they may be schoolteachers. They are mentally ill . . . and their philosophies and morals spill over." Harris asked if the law should include the death penalty for homosexuality. " 'If homosexuality could be a reason for the death penalty, you would see almost a stop to the whole thing,' Mr. Sorenson said with conviction."[7]

Sorenson's proposal to eradicate homosexuals was extreme, of course, but it echoed the historic desire of heterosexual society to end homosexuality. While science experimented on homosexuals, often against their will—with shock treatment, aversion therapy, hormone injections, castration, drug therapy, lobotomy—society, too, did its part to eliminate them. Violence, blackmail, social ostracism, imprisonment, and public humiliation were employed against them, especially if they refused to abandon their "degenerate" ways or refused to remain hidden in what, by the sixties, they had come to call the closet. Indeed, it was in the early sixties—one of the most homophobic periods in American history—that the metaphor of the closet first emerged in gay argot. "Nowhere does it appear before the 1960s in the records of the gay movement, or in novels, diaries, or letters of gay men and lesbians."[8] During the 1960s, when 82 percent of American men and 58 percent of the women surveyed believed that only Communists and atheists were more dangerous than homosexuals, many homosexuals felt that the closet was the safest place to be.[9]

Surveys provide bare statistics. A glance at some randomly chosen writings about homosexuality from the late 1960s and early 1970s demonstrates the hatred behind the numbers. In these writings, homosexuals are "vermin," "perverts," "inferior," "cowards," "unconstrained," "socially worthless," "dangerous," "pitiful," "misfits," "timid," "shy," "retiring," "girlish," "fastidious," "domineering," "abnormal," "sinister," "decadent," "disgusting," "unmanly," "un-American," "foreign," "immoral," "diseased," "insane," "psychopathic," "neurotic," "sterile," "uncreative," "queer," "degenerate," "criminal."[10] This lexicon of vilification expressed an attitude that had not been named; the invention of "homophobia" had to wait until the 1970s.

Perhaps cowed by the virulence of American attitudes, some homosexual activists in the late 1950s and throughout the 1960s urged that assimilation, rather than assertion of difference, was the best road to acceptance. They argued that homosexuals were no different from heterosexuals, except in the incidental matter of sexual desire. Some, however, were impatient with assimilationist theories, which, they felt, only pushed them deeper into the closet. They began to invent new ways to define themselves.

The most spectacular manifestation of a new consciousness occurred on June 27, 1969. On that night, the New York police raided the Stonewall Inn, a gay bar on Christopher Street in Greenwich Village. They expected the usual docile response to what was, after all, a familiar event in New York City's gay bar culture: a few snide remarks, some campy bitchery, but general acceptance of the law. But instead of fading into the Village streets to seek out other haunts, the bar's patrons fought back. The crowd outside the Stonewall grew larger, louder, and increasingly defiant. Bitchy remarks became jeering shouts; hostility grew. A bottle was thrown, a window broken; a paddywagon arrived, blows were exchanged, arrests were made, and suddenly a riot exploded. The *Village Voice* story about the event reported it with a prescient headline: "Gay Power Comes to Sheridan Square." The reporter, Lucian Truscott, noted that "limp wrists were forgotten."[11]

Another *Voice* reporter, Howard Smith, filled out the picture: "The door is smashed open again. More objects are thrown in. . . . By now the mind's eye has forgotten the character of the mob; the sound filtering in doesn't suggest dancing faggots anymore. It sounds like a powerful rage bent on vendetta."[12] Three nights of rioting followed. Many dismissed the event—called the Stonewall riots by detractors, the Stonewall Rebellion by sympathizers—as an unsavory skirmish against authority by a freakish minority. Some gay people condemned the violence, fearing that it would destroy the hard-won "right" of homosexuals to assimilate into straight society. For those present, it was intoxicating and empowering. For the first time in American memory, gay people had refused to accept the law, which indicted them as second-class citizens, as sick, perverted criminals, as undeserving of its protection as they were of the compassion of the righteous. Instead someone shouted, "Take your hands off me!"

After the Stonewall Rebellion, the new liberationist movement, chanting "Gay power!" found its definition in difference, and rejected assimilation in favor of a separatist culture informed by what many thought of as a gay sensibility. The notion of a gay sensibility, which could be identified in life and in literature, in art, even in preferences concerning décor, suggested the possibility that gay people might have a history as well as a shared sexuality. From this conviction gay activism was born.

Antigay protesters express their views at the funeral of Matthew Shepard at St. Mark's Episcopal Church, Friday, October 16, 1998, in Casper, Wyoming. AP photo/Michael S. Green

Epilogue

The Last Acceptable Prejudice

In the decades since Stonewall, some of the promise of that electric time has been fulfilled. Identity became an issue; in the 1980s, the "gay people" of the 1970s became "lesbians and gay men." In the 1990s out "queers" challenged society—and disturbed some now old-fashioned "gays"—by including transgendered and bisexual people under the rubric of difference. Buff and brawny "men for men" contact one another on the Internet, exercise in all-gay gyms, or peer out from gay and straight magazines and fashion ads, muscles toned, complexions perfect, the very image of the all-American male. Lesbians—both lipstick and butch—walk arm-in-arm in the streets. Far-out queers at academic conferences try to define a "postgay" world. Traditional suit-and-tie gays and domesticated Republican male couples vie with their straight middle-class neighbors as to which can be assimilated more quickly into consumer culture. The North American Man-Boy Love Association still makes everyone uncomfortable. The Sisters of Perpetual Indulgence—men in the habit—bless "us" even as they outrage "them." Drag queens appear on every talk show, and funny and happy gay or lesbian characters make sitcoms bearable.

The changes go deeper than lifestyle. The first decade of activism saw tremendous strides in gay and lesbian liberation. Now gay advocates monitor and challenge homophobia on every front. Antigay legal initiatives brought by city, state, or federal agencies are challenged in the courts. Political action groups mount successful campaigns to elect lesbians and gay men to every level of government. Lesbians and gay men confront the crisis of AIDS through charitable and educational initiatives and by the continued pressure of public activism. Religious groups within the established churches are vigilant in confronting homophobia where it has long had its habitation. If the national media have rarely been a congenial forum for gay people, advocates have created their own forum in the gay and lesbian press. Gay men and lesbians have occasionally begun to appear in the popular media in roles other than the tragic victim, the predatory lesbian, or the eccentric odd man out.

The very notion of gay identity has been theorized and challenged by a body of political, literary, and critical work. In this project of historical reevaluation, a rich tradition has been discovered and claimed, its value upheld against the academy's denial of that history and its impulse to trivialize it or treat its study as a form of special pleading, not serious scholarship. Investigations of gay life in early twentieth-century New York, of lesbian texts and writers in modern Europe, of homosexuality in nineteenth- and twentieth-century English and American literature stand next to studies of Greek homosexuality, and of homosexual behavior and literature in Europe's Middle Ages and the Renaissance.

The terminology of sexuality has come under scrutiny. Many insist that "homosexuality" itself needs redefinition: for some a transhistorical category recognizable at all times in all places, homosexuality to others assumes distinct forms at specific historical moments; thus "gay" and "lesbian" refer only to the modern homosexual, since they incorporate the medical and scientific paradigms of recent times. Some contemporary theory urges that we abandon any notion of a fixed gay and lesbian "sexual identity"—an idea ascendant since Stonewall—in favor of a politics of "difference" in which "gay" and "lesbian" identity is constantly renegotiated by race, class, and gender, and may at times be better defined by "queer" or "transgendered."

Nothing signals the shifting perception and self-perception of homosexuality as vividly as the changing fortunes of the words "queer" and "gay." In his "Notes on Homosexuality" (1913), Dr. Douglas McMurtrie described a young homosexual as having been "regarded as 'queer' by his classmates." During the 1920s, many homosexual men used the term to distinguish themselves from "fairies"—a term in use since the late nineteenth century—or from "faggots" or "pansies," as effeminate homosexuals were called in the 1920s and 1930s.[1] By the 1940s, "gay"—though current since the 1920s—had became the term favored by homosexual men, and "queer" fell into increasing disfavor. "The word 'queer' is becoming more derogatory," reported Will Finch in a 1951 diary recounting his emergence into New York homosexual life in the 1930s. "Queer" was "less and less used . . . by the homosexual[s], especially the younger ones."[2] Even as gay people used it less, the term appeared increasingly in the media as synonymous with "deviate" and "pervert." By the 1960s and into the liberation years of the 1970s and 1980s, "queer" had been effectively banished from homosexual speech, replaced by "gay," and then in the 1990s by "gay and lesbian." The nineties also saw, among some academics and younger, more radical gay people, the rejection of "gay" in favor of "queer," now co-opted and used to reflect a spectrum of variant sexualities—gay, lesbian, transgendered, transsexual, and bisexual. But among most homosexuals, the primacy of "gay" has yet to be seriously challenged.

Since Stonewall, lesbians and gay men have celebrated their increased public presence, as well as the effrontery, subversion, and difference of queer style and politics. They now challenge homophobia by chanting, "We're queer, we're here, get used to it." No longer anxious to assimilate, no longer interested in self-definitions bounded by the sexual and stylistic ghettos of the 1980s, or the emotional and intellectual limits inscribed within the idea of "sexual identity," lesbians, gay people, queer people—including those who occupy the most contested sites, the "bisexual" and "transgendered"—now celebrate difference.

1 Homophobia

But the new confidence and social visibility of homosexuals in American life have by no means conquered homophobia. Indeed, it stands as the last acceptable prejudice. In July 1993, *Newsweek* ran a report on American sexual diversity, in which homosexuality was positively discussed. One outraged reader responded: "Homosexuality is abnormal behavior. In no way, shape, or form is it a moral equivalent of heterosexuality. If this makes me a homophobe, I wear the label with pride."[3] She was not alone.

As activist gay people battled homophobia, homophobes fought the social acceptance of homosexuality. Determined to protest any attempt to change traditionally antihomosexual positions, homophobes made their voices heard in houses of worship, science and medicine, and law enforcement. Religious institutions have always considered homosexual practice a matter for discipline, though some groups have made reforms. The Episcopal Church, for example, looks kindly on homosexuals, informally sponsoring gay religious groups, such as Integrity; some Episcopal priests perform "ceremonies of union" between gay couples. Some Reform Jewish groups sponsor gay synagogues and even support the right of gays and lesbians to enjoy civil marriage.[4] The United Church of Christ allows noncelibate homosexuals to be ordained. The United Methodist Church, while insisting that it does not "condone the practice of homosexuality and consider[s] this practice inconsistent with Christian teaching," nevertheless concedes that homosexuals are people of "sacred worth."[5]

For the most part, however, practicing homosexuals are not welcomed at God's table. The Roman Catholic Church continues to treat homosexuality as a violation of "moral" and "natural" law. An article in the Vatican's official newspaper, for example, urged Christians not to support political candidates who endorse same-sex marriages. The author, one Reverend Gino Concetti, insisted that all who support such candidates are open to "moral censure," since homosexual marriage would "undermine the foundation of the family model upon which human civilization was built." Concetti drew on the authority of Pope John Paul II, who has called such marriages catalysts for "moral disorder": "If the unions of homosexuals are a moral disorder, neither can they ever be legitimate on the legal or civil level."[6]

Like conservative Catholics, most conservative Protestants (as well as Orthodox Jews) condemn homosexuality on the basis of the biblical prohibition. They argue that practicing homosexuals, having willfully chosen perversion, stand outside the divinely created natural order. So long as they persist in engaging in homosexual acts, they will be foreclosed from God's grace. While claiming to hate the sin but love the sinner, most conservative religious sects do the latter only if the homosexual agrees to reject the "homosexual lifestyle." That rejection can take many forms. Heterosexual marriage is one prescription for sexual salvation. Once homosexuals are, as it were, out of practice, they will supposedly cease to be homosexual. The practice of heterosexuality washes away homosexuality as baptism does sin. Homosexuals unable to find suitable partners can still achieve forgiveness, either through abstinence or through treatment by a number of "transformation ministries" dedicated to changing sexual orientation by a combination of prayer and "reparative therapy." It does not disturb the reparative therapists that at least thirteen ministries of one recovery group, Exodus, have closed because their directors reverted to homosexuality.[7] Those who persist in homosexual activity, the conservatives affirm, deserve the judgment that God has surely intended for them.

Religious homophobes use any means that come to hand to punish homosexuals on earth, while confidently proclaiming that God's last judgment will fall upon them from heaven. And numerous religious leaders have preached against homosexuals from the pulpit, excoriated them in the media, initiated antigay programs in the schools, sponsored and funded attacks on their rights in the courts and the legislature. They have condoned—by silence—violence against homosexuals; some extreme sectarian homophobes actually incite and participate in antihomosexual violence. Some have even advocated a return to ancient punishments. George Grant, in *Legislating Immorality: The Homosexual Movement Comes out of the Closet* (1993), approvingly cites biblical and historical precedents for the execution of homosexuals. "Sadly," as Grant notes, "the 20th century saw this remarkable 2,000-year-old commitment suddenly dissipate."[8] Grant's opinions are not unique. The antigay preacher Reverend Fred Phelps, prompted by the death penalty given one of the men who bombed the Federal Building in Oklahoma City in 1995, announced that "homosexuals, also, should have the death penalty."[9] A Topeka, Kansas, religious organization that holds antigay demonstrations near the funerals of people who have died from AIDS carries placards asserting, "Gays Deserve to Die."

Perhaps in obedience to injunctions like this, a religious group calling itself STRAIGHT (Society to Remove All Immoral Gross Homosexual Trash) has dedicated itself to the cause of a "fag free America," and a Southern Baptist leader has threatened "the wrath of God on our nation if the government pursues civil rights for homosexuals." In the 1990s a bomb exploded in a lesbian bar in Atlanta, injuring a number of patrons; in Washington, five black gay men were murdered by someone authorities believe to be an antigay serial killer; two lesbians in Oregon were murdered "execution style," and the murder rate of gay men in Texas has risen so high that a magazine article in *Vanity Fair* refers to "The Killing Fields."[10] The murder of Matthew Shepard—bound, tied to a fence, and beaten to death with a pistol by two men on a bleak winter night in 1998 in Wyoming because he was gay—was celebrated by a Kansas minister who praised God for the murder on his Web site, godhatesfags.com.

Not every homophobe relies on religious doctrine. Many turn to science instead. Pointing to homosexuals' "abnormal" sexual practices, the real or imagined promiscuity of the "homosexual lifestyle," or their supposed gender-role confusion or effeminate manner, they argue that homosexuals should be classified as psychological deviants and urged—or compelled—to seek treatment. In this perspective, homosexuality is not a sin but a psychological fault, neither a choice nor an inherent condition, but the result of something going terribly awry in early childhood. As Charles Socarides, a conservative psychiatrist and author of *Homosexuality: A Freedom Too Far* (1995) puts it: homosexuality is a "neurotic adaptation" resulting from "smothering mothers and abdicating fathers."[11] There are several variations on the theme that nurture is at fault, and although the American Psychiatric Association removed homosexuality from its official list of mental illnesses in 1973, a number of vocal practitioners still insist that homosexuality is a sickness, which can be cured through counseling or extensive psychoanalysis.

Other homophobes look to the law to control—and to criminalize—homosexuals, enlisting what could be called official or state-sponsored homophobia. For them, homosexuals pose an imminent—and constantly growing—danger to the institutions of society. Many claim that the government has the right and the duty to control homosexuals, to cast a watchful eye over their private as well as public activities, and to punish them for their sexual infractions. This attitude has infected even the U.S. Supreme Court, which in 1986 heard the case of *Bowers v. Hardwick,* brought under a Georgia law that defined as "sodomy" and declared criminal "any sexual act involving the sex organs of one person and the mouth or anus of another."[12] That is, anyone, male or female, heterosexual or homosexual, could be prosecuted as a sodomite. In *Bowers v. Hardwick* the person discovered in such an act—Hardwick—was a homosexual; the act took place in his home. The illegal entry of police into his bedroom brought the case to the attention of gay civil rights lawyers, who argued that Hardwick's rights as an individual—not as a homosexual—had been violated. To much shock and outrage, the Supreme Court ruled that the invasion of Hardwick's privacy was justified on the grounds that what the court called "homosexual sodomy" was not protected even in private, because "the majority of the electorate of Georgia" believed "that homosexual sodomy is immoral."[13] Though the Georgia sodomy statute does not penalize homosexuals per se, and though Hardwick did not appear before the court *as* a homosexual, it was as a homosexual that he was judged. His homosexuality as much as his homosexual activity figured in the decision of the court, which essentially asserted that no fundamental right of privacy attaches to consensual homosexual sodomy.[14]

On behalf of its armed forces, the U.S. government has also translated homophobia into law. Evidence of homosexual acts or of homosexuality had always been a legal reason for dishonorable discharge from the armed services. In 1996 the federal government allowed homosexuals to serve on the following terms: they would not be asked about their orientation, but they must not state it—the now infamous "don't ask; don't tell" compromise. Under this law, uniformed homosexuals must continue to hide if they wish to continue to serve. Obviously, the "don't ask; don't tell" policy is blatantly discriminatory, nor should anyone be surprised to learn that since its inception, witch-hunts to find evidence of gay sexual activity have continued and the number of men and women discharged for homosexuality has dramatically increased.[15] Between 1998 and the end of 1999, more than 1,600 military careers were ended because of "don't ask; don't tell," and harassment of gay soldiers doubled. This law collaborates in sustaining the most oppressive kind of homophobia by creating the most oppressed kind of homosexuals: forced to be both invisible and silent.

Homophobia is especially evident in antihomosexual legislation, such as anti–gay rights initiatives, which deny to homosexuals the rights granted to other citizens. Bills prohibiting same-sex marriages have been introduced in more than half the state legislatures. In 1996 federal legislators passed, and the president signed, the "Defense of Marriage Act" (DOMA). DOMA turns heterosexuality into law. It declares that, legally, marriage may be defined only as the union of one man and one woman. Its effect is to ban same-sex marriage in the United States. Same-sex marriage would give to some homosexuals a chance to solemnize a lifelong union. That is the emotional and spiritual issue. Legally recognized same-sex marriage would obtain for gay and lesbian partners the legal benefits enjoyed by heterosexual couples, which they are now denied. That is the legal issue. The moral issue is that the Defense of Marriage Act—like all attempts to deny same-sex couples or gay or lesbian individuals equal rights—valorizes blatant heterosexism even as it promotes homophobia.

In 1999, the Arizona legislature considered a bill to bar domestic partner benefits and strip them from gay couples who already enjoyed them. Judicial decisions favoring gay marriage have been handed down in Hawaii and Alaska; but in both states, popular initiatives effectively overturned the courts' decision. Nearly two-thirds of each state's voters chose to uphold only heterosexual marriage. A ruling by the Vermont Supreme Court in December 1999 sweepingly declared that under the state's constitution the Vermont legislature must legalize gay marriage or offer gay couples the benefits that heterosexual couples enjoy. Strangely, the court was unwilling to rule that gay people should be given marriage licenses. Instead, it handed the choice to the state legislature—that is, in effect, to the voters. By millennium's end, thirty state legislatures had enacted laws against gay marriage, and antigay groups in twenty other states were moving to introduce statutes against both gay marriage and domestic partnerships benefits.[16] Maine recently attempted to reverse a state law that prohibited discrimination against gay people in housing and employment. Forty states still allow employers to fire homosexuals summarily.[17]

A much decorated and honored officer loses her commission on the grounds that homosexuals who reveal the fact are no longer fit to serve; a lesbian couple is denied custody of a child, who goes to the abusive father; the inheritance of the surviving partner of a long-term gay relationship is challenged by a distant and hostile family. The murderer of a gay man claims outraged manhood, and homophobia itself, as a defense: "Being a verry [sic] drunk homophobik [sic] I flipped out and began to pistol whip the fag with my gun."[18] When homophobia taints the law, the government's claim to represent all of the people is fatally vitiated; only some of the freedoms available to the heterosexual many are available to the homosexual few.

2 Prancing Activists

For students of homophobia—and most gay people are such students, however unwilling—the evidence of prejudice is everywhere. In June 1995, as gay people celebrated the anniversary of the Stonewall Rebellion, the *New York Post* published an editorial headlined "Saying No to the Gay Crusade." It praised a court decision to exclude gay groups from the St. Patrick's Day parade and argued that "there are plenty of other parades in which gay activists can prance about to their heart's content"; they should not use the St. Patrick's Day parade in "a deliberate attempt to secure legitimacy for a lifestyle millions of Americans consider unnatural and unhealthy." Though homosexuals "should not be subjected to illegal discrimination," the *Post* admits, yet the decision of the court has "significance" that "extends beyond constitutional law," since "society has sound reason not to treat their relationships as morally equivalent to heterosexual bonds." "In our view," the editorial continued, "the goal of the homosexual litigants is to secure judicial affirmation of homosexuality as a morally valid alternative lifestyle. . . . There's only one kind of famiiy society should actively encourage: two-parent homes featuring a mother and father. Such arrangements are crucial to social cohesion."[19]

Calling upon the terrors of the unnatural and the epidemic, conjuring the danger of an uncontrolled populace engaged in a destructive and perversely chosen lifestyle, the *Post* pictures homosexuals as an immoral minority crusading against the moral precepts and family values that millions of Americans, a moral majority, believe to be immutably true.

Homosexuals are confirmed in this inequality not by mere constitutional law, but by a higher tribunal—the moral law itself—from which there is no appeal. Society has "sound reason" not to treat homosexual relations as equivalent to heterosexual "bonds." That sound reason is the protection of "millions of Americans," of the heterosexual family, and of social cohesion. Such an overwhelming imperative can support a final, chilling implication—one all too familiar in the history this book has charted: to protect itself, society has equally sound reason to take whatever action may be necessary against those whose presence endangers it.

In daily life homophobia finds a habitation in newspaper editorials like the one in the *Post,* another in a declaration by U.S. senator Trent Lott that homosexuals are akin to alcoholics, sex addicts, and kleptomaniacs. Homophobia resides in fulminations against homosexuals delivered by TV evangelists, in slurs hurled from passing cars, in graffiti scrawled on walls, in a discharge from the armed forces after a painful investigation, in a summary eviction from an apartment, or in the loss of a job. Homophobia is a national issue and a national threat when politicians approve it, lobby for it, and legislate it, as has now happened in a majority of state legislatures and in Congress. A homophobic lobby in the House of Representatives has helped pass one measure denying federal housing money to a city because it supports homosexual domestic partners, and forced through another measure that takes away federal money from housing programs for people with AIDS so as to allocate it elsewhere.[20] Homophobia threatens the fabric of the nation when school boards mandate that school districts shall "neither implement nor carry out any program or activity that has either the purpose or effect of encouraging or supporting homosexuality as a positive lifestyle alternative."[21] Homophobia touches our lives when a group called the Family Research Council declares its intention on its Web page to "wage war on the homosexual agenda."[22]

It is in physical violence against lesbians and gay men that homophobia shows its most vicious face and its most terrible consequences. Homophobes in federal and state legislatures have opposed legislation that would punish *all* hate crimes, because the proposed laws would punish violence based on sexual orientation. Indeed, in only eleven states is discrimination against homosexuals actually illegal; barely half have enacted any hate-crime laws directed against antigay violence. Across America, even as gay people registered political and social progress in the nineties, antigay violence increased. In 1995, the National Coalition of Anti-Violence Programs predicted that 1996 would show an increase in violence against gay men. The prediction was fulfilled. Antigay violence rose by 6 percent when general violence seemed to decline. In 1998 antigay violence rose 7 percent over the previous year—even as crime nationwide dropped by 4 percent.[23] At this writing, the preliminary statistics for 1999 are no better.

Antigay violence increased not only against gay white men but against lesbians, gay people of color, and gay people younger than eighteen and older than sixty-five. Violence directed against gay people with AIDS increased by 32 percent. Nearly half of the perpetrators are white males (47 percent), with Latinos and African Americans being responsible for 22 percent and 21 percent of assaults respectively. Street attackers are usually groups of two or more young males in their teens and twenties, though violence committed by males under eighteen has increased by 21 percent. There is also an increase in the number of women willing to attack lesbians and gay men.

Not only did violence increase, but the intensity of the violence increased also. More and more of the attacks were physical assaults intended to inflict serious injury or death. Thirty-five percent of attacks *did* end in severe injury or death, while the incidence of simple harassment decreased. If words were used less, weapons were used more. The bricks and bottles of the past became clubs, baseball bats, lead pipes, and guns. Since the murder of Matthew Shepard in October 1998, thirty gay men have been murdered in America. In July 1999, Pfc Barry Winchell, an openly gay soldier who had been harassed by members of his U.S. Army company, was murdered by one of them, an eighteen-year-old private who beat him to death with a baseball bat while he slept. As the Coalition report observes: "The threat of homophobic violence exists everywhere—on the streets, in people's homes and at their place of work. This means that lesbians and gay men are being attacked by people they know and see on a regular basis, as well as by complete strangers. This reality robs lesbians and gay men of any safe places—even their homes—where they can feel free of the threat of violence."[24]

3 From Tolerance to Acceptance?

Of course, as Dennis Altman observes in *Homosexual Oppression and Liberation* (1971), "Most intelligent heterosexuals reject, intellectually, their hostility to homosexuals, while unable to conquer their emotional repugnance. The outward result is tolerance."[25] Such people probably reject the authoritarian prejudices of the religious right and the conservative right wing. They doubt that homosexuality is "abnormal" and may think that homosexuals are "that way" by "nature" or have come to be that way because of some quirk of nurture. They scoff at the gender-bound rigidities of sexism, urge equality for women, and support gay rights. They are concerned about the judicial and legislative injustice aimed at gay people and distressed by the violence daily perpetrated against them. Many such Americans, indeed, would be quick to deny that antihomosexual prejudice could contaminate their principles. They have gay friends. They don't think of themselves as homophobes.

But even for these Americans, tolerance can be a challenge. An incursion into a church by a gay activist group provokes anger and resentment. A news story about the murder or molestation of a child by an adult of the same sex may make intellect and conviction retreat before raw anger, hatred, or disgust; soon the blameless many are conflated with the guilty individual. The increased visibility of lesbians and gay men is said to have made inroads against homophobia. But visibility can also erode tolerance: an encounter on the street—two women kissing, two men holding hands—is still disturbing, as revealed by a poll that asked people how they reacted to such sights. Half of those polled said that they were "very bothered."[26] Closer to home, too, tolerance is tested: a fellow worker comes out; a local teacher is seen with her longtime companion in the supermarket; the priest at the altar declares what he can in conscience no longer hide; two gay men move in next door. These are tests, and sometimes Americans fail them. Even among the most liberal, tolerance, as Altman notes, is still different from acceptance.

Will acceptance come when gay people are seen to be everywhere, when a popular rock star comes out, when a gay politician takes a public stand for what she believes, when the nice gay boys down the block are invited to the neighbor's party? These things have already happened, and consequently some claim that homophobia is loosening its poisonous grip. Some hope that homophobia will disappear from the nation's living rooms when the family that watches together laughs at the amusing lesbian, the kooky queer, or the giddy gay on the TV sitcom. But the laughter is not always friendly, and there are many—very many—who don't laugh at all.

Indeed, homophobia remains nearly untouched by the other battles fought against social and religious hostilities, against racism, against sexism, against prejudice itself. It is contested, but it is still unconquered. Many endorse and embrace it, like the proud homophobe of *Newsweek,* or like those whose cars sport bumper stickers declaring "Hatred is a family virtue."[27] In 1997, 44 percent of Americans surveyed believed that homosexual relations between consenting adults should not be legal; of those who called themselves Christians, 69 percent believed this. In 1998, though 84 percent of the sample were willing to extend equal rights in the workplace to homosexuals, 64 percent of Christians would not. Also in 1998, 54 percent of those surveyed still believed homosexuality to be a "sin," and even more—59 percent—believed it to be morally wrong.[28] As the new millennium begins, these figures have hardly changed. Homophobia is both defensive and on the offensive, both hysterical and wary; it is mobilized and powerful, championed by some influential and privileged people whose advocacy of discrimination legitimates hatred and gives moral and legal authority to bigotry.

There is no doubt that the roots of this prejudice are deep. Some homophobes contend that since homosexuality has "always" been a target of religious condemnation, of state repression and punishment, and of social abhorrence, homophobia, rather than being a form of bigotry or intolerance, ratifies the values of society and of the institutions that constitute and govern it. This appeal to Scripture, law, and centuries of custom reinterprets the history of persecution as a history of the proper application of justice and the maintenance of morality, virtue, and civic order against a subversive form of sexual conduct and an equally dangerous sexual species.

Though homophobes look to ancient doctrines and customs, it often seems that the horror of difference goes deeper than that. It cannot be explained merely by recourse to faith and custom no matter how ancient. And indeed, the near-hysteric vehemence of some homophobes suggests that homophobia is more than learned (if unexamined) bigotry and intolerance. For some, it seems to have the force of a command of nature, to speak from the deep structures of the inner self, and in these psychological or even pathological dimensions, homophobia emerges as a condition, even a disease, of the psyche as well as a disorder of the imagination, the spirit, and the soul.

However ancient homophobia is, and whatever its source, the fact remains that no matter how visible or successful individual gay men and lesbians become, no matter how encouraging is their social progress in America today, they remain second-class citizens without full protection of the law. In America today, no gay men or lesbians can enter into legally recognized unions, and therefore they are denied the benefits that marriage offers to Americans who are not homosexual. No lesbian or gay man can serve the nation in its armed forces without submitting to a legal test not required of heterosexual applicants. In many states, gay people are unprotected against discrimination in getting or keeping jobs, or in finding or keeping a place to live; they can be denied both job and home solely on the basis of sexual orientation. Whereas sexual activity between consenting heterosexual adults is considered to be protected by privacy laws, sexual activity between gay people, even in private, remains criminal in much of the nation. Half the country still believes that homosexuality is wrong and that all homosexuals are sinners. Across the nation, the homophobia that law mandates, government enforces, and many people and institutions seemingly approve is most terribly manifest in the increasing incidents of violence directed against some Americans, exclusively because they are gay.

Lesbians and gay men will remain second-class citizens so long as they—we—are denied the same right to privacy, the same equality under law, the same protection and recognition in employment, religion, housing, and military service, and the same legitimacy in establishing a family, as is accorded without question to heterosexuals. We demand equal, not special civil rights, but we will not have them so long as our lives, characters, and actions are judged by ancient and unquestioned prejudices and scrutinized in the light of a corrosive and persistently negative social mythology. Homophobia alienates mothers and fathers from sons and daughters, friend from friend, neighbor from neighbor, Americans from one another. So long as it is legitimated by society, religion, and politics, homophobia will spawn hatred, contempt, and violence, and it will remain our last acceptable prejudice.

NOTES

Introduction: The Last Acceptable Prejudice

1. Many scholars have made this point, including Craig A. Williams in *Roman Homosexuality: Ideologies of Masculinity in Classical Antiquity* (New York, Oxford: Oxford University Press, 1999), 17. See also David A. Greenberg, *The Construction of Homosexuality* (Chicago and London: University of Chicago Press, 1988) 1–21.

2. Jonathan Ned Katz, *Gay/Lesbian Almanac* (New York: Harper & Row, 1983), 231–32.

3. Some twentieth-century discussions of sexual orientation claim that "homosexuality" is "essential"—that is, always present in every society—and that "homosexuals" are also present as an unchanging and self-identified sexual group. Others argue that both "homosexuality" and "the homosexual" are "social constructions" contingent on social and political forces. Mary McIntosh first discussed homosexuality in terms of social constructionism in 1968, defining it as a social rather than a medical category (Mary McIntosh, "The Homosexual Role," *Social Problems* 16 [fall 1968], 182–92). The French historian Michel Foucault claimed, in *The History of Sexuality,* vol. 1 (New York: Random House, 1978), part 2, chap. 2, that since "sexuality" is an invention of nineteenth-century medicine and science, it was the act of naming and categorizing that actually invented the modern homosexual. He argued that homosexual people with a homosexual identity—he called them

a "species"—could not have existed before the concept of sexuality and the corollary idea of a sexual identity based on the object of desire. Before this categorization, there was homosexuality but no homosexuals. Not only that, but if "homosexual identity" is a modern invention, then persons identifying themselves as homosexual "others" and even as "oppressed" could not have existed before the invention of notions of sexual oppression and difference.

Social constructionists have not always convinced essentialists, who point to Western history to show that some individuals were imagined by their society as different because of their sexuality, and that some of these individuals also identified themselves in that way. Recent tantalizing though inconclusive studies suggest that there may be a genetic basis for sexual orientation—that is, what is often popularly called a "gay gene" or a "gay brain." Perhaps in some way still unclear, people are "wired" for sexual orientation.

For discussions of social constructionism, see Edward Stein, ed., *Forms of Desire: Sexual Orientation and the Social Constructionist Controversy* (New York and London: Routledge, 1992).

4. Among men, different forms of homosexual behavior can be discerned at different times in history: pederastic relationships, between older and younger males; transgendered relationships, which emphasize the "masculinity" of one partner and the "effeminacy" of the other; and intragenerational relationships, between males of roughly the same age. Because of this, "homosexualities" rather than "homosexuality" may best describe same-sex behavior. For a discussion of homosexualities in modern times, see Alan P. Bell and Martin S. Weinberg, *Homosexualities* (New York: Simon & Schuster, 1978). For more recent discussions see Diana Fuss, ed., *Inside/Out: Lesbian Theories, Gay Theories* (New York and London: Routledge, 1991); Michael Warner, ed., *Fear of a Queer Planet: Queer Politics and Social Theories* (Minneapolis and London: University of Minnesota Press, 1993).

5. "Homophobia" names antipathy to homosexuality and to those who engage in it. To discuss that antipathy while avoiding locutions like "disapproval of boy-lovers," "disgust with effeminacy in males," "hatred of sodomites," "fear of people who engage in homosexual behavior," or "prejudice against gay people," I use "homophobia." But the term is even more recently invented than "homosexual" and its precision and accuracy are still open to question. It is not satisfactory, constructed as it is from a slang abbreviation for "homosexual" joined with "*phobia,*" which means fear but not dislike. For lack of a better term, I will use it, usually anachronistically, to name what I look for in history.

6. In *Psychological Reports* 29 (1971), 1091–1094.

7. George Weinberg, *Society and the Healthy Homosexual* (New York: St.

Martin's Press, 1972), 4; Mark Freedman, "Homophobia: The Psychology of a Social Disease," *Body Politic,* no. 24 (June 1975), 19.

8. Elisabeth Young-Bruehl, *The Anatomy of Prejudices* (Cambridge, Mass.: Harvard University Press, 1996), 137ff.

9. Ibid., 33–35.

10. Ibid., 36ff.

11. Feminist and queer theorists question the sex and gender systems that only seem to be confirmed by the terms "heterosexuality" and "homosexuality." Their critiques question the utility of the terms, note their destructive rather than positive effects, and ask whether the dichotomy really describes sexual truth. They argue that demarcation of individuals and behavior into one thing *or* the other distorts sexual reality. They argue further that the dichotomy constructs and enforces social and sexual role-playing that strengthens the already powerful, oppresses the weak, and fosters hatred, violence, discrimination, and homophobia. Homophobia is discussed in Young-Bruehl (1996); Eve Kosofsky Sedgwick, *Epistemology of the Closet* (Berkeley and Los Angeles: University of California Press, 1990); Warren J. Blumenfeld, ed., *Homophobia: How We All Pay the Price* (Boston: Beacon Press, 1992); John de Cecco, ed., *Bashers, Baiters, and Bigots: Homophobia in American Society* (New York and London: Harrington Park Press, 1985); Didi Herman, *The Antigay Agenda* (Chicago and London: University of Chicago Press, 1997).

12. See Lillian Faderman, *Surpassing the Love of Men: Romantic Love and Friendship Between Women from the Renaissance to the Present* (New York: William Morrow, 1981) and *Chloe Plus Olivia: An Anthology of Lesbian Literature from the Seventeenth Century to the Present* (New York; Viking, 1994); Diana Fuss, ed., *Inside/Out: Lesbian Theories, Gay Theories* (New York and London: Routledge, 1991).

13. See John J. Winkler, "Laying Down the Law: The Oversight of Men's Sexual Behavior in Ancient Athens" and other essays in *Before Sexuality: The Construction of Erotic Experience in the Ancient World,* David M. Halperin, John J. Winkler, and Froma Zeitlin (Princeton, N.J.: Princeton University Press, 1990), 173; Robert Graves, *The Greek Myths* (Harmondsworth, Eng.: Penguin Books, 1955); K. J. Dover, *Greek Homosexuality* (Cambridge, Mass.: Harvard University Press, 1978); John Boswell, *Christianity, Social Tolerance and Homosexuality* (Chicago and London: University of Chicago Press, 1980).

14. See Alan Bray, *Homosexuality in Renaissance England* (London: Gay Men's Press, 1982).

15. Dennis Altman, *The Homosexualization of America, the Americanization of the Homosexual* (New York: St. Martin's Press, 1982).

16. *The Advocate,* April 1, 1997, 25.

17. *The Advocate,* Feb. 4, 1997, 14.
18. *The New York Times,* April 4, 1999, 14.

Chapter One: Inventing Eros

1. Homosexual behavior was known to the Greeks, as was disapproval of it in certain forms. Most historians of Greek sexuality argue that the Greeks had homosexuality, but no homosexuals in the modern sense of the word. For sources, see Introduction n. 13, above.
2. Winkler (1990).
3. For Ganymede, see Robert Graves, *The Greek Myths* (Harmondsworth, Eng.: Penguin Books, 1955), I, 29, 115–18. For Laius and Chrysippus, see K. J. Dover, *Greek Homosexuality* (Cambridge, Mass.: Harvard University Press, 1978), 199–200.
4. Wayne Dynes et al., eds. *Encyclopedia of Homosexuality* (New York: Garland, 1990), "Solon," 1234–35.
5. Also see Dover (1978), 9–13, 57–60, 196–203, on homoeroticism in Greek literature, and 4–9 and 111–24 for a discussion and illustration of homoeroticism in vase paintings.
6. Its practice, this argument asserts, was ritualized, but not homoerotic. It was pederasty without homosexual desire, as some scholars have argued, most notably Harald Patzer in *Die griechische Knabeliebe* (Weisbaden, 1982).
7. See Dover (1978), 1–19.
8. David M. Halperin, *One Hundred Years of Homosexuality* (New York and London: Routledge, 1990), 58.
9. See John R. Clarke, *Looking at Lovemaking: Constructions of Sexuality in Roman Art 100 B.C.–A.D. 250* (Berkeley: University of California Press, 1998); John Boswell, *Christianity, Social Tolerance and Homosexuality* (Chicago and London: University of Chicago Press, 1980), 28. Boswell argues that the "apparent prevalence of erotic relationships between adults and boys" in literature was an "idealized and cultural convention" that may not have corresponded to reality.
10. On the age of lovers, see Boswell (1980), 28–29 and 28 n. 52, and Dover (1978), 84–87.
11. Strato, *Greek Anthology* 12:4, translated in James J. Wilhelm, ed., *Gay and Lesbian Poetry* (New York: Garland, 1995), 31.
12. Xenophon, *Symposium,* trans. E. C. Marchant and O. J. Todd (Cambridge, Mass.: Harvard University Press, 1923), 4, 17.
13. Dover (1978), 86–87.
14. Dover (1978), 79–80, notes that Hellenistic poetry after the fourth century B.C.E. showed "a certain shift of taste toward feminine characteristics" in descriptions of the ideal *eromenos.*

15. Plato, *Symposium,* Walter Hamilton, trans. (Harmondsworth, Eng.: Penguin, 1951), 44–45.
16. There are two forms of love, he says. "One is the elder and is the daughter of Uranus and had no mother; her we call Heavenly Aphrodite." The other is younger, the child of Zeus and Dione, and is called the Common Aphrodite. Love inspired by the latter is the love that the "baser sort of men feel. It . . . is directed toward women quite as much as young men . . . and its aim is the satisfaction of its desires." But the Heavenly Aphrodite, having no mother, has no "female strain in her" and this love "springs entirely from the male. . . . Hence those who are inspired by this Love are attracted toward the male sex, and value it as being naturally the stronger and more intelligent" (180e–182a).
17. See Dover (1978), 84–91, on the ages of Greek male lovers.
18. It is possible, however, that Pausanias' comments are delivered tongue in cheek. Greek poetry commonly portrayed boys as notoriously fickle and men as notoriously desirous only of having sex with them.
19. For an excellent discussion see David Halperin, "Why Is Diotima a Woman? Platonic *Eros* and the Figuration of Gender" in Halperin, Winkler, and Zeitlin (1990), 257–308.
20. Jeffrey Henderson, *The Maculate Muse: Obscene Language in Attic Comedy* (New Haven: Yale University Press, 1975), 205.
21. Michel Foucault, *The Uses of Pleasure* (New York: Random House, 1985), 85–86.
22. Halperin (1990), 133.
23. Ibid., 30–32, and see 163 n. 53 for a bibliography of classical sources mentioning men who preferred exclusively homosexual behavior.
24. James Davidson, *Courtesans and Fishcakes: The Consuming Passions of Classical Athens* (New York: St. Martin's Press, 1997), 178–79.

Chapter Two: Against Nature

1. See John Boswell, *Christianity, Social Tolerance, and Homosexuality* (Chicago: University of Chicago Press, 1980), 24 n. 43 and 339–41, for a survey of ancient texts in which *malakoi / malakos* appears.
2. Boswell (1980), 24–25; K. J. Dover, *Greek Homosexuality* (Cambridge, Mass.: Harvard University Press, 1978), 68ff.
3. Aristotle (*Nichomachean Ethics,* 1148b 15–9a 20) theorized that pleasure in sex comes about for some males by nature and for others by habituation. See Dover (1978), 168.
4. On sex roles, see Dover (1978), 68–81.
5. Euripides, *Antiope,* frr. 184, 185, 187, quoted in Dover (1978), 74.
6. Dover (1978), 137.
7. And in Greek, more or less, he did. Though Greek was rich in metaphoric

terms relating to sex and sex acts, it was satisfied with a few names or deri-sive metaphors for those who deviated from expected male sexual practice. These terms asserted that such men were anally assaulted by other men, so they were described as wide-assed (*euruproktos*) or cistern-assed (*lakko-proctos*) or, if effeminate, as smooth-assed (*leukoproctos*) in reference to the idea that smooth, hairless, white skin is effeminate. They were some-times simply called pale men (*leukov androv*). Greek also employed *leios* (soft) and sometimes *malthakos* (soft, implying unmanly) to indicate weak or effeminate men. See Jeffrey Henderson, *The Maculate Muse: Obscene Language in Attic Comedy* (New Haven: Yale University Press, 1975), 209ff. for additional terms. While Greek comedy employs numerous phrases that implicate men in disapproved forms of homosexual activity, Greek poetry is generally more circumspect. In Books XI and XII of the *Greek Anthology,* the chief source of epigrams dealing with homosexual-ity, few obscenities are used, usually *binein* (fuck) or *puge* (ass). Relatively few of the epigrams in the anthology directly describe homosexual sex at all. (Though see XI. 21, 22; XII. 3, 95, 207; and Jeffrey Henderson [1975], 30–56.)

8. Aristophanes, *Thesmophoriazusae,* Dudley Fitts, trans., quoted in *Eros: An Anthology of Male Friendship,* ed. Alistair Sutherland and Patrick Anderson (New York: Citadel Press, 1963), 70–71.

9. Plato, *Symposium,* Walter Hamilton, trans. (New York and London: Pen-guin Books, 1951), 208–209e, 90–91.

10. Plato, *Laws* (636a–c), Trevor J. Saunders, trans. (New York and London, Penguin Books, 1970), 61. References hereinafter in the text.

11. What has changed since Plato wrote is the understanding of the meaning of "natural." What does Plato mean by "natural," by "against nature"? Plato's commentary on homosexuality is framed within the context of Greek ideas about "nature." The Greeks maintained a general distinction between what exists in nature (*physis*) and what is a product of culture, or what is man-made convention (*nomos*). The writings under discussion here assume a contrast between the two, but in fact the concept of nature in much Greek writing often seems closer in meaning to "convention" than to a concept of "natural law" as an ordering cosmic principle. Indeed, the meaning of "nature" is not at all precise; Greek writers employed the term in a variety of ways, to refer to innate individual physical or character traits, or to the social status of the individual, or more simply to that which is conventional or expected. Though many Greek writers talk about nature, few would have imagined that there were some kinds of behavior that were outside of nature or some kinds of individuals whose acts were contrary to a presumed natural law. Nor did Greek *para physin* (contrary [to] nature, or against nature) mean sexually abnormal. As Winkler argues, "The nature/culture contrast, as it applies to sex," did not "possess

the same valence" for the Greeks as it does today. For them, the terms "natural" and "unnatural" did not "function" as they do today, "as equivalents of 'normal' and 'abnormal.'" John J. Winkler, "Laying Down the Law: The Oversight of Men's Sexual Behavior in Ancient Athens," in *Before Sexuality: The Construction of Erotic Experience in the Ancient World,* David M. Halperin, John J. Winkler, and Froma Zeitlin, eds. (Princeton, N.J.: Princeton University Press, 1990), 175. See also Boswell (1980), 13 n. 22.

12. Introduction, Plato, *Laws,* Trevor Saunders (1970), 27.
13. Dover (1978), 167.
14. Winkler (1990), 173.
15. Ibid., 191.
16. Dover (1978), 13–14.
17. *The Speeches of Aeschines,* Charles Darwin Adams, trans. (Cambridge, Mass.: Harvard University Press) 1919; 1988, sec. 38, p. 35; references hereinafter in text.
18. Henderson (1975), 11.
19. Aeschines, 41, in Dover's translation, Dover (1978), 73.
20. Dover (1978), 17, 74.
21. Aeschines, 1.131.
22. Plato, *Gorgias,* 493a–494e. Quoted in Winkler (1990), 185.
23. Aristophanes, *Frogs,* 422–27. Quoted in James Henderson, *Courtesans and Fishcakes: The Consuming Passions of Classical Athens* (New York: St. Martin's Press, 1997), 179.
24. They have also been called *katapugones*—a term that in Euripides and Aristophanes sometimes refers to outlandish and effeminate attire. On *kinaidoi,* see Winkler (1990), 176ff. and James Henderson (1997), 168–174.

Chapter Three: Making Monsters

1. Juvenal, Satire II, ll. 9–10. *The Sixteen Satires of Juvenal,* Peter Green, trans. (London: Penguin Books, 1967).
2. John Clarke, *Looking at Lovemaking: Constructions of Sexuality in Roman Art 100 B.C.–A.D. 250* (Berkeley: University of California Press, 1998), 59–91.
3. See Craig Williams, "Homosexuality and the Roman Man: A Study in the Cultural Construction of Sexuality" (Yale University, Ph.D. diss., 1991) 9–10, and his *Roman Homosexuality: Ideologies of Masculinity in Classical Antiquity* (New York: Oxford University Press, 1999).
4. Clarke (1998), 8–12.
5. Ibid., 3.
6. Williams (1999), 97.

7. Williams (1999), 110.

8. On this law, see Williams (1999), 120, who argues for this position and John Boswell, *Christianity, Social Tolerance, and Homosexuality* (Chicago: University of Chicago Press, 1980), 65ff.

9. See Boswell (1980), 68, and his cautionary n. 30 on Clement's veracity.

10. See Williams (1999), 62–97, on pederasty and the differences between Greek and roman homosexuality.

11. See *Epigrams of Martial by Divers Hands,* J. P. Sullivan and Peter Whigham, eds. (Berkeley and London: University of California Press, 1987), 12.96; 11.43. See also 2.47, 62; 6.16, 54; 8.46, 73; 9.32, 56; and 11.45, 46. See Boswell (1980), 73ff.

12. Translated by Brian Hill, quoted in *The Columbia Anthology of Gay Literature,* Byrne R. S. Fone, ed. (New York: Columbia University Press, 1998), 83.

13. Boswell (1980), 69 and n. 37.

14. John Boswell, *Same-Sex Unions in Pre-Modern Europe* (New York: Villard Books, 1994), 80.

15. Juvenal, Satire II, 137ff.

16. Boswell (1994), 80–85.

17. See Martial 6.16. and 7.58.

18. Translation by James J. Wilhelm, *Gay and Lesbian Poetry* (New York: Garland, 1995), 117, 128.

19. Juvenal, 2.122. See Amy Richlin, *Sexual Terms and Themes in Roman Satires and Related Genres* (Yale University, Ph.D. diss., 1978), 59, 289, 260.

20. I am indebted to Richlin (1978) for this summary of Latin sexual terminology.

21. Richlin (1978), 311.

22. Boswell (1980), 21 n. 41, and Richlin (1978), 319. As Richlin says, "Irrumation is not irrumation if the victim enjoys it."

23. John J. Winkler, "Laying Down the Law: The Oversight of Men's Sexual Behavior in Ancient Athens," in *Before Sexuality: The Construction of Erotic Experience in the Ancient World,* David M. Halperin, John J. Winkler, and Froma Zeitlin, eds. (Princeton, N.J.: Princeton University Press, 1990), 175.

24. On effeminacy see Boswell (1980), 76 and n. 72.

25. Richlin (1978), 299.

26. Juvenal, Satire VI, 8 (Housman's emendation). Martial X, 65. See Richlin (1978), 308.

27. Juvenal, Satire VI, 27–30.

28. See Richlin (1978), 309 for references.

29. See ibid., 295, 273.

30. See ibid., 297–98.

31. Martial, 10.65, in Wilhelm (1994), 127.
32. Martial 1.96, ll. 9–14, in Wilhelm (1994), 120. And see Richlin (1978), 285.
33. Juvenal, Satire I, 16–18.
34. Though it is hard to find much that Juvenal admires save for the long-dead past, in Satire VI he warns a young man soon to marry about the tyranny of domestic life and slyly asks: "Isn't it better to sleep with a pretty boy? / Boys don't quarrel all night, or nag you for little presents / While they're on the job, or complain that you don't come / Up to their expectations, or demand more gasping passion" (VI, ll. 35–38).
35. See K. J. Dover, *Greek Homosexuality* (Cambridge, Mass.: Harvard University Press, 1978).
36. Dover (1978), 168.
37. See pseudo-Aristotelian *Problemata,* iv, 26. Quoted in Dover (1978), 169ff.
38. Dover (1978), 168, makes this observation. See also Boswell (1980), 51.
39. Some of this material dates from the third century B.C.E.; some is a later translation or reworking of lost earlier texts from the second and third centuries of the Common Era. In these works the *kinaidos* is viewed as a sexually deviant male; it is the task of manuals of physiognomy to identify the distinguishing physical traits of such deviants. See J. Barnes, *Complete Works of Aristotle* (Princeton, N.J.: Princeton University Press, 1984), 1:1237–50.
40. Quoted in Winkler (1990), 200.
41. Though the original Greek text of Polemo's *Physiognomy* has been lost, it has been preserved in an Arabic translation, in a Greek paraphrase by Adamantios the Sophist, and in an anonymous Latin physiognomy written in the fourth century C.E. See Maud W. Gleason, "The Semiotics of Gender: Physiognomy and Self-Fashioning in the Second Century," in *Before Sexuality: The Construction of Erotic Experience in the Ancient World,* David M. Halperin, John J. Winkler, and Froma Zeitlin, eds. (Princeton, N.J.: Princeton University Press, 1990), 312–413, to whom I am indebted for details of my discussion. Gleason translates Polemo but notes that the result is often a composite of Polemo himself, a summary of Polemo, and the Latin physiognomy. See Gleason, 395 n. 24.
42. Ibid., 391–92.
43. Ibid., 390.
44. Ibid.
45. Ibid., 395.
46. Ibid., 408–409.
47. Ibid., 409.
48. Soranos' comments were summarized and translated into Latin by Caelius Aurelianus. English translation quoted in Vern Bullough, *Sexual Variance in Society and History* (New York: John Wiley & Sons, 1976), 143.

Chapter Four: The End of Antiquity

1. Plutarch, "Dialogue on Love." In *Moralia,* vol. 9, W. C. Helmbold, trans. (Cambridge, Mass.: Harvard University Press, 1961), 425.
2. *Erotes* has been attributed to the satirist Lucian of Samosata (120–185 C.E.). This attribution is probably incorrect; the style of the work suggests composition by an imitator. The date of composition is no more certain than the identity of the author, but a specific reference to Gothic invasions of the empire at the end of the third century C.E. gives reason to date the book near that time or at the beginning of the fourth century. See pseudo-Lucian, *Affairs of the Heart* [*Erotes*], M. D. McLeod, trans. (Cambridge, Mass.: Harvard University Press, 1967), 148–49.
3. Derrick Sherwin Bailey, *Homosexuality and the Western Christian Tradition* (Garden City, N.Y.: Doubleday 1955), 70.
4. Boswell (1980), 71, and Bailey (1955), 68–70.
5. *Erotes* 3. Subsequent references in the text.
6. On Lesbianism, see Juvenal, Satire VI, 301–49, Martial, 7, 67, and Charicles in this debate, Sec. 28.
7. On Alcibiades, see *Erotes* 188 n. 1.
8. Also see Juvenal, Satire VI.
9. The quotation is from Homer, *Iliad* 1, 156–57.

Chapter Five: The Sodom Story

1. Genesis 18:20–21 (King James Version).
2. Bailey, *Homosexuality and the Western Christian Tradition* (Garden City, N.Y.: Doubleday 1955), 2–3.
3. Genesis 19 in *The Jerusalem Bible* (Garden City, N.Y.: Doubleday, 1966) and *The New English Bible* (New York: Oxford University Press, 1971). I indicate English translations of biblical texts as follows: King James Version (KJV); *New English Bible* (NEB); *Jerusalem Bible* (JB). Rather than employ one translation only, I have tried to choose the English translation that most clearly renders the text I quote.
4. Bailey (1955), 2–3; John Boswell, *Christianity, Social Tolerance, and Homosexuality* (Chicago: University of Chicago Press, 1980), 94.
5. Bailey (1955), 29ff.; Boswell (1980), 91–169.
6. This argument is advanced by Bailey (1955), 1–8, and by Boswell (1980), 93–97; it is opposed by David F. Greenberg, *The Construction of Homosexuality* (Chicago: University of Chicago Press, 1988), 136.
7. Bailey (1955), 6.
8. On women, see *The Jerusalem Bible,* Genesis 19 n. *c.*
9. See Greenberg (1988), 133–34.

10. Greenberg (1988), 135, argues for a postexilic date for the story, making it later than Genesis by several hundred years.

11. Mark D. Jordan, *The Invention of Sodomy in Christian Theology* (Chicago: University of Chicago Press, 1997), 30, 30–37, argues against a "homosexual" interpretation of the Sodom story.

12. Bailey (1955), 4.

13. *Yadha* is translated variously. In the KJV it is, as we have seen, translated as "know"; in NEB, as "have intercourse with"; and in JB, as "abuse."

14. John J. NcNeill, S.J., *The Church and the Homosexual* (Kansas City: Sheed, Andrews and McMeel, 1976), 50.

15. Boswell (1980), 96.

16. *The New English Bible,* Leviticus 17:22, 20:13. *The Jerusalem Bible* translates the text: "The man who lies with a man in the same way as with a woman, they have done a hateful thing together; they must die, their blood shall be on their own heads." Boswell (1980), 100, argues that the Hebrew word *toevah (to'ebhah)*—usually translated as "abomination"—does not refer to something that is "intrinsically evil" but instead to something that is "ritually unclean" and has to do with offenses involving idolatry. Hence the homosexuality forbidden by Leviticus may be the homosexual prostitution that some scholars believe characterized the rituals of Semitic peoples who were seen by the Jews as heathens. It has also been suggested that this homosexuality is associated with the sexual profligacy of the Gentiles, whose acts are deemed by Judaism to be unclean. Greenberg (1988), 195, disagrees with Boswell about the Jewish view of homosexuality, arguing that the ancient Hebrews believed it to be both evil *and* unclean.

17. These events were probably orally transmitted, then committed to writing around the ninth century B.C.E. See Greenberg (1988), 193, on this date, and Bailey (1955), 30, on differing dates.

18. See Bailey (1955), 29–30, and *The Jerusalem Bible,* Introduction, 12, on the dating of Leviticus.

19. *The New English Bible,* Leviticus, 18:1, 2.

20. Boswell (1980), 101 n. 34.

21. See Greenberg (1988), 94, for a summary of evidence concerning homosexual prostitution in religious rites, and Deut. 23:18–19, and 1 Kings 13:23–24, 15:12–23, for attempts to end it.

22. See Greenberg (1988), 140–41. Bailey (1955), 30–37, argues that both the Caananites and the Egyptians found homosexuality as repugnant as the Jews did.

23. Translations from *The Jerusalem Bible* cited as JB.

24. Bailey (1955), 21, cites a mysterious 3 Maccabees 2:5 (there are only two books of Maccabees) as concurring with this opinion: "Thou didst burn

up with fire and brimstone the men of Sodom, workers of arrogance, who had become known of all for their crimes and didst make them an example for all who came afterward."

25. Greenberg (1988), 141.
26. See ibid., 139–40.
27. Pseudo-Phocylides (first century B.C.E.) added antisexual commandments. See ibid., 199.
28. Ibid., 200.
29. The Watchers are called "sons of God" in Gen. 4:1–4 and "angels" in 2 Peter 2. See Bailey (1955), 11–16.
30. Primary translation by W. R. Morfill and R. H. Charles, quoted in Bailey (1955), 20. Second translation by James H. Charlesworth, *The Old Testament Pseudepigrapha,* 2 vols. (Garden City, N.Y.: Doubleday, 1985). Quoted in Greenberg (1988), 199.
31. The concept of the law of nature would not be fully elaborated for several more centuries. See Boswell (1980), 110 n. 61.
32. Philo, *Works,* F. H. Colson, trans. (Cambridge, Mass.: Harvard University Press), vol. 7, 499.
33. Ibid., vol. 6, 69–71.
34. Bailey (1955), 21.
35. On Philo, see ibid., 21ff. As Bailey says about *On Abraham,* "Here at last is the Sodom of nameless and unmentionable vice which has obsessed the minds of the theologian and the legislator for so many centuries."

Chapter Six: Gospel Sodomy

1. Mark Jordan, *The Invention of Sodomy in Christian Theology* (Chicago: University of Chicago Press, 1997), 32.
2. Matthew 8 5:13; John 11:13, 13:23, 18:26, 20:2, 21:7, and 21:20.
3. See "Jesus" in Wayne R. Dynes, ed., *Encyclopedia of Homosexuality* (New York: Garland Publishers, 1990), vol. 1, 637.
4. For a good summary of the transmission of the text of the Gospels, see the introduction to *The Jerusalem Bible* (Garden City, N.Y.: Doubleday, 1966), pp. 5–15.
5. See *The Jerusalem Bible,* Matthew 5:22–23i, which translates *raca* as "empty-headed" and "nitwit."
6. My thanks to Sara Bershtel for pointing out the modern usage.
7. Warren Johansson, "Whosoever Shall Say to His Brother," *The Cabirion and Gay Books Bulletin,* no. 10 (winter–spring 1984), 2–10. David F. Greenberg, *The Construction of Homosexuality* (Chicago: University of Chicago Press, 1988), 211.
8. Johansson (1984), 3.
9. *The Jerusalem Bible* (Matthew 5:22k) translates "moros" as "renegade"

and notes that to the Greek meaning "Jewish usage added the more insulting one of 'impious.'"

10. Johansson (1984), 4, comments that "if *rachas* denotes the passive–effeminate homosexual, then *moros* = *nabhal* could apply to the active one."

11. Liddell and Scott, *Greek-English Lexicon* (Oxford, Eng.: Clarendon Press, 1953), 424.

12. Johansson (1985), 3.

13. Phaedrus, 239c.

14. See John Boswell, *Christianity, Social Tolerance, and Homosexuality* (Chicago: University of Chicago Press, 1980), 106; Greenberg (1988), 212; Derrick Sherwin Bailey, *Homosexuality and the Western Christian Tradition* (London: Longmans, Green and Co., 1955), 38.

15. Liddell and Scott (1953), 104.

16. See Bailey (1955), 38; Boswell (1980), 342–50; Greenberg (1988), 213.

17. In an attempt to clear early Christianity of homophobia, Boswell (1980) has argued that neither Paul nor other Greek writers used *malakoi* "to designate gay people as a group or even in reference to homosexual acts generically" (107). Nor, Boswell also argues, is there any reason to believe that *arsenokoitai* or *malakoi* "connoted homosexuality in the time of Paul or for centuries thereafter, and [there is] every reason to suppose . . . that they were not determinative of Christian opinion on the morality of homosexual acts" (353). Boswell claims, despite the occasional usage in antiquity, that in Paul's terminology *malakoi* is used only to nominate morally weak people and that it does not ever, in Greek, refer to homosexuals as a class (340). In a discussion of the meaning of *arsenokoitai,* he argues that it too does not refer to specific homosexual acts, or to people who might have been recognized as a class as exclusively preferring homosexual behavior. Instead it is meant only to name active male prostitutes whose clients were both men and women. The argument that *malakoi* and *arsenokoitai* did not refer to homosexuals as a class is, however, irrelevant to what Paul intends and certainly to the effect his words have had on opinions about homosexuality.

18. Quoted in Louis Crompton, "The Myth of Lesbian Impunity: Capital Laws from 1270–1792," *Journal of Homosexuality* 6 (fall–winter 1980–81), 14.

19. Greenberg (1988), 207.

20. Boswell (1980), 145 ff.

21. Boswell argues that rather than condemning homosexuals *per se,* Paul only intends to target homosexual practices (112).

22. Boswell (1980), 109, questions Paul's conception of the people whose acts he condemns, and claims that Paul was not speaking about homosexual persons: he could have had no conception of them and therefore could not condemn them. Nowhere in Paul, or indeed in the New Testament, is

homosexuality condemned, Boswell argues. He asserts that Paul did not find "mere homoerotic attraction or practice morally reprehensible."

23. Bailey (1955), 83; Greenberg (1988), 194; Boswell (1980), 137, 139 n. 9.

24. Boswell (1980), 357. "Incomplete" union may mean coitus interruptus; "androgynous" might refer to a heterosexual couple, as it can in modern Greek.

25. James B. De Young, "The Source and Meaning of *Arsenokoitai*, with Implications for the Christian Ministry." Website lcrew@andromeda. rutgers.edu.com.

26. Clement of Alexandria, *Paidagogos*, 3.15.1, 3, 8. Quoted in Bailey (1955), 25.

27. Boswell (1980), 358.

28. Clement, 3.15.2; 3.20.3. In Bailey.

29. Bailey (1955), 86; Greenberg (1988), 227–28.

30. Boswell (1980), 178 n. 33.

31. Bailey (1955), 82.

32. Boswell (1980), 359–83.

33. St. Basil, *De renuntiatione saeculi*, Sister M. Monica Wagner, trans. In *The Fathers of the Church* (Washington, D.C.: Catholic University of America), vol. 9, 23–24.

34. Ibid.

35. Bailey (1955), 89–90.

36. See Augustine, *Confessions*, 3.i.

37. Augustine, *Contra mendicam*, 7.10, quoted in Boswell (1980), 157.

38. *Confessions* 3.viii, quoted in Greenberg (1988), 225.

39. Boswell (1980), 161; Bailey (1955), 83.

Chapter Seven: Avenging Flames

1. David F. Greenberg, *The Construction of Homosexuality* (Chicago: University of Chicago Press, 1988), 231.

2. John Lauritsen, "Culpa Ecclesiae: Boswell's Dilemma," Gai Saber Monograph No. 1 (New York: Gay Academic Union, 1981), 20.

3. John Boswell, *Christianity, Social Tolerance, and Homosexuality* (Chicago: University of Chicago Press, 1980), 61ff.; Greenberg (1981), 228.

4. Lauritsen (1981), 18.

5. Boswell (1980), 123, believes this to be a prohibition of homosexual marriage. Lauritsen (1981), 18, declares Boswell's position to be "ridiculous"; he argues that the verb *nubere*, which Boswell translates as "to marry," can also simply mean "to have sex." Greenberg (1988), 229, argues that if applied to marriage alone and not to other homosexual acts the punishment is extreme.

6. Lauritsen (1981), 18.

7. Derrick Sherwin Bailey, *Homosexuality and the Western Christian Tradition* (London: Longmans, Green and Co., 1955), 69.

8. Edward Westermarck, *Christianity and Morals* (1917, reprinted Freeport, N.Y.: Books for Libraries Press, 1969), 362–72. Boswell (1988), 127–28, and Bailey (1955), 70, minimize what Westermarck maximizes.

9. Greenberg (1988), 233.

10. Ibid., 242; Wayne R. Dynes, ed. *Encyclopedia of Homosexuality* (New York: Garland Publishers, 1990), vol. 2, 1275.

11. *Encyclopedia of Homosexuality*, 687–89; Greenberg (1988), vol. 1, 242–55.

12. Procopius, *History of the Wars*, H. B. Dewey, trans. (New York: Macmillan, 1914), 1:487, 2:14.

13. The Visigoths were Arians, followers of Arius, who taught that Christ was not of the same divine substance as God, but was only the best among created beings.

14. Bailey (1955), 92–93.

15. Bullough (1976), 349–53, believes the penalty was death. Boswell (1980), 176, argues that the Visigothic laws were not prompted by Christian doctrine, insisting that "the church took no part in their passage; they were purely civil laws." Greenberg (1988), 252, urges that the role of Christianity in the enactment of these laws ought not to be minimized, because the Visigothic kings ruled a theocratic state.

16. Boswell (1980), 177.

17. Greenberg (1988), 254; *Encyclopedia of Homosexuality*, 811.

18. Greenberg (1988), 263.

19. Bullough (1976), 357.

20. Ibid., 195.

21. Ibid., 361; Bailey (1955), 109.

22. Bullough (1976), 361; Bailey (1955), 100–110.

23. Bullough (1976), 363.

24. Michael Goodich, *The Unmentionable Vice: Homosexuality in the Later Medieval Period* (Santa Barbara, Calif.: Ross-Erikson Publishers, 1979), 27.

25. Bullough (1976), 357.

26. Boswell (1980), 181.

27. Bailey (1955), 106; Bullough (1976), 362.

28. Bullough (1976), 361.

29. For a discussion of homoerotic literature in this period, see Boswell (1980), 169–207.

30. Meleager, *Greek Anthology*, 11:225. My translation.

31. Translated by James J. Wilhelm, in Wilhelm, ed., *Gay and Lesbian Poetry* (New York: Garland, 1995), 137.

32. Translation by Stephen Coote, in *The Penguin Book of Homosexual Verse* (London: Penguin Books, 1983), 111.

33. For a convincing discussion of the likelihood of same-sex marriage, see John Boswell, *Same-Sex Unions in Premodern Europe* (New York: Villard Books, 1994), 141.

34. Ibid., 150.

35. See ibid., chapter 4 *passim,* for a discussion and translations of various saints' lives.

36. See Wilhelm (1995), 139–41, for translations of Ennodius and Luxorius by Thomas Stehling. Unless noted, translations cited in Wilhelm are those by Stehling from *Medieval Poems of Male Love and Friendship* (New York: Garland, 1984).

37. Bailey (1955), 98–99, and Boswell (1980), chap. 7, point out that there was little legislation or commentary about homosexuality, compared with the vast amount of commentary concerning other sinful acts; this demonstrates, they argue, that the church was relatively unconcerned about it.

Chapter Eight: The Plague of Sodomy

1. Michael Goodich, *The Unmentionable Vice: Homosexuality in the Later Medieval Period* (Santa Barbara, Calif.: Ross-Erikson Publishers, 1979), 25.

2. Burchard, *Decretorum libri* XX, quoted in Bullough.

3. Mark Jordan, *The Invention of Sodomy in Christian Theology* (Chicago: University of Chicago Press, 1997), 52.

4. Jordan (1997), 43, claims that *sodomia* first appeared in this text.

5. John Boswell, *Christianity, Social Tolerance, and Homosexuality* (Chicago: University of Chicago Press, 1980), 211.

6. Quoted in ibid.

7. Derrick Sherwin Bailey, *Homosexuality and the Western Christian Tradition* (London: Longmans, Green and Co., 1955), 112.

8. See ibid., 111–15, and Boswell (1980), 210–13, on Peter Damian.

9. Ivo of Chartres, *Decretum,* para. IX, cols. 685–86. Quoted in Vern Bullough, *Sexual Variance in Society and History* (New York: John Wiley and Sons, 1976), 381 and nn. 16, 17.

10. Boswell (1980), 316.

11. Albertus Magnus, *In evangelium Lucae,* 17:29. In his *Opera omnia,* vols. 22, 23. Discussed in Bailey (1955), 119–20; Bullough (1976), 379; and Boswell (1980), 316 n. 52.

12. Boswell (1980), 318.

13. Ibid., 326. See also his pp. 318–30 for a discussion of contradictions in Thomas' argument; and Jordan (1997), 136–58, for a discussion of Thomas on sodomy.

14. Arthur N. Gilbert, "Conceptions of Sodomy in Western History," in *The Gay Past,* Salvatore J. Licata and Robert P. Petersen, eds. (Binghamton, N.Y.: Harrington Park Press, 1985), 57–68.

15. Joan Cadden, "Sciences/Silences: The Natures and Languages of 'Sodomy' in Peter of Abano's *Problemata* Commentary," in *Constructing Medieval Sexuality,* Karma Lochrie, Peggy McCracken, and James A. Shultz, eds. (Minneapolis: University of Minnesota Press, 1997), 47.

16. Ibid., 50.

17. Ibid., 51.

18. Ibid., 47 n. 30.

19. Boswell (1980), 294.

20. Bailey (1955), 123–24.

21. Boswell (1980), 230.

22. Ibid., 215.

23. Bailey (1955), 96.

24. Ibid.

25. Boswell (1980), 277.

26. Goodich (1979), 43.

27. Boswell (1980), 277, 375.

28. I have drawn upon overviews of this period by Goodich (1979), 79–88, and David F. Greenberg, *The Construction of Homosexuality* (Chicago: University of Chicago Press, 1988), 297–98.

29. Greenberg (1988), 298.

30. Bailey (1955), 143.

31. Goodich (1979), 77–78; Bailey (1955), 141–42.

32. Boswell (1980), 288.

33. Ibid., 289.

34. Bruce R. Smith, *Homosexual Desire in Shakespeare's England: A Cultural Poetics* (Chicago: University of Chicago Press, 1991), 42–43.

35. Greenberg (1988), 273 n. 162.

36. Goodich (1979), 85.

37. Wilhelm, *Gay and Lesbian Poetry* (New York: Garland, 1995), 157.

38. Ibid., 190.

39. For a fuller discussion of Richard of Devizes, see Wayne Dynes and Warren Johansson, "London's Medieval Sodomites," *The Cabirion* (no. 10, winter–spring 1984), 5–7.

40. Wilhelm (1995), 168.

41. Ibid., 174.

42. Ibid., 172.

43. Boswell (1980), 213.

44. Greenberg (1988), 293.

45. Boswell (1980), 229–30.

46. Goodich (1979), 10. The medieval antipope John XXIII is not included in the roster of legitimate popes.

47. See Jordan (1997), 10–29, for a discussion of the legend.

48. Greenberg (1988), 176.

49. Quoted in Boswell (1980), 368.
50. Quoted in ibid., 282.
51. Ibid., 273–75.
52. Bailey (1955), 145.
53. Greenberg (1988), 176.
54. Bullough (1976), 392.
55. Bailey (1955), 141.
56. Boswell (1980), 297. But see Goodich (1979), 12, for contradictory testimony.
57. Bullough (1976), 397.
58. Goodich (1979), 95.
59. Ibid., 115–17.
60. Ibid., 106.
61. Ibid., 123.
62. See Boswell (1980), chap. 8, and 210 n. 7. Also, Homer Haskins, *The Renaissance of the Twelfth Century* (Cambridge, Mass.: Harvard University Press, 1927).
63. For a good brief note on the bibliography of courtly love see Boswell (1980), 209 n. 6. And on a possible homosexual subculture see Boswell (1980), chapters 8, 9.
64. Greenberg (1988), 267 n. 129, warns against the careless use of the sociological term "subculture," with reference to Boswell's assertion that homoerotic poetry of the tenth and twelfth centuries is evidence of a homosexual subculture. Greenberg prefers to call it a culture of marginality rather than one based on homosexuality.
65. See Judith Brown, "Lesbian Sexuality in Medieval and Early Modern Europe," in Martin Bauml Duberman, Martha Vincius, and George Chauncey, Jr., *Hidden from History: Reclaiming the Gay and Lesbian Past* (New York: New American Library, 1989), 67–75.
66. Boswell (1980), 185. Boswell's translation.
67. Wilhelm (1995), 174–76.
68. Ibid., 190.
69. Boswell (1980), 222.
70. Ibid., 223–24.
71. Wilhelm (1995), 152.
72. Boswell (1980), 248.
73. Wilhelm (1995), 155.
74. Ibid., 156–57.
75. Ibid., 158.
76. My translation.
77. Boswell (1980), 247.
78. Wilhelm (1995), 153.
79. Ibid., 153–54.

80. Boswell (1980), 237.
81. Wilhelm (1995), 158.
82. From *De contemptu mundi,* Book 3, Wilhelm trans. (1995), 166–67.
83. Ganymede's response is an example of the misogyny also common to classical texts.
84. Wilhelm (1995), 176–85.
85. Bullough (1976), 393.
86. Goodich (1979), 26.
87. Ruth Mazo Karras and David Lorenzo Boyd, " 'Ut cum muliere': A Male Transvestite Prostitute in Fourteenth-Century London," in *Premodern Sexualities,* Louis Fradenberg and Carla Freccero, eds. (New York: Routledge, 1996), 108.
88. Quoted in Boswell (1980), 306.
89. Monica McAlpine, "The Pardoner's Homosexuality and How It Matters," *PMLA* 95: 8–22.
90. E. William Monter, "Sodomy and Heresy in Early Modern Switzerland," in Licata and Petersen (1985), 51 n. 5.
91. Bullough (1976), 390; Bailey (1955), 142–44.
92. Bullough (1976), 386; Greenberg (1988), 314.
93. Louis Crompton, "Gay Genocide from Leviticus to Hitler," in *The Gay Academic,* Louis Crew, ed. (Palm Springs, Calif.: ETC Publications, 1978), 72.

Chapter Nine: Reinventing Sodomy

1. Bruce Smith, *Homosexual Desire in Shakespeare's England: A Cultural Poetics* (Chicago: University of Chicago Press, 1991), 13–14.
2. James Saslow, *Ganymede in the Renaissance: Homosexuality in Art and Society* (New Haven: Yale University Press, 1986), 7–8.
3. Ibid., 30–31.
4. James M. Saslow, "Homosexuality in the Renaissance: Behavior, Identity and Artistic Expression," in Martin Bauml Duberman, Martha Vincius, and George Chauncey, Jr., *Hidden from History: Reclaiming the Gay and Lesbian Past* (New York: New American Library, 1989), 90–106.
5. Quoted in Byrne Fone, ed., *The Columbia Anthology of Gay Literature* (New York: Columbia University Press, 1998), 151–53.
6. See Giovanni Dall'Orto, "Dante Alighieri," in Wayne R. Dynes, ed., *Encyclopedia of Homosexuality* (New York: Garland Publishers, 1990), 295.
7. Wilhelm, *Gay and Lesbian Poetry* (New York: Garland, 1995), 279–80.
8. Panormita's poems are translated by James J. Wilhelm in ibid., 286–89.
9. Translated by Wilhelm, in ibid., 291.
10. *The People's Chronology,* compiled by James Trager (New York: Henry Holt and Company, 1992), 129.
11. Michael J. Rocke, *Forbidden Friendships: Homosexuality and Male*

Culture in Renaissance Florence (New York: Oxford University Press, 1996), 20. I am indebted to Rocke's essay for much of the material in this chapter.

12. See Vern L. Bullough, "Christianity," in *Encyclopedia of Homosexuality,* 221–24.

13. Bryant T. Ragan, Jr., "The Enlightenment Confronts Homosexuality," in *Homosexuality in Modern France,* Jeffrey Merrick and Bryant T. Ragan, Jr. eds. (New York: Oxford University Press, 1996), 9.

14. William A. Percey, "Protestantism," in *Encyclopedia of Homosexuality,* 1058–1069.

15. Guido Ruggiero, *The Boundaries of Eros: Sex, Crime and Sexuality in Renaissance Venice* (New York: Oxford University Press, 1985), 4–5.

16. Alan Bray, *Homosexuality in Renaissance England* (London: Gay Men's Press, 1982), 20. Buggery was originally a description for a kind of heresy. It probably here means sex with animals, though it is also used to mean sodomy—homosexual acts. Sodomy, originally any unnatural sexual act, here means homosexual acts.

17. John Boswell, *Christianity, Social Tolerance, and Homosexuality* (Chicago: University of Chicago Press, 1980), 299.

18. Michael Drayton, *Piers Gaveston* (1593), quoted in Byrne Fone, ed., *The Columbia Anthology of Gay Literature* (New York: Columbia University Press, 1998), 163ff.

Chapter Ten: A Continental Epidemic

1. Michael J. Rocke, *Forbidden Friendships: Homosexuality and Male Culture in Renaissance Florence* (New York: Oxford University Press, 1996), 3.

2. Ibid., 28.

3. Ibid., 7.

4. Goodich, *The Unmentionable Vice: Homosexuality in the Later Medieval Period* (Santa Barbara, Calif.: Ross-Erikson Publishers, 1979), 27.

5. Guido Ruggiero, *The Boundaries of Eros: Sex, Crime and Sexuality in Renaissance Venice* (New York: Oxford University Press, 1985), 109.

6. Ibid., 139.

7. Rocke (1996), 112.

8. Ibid., 59.

9. Ibid., 7.

10. Michael Rocke, "Sodomites in Fifteenth-Century Tuscany: The Views of Bernardino of Siena," in *The Pursuit of Sodomy: Male Homosexuality in Renaissance and Enlightenment Europe,* Kent Gerard and Gert Hekma, eds. (Binghamton, N.Y.: Harrington Park Press, 1989), 7. Rocke's article, to which I am indebted for material in this section, provides a detailed pic-

ture of Bernardino's antisodomitical campaign. See his expansion of the material in Rocke (1996).

11. James Saslow, *Ganymede in the Renaissance: Homosexuality in Art and Society* (New Haven: Yale University Press, 1986), 49.
12. *Prediche* (Florence, 1425), 3:42, in Rocke (1989), 12.
13. *Prediche* (Florence, 1425), 3:42, in Rocke (1989), 15.
14. *Opera Omnia,* 2:83, in Rocke (1989), 17.
15. *Prediche* (Siena, 1425), 2:109, in Rocke (1989), 17.
16. *Prediche* (Florence, 1424), 1:416, in Rocke (1989), 18.
17. Rocke (1989), 19, and n. 54.
18. *Prediche* (Florence, 1425), 2:276, in Rocke (1989), 21.
19. *Prediche* (Siena, 1427), 897, in Rocke (1989), 21.
20. *Prediche* (Siena, 1425), 2:105, in Rocke (1989), 20.
21. *Prediche* (Siena, 1427), 410, in Rocke (1989), 21.
22. *Prediche* (Florence, 1424), 2:141, in Rocke (1989), 21.
23. Rocke (1989), 16.
24. Rocke (1996), 44.
25. Ibid., 196.
26. Ibid., 205.
27. Ibid., 197.
28. See Goodich (1979), chapter 5, for a detailed account of thirteenth-century legal developments.
29. Saslow (1986), 47.
30. Rocke (1996), 221.
31. The eyewitness was Jacopo Nardi, who recorded the incident in his *Istorie della città di Firenze* (1:161). Quoted in Rocke (1996), 223.
32. Rocke (1996), 233.
33. This is not to say that sex between adult males was not condemned and punished in earlier times, only that the specification of it in Florentine law was new. See ibid.
34. Ibid., 43.
35. Louis Crompton, "The Myth of Lesbian Impunity: Capital Laws from 1270–1792," in *The Gay Past,* Salvatore J. Licata and Robert P. Petersen, eds. (Binghamton, N.Y.: Harrington Park Press, 1985), 18.
36. William A. Percy, "Inquisition," in Wayne R. Dynes, ed., *Encyclopedia of Homosexuality* (New York: Garland Publishers, 1990), 605.
37. Mary Elizabeth Perry, "The 'Nefarious Sin' in Early Modern Seville," in Gerard and Hekma (1989), 76–89. I am indebted to Perry's article for material summarized in this section.
38. Ibid., 87, n. 27.
39. Ibid., 71.
40. Ibid., 71ff.
41. Ibid., 71.

42. For a discussion, see Crompton (1985), 18.

43. Perry (1989), 79.

44. Ibid., 81.

45. Ibid., 82.

46. Ibid., 81.

47. Ibid., 83.

48. Ibid.

49. Ibid., 84.

50. Ibid.

51. For the following passages I am indebted to the research summarized in Luiz Mott and Arnoldo Assunção, "Love's Labors Lost: Five Letters from a Seventeenth-Century Portuguese Sodomite" in Gerard and Hekma (1989), 91–101, and to material derived by the authors from Asdrubal D'Aguiar, "A Evolucao da Pederastia e do Lesbianismo na Europe," *Spaerto do Arquivo da Universidadde de Lisbo* 11 (1926), 504, and from information gathered by the authors from the Arquivo Nacional da Tore Tombo, Inquisicao de Lisboa, Processa No 7622 and 5007.

52. Mott and Assunção (1989), 99.

53. Ibid., 92.

54. Ibid., 95–96.

55. Ibid., 93, letter 1. Translations by Mott and Assunção.

56. See ibid., 93.

57. Ibid.

58. Ibid., 94–95, letter 2.

59. Ibid., 94–98, letters 2, 3, 4, 5.

60. Ibid., 94, 97, letters 2, 4.

61. Ibid., 99

62. Ibid., 95.

63. Ibid., 92, 99.

64. Quoted in Stephen Coote, *The Penguin Book of Homosexual Verse* (New York: Penguin Books, 1983), 142.

65. Joseph Cady, "The 'Masculine Love' of the 'Princes of Sodom' 'Practicing the Art of Ganymede' at Henri III's Court: The Homosexuality of Henry III and His *Mignons* in Pierre de L'Estoile's *Memoires-Journaux*," in *Desire and Discipline: Sex and Sexuality in the Premodern West*, Jacqueline Murray and Ronald Eisenbichler, eds. (Toronto: University of Toronto, 1996), 123. I am indebted to Cady's article for much of the material in this section.

66. Cady's translation in ibid., 126.

67. Ibid., 141.

68. Ibid., 133.

69. Ibid., 127.

70. Ibid., 125.

71. Ibid., 134.
72. Ibid., 123.
73. Ibid., 138.
74. See E. William Monter, "Sodomy and Heresy in Early Modern Switzer-land," in *The Gay Past,* Salvatore J. Licata and Robert P. Petersen, eds. (Binghamton, N.Y.: Harrington Park Press, 1985), 41–53. I am indebted to this essay for material I use in this section.
75. Ibid., appendix 1, 54–55.
76. Ibid., appendix 1, cases 9, 17, 69, 54–55.
77. Ibid., appendix 1, cases 1, 24, 38, 54–55.
78. See ibid., appendix 1, 54–55.
79. Quoted in Monter (1985), 46–47.
80. Louis Crompton, "Gay Genocide from Leviticus to Hitler," in *The Gay Academic,* Louis Crew, ed. (Palm Springs, Calif.: ETC Publications, 1978), 67–92, argues that executions of sodomites constituted a kind of genocide. This view is criticized by Arthur Gilbert, who rightly suggests that it is anachronistic to describe those executed as "gay" and that the number of sodomites executed is too small to constitute "genocide." See Arthur Gilbert, "Conceptions of Homosexuality and Sodomy in Western History," in Licata and Petersen (1985), 57–69. Gilbert's comments appear on p. 61.

Chapter Eleven: England's Abominable Vice

1. Derrick Sherwin Bailey, *Homosexuality and the Western Christian Tradi-tion* (London: Longmans, Green and Co., 1955), 146; Bruce Smith, *Homosexual Desire in Shakespeare's England: A Cultural Poetics* (Chicago: University of Chicago Press, 1991), 45.
2. Smith (1991), 42–43.
3. Ibid., 43.
4. Bailey (1955), 147.
5. Smith (1991), 44.
6. Ibid.
7. Bailey (1955), 148; Smith (1991), 45.
8. Ed Cohen, "Legislating the Norm: From Sodomy to Gross Indecency," in *Displacing Homophobia,* Ronald R. Butters, John M. Clum, and Michael Moon, eds. (Durham, N.C.: Duke University Press, 1989), 174.
9. Smith (1991), 46.
10. Bailey (1955), 150.
11. Smith (1991), 46–47, outlines this history, as does Bailey (1955), 149–50.
12. Sir Edward Coke, *The Third Part of the Institutes of the Laws of England.* Quoted in Smith (1991), 31.
13. Alan Bray, *Homosexuality in Renaissance England* (London: Gay Men's Press, 1982), 20.

14. Gregory W. Bredbeck, *Sodomy and Interpretation: Marlowe to Milton* (Ithaca: Cornell University Press, 1991), 10–17.

15. Ibid., 90.

16. Ibid., 35.

17. Ibid., 17.

18. "Ingle" is a Gaelic word meaning "fire"; hence "inglenook," the chimney corner. Whether "ingle" in the sense of "catamite" derives from some notion that ingles were kept boys and thus like women who stayed by the fire, or whether it comes from Latin *angelus* or Scots *aingeal,* both meaning "angel"—and angels being depicted as beautiful and androgynous—is not decided. See Warren Johansson, "Ingle," in *Encyclopedia of Homosexuality,* Wayne R. Dynes, ed. (New York: Garland Publishers, 1990), 601.

19. E.K. means to say that the pederasty is not what the author means. But E.K. objects to the classical approval of pederasty, even as he defines it in a Christian context as "disorderly love."

20. Bredbeck (1991), 149–60.

21. Smith (1991), 13–14.

Chapter Twelve: Societies of Sodomites

1. Randolph Trumbach, "Sodomitical Subcultures, Sodomitical Roles, and the Gender Revolution of the Eighteenth Century: The Recent Historiography," in *Unauthorized Sexual Behavior During the Enlightenment,* Robert P. Maccubin, ed., in *Eighteenth-Century Life* (vol. 9, n.s., no. 3 [May 1985]), 110.

2. Louis Crompton. Quoted in *Byron and Greek Love: Homophobia in 19th-Century England* (Berkeley: University of California Press, 1985), 35.

3. Michael Rey, "Police and Sodomy in Eighteenth-Century Paris: From Sin to Disorder," in Kent Gerard and Gert Hekma, eds., *The Pursuit of Sodomy: Male Homosexuality in Renaissance and Enlightenment Europe* (Binghamton, N.Y.: Harrington Park Press, 1989), 134.

4. Johann Michaelis, *Grundliche erklärung des mosaischen rechts in sechsen theilen (1770–1775),* quoted in Greenberg, *The Construction of Homosexuality* (Chicago and London: University of Chicago Press, 1988), 322.

5. Wayne Dynes, "Enlightenment," in *Encyclopedia of Homosexuality,* Wayne R. Dynes, ed. (New York: Garland Publishers, 1990), 358.

6. Randolph Trumbach, "London's Sodomites: Homosexual Behavior and Western Culture in the 18th Century," *Journal of Social History* 11, no. 1 (1977), 1–33.

7. Randolph Trumbach, "Sodomitical Assaults, Gender Role, and Sexual Development in Eighteenth-Century London," in Gerard and Hekma

(1989), 409. Raids took place in 1698, 1707, 1726–27, 1763–65, 1776, 1798, and 1810.

8. Michael D. Sibalis, "Paris," in *Queer Sites: Gay Urban Histories Since 1600,* David Higgs, ed. (New York: Routledge, 1999), 18.

9. Ibid., 23.

10. Rey (1989), 130–31.

11. L. J. Boon, "Those Damned Sodomites: Public Images of Sodomy in the Eighteenth-Century Netherlands" in Gerard and Hekma (1989), 246.

12. G. S. Rousseau, "The Pursuit of Homosexuality in the Eighteenth Century: Utterly Confused Category and/or Rich Repository," in Robert P. Maccubbin, ed., *Unauthorized Sexual Behavior During the Enlightenment in Eighteenth-Century Life* (vol. 9, n.s., no. 3 [May 1985]), 147.

13. The Anglo-Saxon word *baedling* refers to an effeminate fellow. Homophobia may have been inscribed into the language itself, if *baedling* is the source of Middle and Modern English "bad." See Wayne Dynes, "Anglo-Saxon," in *Encyclopedia of Homosexuality* (1990), 60.

14. Wayne Dynes and Warren Johansson, "London's Medieval Sodomites," *The Cabirion and Gay Books Bulletin* (no. 10, winter–spring 1984), 5.

15. Ned Ward, *The London Spy,* quoted in Paul Hallam, *The Book of Sodom* (London: Verso, 1993), 111–13.

16. Rey (1989), 186.

17. Dirk Noordam, "Sodomy in the Dutch Republic, 1600–1725," in Gerard and Hekma (1989), 216.

18. Trumbach (1977), 18.

19. Rey (1989), 188.

20. James Dalton, *A Genuine Narrative of All the Street Robberies Committed Since October Last* (London, 1728), quoted in Rictor Norton, *Mother Clap's Molly House: The Gay Subculture in England 1700–1830* (London: Gay Men's Press, 1992), 98.

21. Norton (1992), 55.

22. Trumbach (1989), 428 n. 27.

23. Norton (1992), 45–46.

24. Ibid., 109.

25. Rey (1989), 134.

26. Ibid., 145.

27. Boon (1989), 424.

28. Arend H. Huussen, "Prosecutions of Sodomy in Eighteenth-Century Frisia, Netherlands," in Gerard and Hekma (1989), 255.

29. Boon (1989), 243–45.

30. Theo Van der Meer, "The Persecution of Sodomites in Eighteenth-Century Amsterdam: Changing Perceptions of Sodomy." In Gerard and Hekma (1989), 297.

31. Louis Crompton, "Gay Genocide from Leviticus to Hitler," in *The Gay Academic*, Louis Crew, ed. (Palm Springs, Calif.: ETC Publications, 1978), 89–90.

32. Van der Meer (1989), 281–82.

33. Crompton (1977), 88–90.

34. Crompton (1985), 14.

35. Michael S. Kimmel, ed., *Love Letters Between a Certain Nobleman and the Famous Mr. Wilson* (Binghamton, N.Y.: Harrington Park Press, 1990), 113.

36. Kimmel (1990), 2–3.

37. Ibid., 115.

38. Crompton (1985), 55–56.

39. Tobias Smollett, *Roderick Random* (New York: New American Library, 1964), 223–27.

40. Randolph Trumbach, "Sodomy Transformed: Aristocratic Libertinage, Public Reputation and the Gender Revolution of the 18th Century," in Kimmel (1990), 106.

41. Rousseau (1985), 150.

42. Norton (1992), 46.

43. See Anonymous, *Don Leon* (Fortune Press, n.d. [1833], note, p. 58: "A lad who had been tampered with in the streets . . . was taught how he should deliberately lead his seducer into a snare."

44. For September 24, p. 4, col. 2; in Crompton (1985), 163.

45. Ibid.

46. "The Trying and Pillorying of the Vere Street Club" (London: J. Brown, 1810), quoted in Crompton (1985), 165.

47. *The Annual Register* (1810) and *The Times* (September 28, 1810) reported it. See Norton (1992), 191–93.

48. *Don Leon*, 93–94.

49. Crompton (1985), 168.

50. *General Evening Post* (September 27–29, 1810), quoted in Crompton (1985), 167.

51. Matthew Bacon, *New Abridgement of the Law*, C. E. Dodd, ed. (London: J. & W. T. Clarke, et al., 1832), 374; Crompton (1985), 50–51.

52. Crompton (1985), 14–15.

53. Ibid., 33.

54. Norton (1992), 58.

55. Crompton (1985), 18.

56. Ibid., 403.

57. Jeremy Bentham, "Offenses Against One's Self: Paederasty," Louis Crompton, ed., *Journal of Homosexuality* 3, no. 4 (1978), 394.

58. Ibid., 396–97.

59. Ibid., 399.

60. Ibid., 384.
61. Jeremy Bentham, "Jeremy Bentham's Essay on 'Paederasty' (Part 2)," Louis Crompton, ed., *Journal of Homosexuality* 4, no. 1 (1978), 94.
62. Ibid., 94.
63. Ibid., 95–98.
64. Crompton (1985), 27.
65. Ibid., 21.
66. Ibid., 38.
67. Bentham, 385.
68. Crompton (1985), 30.
69. Ibid., 161–62.
70. *Don Leon* was probably written in 1833. If a printed edition existed it is lost. *Notes and Queries* 7 of 1853 mentions a poem about Byron addressed to Thomas Moore and "printed abroad many years since." The earliest known edition is that of William Dugdale (London, 1866).
71. Crompton (1985), 360.
72. *Don Leon,* 57.
73. *Don Leon,* ll. 60–76. References hereinafter in the text.
74. See Crompton (1985), 142ff., for Byron and Hobhouse in the East.
75. Crompton (1985), 151–52.
76. Ibid., 152.
77. In the anonymous *Commentary* (1766) and in *"Prix de la justice et de la humanité"* (1785).
78. Greenberg (1988), 320 n. 120.
79. Ibid., 352.
80. Crompton (1985), 16–18.
81. From *La Philosophie dans le boudoir* (1795), translated by Austryn Wainhouse and Richard Seaver (New York: Grove Press, 1965), 325–29.

Chapter Thirteen: Inverting Perversion

1. Crompton. Quoted in *Byron and Greek Love: Homophobia in 19th-Century England* (Berkeley: University of California Press, 1985), 35.
2. Derrick Sherwin Bailey, *Homosexuality and the Western Christian Tradition* (London: Longmans, Green and Co., 1955), 152.
3. Timothy d'Arch Smith, *Love in Earnest: Some Notes on the Life and Writings of English "Uranian" Poets from 1889 to 1930* (London: Routledge & Kegan Paul, 1970), 58.
4. Smith, *Homosexual Desire in Shakespeare's England: A Cultural Poetics* (Chicago: University of Chicago Press, 1970), 86.
5. Wayne Dynes, "Inversion," in *Encyclopedia of Homosexuality,* Wayne Dynes, ed. (New York: Garland Publishers, 1990), 610–11.
6. Wayne Dynes, "Kertbeny," in *Encyclopedia of Homosexuality,* 659–60.

7. Carl Westphal, "Die konträre Sexualempfindung: Symptom eines neuro-pathologischen (psychopathischen) Zustandes," *Archiv für Psychiatrie und Nervenkrankheiten* 2 (1870), 73–108.

8. Warren Johansson, "Perversion," in *Encyclopedia of Homosexuality* (1990), 976–77.

9. Jeffrey Weeks, *Coming Out: Homosexual Politics in Britain, from the Nineteenth Century to the Present* (London: Quartet Books, 1979), 26.

10. Katz, *Gay/Lesbian Almanac* (New York: Harper & Row, 1983), 245.

11. E. M. Forster, *Maurice* (New York: New American Library, 1971), 159.

12. John Addington Symonds, *A Problem in Modern Ethics* ([Davos:] Privately printed, [1891]), 3.

13. Warren Johannson, "Uranianism," *Encyclopedia of Homosexuality* (1990), 1352–53.

14. John Addington Symonds, *The Memoirs of John Addington Symonds,* Phyllis Grosskurth, ed. (New York: Random House, 1984), 117.

15. Forster (1971), 19, 137.

16. Smith (1970), 91.

17. Ibid., 73, 102 n. 80.

18. Brian Reade, *Sexual Heretics: Male Homosexuality in English Literature 1850–1900* (New York: Coward, McCann, 1970), 357–58.

Chapter Fourteen: Modern Ethics

1. Edward Carpenter, *Homogenic Love* (1894), quoted in Brian Reade, *Sexual Heretics: Male Homosexuality in English Literature 1850–1900* (New York: Coward, McCann, 1970), 343.

2. Phyllis Grosskurth, *The Woeful Victorian: A Biography of John Addington Symonds* (New York: Holt, Rinehart & Winston, 1964), 268.

3. John Addington Symonds, *A Problem in Greek Ethics* ([Bristol: Privately printed by Ballantyne and Hanson, 1883]), 1.

4. John Addington Symonds, *The Memoirs of John Addington Symonds,* Phyllis Grosskurth, ed. (New York: Random House, 1984), 99.

5. Havelock Ellis and John Addington Symonds, *Sexual Inversion* (New York: Arno Press, 1975; originally published 1897), case 18, 58–63.

6. Symonds (1883), 1.

7. Ibid., 69.

8. John Addington Symonds, *Studies of the Greek Poets* (London: A & C. Black, 1920), 554–55, 570–78.

9. Symonds (1883), 30–32.

10. Symonds (1891), 1–3.

11. Ibid., 77.

12. Ibid., 5.

13. Ibid., 4.

14. Ibid., 11.

15. Ibid.

16. Ibid., 13

17. Ibid., chap. 7, 84–114.

18. Ibid., 13–14.

19. Brian Masters, *The Life of E. F. Benson* (London: Chatto & Windus, 1991), 75.

20. Symonds (1984), 218.

21. Ibid., 283.

22. Carpenter (1894), 324ff.

23. Ibid., 344.

24. Carpenter, "The Intermediate Sex" (1908), in *Edward Carpenter, Selected Writings,* vol. 1: *Sex* (London: Gay Men's Press, 1984), 186.

25. Ibid.

26. Ibid., 242.

27. Ibid., 217.

28. Ibid., 196.

29. Ibid., 197.

30. Ibid., 200.

31. See "Intermediate Types Among Primitive Folk," in *Edward Carpenter, Selected Writings,* 1:247–89.

32. Carpenter, "Intermediate Sex" (1908/1984), 194.

33. Ibid., 220.

34. Grosskurth (1964), 285.

35. Because Ellis added a number of valuable histories to the 1901 edition (Philadelphia: F. A. Davis), which was volume 2 of *Studies in the Psychology of Sex,* I have drawn my citations from it except where otherwise indicated.

36. Ellis and Symonds (1897), 79–80.

37. Ibid., 88–91.

38. Ibid., 92–93.

39. Ellis (1901), case 10:66.

40. Ellis and Symonds (1897), case 18:58.

41. Quoted in Richard Ellmann, *Oscar Wilde* (New York: Knopf, 1988), 463.

42. Ed Cohen, *Talk on the Wilde Side* (New York: Routledge, 1993), 171–72.

43. E. M. Forster, "Terminal Note," *Maurice* (New York: New American Library, 1971), 250.

44. Ibid., 22.

45. Ibid., 255.

Chapter Fifteen: Colonizing Sodom

1. See Jonathan Ned Katz, *Gay American History* (New York: Crowell, 1976), 281–335, which includes a collection of primary texts and bibliography of

research on Native American homosexuality to which I am indebted for materials I use in this chapter.

2. See Jonathan Goldberg, *Sodometries: Renaissance Texts, Modern Sensibilities* (Stanford, Calif.: Stanford University Press, 1992), 179–249, a discussion of the importation of the idea of "sodomy" to the New World to which I am indebted for material I use in this chapter.

3. Pietro Martire d'Anghiera, *De rebus oceanicis et orbe novo decades tres,* translated by Richard Eden as Peter Martyr's *Decades of the Newe Worlde or West India* (1555), March of America Facsimile Series, no. 4 (Ann Arbor: University Microfilms, 1966). See also Goldberg (1992), 180.

4. Theodore de Bry, *Americae, Pars Quatra* (Frankfurt, 1594), vol. 4, pl. xxii.

5. Martyr, 89v; Goldberg (1992), 181 n. 4.

6. Martyr, 90r; Goldberg (1992), 182.

7. See Goldberg (1992), 182.

8. Hernán Cortés, *Letters from Mexico,* Anthony Pagden, ed. and trans. (New Haven: Yale University Press, 1986), 37; Goldberg (1992), 193.

9. Goldberg (1992), 203.

10. Francisco Lopez de Gomara, *Cortés,* Lesley Byrd Simpson, ed. and trans. (Berkeley and Los Angeles: University of California Press, 1964), 4, 13; Goldberg (1992), 198.

11. Bernal Díaz, *The Conquest of New Spain,* J. M. Cohen, trans. (Baltimore: Penguin, 1963), 19; Goldberg (1992), 201.

12. Díaz, 124; Goldberg (1992), 202.

13. Jonathan Ned Katz (1976), 282, observes that "before the inroads of Christianity homosexuals generally occupied an institutionalized, important and often respected position within many Native groups." However, he cautions, these berdaches were only the most obvious variety of Native American homosexual, and are so often mentioned because they fascinated white spectators and because other forms of homosexual behavior—between adult non-berdache males or between women—were less visible.

14. Translation of *The Journey of Alvar Nuñez Cabeza de Vaca* in Samuel Purchas, *Purchas His Pilgrimes,* [1613], 20 vols. (Glasgow: James McLehose & Sons, 1905–07), 17:495; Goldberg (1992), 215.

15. Jacques Marquette, "Of the First Voyage Made by Father Marquette Toward New Mexico," *The Jesuit Relations and Allied Documents,* Reuben Gold Thwaites, ed., 73 vols. (Cleveland: Burrows, 1896–1901), 59:129; Katz (1976), 287.

16. Pierre Liette, "Memoir of Pierre Liette on Illinois Country," in *The Western Country in the 17th Century,* Milo Quaife, ed. (New York: Citadel, 1962), 112–13; Katz (1976), 288.

17. Pierre François Xavier de Charlevoix, *Journal of a Voyage to North America,* 2 vols. (London: R. and J. Dodsley, 1761), 2:80; Katz (1976), 290.

18. *Jean Bossu's Travels in the Interior of North America, 1751–1762,* Seymour Feiler, ed. and trans. (Norman: University of Oklahoma, 1962), 169; Katz (1976), 290.

19. Pedro Font, *Font's Complete Diary of the Second Aztec Expedition,* Herbert Eugene Bolton, ed. and trans.; vol. 4 of *Anza's California Expeditions,* 5 vols. (Berkeley: University of California Press, 1930–31), 105; Katz (1976), 291.

20. Francisco Palóu, *Relación histórica . . . de la vida y apostolicas . . . Junipero Serra* (Mexico: 1787), 222; Katz (1976), 292.

21. Edwin James, *Account of an Expedition from Pittsburgh to the Rocky Mountains . . .* 2 vols. (Philadelphia: H. C. Carey and I. Lea, 1822–33), 1:129, 267; Katz (1976), 299.

22. Isaac McCoy, *History of the Baptist Indian Missions* (New York: H. & S. Raynor, 1840), 360–61; Katz (1976), 300.

23. George Catlin, *Letters and Notes on the Customs and the Conditions of the North American Indians* (London: Henry G. Bohn, 1866), 2:214–15; Katz (1976), 302.

24. Michael Warner, "New English Sodom," in *Queering the Renaissance,* Jonathan Goldberg, ed. (Durham, N.C.: Duke University Press, 1994), 331.

25. Samuel Whiting, *Abraham's Humble Intercession for Sodom* (Cambridge, 1666), 46; Warner (1994), 335.

26. Warner (1994), 348.

27. Robert Ryece to John Winthrop, *Winthrop Papers,* Stewart Mitchell, ed. (Boston: Massachusetts Historical Society, 1929–47), 2:127–32, 129–30; Warner (1994), 330.

28. John Winthrop, "A Modell of Christian Charity," *Winthrop Papers,* 2:294–95; Warner (1994), 338.

29. Peter Bulkeley, *The Gospel-Covenant,* 2d ed. (London, 1651), 11, 16; Warner (1994), 338.

30. "Francis Higginson's Journal" in *The Founding of Massachusetts* (Boston: Massachusetts Historical Society, 1930), 71; Katz (1983), 73.

31. Nathaniel Bouton, ed., *Provincial Papers . . . 1623–1687* (Concord, N.H.: G. E. Jenks, 1867), 1:106; Katz (1983), 73.

32. William R. Staples, ed., *The Colonial Laws of Massachusetts . . .* (Boston: Rockwell and Churchill, 1890), 35n.; Katz (1983), 74.

33. Nathaniel Shurtleff and David Pulsifer, eds., *Records of the Colony of New Plymouth* (Boston: William White, 1855), 1:64, 68, 2:6; Katz (1983), 75.

34. William Bradford, *Of Plymouth Plantation,* Samuel Eliot Morison, ed. (New York: Knopf, 1952), 316.

35. Thomas Shepard, "The Sincere Convert," in *The Works of Thomas Shepard,* John Albro, ed. (Boston: Doctrinal Tract and Book Society, 1853), 1:28, 29; Katz (1983), 83.

36. Bradford (1952), 321.

37. Katz (1983), 79–82, 674 n. 14.

38. John Winthrop, *History of New England from 1630 to 1649,* James Savage, ed. (Boston: Little, Brown, 1853), 2:324; Katz (1983), 90–91.

39. Katz (1983), 40.

40. Louis Crompton, "Homosexuals and the Death Penalty in Colonial America," *Journal of Homosexuality* 1 (1976), 277–93.

41. Katz (1976), 24.

Chapter Sixteen: The Discord Young Men Feel

1. Thomas Harris and Revredy Johnson, *Report of Cases Argued . . . 1810* (Annapolis, Md.: Jonas Green, 1826), 3:154; Jonathan Ned Katz, *Gay American History* (New York: Crowell, 1976), 26.

2. Carroll Smith-Rosenberg, "The Female World of Love and Ritual: Relations Between Women in Nineteenth-Century America," *Signs,* vol. 1, no. 1 (fall 1975), 1–29.

3. Carroll Smith-Rosenberg, *Disorderly Conduct: Visions of Gender in Victorian America* (New York: Oxford University Press, 1985), 106.

4. Ralph Waldo Emerson, *The Journals and Miscellaneous Notebooks of Ralph Waldo Emerson,* William H. Gilman, Alfred P. Ferguson, George P. Clark, Merrell R. Davis, eds. (Cambridge, Mass.: Belknap Press of Harvard University, 1960), 1:353, 39–40, 291–92, 3:289–90; Katz (1976), 456–61.

5. Henry David Thoreau, *The Journals of Henry David Thoreau,* Bradford Torrey and Francis H. Allen, eds., 14 vols. (Cambridge, Mass.: Houghton Mifflin, 1906); Katz (1976), 481–94.

6. Edwin Haviland Miller, ed., *The Correspondence of Walt Whitman,* in *The Collected Writings of Walt Whitman* (New York: New York University Press, 1961), 1:295.

7. Bayard Taylor, "The Poet's Journal," *The Poetical Works of Bayard Taylor* (Boston and New York: Houghton Mifflin, 1862), 11.

8. William White, ed., *Daybooks and Notebooks,* in *The Collected Writings of Walt Whitman,* 3:740–41.

9. Ibid., 745.

10. Sculley Bradley and Harold Blodgett, eds. *Leaves of Grass* (New York: Norton, 1973), 741.

11. Ibid., 736–39.

12. White (1978), 3:746.

13. Bradley and Blodgett (1973), 739–40.

14. Sculley Bradley, Harold Blodgett, Arthur Golden, and William White eds., *Leaves of Grass: A Textual Variorum of the Printed Poems* (New York: New York University Press, 1980), 1:230, l. 91.

15. Quoted in Byrne Fone, *Masculine Landscapes: Walt Whitman and the Homoerotic Text* (Carbondale: Southern Illinois University Press, 1992), 43–44.

16. Miller (1961), 97.

17. Floyd Stovall, ed., *Prose Works 1892* in *The Collected Writings of Walt Whitman*, 2:414–15.

18. Records of the Unitarian Church, Brewster, Mass., quoted in Richard M. Huber, *The American Idea of Success* (New York: McGraw-Hill, 1971), 45–46; Katz (1976), 33–34.

19. Martin Duberman, *About Time: Exploring the Gay Past* (New York: Gay Presses of New York, 1986), 43–45.

20. Milton Hindus, *Whitman: The Critical Heritage* (London: Routledge & Kegan Paul, 1971), 244–45.

Chapter Seventeen: In Fear of Fairies

1. William Howard, "Sexual Perversions in America," *American Journal of Dermatology and Genito-Urinary Diseases* 8, no. 1 (1904), 14; Katz, *Gay/Lesbian Almanac* (New York: Harper & Row, 1983), 312.

2. George Shrady, "Perverted Sexual Instinct," *Medical Record* (1884); Katz (1983), 197–98.

3. George Chauncey, *Gay New York: Gender, Urban Culture, and the Making of the Gay Male World, 1890–1940* (New York: Basic Books, 1994), 50.

4. Griswold T. Comstock, *New York Medical Times,* September 1892; Katz (1983), 227.

5. C. H. Hughes, "Erotopathia—Morbid Eroticism," *Alienist and Neurologist* 14, no. 4 (1893), 148–57; Katz (1983), 245.

6. G. Frank Lydston, "Sexual Perversion, Satyriasis, and Nymphomania," *Medical and Surgical Reporter* (1889); Katz (1983), 213–14.

7. Chauncey (1994), 38–39.

8. Allan Hamilton, "Insanity in Its Medico-Legal Bearings," *A System of Legal Medicine* (1894); Katz (1983), 258.

9. Colin Scott, "Sex and Art," *The American Journal of Psychiatry* (1896); Katz (1973), 44.

10. Francis Anthony, "The Question of Responsibility in Cases of Sexual Perversion," *Boston Medical and Surgical Journal* 139, no. 12 (1898); Katz (1983), 294.

11. F. E. Daniel, "Should Insane Criminals and Sexual Perverts Be Permitted to Procreate?" *Medico-Legal Journal* (1893); Katz (1983), 241–42.

12. George Monroe, "Sodomy and Pederasty," *Saint Louis Medical Examiner* (1899); Katz (1983), 301.

13. "Xavier Mayne" (Edward Prime Stevenson), *The Intersexes* (1908); Katz (1983), 330.

14. Katz (1983), 243–44.
15. Hughes (1893) in Katz (1983), 246–47.
16. Anthony (1898) in Katz (1983), 294.
17. Quoted in "Earl Lind," *Autobiography of an Androgyne* (New York: Medico-Legal Journal, 1918), 24–25.

Chapter Eighteen: The Riddle of Homosexuality

1. Professor X was identified by Symonds (*Letters of John Addington Symonds,* Herbert M. Schueller and Robert L. Peters, eds. [Detroit: Wayne State University, 1968], 3:579–80) as Benjamin Osgood Pierce. Jonathan Katz advocates James Mills Pierce. See *Dictionary of American Biography,* "J. M. Pierce."
2. Havelock Ellis and John Addington Symonds, *Sexual Inversion* (New York: Arno Press, 1975; originally published 1897), 273.
3. *Monatsberichte des wissenshaftlich-humanitaren Komitees,* vol. 6 (1907), 98–99; Katz (1976), 382–83.
4. "Xavier Mayne" (Edward Prime Stevenson), *Imre* (Naples, 1906), 110.
5. Mayne (1906), 111–17. I have silently emended Mayne's erratic punctuation.
6. Ibid., 113–14.
7. Ibid., 121.
8. "Xavier Mayne" (Edward Prime Stevenson), *The Intersexes* (Naples, 1908), 43–44.
9. Ibid., 16–18.
10. Ibid., 18–20.
11. Ibid., 25–27.
12. Ibid., 27.
13. Ibid., 62–71.
14. "Earl Lind," *Autobiography of an Androgyne* (1918) and *The Female Impersonators* (1922). Reprinted in *Homosexuality: Lesbians and Gay Men in Society, History and Literature,* Jonathan Ned Katz, ed. (New York: Arno Press, 1975).
15. Lind (1918), 30.
16. Ibid., 40.
17. Ibid., 41.
18. Ibid., 62.
19. Ibid., 46.
20. Ibid., 59.
21. Ibid., 60–62.
22. Ibid., 63–66.
23. Ibid., 69–71.
24. George Chauncey, *Gay New York: Gender, Urban Culture, and the*

Making of the Gay Male World, 1890–1940 (New York: Basic Books, 1994), 69.

25. Lind (1918), 71–72.
26. Ibid., 74.
27. Chauncey (1994), 180, locates "cruise" as early as the 1920s.
28. Lind (1922), 159–60.
29. Lind (1918), 82–83.
30. Lind (1922), 270.
31. Ibid., 36–39.

Chapter Nineteen: Hit Them! Hit Back!

1. Vice Commission of Chicago, *The Social Evil in Chicago: A Study of Existing Conditions. With Recommendations* (Chicago: Guntrop-Warren, 1911); Katz, *Gay/Lesbian Almanac* (New York: Harper & Row, 1983), 334.
2. Dr. William Lee Howard, *Confidential Chats with Boys* (New York: Edward J. Clode, 1911); Katz (1983), 337–38.
3. Dr. Alfred Adler, "The Homosexual Problem," *Alienist and Neurologist* 38, no. 3 (1917), 268–87; Katz (1983), 374–77.
4. Dr. William Robinson, "My Views on Homosexuality," *American Journal of Urology* 10 (1914), 550–52; Katz (1983), 357–58.
5. Dr. E. S. Shepherd, "Contribution to the Study of Indeterminacy," *American Journal of Urology and Sexology* 14, no. 6 (1918), 241–52; Katz (1983), 379–80.
6. George Chauncey, Jr., "Christian Brotherhood or Sexual Perversion? Homosexual Identities and the Construction of Sexual Boundaries in the World War I Era," in Martin Bauml Duberman, Martha Vincius, and George Chauncey, Jr., *Hidden from History: Reclaiming the Gay and Lesbian Past* (New York: New American Library, 1989), 316.
7. Sherwood Anderson, "Hands," in *Calamus: Male Homosexuality in Twentieth-Century Literature: An International Anthology,* David Galloway and Christian Sabisch, eds. (New York: Quill, 1982), 93–100.
8. Carl Van Vechten, *The Blind Bow-Boy* (New York: Knopf, 1923), 56.
9. Ibid., 160.
10. Robert McAlmon, "Miss Knight," reprinted (with "Distinguished Air") in *There Was a Rustle of Black Silk Stockings* (New York, 1963), 50.
11. McAlmon, "Distinguished Air," 10.
12. McAlmon, "Miss Knight," 59.
13. *The New York Times,* April 5, 1902; Katz (1983), 307.
14. *The New York Times,* September 30, 1926; Katz (1983), 426–27.
15. Jonathan Ned Katz, *Gay American History* (New York: Crowell, 1976), 82–91.

16. *The New York Times,* November 1, 1932; Katz (1983), 471.
17. *The New York Times,* January 29, 1933; Katz (1983), 473.
18. *The New York Times,* October 21, 1933; Katz (1983), 488.
19. *The New York Times,* February 21, 1937; Katz (1983), 529.
20. Henry Gerber, "The Society for Human Rights—1925," *ONE Magazine* (Los Angeles) 10, no. 9 (Sept. 1962), 5–10; Katz (1976), 389–93.
21. Dr. Joseph Collins, "Homosexuality," in *The Doctor Looks at Love and Life* (New York: Doran, 1926); Katz (1983), 428–36.
22. Katz (1983), 428n., 463.
23. Dr. William J. Robinson, "Nature's Sex Stepchildren," *Medical Critic and Guide* (New York) 25 (1925), 475–77; Katz (1983), 424.
24. John F. W. Meagher, "Homosexuality: Its Psychobiological and Psychopathological Significance," *Urologic and Cutaneous Review* 33, no. 8, 505–15; Katz (1983), 455.
25. Clarence P. Oberndorf, "Diverse Forms of Homosexuality," *Urologic and Cutaneous Review* 33, no. 8, 518–23; Katz (1983), 459.
26. *The New York Times,* June 3, 1936, 46:2; Katz (1983), 523.
27. Katz (1983), 523.
28. Dr. Aaron J. Rosanoff, "Sexual Psychopathies," *Manual of Psychiatry,* 6th ed. (New York: Wiley, 1927), 193–208; Katz (1983), 439.

Chapter Twenty: American Masculinity

1. Dr. Joseph Collins, *The Doctor Looks at Love and Life* (New York: Doran, 1926), 64; Katz, *Gay/Lesbian Almanac* (New York: Harper & Row, 1983), 428.
2. La Forest Potter, *Strange Loves: A Study in Sexual Abnormalities* (New York: Padell, 1933), 4–5.
3. Ibid., 93.
4. Ibid., 176.
5. Ibid., 107.
6. Ibid., 100–101.
7. Ibid., 178.
8. Ibid., 235–36.
9. Roger Austen, *Playing the Game: The Homosexual Novel in America* (Indianapolis: Bobbs-Merrill, 1977), 57.
10. Potter (1933), 4–5.
11. *The New York Times,* March 4, 1938; Katz (1983), 537.
12. George Henry, *Sex Variants: A Study of Homosexual Patterns* (New York: Paul B. Hoeber, 1948), ix.
13. Ibid., xv.
14. *Parents,* October 1948, 144–47; Katz (1983), 632–33.
15. *Time,* June 4, 1948; Katz (1983), 630–33.

16. *Newsweek,* October 10, 1949; *Queer People,* 52; Katz (1983), 652.

17. Max Lerner, *New York Post,* July 11, 1950. Reprinted in Max Lerner, *The Unfinished Country: A Book of American Symbols* (New York: Simon & Schuster, 1959), 311–13; Jonathan Ned Katz, *Gay American History* (New York: Crowell, 1976), 94, 98.

18. Jack Lait and Lee Mortimer, *Washington Confidential* (New York: Crown, 1951) 90, 94; Katz (1976), 100.

19. Lait and Mortimer, 91; Katz (1976), 101.

20. See Drew Pearson, *Diaries, 1949–1959,* Tyler Abell, ed. (New York: Holt, Rinehart & Winston, 1974), 188–89, 190, 192; Katz (1976), 101.

21. Henry Hay, taped interview with Jonathan Ned Katz, March 31, 1974, in Katz (1976), 408.

22. Mattachine Society, "Missions and Purposes," [28] April 1951. In Katz (1976), 412.

23. "Donald Webster Cory" (Edward Sagarin), *The Homosexual in America* (New York: Greenberg, 1951), 228–35.

Chapter Twenty-one: A Panic Close to Madness

1. James Baldwin, "Preservation of Innocence: Studies for a New Morality," *Zero* (Tangier, Morocco) 1, no. 2, 14–22; Jonathan Katz (1983), 647–50.

2. John W. Aldridge, *After the Lost Generation: A Critical Study of the Writers of Two Wars* (New York: Noonday Press, 1951, 1958), 101–102.

3. Roger Austen, *Playing the Game: The Homosexual Novel in America* (Indianapolis: Bobbs-Merrill, 1977), 119.

4. James Levin, *The Gay Novel in America* (New York: Garland Publishing, 1991), 198.

5. Robert Duncan, "The Homosexual in Society," *Politics* 1 (1944), 209–11; Katz (1983), 592.

6. John D'Emilio and Estelle B. Freedman, *Intimate Matters: A History of Sexuality in America* (New York: Harper & Row, 1988), 276–77.

7. Sara Harris, *The Puritan Jungle: America's Sexual Underground* (New York: Putnam, 1969), 165–69, 171–72. Jonathan Ned Katz, *Gay American History* (New York: Crowell, 1976), 123–25.

8. George Chauncey, *Gay New York: Gender, Urban Culture, and the Making of the Gay Male World, 1890–1940* (New York: Basic Books, 1994), 6 n. 7.

9. Joseph E. Aguero, Laura Bloch, and Donn Byrne, "The Relationships Among Sexual Beliefs, Attitudes, Experience, and Homophobia," in *Bashers, Baiters and Bigots: Homophobia in American Society,* John de Cecco, ed. (Binghamton, N.Y.: Harrington Park Press, 1985), 95.

10. Terms taken at random from various articles in Katz (1976), 11–209.

11. Quoted in Byrne Fone, ed. *Hidden Heritage: History and the Gay Imagination* (New York: Avocation Press, 1979), 320.
12. Quoted in ibid., 322.

Epilogue: The Last Acceptable Prejudice

1. George Chauncey, *Gay New York: Gender, Urban Culture, and the Making of the Gay Male World, 1890–1940* (New York: Basic Books, 1994), 13–22.
2. Will Finch Diary, Nov. 18, 1951, Kinsey Institute for Research in Sex, Gender and Reproduction Library, Indiana University, Bloomington, Ind. Quoted in ibid., 19.
3. *Newsweek,* July 1993.
4. David W. Dunlap, "Reform Rabbis Vote to Back Gay Marriage," *The New York Times,* March 29, 1996.
5. Gustav Niebuhr, "Methodists Keep Rule Against Homosexuality," *The New York Times,* April 25, 1996.
6. "Vatican Denounces Gay-Marriage Idea," *The New York Times,* March 29, 1996.
7. John Leland and Mark Miller, "Can Gays Convert?" *Newsweek,* August 17, 1998, 46–50.
8. "Thousands Support Judge on Religion in Courtroom," *The New York Times,* April 13, 1997.
9. *The Advocate,* July 22, 1997, 12.
10. *Newsletter of the National Gay and Lesbian Task Force,* July 1997.
11. David W. Dunlap, "An Analyst, Father, Battles Homosexuality," *The New York Times,* December 24, 1995.
12. Janet Halley, "The Politics of the Closet: Toward Equal Protection for Gay, Lesbian, and Bisexual Identity," in *Reclaiming Sodom,* Jonathan Goldberg, ed. (New York: Routledge, 1994), 169.
13. Justice White in *Bowers v. Hardwick,* 478 U.S. 186. reh'g denied. 487 U.S. 1039 (1986).
14. Halley (1994), 145.
15. *The New York Times,* March 3, 1996.
16. Carey Goldberger, "Redefining a Marriage Made in Vermont," *The New York Times,* December 26, 1999.
17. *The Advocate,* April 1, 1997, 25.
18. Aaron McKinney, the murderer of Matthew Shepard, quoted in JoAnn Wypijewski, "A Boy's Life," *Harper's,* September 1999, 63.
19. *New York Post,* June 21, 1995.
20. Richard L. Berke, "Chasing the Polls for Gay Rights," *The New York Times,* August 2, 1998.
21. Jill Smolowe, "The Unmarrying Kind," *Time,* April 29, 1996, 69.

22. Richard Lacayo, "The New Gay Struggle," *Time,* October 26, 1998, 35.
23. Marc Peyser, "Battling the Backlash," *Newsweek,* August 17, 1998, 50–51.
24. *National Coalition of Anti-Violence Programs* (New York, 1998), 15.
25. Dennis Altman, *Homosexual: Oppression and Liberation* (New York: Outerbridge & Dienstfrey, 1971), 42.
26. Peyser (1998), 52.
27. Steve Lopez, "To Be Young and Gay in Wyoming," *Time,* October 26, 1998, 38–40.
28. Berke (1998), 34; Lacayo, (1998), 35.

INDEX

Entries in *italics* refer to illustrations.

effeminacy (*cont'd*)
209–10; "naturally" disposed to homosexuality, 138–39; in 19th century literature, 282; in Rome, 44–45, 50–54;
satirized in England, 242–46; as social
construction, 292; in Spain, 204; stereotype countered by gay authors, 292, 295,
299, 338–39, 358–60, 398–99; as stock
character, 30–32; Vidal on, 398–99
effeminatus, 52
Effen, Justus van, 232
Egica, King of Visigothic Spain, 120–21
Elagabalus, Emperor of Rome, 48
Elizabeth I, Queen of England, 218
Ellis, Havelock, 275, 278, 279, 290, 302–6,
309, 355–57
Emerson, Ralph Waldo, 334–35, 339, 341
"Employment of Homosexuals and other
Sex Perverts in Government," 391
England: abnormality of sodomy in, 273–
77; antisodomy laws, 140–41, 144, 215–
19, 224–25, 271–73, 313; Bentham's
defense of sodomites in, 254–57; Carpenter argues for rights, 297–302; Ellis
studies of homosexuals, 302–6; in
Enlightenment, 229–32, 242–54, 258–66;
homoeroticism during Victorian era,
9–10, 277–81; literary sodomy, 220–24;
literature on homosexual themes, 278,
281–87; newspapers, 249–54; Parliament, 217, 218; Renaissance, 215–25;
rights advocates suppressed, 309–16;
sodomy redefined, 219–20; Symonds
argues against homophobia, 288–97; Victorian era, 9–10, 271–315; Wilde trial,
306–9
Enlightment, 8–9, 229–67; antisodomy
laws challenged in *Don Leon*, 258–65;
Bentham's defense of sodomites in England, 254–57; decriminalization during,
265–67; Dutch Republic persecutions,
236–42; press spreads homophobia,
249–54; sodomites satirized in *Roderick
Random*, 242–49; subcultures during,
231–36
Ennodius of Arles, Bishop of Ticinum,
129–30
entrapment, 249, 254–55, 260, 272,
374–75
Ephesiaca (Xenophon of Ephesus), 47
Epigrams (Catullus), 50
Episcopal Church, 412
Epistle of Barnabas, 101
Epistles, 96–101, 103
erastes (lover or mentor), 19, 31
Eric, or, Little by Little (Farrar), 280

eromenos (beloved), 19, 31
Erotes (Lucian of Samosata), 61–70, 71
Erotikos (Plutarch), 61
Eryximachus, 22
"Euliades" (Symonds), 282–83
Euripides, 30, 31–32, 33–34, 35, 40
exclusively homosexual, in Greece, 27, 40,
50, 54, 55
excommunication, 119, 120
Exodus, 413
exoleti (prostitutes), 49
"extreme" homosexual, 299
Ezekiel, 84–85

Faan, Netherlands, 238–39
Faerie Queene (Spenser), 220
"fag," in Rome, 49
"faggots," 410
"fairy," 346, 363–71, 378, 410
False Capitularies, 122
family, homosexuals as enemy of, 120, 192,
230
Family Research Council, 418
Fanchono, Rafael, 205
fanchonos (effeminate homosexuals), 204–5
Farrar, Dean, 280
Favola d'Orfeo (Poliziano), 181–82
fellatio, 48–50, 125, 136–37, 234
fellator, in Rome, 50
Female Impersonators, The (Lind), 10, 363,
369–71
femininity, 56–57, 345
Ferdinand of Aragon, 201
Ferlinghetti, Lawrence, 402
Fernández de Oviedo, Gonzalo, 321
Ficino, Marsilio, 183
Finch, Will, 411
Finiguerri, Stefano ("Lo Za"), 185
Fitzroy, A. T., 314
Fleta (English legal treatise), 144, 215
Florence, 192–99; Officers of the Night,
187, 189, 194, 198, 199, 224
Florio, John, 219
Font, Pedro, 324
Ford, Charles Henri, 398
Forster, E. M., 277, 281, 283, 289, 309–15
Foucault, Michel, 26
France, 9, 143–44, 150–51, 208–10, 214,
224, 229, 265
Francis, Richard, 250
Franciscan orders, 143, 152
Frank, Waldo, 377
Franks, 118, 121–22
frater ("brother"), 49
Freedman, Mark, 5
Freud, 373

ostracism or outcasts, 260, 349. *See also* banishment
Ostrogoths, 118
Oswald (character), 357–60
Other Voices, Other Rooms (Capote), 399
Ovid, 46, 181, 219

"Paean to Dawn, A" (Taylor), 337
paederastia, 64, 183
"paederasty," Bentham on, 255–58
pagan(s): 104, 107, 112–13, 127–28; homosexuality as, 8, 97–98. *See also* Greece; Rome
Paidagogos (Clement of Alexandria), 101–2
paiderastia, in ancient Greece, 18–21, 31, 66; Symonds on, 291
pais or *paidika* (beloved boy), 19
"Palaestral Study, A" (Lefroy), 283
Palóu, Francisco, 324, 326
Pamiers, Bishop of, 155
Panamanian Indians, 320
Panormita, Antonio (Antonio Beccadelli), 185
"pansies," 410
Parents magazine, 389
Paris, France, 231–33
Partidas (1555), 201
Partridge, Rev. Ralph, 331
Passing the Love of Women and Other Poems (Barford), 283–85
"Passionate Shepherd to His Love, The" (Marlowe), 220–21
Passion of St. Pelagius (Hrosvitha of Gandersheim), 149
passive homosexuality: in Greece, 27–28, 29–31, 33, 55–59; in Middle Ages, 125; Paul on, 97; in Renaissance, 194; in Rome, 44, 48– 51; and Victorians, 277
Pater, Walter, 278, 279, 280, 283, 310
pathicus/i (men enjoying passive sex or performing fellatio), 49, 50–52, 54
pathology concept, 272–73, 275–76, 277. *See also* disease; insanity
Patrick, Robert, 404
Patroclus, 21
Paul, Apostle, 8, 96–101, 103, 123, 210
Pausanias, 20, 21–23
Pearson, Drew, 392
pecado nefando (unmentionable sin), 200
Pech, Guillaume, 156
pederasty: and Christianity, 71, 101; and Enlightenment, 232; in Florence, 193; Gentiles accused of, 87, 88, 89; and Neoplatonists, 89–90; and Romans, 47
pedophilia, vs. *paiderastia*, in Greece, 19

Pelagius, St., 149
penitentials and penances, 123–26, 134–35
Pérez de Mansilla, Juan, 203
Perpetua and Felicity, saints, 129
Perry, Elizabeth, 204
persecutions, in Enlightenment, 236–42; in Renaissance Italy, 193–200
perversion, homosexuality seen as, 10, 275–77, 344
pervertimenti dell'amore, I (Mantegazza), 275
"perverts": in America, 346–47, 350–51; named, in Latin, 49–54; term invented, 273, 276–77
Peter of Abano, 138
Petronius, Gaius, 47, 246
Phaedrus, 21, 22, 61, 69
Phaedrus (Plato), 96, 289–90
Phelps, Rev. Fred, 413
Philip, Emperor of Rome, 46
Philip, King of France, 147
Philip II, King of France, 148
Philip IV, King of France, 153–55, 174
Philip of Macedon, 38
Philo Judaeus, 89–92, 98, 99, 100, 101, 172
Philosophical Dictionary (Voltaire), 230–31
Physiognommonics, 55–56
physiognomy, 55–56, 102
Physiognomy (Polema), 56
Pierce, James Mills, 355–56
Piers Gaveston (Drayton), 189
Pilgrims, 328
pillory, 250, 251, 252, 253–54
plague, 116, 186–87, 192, 195, 201
Plaine, Willim, 331
Plato, 18, 20, 31, 33–34, 41, 89, 96, 99, 115, 261, 288; Americans and, 335; analysis of homosexual desire in, 54; cited by Clement, 102; condemns homosexual sex in *Laws*, 34–38, 55, 60, 61, 66, 70, 119; "contrary to nature" in, 99–100; on proper homosexual acts in *Symposium*, 21–25, 66, 289–90; reexamined in Renaissance, 183, 222; *Uranismus* term in, 278; Victorians and, 288–90, 310
Plutarch, 61, 261
Plutus (Aristophanes), 31
Plymouth Colony, 329–30
Poems of the Orient (Taylor), 336–37
Poet in the East, A (Taylor), 337
Poets Journal, The (Taylor), 336
Polemo, 56–57
police raids, 231, 250, 380, 402, 407